PRUSSIAN NETZELANDERS

AND OTHER GERMAN IMMIGRANTS IN GREEN LAKE, MARQUETTE AND WAUSHARA COUNTIES WISCONSIN

Schleswig-Holstein
M.S.
Mecklenburg Schwerin
Olden-burg
Ham-burg
Pommern (Pomerania)
Westpreussen (West Prussia)
Ostpreussen (East Prussia)
Hannover (Hanover)
M.S.
Westfalen (Westphalia)
Li
B
B
B
Prov.
A
Brandenburg
NEUMARK
Posen
Rheinland
Hessen
Schw
Sachsen
Nassau
H.D.
Thur-ingia) Thüringen
Königreich Sachsen (Saxony)
Schlesien (Silesia)
O
H.D.
Lothringen
Pfalz
Bayern (Bavaria)
Elsass
Baden
(Wuert-temberg) Württemberg
H

Compiled by

Brian A. Podoll, C.G.R.S.

HERITAGE BOOKS
2010

HERITAGE BOOKS

AN IMPRINT OF HERITAGE BOOKS, INC.

Books, CDs, and more—Worldwide

For our listing of thousands of titles see our website
at
www.HeritageBooks.com

Published 2010 by
HERITAGE BOOKS, INC.
Publishing Division
100 Railroad Ave. #104
Westminster, Maryland 21157

International Standard Book Numbers
Paperbound: 978-1-55613-954-3
Clothbound: 978-0-7884-8365-3

CONTENTS

Maps (continued)

FOREWORD

In researching my own paternal ancestry in Green Lake, Marquette, and Waushara Counties, Wisconsin, I discovered a pattern of settlement among German immigrants there. This pattern indicated that the majority originated from the same vicinity of the former Prussian kingdom.

When listening to older relatives reminisce or looking over old photographs, it is easy to form a picture of pioneer days in your mind. For these central Wisconsin residents of German ancestry now, some may be surprised to learn that their immigrant forefathers to America weren't the first in their families to move to a"new frontier". On behalf of their Prussian homeland, many of these immigrants' parents and grandparents staked out their own frontier-- on the Polish frontier, that is.

Part of this text is drawn from two articles that I wrote, which were published in the 7 February 1985 Marquette County Tribune (printed at Montello, Wisc.) and the December 1986 National Genealogical Society Quarterly. Originally, in preparing this book project, serious consideration was given to including Adams County, adjacent west to the other three; and to Waupaca County, adjacent to northeastern Waushara County. Even though my own Podoll ancestors forged their way from the village of Marquette, in Green Lake County in 1873, onto New Chester Township in Adams County nine years later; Adams County Germans were fewer in number and did not neatly fit the larger pattern that I was trying to establish.

Adams County is largely a mix of Yankees, Norwegians and other Scandinavians, plus Bohemians. Germans probably fall somewhere below that pecking order as the 1890 map indicates that only 21-40% of the immigrant population was German. Only in New Chester and Quincy Townships does there appear to be any semblance of German "communities".

In both cases, there seems to be a smattering extension of the Prussian influence in Marquette County, yet those in New Chester appeared to Americanize themselves with the local Congregational Church community, as many are buried in that cemetery there. In Quincy, however, there appears to be more of a Pomeranian influence, including an Evangelical Lutheran Church shared with some of the local Scandinavians. But, again, no overwhelming pattern is evident.

As you will later see in the Waushara County listings of this book, Prussians from Waupaca County, particularly Lind Township, make up a significant number of those marrying at adjacent Bloomfield Township. My original knowledge of Waushara County Prussians (including Podoll people) revealed a pattern in the southwestern townships of Coloma, Richford, Dakota, Deerfield, and Dakota. Since then, I've learned that many of those people may have been Marquette County Prussians pressing to settle in around the turn of this century. To my surprise, and although it is somewhat detached from the southwest townships, Bloomfield appears to have been something of a center for Prussian/German culture in Waushara County.

As for Waupaca County, itself, I've decided to include it in a future book on Germans in Wisconsin's Fox River Valley counties. This Green Lake-Marquette-Waushara Counties book, here and now, is to be the first of a series on German settlements in different regions of Wisconsin.

Brian A. Podoll, C.G.R.S.

THE PRUSSIANS ARE COMING! THE PRUSSIANS ARE COMING!

-AN OVERVIEW

There are at least a half-dozen excellent books on the background
and development of the Prussian colonization of the Polish frontier.
In German, the Walther Maas book SIEDLUNGEN ZWISCHEN WARTHE UND NETZE
(Settlement Between the Warthe and Netze Rivers) explains in great de-
tail, the succeeding waves of German colonization. From a trickle of
Germans amongst established Polish villages in the Middle Ages to a
flood after Prussian annexation, he leaves no stone unturned. His ap-
proach is constructed, in large part, on how farming colonies were
determined by terrain, i.e., sandy marshlands, ground moraine plattes,
and the overall geography of the region. He also gives a thorough ac-
count of the evolution of Polish and German names for each locale, as
well as many somewhat complex maps.

Another superb German book ANTLITZ UND GESCHICHTE DES KREISES
KOLMAR (POSEN), or The Face and History of County Kolmar, Posen (published 1970 by Heimatkreisgemeinschaft Kolmar and available c/o Frau
Margot Derwanz, address Müdenkamp 11, D-4920 Lemgo, Federal Republic
of Germany); provides a more aesthetic look, with many photos and men-
tions many family names, as well as a mini-history of each locale in
the county. It has one of the few modern articles that I've seen published in Low German, plus a finely detailed map tucked into its back
cover.
Hans Bahlow is probably the foremost author on the origins of
German names and his DEUTSCHES NAMENLEXICON is probably the best, all-
encompassing work on the subject. Many of the family names listed in
this book can be found in Bahlow's books, which are printed in German.
Among the genealogical set in America, Professor Jürgen Eichhoff of
the University of Wisconsin is best known for his lectures in deline-
ating regional differences among German surnames, I might add.

Among American books, however, the GENEALOGICAL GUIDE TO GERMAN
ANCESTORS FROM EAST GERMANY AND EASTERN EUROPE (translated by Joachim

O.R. Nuthack of Edmonton, Canada and Adalbert Goertz of Waynesboro, Pennsylvania, published as the AGoFF-Wegweiser-English Edition by Verlag Degener & Co., Inh. Gerhard Gessner in 1984 at Neustadt/Aisch, West Germany) provides a very fine breakdown of the provincial and county structure for the eastern part of Prussia, as well as modern German sources for genealogists to pursue.

GERMANS, POLES, AND JEWS: The Nationality Conflict in the Prussian East, 1772-1914, by Wm. W. Hagen (University of Chicago Press 1980) is by far the best American work in understanding the land and legal reforms which evolved during the process of Prussia's Polish frontier colonization. In many ways, the book lays the social and economic groundwork for what prompted so many to emigrate to America, and in this case, central Wisconsin in particular. I could not recommend these books strongly enough, for both the genealogist and those with an interest in German-American history.

It is from these sources that I will attempt to provide a condensed overview of these people, their motivation, and their pattern of moving first onto the Polish frontier and then onto central Wisconsin. In addition, a few examples will be shown how this pattern moved onto southern Minnesota and both Dakotas, as well.

In September 1989, I compiled and published the 653-page hardbound book BOUND BY BLOOD AND NAME: A History and Genelaogies of the Podoll Families in Prussia and America. I mention it here only because, besides its obvious value to the family itself, I like to think of it as a prime example of Prussian immigrants fulfilling that migratory pattern. When applicable, I may make limited references from that work, which if I may be so indulgent, received an Award of Commendation from from the Concordia Historical Institute (Lutheran Archives) in November 1990 at St. Louis, Missouri.

This overview is as follows:

In the mid-to-late 18th Century, Germans-mostly Protestants-along with Dutch Mennonite refugees, were invited by the Polish government to settle previously uncultivated lands in Great Poland (or Poznan) and Pomerelia. Usually, because their purpose was to bolster a sagging farm economy, these German and Dutch settlers often received better treatment and were granted more rights than the Polish peasantry themselves!

Although the Dutch Mennonites were far fewer in number than their German counterparts, they would leave their imprint on the area in two ways: Germans who would later colonize the area were referred to as "Hauländer", a corruption of "Holländer", which was how the Germans referred to the Dutch. As a result, many small villages and colonies throughout the area carried the suffix "Hauland", as in Borowo-Hauland or Gembitz-Hauland.

Between 1772-1795, the warring powers of Austria, Russia, and Prussia partitioned the defeated Polish nation, literally "wiping it off the map". For Prussia (in German, Preussen="Proys-sen"), the territory they gained from these treaties meant that the Prussian king-

THE GERMAN EMPIRE   1871 - 1918

TO LITHUANIA AFTER W.W.I

TO U.S.S.R. AFTER W.W.II

Ostpreussen (East Prussia)

Westpreussen (West Prussia)

TO POLAND AFTER W.W.I

ODER-NEISSE LINE AFTER W.W.II

TO POLAND

TO E.GERMANY

Pommern (Pomerania)

Posen

NEUMARK

Brandenburg

Schlesien (Silesia)

M.S.

M.S.

Mecklenburg Schwerin

Schleswig-Holstein

TO DENMARK AFTER W.W.I

Ham-burg

Hannover (Hanover)

Olden-burg

L

B

Li

B

Prov. Sachsen

A

B

Schw

Königreich Sachsen (Saxony)

(Thur-ingia) Thüringen

Westfalen (Westphalia)

W

Rheinland

Hessen

Nassau

H.D.

H.D.

O

Pfalz

Bayern (Bavaria)

(Wuert-temberg) Württemberg

H

Baden

Lothringen

Elsass

Alsace-Lorraine

TO FRANCE AFTER W.W.I

TO BELGIUM AFTER W.W.I

Abbreviations:

A   = Anhalt
B   = Braunschweig
H   = Hohenzollern
H.D. = Hessen-Darmstadt
L   = Lubeck
LI = Lippe
M.S. = Mecklenburg-Strelitz
O   = Oldenburg
Schw = Schwarzburg
W   = Waldeck

MOST OF POSEN AND WEST PRUSSIA WAS LOST TO POLAND AFTER WORLD WAR I. PART OF THE WESTERNMOST COUNTIES OF BOTH PROVINCES, PLUS THE NORTHEAST PART OF WEST PRUSSIA, WERE RETAINED BY GERMANY UNTIL THE END OF WORLD WAR II.

dom's previously separated provinces of Brandenburg and East Prussia (Ostpreussen) would now be connected. Poznan would evolve into the Grand Duchy of Posen and Pomerelia became the Province of West Prussia. When Prussia first annexed West Prussia in the Polish partitions of 1772, they also received a territory called the Netze District, encompassing uncultivated marshlands along the Netze River. This Netze District was composed of two "Grand Counties", Deutsch Krone and Kamin bei Flatow. Posen, which was also sometimes called "South Prussia" (Südpreussen) in those early years, was annexed in 1793. An additional area, "New East Prussia" (Neuostpreussen), was temporarily held until the end of the Napoleonic Wars in 1815. When the Congress of Vienna determined the outcome of those wars, under which the occupying French made the Netze/Posen area part of a "Grand Duchy of Warsaw", the old Netze District was divided into smaller county units.

From the old Netze District, the counties of Filehne, Czarnikau, Kolmar. Wirsitz, Schubin, Bromberg, and Hohensalza arose under the reorganized Grand Duchy of Posen (which became a Province in 1836). The counties of Deutsch Krone and Flatow were adjoined to the Province of West Prussia. These boundaries were obviously altered a great deal by both World Wars, but it was under this alignment, during most of the 19th Century, when the emigrants made their move to Wisconsin.

It would be Posen, in particular, and West Prussia, along with Pomerania and Brandenburg, which would provide Green Lake, Marquette, and Waushara Counties with the vast majority of their German settlers.

Those Germans who originally colonized the Netze District, some before the Prussian annexation, came primarily from adjacent counties to the immediate west, in southern Pomerania and the Neumark region of Province Brandenburg, although some came from all parts of the Germanies. These Pomeranian and Neumarkish "Hauländer" colonists brought with them their corrupted Kashubian-Low German dialects (Kashubian a very separate dialect of Polish), which were still taught in some local schools as late as 1900. The pattern of some families moving eastward, during the very early 1800's, from say the Evangelical Lutheran parishes of Czanikau to Kolmar, is evident in the church books of these places, which have been microfilmed by the LDS (Mormon) Church. This "migrating neighborhood", where some intermarriages within families occured, carried all the way to Wisconsin.

Led by nobility-organized groups, such as the Eastern Marches Society, Posen and West Prussia would be the focus of a massive colonization program over the next 100 years, an effort which was never popular with the Polish Catholic majority in the region.

Because Germany was not a unified nation, itself, at that time, regional differences between Germans, themselves, were more apparent. Roughly divided, southern Germans, like Bavarians, Hessians, and Swabians, were predominantly Catholic and spoke the most extreme High German (Hochdeutsch) dialects. To the north and east, Protestants in the Prussian provinces and Lower Saxony area spoke versions of Low German (Plattdeutsch). The Evangelical Lutheran Church was state-supported in Prussia.

An example of the similarities between Low German and English can be found in this simple sentence, "There is the ship". In the modern, written language of Standard High German, that same sentence would read, "Da ist das Schiff", but in the spoken-only tongue of Low German, "Da is dat Schipp" is not far removed from English. One word still known to German descendants in central Wisconsin is "Tüfte" (like"tif-tä"). Although it sometimes sounds like "tif-ka", it is a Low German dialect word for "potatoes", and that is very different from the Standard High German "Kartoffeln".

Posen and West Prussia were, to a degree, the Prussian equivalent of being sent to Siberia. Life on the Polish frontier was usually reserved for incompetent bureaucrats and colonists who were displaced in Prussia proper. Animosity between Polish Catholics, German Protestants, and the sizable Jewish minority was commonplace, but rarely violent. "Polack" was a common term of disdain and the Polish retaliated by condemning the "German Fritz" as a "szwab" (like shvahb). The Polish squelched Prussian efforts at purchasing-up their land, with their own land-buying cooperatives, but all three ethnic groups did conduct some business between themselves. They just rarely socialized with each other.

There are also some parallels between the "Hauländer" forebears and today's generation in central Wisconsin: Posen and West Prussia were among the least industrially developed provinces in Prussia, relying on an agriculture which was farmed on sandy, marshy lowlands, not unlike that part of Wisconsin. The demonstration of support for Republican conservatism in our most recent elections may also be hereditary. The agrarian ancestors were, for the most part, fiercely conservative, and looked to the Prussian royal government for protection on the hostile Polish frontier.

Most German family names in central Wisconsin can trace their origins to Prussia's Netzeland, or the Netze River valley marshlands region, where many of the colonists, including my 4th-great-grandfather, were military veterans receiving land grants as a form of pension. In Marquette County, the largest specific group came from County Kolmar, Province Posen; in Green Lake County, the most were from County Arnswalde, in Province Brandenburg's Neumark region.

In all three Wisconsin counties, Posen's northern Netzeland counties: Wirsitz, Obernick, Wongrowitz, besides Filehne, Czarnikau, and Kolmar, plus Bromberg provided fewer, but still significant numbers of immigrants, as did the adjacent West Prussian counties of Deutsch Krone and Flatow along the Netzeland.

For people who **do** research their families without the benefit of a genealogist, a point should be made: If you stumble upon the term "Bromberg" or "Bromberg, Prussia", that may not necessarily refer to the city or county of Bromberg, itself, but rather, the administrative district (Regierungsbezirk) of Bromberg, which included counties in the northern third of the province. The remaining two-thirds of the province came under the administrative district of Posen, the city itself. When villages in adjoining counties may have the same name, this knowledge can help pinpoint the exact location of an ancestors' hometown.

WISCONSIN

PERCENTAGE OF GERMAN-BORN
WITHIN FOREIGN-BORN POPULATION
1890

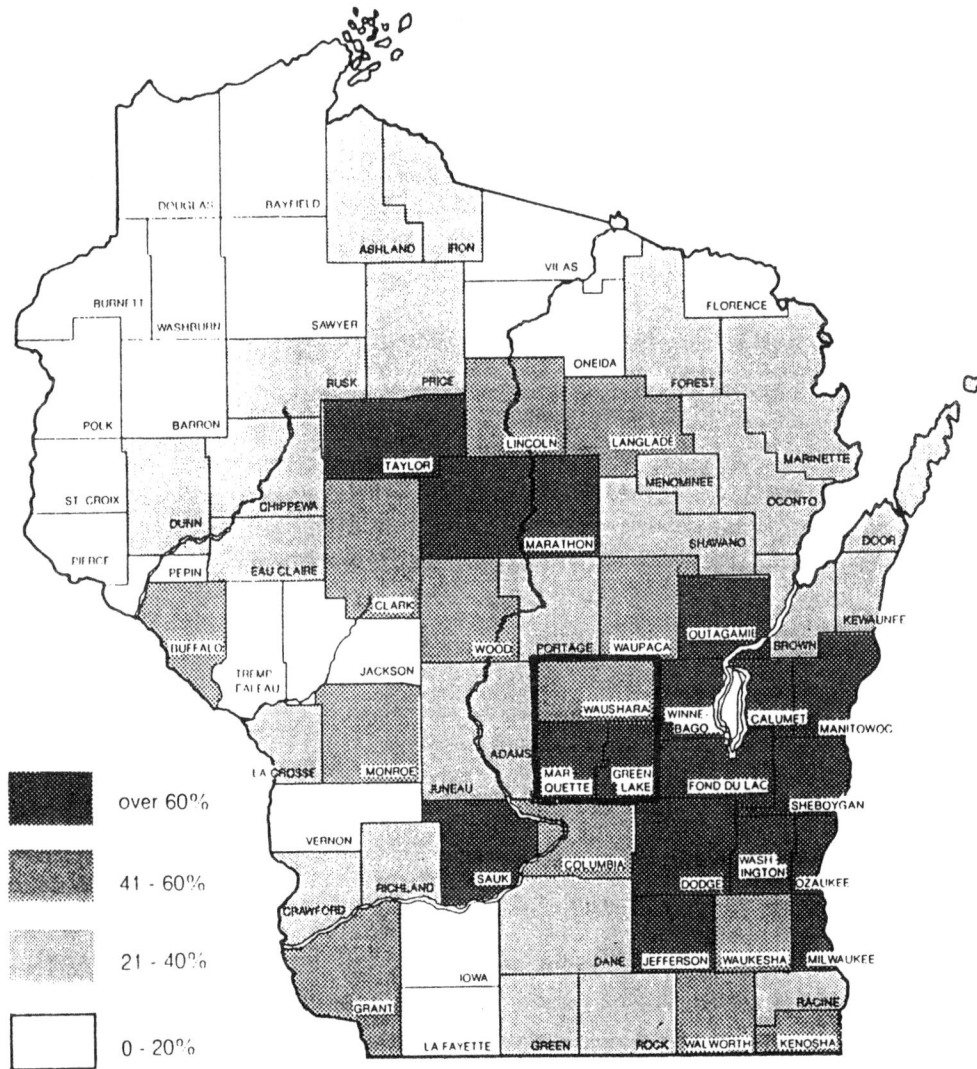

over 60%

41 - 60%

21 - 40%

0 - 20%

(From the monograph, GERMANS IN WISCONSIN by
Richard H. Zeitlin, published by State
Historical Society of Wisconsin, Madison:1977)

Maybe it should be mentioned here, but, to my surprise, it seems
that the Province of East Prussia was not the same voluminous source
for immigrants to America, that the other eastern provinces were.
This may be attributed to the fact that East Prussia has a more entren-
ched German history for 700 years, whereas even Pomerania (mid-1600's),
and of course Posen and West Prussia were later acquisitions. East
Prussian culture had evolved from the conquest of heathen Baltic Prussian natives in the 1200's by the Teutonic Knights.

Michael Anuta makes the analogy quite well in his book EAST PRUS-
SIANS FROM RUSSIA, where he compares that conquest with the near exter-
mination of some native American cultures. Much like you'll find In-
dian place names in America, especially Wisconsin, today, the influence
of the extinct Old Prussian language on place and family names survived
in East Prussia until the end of the Second World War.

Even though the Neumark region, then on Poland's border, was ob-
tained by the Electorate of Brandenburg as early as the 1400's, the
migratory nature of the ancient peoples in the Pomerania-West Prussia-
Posen area became more of an evolutionary merging of Teutonic and Slavic cultures. With the political merging of Brandenburg and East Prussia into the Kingdom of Prussia in 1701, the delineation and maturation
of these cultures began to crystalize much more. The collapse of Poland
as a political entity at the end of the 18th Century probably opened
the door, albeit in a limited way, to the further intermarrying admixture
of German and Polish, Catholic and Protestant strains. Hence, many of
the family names from the region reflect these influences, Podoll being one of many examples.

In her book, COME BACK IN TIME, VOL. II, central Wisconsin historian Elaine Reetz writes that in Green Lake County, Princeton's J.F.
Warnke, of local lumber fame, came from "Schneidemuhl in the Province
of Bromberg". Well, Schneidemühl was in County Kolmar, but was under
the Administrative District of Bromberg. Mrs. Reetz may be surprised
to know that there were at least two villages in the area named "Reetz",
as well: One in County Arnswalde, Province Brandenburg, the other in
County Tuchel, Province West Prussia.

As possibly the best example, Kolmar was one of the more heavily
German-speaking counties on the Polish frontier, with more than 75%
using "Deutsch" as their mother tongue. Still, the Polish influence,
particularly on place names, could be seen, especially when the county seat of Kolmar, itself, was often called "Chodziesen" (like K'ohj-
yesen). In modern Poland, it is called Chodzież (like H'odzh-yezh).
My own ancestral villages of Nalentscha and Radwonke in County Kolmar,
underwent a variety of spellings during the days of Prussian rule, but
today, they are Nałęcza and Radwanki. The locality of Budsin, in Marquette County's Crystal Lake Township, at the junction of State Highway 22 and County Trunk E, was named after its precedent in County
Kolmar. We may expect some German names to get mangled in their American translations, but even in their Prussian homeland, some family
names weren't safe from "acts of butchery". In 19th Century Evangeli-

cal Lutheran microfilms from the Kolmar area, the Polish influence on "Pawlicka" and "Redecki" made for the same pronounciation as Pavlitzke and Redetzke. Weckwerth was sometimes "Wekkwert" and Wandrey could be "Vandrei" or "Fandrey". Hartwig and Hartwich were also interchangeable and makes for a difficult time in establishing proper family relationships.

In the 1860's, a man named Adam Wilhelm Tucholke altered his last name, in Kolmar parish records, to Tucholl. Despite some questions and debate about whether Podoll was another of those names, perhaps altered from Podolski, Podolsky, or Podolske, I could not find any evidence of that connection, with one exception, but all earlier and other spellings are consistently as Podoll. This, even though there were a few Lutheran Podolsky families in County Kolmar, too.

Just like the "Po-" prefix is usually an indication of an eastern, Slavic bent in names like Poblitz, Podoll, or Porath, so are the "-ow" (Guelzow, Pontow, Sandow, Wittchow), "-in" (Beuthin=boy-teen, Koplin=ko-pleen, Polzin=pol-tseen), and "-zke" (Gatzke, Kopitzke, Neitzke, Schatzke) suffixes representative of Pomeranian origins. Of course, the "-ow" suffix is pronounced like "oh" in English, but for names like Ristau, the German "-au" ending is said like "ow" in English. Other names like Pollack, Pollnow, Pollesch, or Polsfuss are still further evidence of Teutonized Slavs in the Polish regions.

The Netze District also seems to be a source of names which underwent a Low German corruptive influence. I don't know if Mr. Bahlow would wholeheartedly agree, but it looks like some names, namely Bursack, Kop(p)lin, or Moskopp and Ke(r)ntopp were Low German modifications of Biersach (beer sack), Kopflein (little head?, kopf=head), Mooskopf (moor head), and Köntopf (place name in Pomerania). In Adams County, Wisconsin, for example, there was a Bavarian Zimbeck family, which was originally Zümbach, although that looks more like a case of Americanization, but Low German is sort of a step in that Anglicized simplification process.

Another good example of Germanized Polish/Slavic evolution comes in the name Jab(b)usch. This Netzelander name would appear to be a nickname for Jakob, as say, Bogisch would be for Bogislav, or Jarosch for Jaromir. We can see this process in the Polish name Kowalski (blacksmith)= Kowalske (Pomeranian version)= Kowall or Kowald= Kufahl= Kuphal. The Prussian name Pigorsch has a slightly more complex evolution. "Piekarz" (p'ye-kazh) is the Polish word for a baker, which is Bäcker= Becker in German. Pigorsch is then the German corruption of piekarz. For names with the "Po-" prefix, as mentioned above, "po" usually means "on" the something, like Podoll can mean "on the valley" (dolina=valley or lowland), although in its case, it can also mean someone from Podolia, an historic region now in the western Ukraine.

Such meanings of family names can shed some additional light on a family's history. Among Netzelander-Wisconsinite names, Floet(h)er refers to someone who played a flute. Mittelstaedt meant that someone lived "in the middle of town". Some, like Arendsee, Kemnitz, Salzwedel,

9

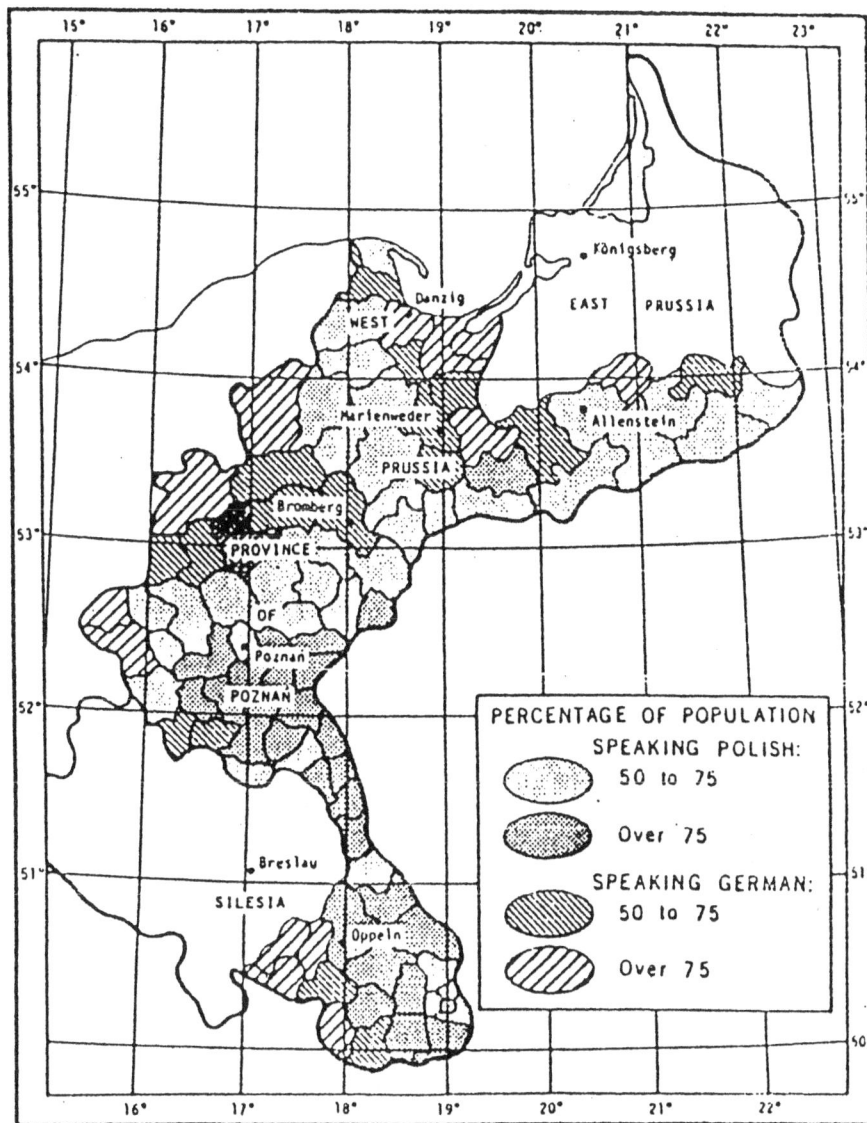

—County Kolmar (over 75% German speaking)

(Reprinted from GERMANS, POLES, AND JEWS: The Nationality
Conflict in the Prussian East by Wm. W. Hagen, U. of Chicago
Press, 1980)

or Burgdorff, may pertain to pre-Netzeland origins in central Germany. Beutler is a specific word for a marisupial (a pouch animal, like o-possum), but, in the same context, may relate to someone who makes pouches or bags.

Others, like Abraham or Zacharias, may have Biblical implications, and Gros(s)kreutz was a "great or large cross". Surnames aren't always so flattering. Take Bloede (now Blada?), for instance. Whoever first carried that tag was apparently an "imbecile", who was "stupid, dull, and silly". A regular triple threat! As Casey Stengel used to say, "You could look it up!"

Some names were affected by their Americanization: What was Glock-zien or Klockzin in Prussia became "Clocksene" in Marquette County. Bläsing dropped the "umlaut" (two dots for "ae") over the "a", but kept the same pronounciation. Tagatz, in the "old country", sometimes had two "g's".

Many of central Wisconsin's Prussian settlers came after the American Civil War, some for social reasons, many for economic opportunity, and some to get away from the three wars that Prussia would wage during that decade. Ironically, a few of those Germans who did come earlier, volunteered for the Union cause in our own Civil War!

A grain market crash in 1873, precipitated by American and Russian imports, sent the Prussian economy into a depression which would last until 1890. Some Poseners migrated to central and western Germany for seasonal farm work. Many left for America. It was during this period that the major influx of Prussian settlers came into the western townships of Green Lake County and also the northern townships of Marquette County, particularly Newton, Crystal Lake, Springfield, the Lawrence millpond area of Westfield Township, as well as Mecan and Montello to the east.Many of Waushara County's Prussians, especially in its south-western townships, were a result of a later northward push by Marquette County immigrants. For many, it was the first time they could own their own land.

Some belonged to Evangelical Association and Evangelical United Brethren churches and were called "German Methodists", later merging with the United Methodist churches of the Anglo-Yankees in the area. Ironically, though they didn't coalesce very well back in Prussia, clusters of German Lutherans and Polish Catholics would meet again around Princeton and Berlin in Green Lake County. In Green Lake and Marquette Counties, the Germans made up roughly one-third of the population, outnumbering large groups Yankees, English, and Scotch-Irish. Waushara County also had a significantly numerous amount of Norwegians and other Scandinavians, as well as groups of Finns, Italians, and Welsh to work the quarries around Redgranite.

For people who have grown up in this central Wisconsin area amongst neighbors of German ancestry, the family researcher comes to find that most of these were interrelated and transplanted their "neighborhoods" from the Netzeland to central Wisconsin. In researching my own extended families, I've found that the nomadic tendencies of these people also carried them onto Dunn and Pierce Counties in western Wisconsin.

Not just Podoll, but other names like Draeger, Boelter, Drewitz, and Malzahn can be seen in local cemeteries as examples of this movement. Furthermore, many of these Prussian Netzelanders would go on to the flat prairie lands across southern Minnesota.

When I visited some distant Minnesota relatives during a gathering at Racine, Wisconsin over four years ago, these folks brought along an old portrait photo of their Grandma Podoll, who had lived at Wood Lake, in Yellow Medicine County, southwestern Minnesota. The name of the photo studio on the frame caught me by surprise, for it said "Redetzke Studio, Echo, Minnesota". They weren't aware of it, but I explained to them that their Grandpa Podoll had a first cousin, who married a Redetzke in Marquette County and moved onto northern North Dakota, after the turn of the century. The progenitors, Christoph and Wilhelmine (Martin) Redetzke are buried in "Little Mecan" cemetery in Marquette County, and had come from County Kolmar, Posen. I've since seen that uncommon Redetzke name on a construction firm between Marshfield and Abbotsford, probably in Marathon County, Wisconsin.

That this migrating pattern carried from central Wisconsin, across southern Minnesota, and on into northwestern North Dakota is most evident, but among my many correspondents, Mr. Wayne Fabert of San Diego, California; Ms. Deb Koplen of Grand Prairie, Texas, and others; lend credence to it.

In the case of Mr. Fabert, much of his early extended genealogy came from County Kolmar, Posen to Marquette County. Although he has Illinois roots himself, where the pronounciation of his surname was Americanized to "Fay-bert", he noted that during a trip to Marquette County he kept hearing the traditional German pronounciation of "Fah-bert". He attributed the difference to the central Illinois community being more ethnically mixed, while Marquette County was still very Germanic in nature. Many of his relations spread to places as diverse as Michigan to California, in coming directly from County Kolmar, but besides Illinois and Wisconsin, some of his people also settled in the Blue Earth area of Faribault County, Minnesota. In that Fabert movement from Kolmar to Blue Earth, other family names with mutual Kolmar/Marquette ties are Manthey and Döge (Doege).

Ms. Koplen's immigrant ancestor, whose name was probably also Americanized from Koplin (ko-Pleen) and is pronounced that way, came from at least Posen, whether the province or city, and went first to Ripon, in Fond du Lac County, Wisconsin, near the Green Lake County. However, Ripon came after he may have been in Newton Township, Marquette County, living near a Fratzke relation. These Koplen/Fratzke families went on to the Janesville/Freedom Township areas of Waseca County, Minnesota, circa 1870.

It is a strong hint of the settlement in Yellow Medicine County, Minnesota that, not only is one township named Posen, but two others are Oshkosh and Omro, named after the county seat and a town in Winnebago County, Wisconsin, also home to a large Prussian settlement. Other Podoll-related names in that area of Minnesota with both Prussian roots and Wisconsin connections are Hinz and Warnke.

To further reinforce this trend, the late Mrs. Viola Kroenke De-Witt Podoll had mentioned that her Kroenke family had moved from Green Lake County, Wisconsin out to near Blue Earth, Faribault County, Minnesota, which by the way, is near the Iowa border. Ultimately, her family moved back to Wisconsin.

Another Podoll relation, August Fritz, moved his second wife and two children from Green Lake County, Wisconsin to Wellington Township in the Minnesota River Valley area of Renville County, circa 1871. This German community, where Emmanuel Evangelical Lutheran Church and Cemetery was established, found the Kiecker family name to be prominent, although other Kolmar Posener surnames, such as Splittstoesser, could be seen. It was during a return trip from a 1989 Podoll Family Reunion near Aberdeen, South Dakota that I could see other familiar Prussian names on businesses scattered across southern Minnesota. Along the vicinity of Gaylord-Winthrop-Henderson, there was a Lieske Genetics company, Sando Implement (Sando may be Swedish, or Pomeranian Sandow, without the "w"), a Uecker Bros. garage, and for Milwaukee Brewers baseball fans, there was even a business with the Trebelhorn name (like recently fired manager Tom Trebelhorn). Lieske and Sandow are actually names related to my own pedigree.

In researching another branch of Podoll relations in the Winona, Minnesota area, names appearing in old local newspapers also adhered to this general pattern, but I think the point has been made. If the suggested pattern from this book serves as some sort of impetus for a Minnesota researcher to further follow-up from their side, more power to them!

The pattern is less blatant in North Dakota, but McHenry County in the north central part of the state and Burke County, to the northwest, seems to have some of the same inclinations, as other family names like Erdman, Nickel, Kitzman (Kietzmann in Wisconsin), besides Podoll, keep recurring.

The ethnic melting pot that was Prussia, was complex enough with its Teutonic, Slavic, and Old Prussian elements and I want to add here that many of the same names that I have seen in County Kolmar microfilms and central Wisconsin records could also be found in County Preussisch Holland, Province East Prussia. Besides Podoll again, other examples like Bläsing or Dahlke show a possible eastward internal colonization of similar families farming those lowland areas. One excellent example of Prussian complexity is the family name Bonneur.

French Hugenots and Dutch Mennonites were among other colonists invited into different parts of Prussia. This name Bonneur, which is in County Kolmar Lutheran records, may be derived of the French bonheur, meaning "good fortune" or "good luck". One of my Stelter grand-aunts in Marquette County, of Kolmar ancestry, married a "Bonier" (bo-near), which was probably an Americanized corruption of Bonneur. The aforementioned Mr. Fabert had both a Stelter and a Bonneur woman in his early Kolmar genealogy and I have seen the Bonneur name in recent Minneapolis telephone books. Simply citing your ancestry as "German" or even "Prussian" may not suffice, when those roots may run in some very different directions!

M I N N E S O T A

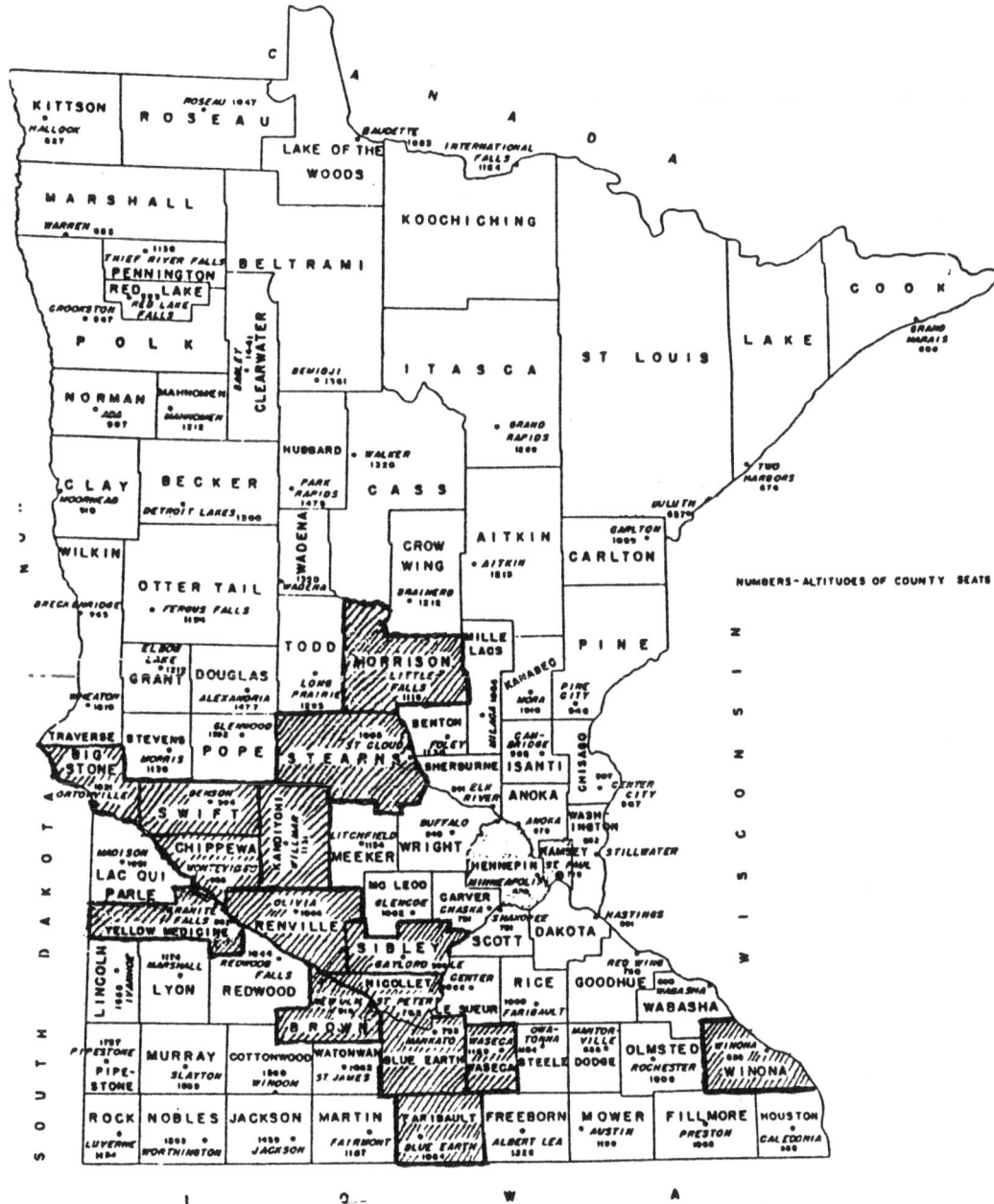

Central and southern Minnesota counties with known Prussian and German settlement are shaded (Map from the ATLAS OF THE STATE OF MINNESOTA, Fergus Falls, Thomas O. Nelson Co., 1971)

The spark for translating this interest in Prussian immigrants into a series of books on Wisconsin was provided in part by Mrs. Beulah Hermann of West Allis, Wisconsin, with help from Mr. Ken Wolske of Racine, Wisconsin. They directed me to the Walther Maas book, as well as to the vast amount of information that Mr. Ron Kruger of Ashland, Nebraska has accumulated on Krüger, Leu, and Ponto(w) lineages from County Kolmar, Dodge County, Wisconsin; plus Illinois and Nebraska. My thanks also goes to Wautoma, Wisconsin historian Michael Bednarek, whose collection of local history memorabilia is truly impressive. Beyond the maps that he has contributed towards this book, we will now peruse some of the obituaries of Prussian immigrants in Waushara County, which he received in a scrapbook from an elderly woman. Although the clippings contain no dates or pages from the newspapers themselves, it is fairly safe to assume that they appeared in the local Waushara Argus weekly, which is still published in Wautoma:

"Frederick Boelke, who was called by death on Friday, May 29th (1931), was the son of Frederick Boelke and his wife Wilhelmine, nee Bock. He was born at Veronika (County Schubin), Province of Posen, Germany, on March 12th, 1849. He was baptized in the Lutheran church in his infancy, and confirmed at the age of fourteen years.

"In 1875 he was united in holy wedlock to Auguste Harke. In 1881 he emigrated to America, settling on a farm about four miles west of Neshkoro, where he resided until 1914, when he erected a new house in Wautoma. He made Wautoma his home until seven years ago, when he was tragically bereft of his wife. From that time until his final summons he lived at the home of his youngest daughter, Elsa, the wife of Emil Bohn, who faithfully attended him during his last illness which lasted about six months. The cause of death was arteriosclerosis. The time of his sojourn on earth was 82 years, 2 months and 17 days.

"Funeral services were held in the home and in Grace Evangelical Lutheran Church, Deerfield Township, conducted by his pastor, Rev. O.G. Renner. Interment was made in Wautoma cemetery on Sunday afternoon, May 31st. The large attendance at both services and at the cemetery betokened the esteem in which he was held by his many acquaintances and friends in this and surrounding communities.

"Mr. Boelke was a member of the Lutheran church all his days, holding voting membership in Immanual church, Neshkoro, Peace church in Wautoma, and Grace church, Deerfield, successively. His wedded life was blessed with thirteen children, eight of whom preceeded him into eternity, namely: Bertha, Hulda, Ida, Julius, Augusta, Edward, and two infants. There survive, to mourn him, two sons, Otto and Emil, and three daughters, Alvina, wife of Emil Boelter, of Coloma, Wis.; Tina, wife of Fred Glode, also of Coloma; and Elsa,wife of Emil Bohn, of Hancock, besides seventeen grandchildren and six great grandchildren." These five examples are being listed in alphabetical order and where necessary, notes in parentheses will explain clarifying information.

POSENER LAND

0 25 50 km

Border of province Posen 1818-1918
Border of „Deutsches Reich" 1920-1939
Border of „Reichsgau Posen (Wartheland)" 1939-1945
Administration District

Counties in what was once the Grand Duchy and later Province Posen in Prussia.
The northern counties of Filehne, Czarnikau, Kolmar, Wirsitz, Schubin, Brom-
berg, & Hohensalza made up the Netze River District, along with the counties of
Flatow and Deutsch Krone in West Prussia, which was annexed by Prussia in
1772. Kolmar was a model county of German colonization, with over 75%
German-speaking inhabitants (Courtesy GENEALOGICAL GUIDE to German
Ancestors from East Germany and Eastern Europe, edited by AGoFF e.V.,
Herne, W. Germany)

"Mrs. Wilhelmine Bruch, nee Knaack, was born on April 13, 1843, in Dreidorf (County Wirsitz), government-district Bramberg (Bromberg) in Posen, Germany. She was the daughter of Christoph Knaack and Eva Knaack.

"She was baptized in infancy and confirmed in the Lutheran Faith on September 27, 1857, in Lobsenz (Lobsens, County Wirsitz), Germany. Here in Lobsenz she also was united in marriage to August Bruch in March 1862. To this union were born eight children, three of whom died in infancy.

"It was approximately 1873, when Mr. and Mrs. Bruch left Germany in order to establish for themselves a new home in America. They came to Ripon, where they lived only a short time before they moved to Germania, but here also they did not remain a long time. They soon came to Richford, which was to become their permanent home.

"Twenty years ago, on October 31, 1915, Mrs. Bruch was widowed through the death of her husband. Again about 2½ years ago, she was called upon to mourn the loss of a daughter, Mrs. Emilie Apps.

"In June 1935, Mrs. Bruch began to fail. Later she was stricken with pneumonia from which, contrary to expectations, she rallied, but never regained her strength. At this time she consented to leave her home of the past 58 years in order to stay with her son, Eduard, in Wautoma. Gradually she became weaker again until three weeks before Christmas her condition became serious. She died at the ripe old age of 92 years, 9 months and 22 days on Monday, February 10 (1936) at 7:55 p.m.

"She leaves to mourn her death four children: Herman in Richford, Eduard in Wautoma, Gustav in Richford and Ida Hennig in Wautoma; 21 grandchildren; 30 great-grandchildren; 2 great-great-children; 2 sisters: Miss Emilie Knaack of Princeton and Mrs. Henrietta Boelke of Wautoma; 1 brother, Gottlieb Knaack of Princeton, also a son-in-law, George Apps of Wild Rose.

"Among those from out of town who attended the last rites were Albert Bruchs and daughter Pearl, Oxford; Elmer Bruchs, Stanley; Evelyn Bruchs, Wisconsin Rapids; George Apps and son George, Mr. and Mrs. Milton Woodward, Mr. and Mrs. John Apps, Wild Rose; Gottlieb Knaack and son William, Mr. and Mrs. Gust Knaack, Mr. Fred Knaack and son Leo, Mrs. Ernest Priebe and Louise Schavey, Princeton."

* * * * *

"FUNERAL SERVICES HELD SUNDAY FOR HERMAN KLABUNDE

Funeral services were held Sunday afternoon at St. Peter's church, Richford, for Herman Frederick Klabunde, 59, who died at his home Thursday evening due to a blood clot. The Rev. L. Vater officiated.

"Mr. Klabunde was born in the village of Schiefelbein, province Pommerania, Germany, Sept. 3, 1890. When he was but 11 months old, the family came to America and settled in Waushara County, in the township of Deerfield, the present Emil Klabunde farm. He married Miss Ida Roeski of Richford on May 19, 1915 and to this union eight children were born, three of whom preceded their father in death.

"Survivors include his wife, a daughter, Mrs. Rollins Clark, Ripon, Ervin, Springfield, O., Edward of Two Rivers, Ruth and Donald at home, three grandchildren, one brother, Emil, Deerfield, and a sister, Anna, of Milwaukee, besides other relatives.

"Interment was in the Richford Cemetery."

* * * * *

"JULIANNA HENRIETTA LIPKE

Julianna Henrietta Lipke, nee Borkenhagen, daughter of Mr. and Mrs. Wilhelm Borkenhagen, was born in Linden Werder (Lindenwerder, County Kolmar), Posen Germany, July 14, 1842. October 18, 1862, she was united in holy wedlock with Fredrich Bliske. To this union nine children were born, five sons and four daughters. One son and two daughters preceded her in death. In 1867 she and her family emigrated to America and settled in Dakota township , Waushara County, Wis. About thirty-five years ago she and her family moved onto a farm in Deerfield township. In 1895 her first husband died. In 1896 she entered a second marriage with Anton Lipke who died April 1, 1909. Last November the deceased went to Montello to visit her relatives. While she was there she took sick and was unable to return to her home. She departed this life at the home of her grandson, Ed Cook, near Montello, May 30, 1927, at eleven o'clock a.m., at the age of 85 years, 10 months, and 19 days. She has through her death, as we confidently hope and trust, because of her Christian faith and life, entered into the church triumphant.

She leaves to mourn her death three sons and three daughters: Wilhelmine, Mrs. Julius Kuck of Montello; Herman Bliske of Wautoma; Auguste, Mrs. Albert Podoll of Wautoma; Alvine, Mrs. Aug. Putzky of Hancock; Friedrich Bliske of Wautoma; Albert Bliske of Wautoma; 51 grandchildren, 42 great-grandchildren, and eight stepchildren: Fred Lipke of Hancock; Mrs. Frank Rohde of Kenosha, Wis.; Mrs. Albert Monroe, of Hancock; Gust. Lipke of Hancock; Mrs. Richard Stratton, New London, Wis.; Leonard Lipke, Hancock; Mrs. Emmett Searls, Green Lake, Wis.; Elmer Lipke of Oshkosh.

"Funeral services were held Tuesday afternoon, June 2, at the home of Albert Bliske and in the Deerfield Lutheran church, of which the deceased was a member, Rev. B.J.E. Stelter officiating. The flowers were carried by the following ladies: Mrs. Otto Reier, Emma Bliske, Mary Podoll, Lillian Cook, Linda Salzwedel and Erna Cook. The community extends to the mourners its heartfelt sympathy."

(followed by card of thanks from "The Children")

* * * * *

"Hanna Henrietta Raatz was born March 16, 1845 at Hertzberg Kreis (County) Dromberg (Dramburg, Province Pomerania), Germany. May 1, 1868 she was married to Wilhelm Albert Raatz. To this union 13 children were born, three passed away. In the year 1875 this family came to this country and have lived on their farm 4 miles north-

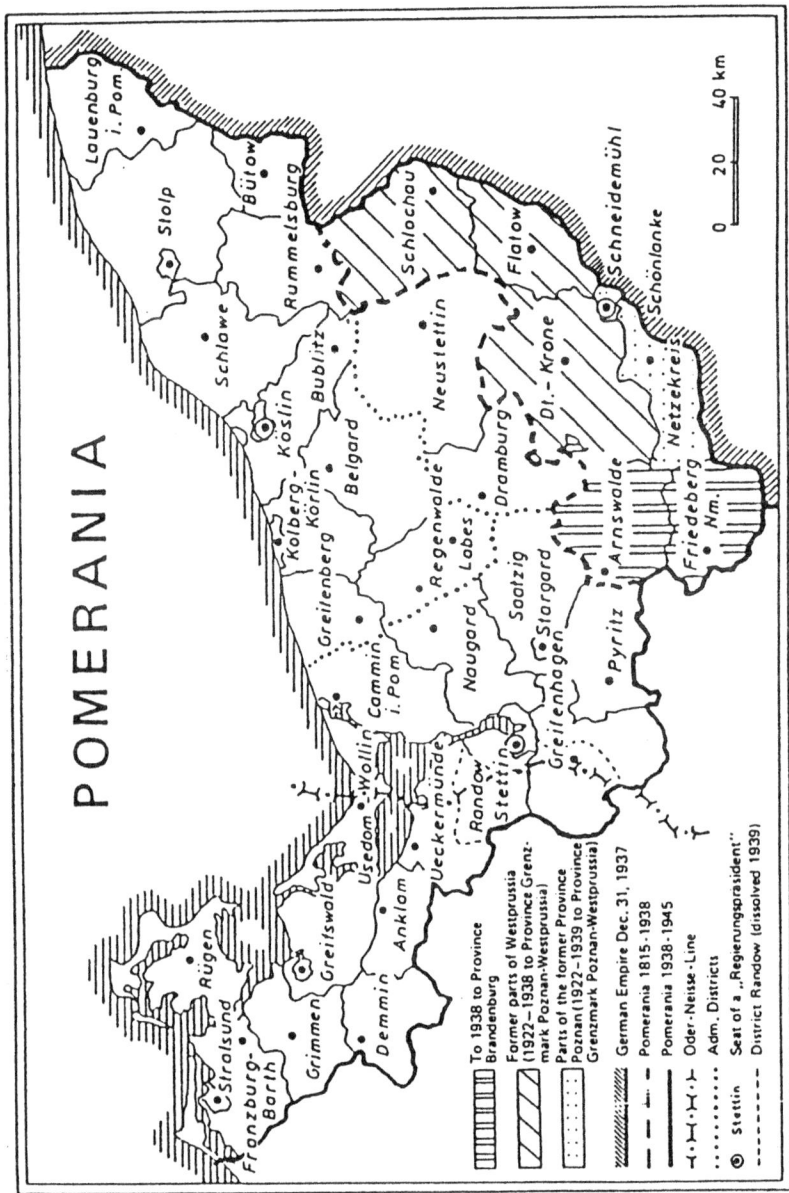

POMERANIA

Legend:

- ▦ To 1938 to Province Brandenburg
- ▨ Former parts of Westprussia (1922–1938 to Province Grenzmark Poznan-Westprussia)
- ⋮ Parts of the former Province Poznan (1922–1939 to Province Grenzmark Poznan-Westprussia)
- ▨▨ German Empire Dec. 31, 1937
- – – Pomerania 1815-1938
- —— Pomerania 1938-1945
- –×–×– Oder-Neisse-Line
- ⋯⋯ Adm. Districts
- ⊙ Stettin Seat of a „Regierungspräsident"
- –·–·– District Randow (dissolved 1939)

Genealogical Guide to German Ancestors in East Germany and Eastern Europe, AGoFF e. V., Herne W. Germany.

18

east of Richford. As they only had small means the time at first was
very hard, but through hard labor they worked themselves up and got
wealthy.

"This family was respected by all who knew them and Mr. Raatz
was for 7 years president of our St. Petri Gemeinde (parish community)
at Richford. Last year, March 4, 1914 Mr. Albert Raatz, her husband,
was called from this world and her words spoken then, "I shall foll-
ow him soon" were soon fulfilled, yea, sooner than we expected for
she was always of good health. She was taken sick about March 18. At
that time we did not think she would leave us for we thought it was
only a bad cold. The doctor was called and when he stated that it was
pneumonia we knew that the end was near. She died March 22, 1915.

"Mrs. Raatz was a lovable character and was held in the highest
esteem and affection by all who knew her. She was a model wife, an af-
fectionate mother, a loving sister, a kind neighbor and a good christian. (nee Brietzke- adds Michael Bednarek)

"She leaves to mourn her loss her children Robert, Mary, Bertha,
Emilie, Emma, Wilhelm, Ida, Herman, Albertine, and Ricdard (sic), and
many relatives and friends. Her age was 70 years and 6 days.

"The funeral services were held in the Lutheran St. Petri church
at Richford. When the remains by pallbearers were tenderly carried in
the church, the choir sang, Droben in des Himonels-- Fernien is ein
seliges Heimat-- Land. Rev. Reu preached the funeral sermon from He-
brews 4:9 : There remaineth therefore a Sabbath for the people of God.
Interment was in Richford cemetery, March 25th. A large funeral pro-
cession followed her. "   (followed by card of thanks)

And so it was for these migratory people, these Netzelanders, Poseners, Pomeranians, West Prussians, Neumarkers (noy-markers), and other
Germans. People with names like Abendroth("sunset"), Buchhol(t)z
("beech wood"),or Dolgner("from Dolgen") meshing with names like Duesterhoeft (lower German for"sullen chief" or polonized as "Disterhaft"),
Ge(h)lha(a)r ("blond hair"), Gollnick (Slavic root for "heath keeper"),
across the Polish frontier with families like Janke (Slavic root nickname for Johann=John), Klatt (lower German for "disheveled hair"),
Klingbeil (lower German, another for "carpenter"), Mag(e)danz (lower
German for "make dance"), Marotz (probably German corruption of Polish
mroz="frost, the cold").

People, families who would take such names to America like Pomplun (Slavic place name), Prellwitz (Slavic place in Mecklenburg &
Pomerania), or Prochnow (Slavic place name, referring to "rotten wood");
on to central Wisconsin, families such as Quade ("bad, evil"), Schrank
(upper German for someone who "lives behind a grating fence"), Sied-
schlag (from Slavic personal name Setslav, slav="glory"), Stellmacher
(Silesian term for "wagon maker"), Tetzlaff (Pomeranian version of Slavic personal name Tetslav), Weckwerth (Hamburg locality name for "swamp
island"), Wruck (lower German, often Hamburg area for "quarrelsome,
pugnacious"), or Zuehlke (nickname for Slavic personal name Zulimir,
Zulislav). Both Wandrey (Wendish version, "vahnd-rye") and Drews (lower
German verison, "draves") are variants of the Christian name Andreas.

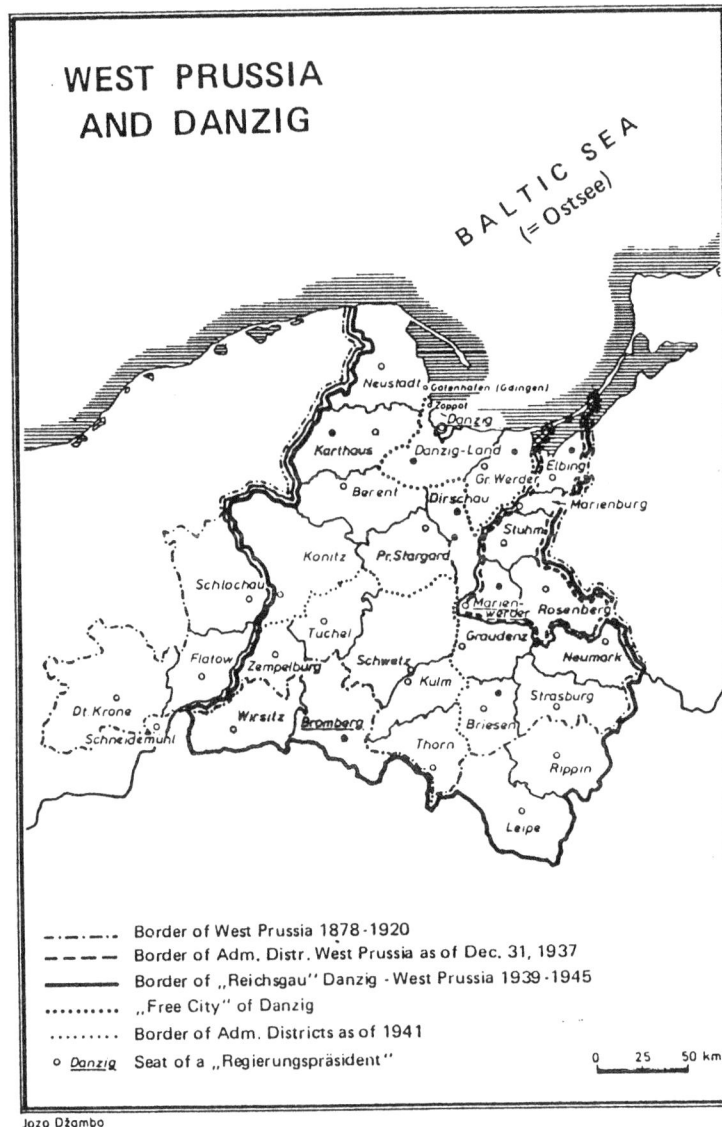

WEST PRUSSIA
AND DANZIG

BALTIC SEA
(= Ostsee)

Neustadt Gotenhafen (Gdingen)
Zoppot
Danzig
Karthaus   Danzig-Land
                                Elbing
Berent   Dirschau   Gr.Werder
                            Marienburg
                        Stuhm
        Konitz   Pr.Stargard
Schlochau   Marien- Rosenberg
                            werder
            Tuchel   Graudenz
Flatow Zempelburg Schwetz   Neumark
                        Kulm
Dt.Krone   Strasburg
        Wirsitz Bromberg   Briesen
Schneidemuhl   Rippin
            Thorn
                    Leipe

_.._.._.. Border of West Prussia 1878-1920
_ _ _ _   Border of Adm. Distr. West Prussia as of Dec. 31, 1937
‾‾‾‾‾   Border of „Reichsgau" Danzig - West Prussia 1939-1945
.... „Free City" of Danzig
.... Border of Adm. Districts as of 1941
o Danzig   Seat of a „Regierungspräsident"

0   25   50 km

Jozo Dżambo

Germany, formed Regierungsbezirk West Prussia within the province of East Prussia. After the occupation of Poland in September 1939 the Regierungsbezirk West Prussia, the Wojewodztwo (administrative district) Pomorze (Pomerellen) and Danzig were combined to form Reichsgau (administrative district) Danzig-West Prussia.

After World War II all territories of West Prussia and Danzig were taken by Poland.

(From GENEALOGICAL GUIDE to German Ancestors from
East Germany and Eastern Europe, edited by AGoFF
e.v. Herne, Germany)

These people would leave an impact on their newly found home, not just with the propagation of their families, but also on place names in these three Wisconsin counties. The best demonstrations of this can be seen to this day in Marquette County: Budsin, still an unincorporated locality in Crystal Lake Township at the junction of highways County Trunk "E" and State Highway 22, was most likely named after its counterpart in County Kolmar, Province Posen. Klawitter's Creek in Newton Township and Fenner's Lake in Westfield Township, at the Adams County border can be known to all, but some now private lakes, also in Westfield Township, used to carry the monickers "Sandow's Lake" and "Bursack's Lake". These Prussian colonists would migrate from strange-sounding places on the Polish frontier, like Polajewo-Hauland or Cziskewo, to equally odd-sounding Native American-influenced places like Neshkoro or Wautoma.

That migratory status, that lack of a strong regional identity among other German groups can be borne out today when the annual "Germanfest" is celebrated in Milwaukee. Pomeranian groups are represented at that affair, and it could be said that the Netzelander cutlture is somewhat an extension of Pomeranian influences. However, as some visiting German cousins pointed out to me, the festival is geared more to the Bavarian, southern Alpine image of Germans, with their "lederhosen" short pants and feathered caps. Other than the local Pomeranian groups, the Low Germans of the north and east, who make up the bulk of Wisconsin's rural German population, are barely seen or heard.

In preparing this book, marriage records provided the best vehicle for these settlers to cite their German hometowns. Naturalization records are helpful, too, but for Green Lake County, access to them had been complicated by the fact that the courthouse transferred the naturalization books to the State Historical Society of Wisconsin, which, in turn, has them at regional facilities, in this case, the University of Wisconsin-Oshkosh. Green Lake County pre-1907 records, in general, are less accessible , because they are folded into packets by year, in contrast to being kept in large record books, as in Marquette and most other Wisconsin counties. Because death records were reported by someone other than the decedants, they were vague and generally useless in providing specifics on settlers' hometowns.

A review was made of the marriage records for all three counties between 1858 and 1907, when reporting vital statistics in Wisconsin became mandatory and German immigration had subsided. It should be noted that Waushara County was carved out of a larger Marquette County in 1851, after Wisconsin statehood in 1848 and that Green Lake County remained part of Marquette County until 1858, when they were divided into the smaller, present units. Countless numbers of these immigrants, especially prior to 1890, still gave their home only as "Germany" or "Prussia", because it was convenient to do so.

From that period of Prussian inner colonization came this saying: "The first worked themselves to death, the next still tolerated misery, but the third were the first to have their bread".

BRANDENBURG (EAST)

POMERANIA

Dt Krone

Arnswalde

Soldin

Königsberg Nm.

Friedeberg Nm.

Landsberg (Warthe)

Schwerin (Warthe)

Posen

Soplow

Oststern-berg

Lebus

Zielenzig

Meseritz

POLAND

West-sternberg

Frankfurt (O)

Rappen

Züllichau-Schwiebus

Crossen (Oder)

Lübben (Spreewald)

Guben

Cottbus

Forst (Lausitz)

Sorau

Glogau

Calau

Spremberg (Lausitz)

SILESIA

——— Germany (as of Dec. 31, 1937)
——— Province of Brandenburg (1815-1938)
–·–·–·– Province of Brandenburg (1938-1945)
▸◂▸◂▸ Oder-Neisse-Line
·········· Administration Districts

0   25   50 km

Jozo Džambo

The counties of eastern Province Brandenburg, including the old
Neumark, now mostly in Poland (Courtesy GENEALOGICAL
GUIDE to German Ancestors from East Germany and Eastern
Europe, AGoFF e.v., Herne, West Germany)

It was that sense of overwhelming difficulty in their homeland that drove these Prussian immigrants to integrate into the Wisconsin frontier so thoroughly, that their numbers made up about half of Green Lake, Marquette, and Waushara Counties' population by the turn of the century.

Despite the severity for immigrants establishing new lives here, friends and relatives left behind in the Netzeland and the rest of Prussia may have been less fortunate. After World War I, the provinces of Posen and West Prussia were turned over by Imperial Germany to the re-established Polish nation, after 1919. The rest of Prussia's old eastern provinces were lost to Poland, and partially the Soviet Union, after World War II.

While some of our distant Prussian relatives and namesakes are dispersed throughout modern Germany (what has been East and West), the ancestral hometowns, common to us all, now carry names like Wągrowiec (Wongrowitz), Czarnków (Czarnikau), Bydgoszcz (Bromberg), and Piła (Schneidemühl). And of course, Kolmar is now Chodżież.

The Netzeland and Prussia may no longer exist, but its memory does carry on in the names of its descendants on both sides of the Atlantic.

(Note: Unless otherwise cited, maps for individual Prussian counties, which appear throughout this book, were extracted from the Pommern map- scale 1:300,000- available thru Genealogy Unlimited, Inc. of Orem, Utah. Also, the Waushara County maps of the Michael Bednarek Collection, from Wautoma, Wisc., are believed to be from a 1919 Plat Book.)

GREEN LAKE COUNTY MARRIAGES

Immigrants from County Kolmar, Province Posen, Prussia:

1) BLOCH nee Sommerfeld, Emilie- b. "Lindenwerder in Kolmar, Prussia", marr. John August Bedke- b."Lobsintz (Lobsens, Co. Wirsitz) Germany"; at Utley 24 August 1892/ No. 69978 (Vol. 5, p. 142).

2) BRAUN, Gustav- b. "Kolmar Prov. Posen Germany", marr. Emilie Linke- b. "Schloppe, Prov. Posen (actually Co. Deutsch Krone, Prov. West Prussia) Germany"; at the Town of Mackford 19 November 1888/ No. 64732 (Vol. 5, p. 120).

3) BUS(C)HO(W), Martin Jacob of Shields, Marquette Co.- b. "Aradowanka (Radwonke) Prussia", marr. Miss Louisa Gehring (no location given),30 October 1855/ Early Vol. 3 (1852-1855), p. 240.

4) GEHRING, Godfried of Shields, Marquette Co.- b. "Kinkolowo (Kunkolewo) Prussia", marr. Miss Augusta Bus(c)ho(w) (no location given), 30 October 1855/ Early Vol. 3 (1852-1855), p. 239.

5) GLENZ, Johann Gottlieb- b. "Braknitz Hauland, Circ. (Circuit= literal translation of Kreis=County) of Chodziesen (Kolmar) Prov. of Posen Pr.", marr. Eva Rosine Steinke at Princeton 1 June 1859/ Early Vol. 3 (1858-1867), p. 19.

6) GOETZ, John Julius- b. "Zachasberg (Chodziesen) Preussen", marr. Wilhelmine Heidel at Manchester 1 January 1874.

7) GRIEGER, Johan Julius of Casselton, Cass Co."Dacota T.(erritory)"- b. "Bra(c)knitz Hauland Prussia", marr. Emilie Zierke- b. "Deutschbriesen (Deutsch Briesen, Co. Wongrowitz), Prussia"; at Manchester 31 December 1882/ No. 56169 (Vol. 5, p. 83).

8) HAASE, Emilie Auguste- b. "Zachasberg Kreis Kelmine (Kolmar) Prussia", marr. Franz August Grams at Green Lake County 4 p.m.- 30 September 1897/ Vol. 7 (1897-1900), p. 71.

9) HADEL, Heinrich of Oshkosh (Winnebago Co. seat), Wisc.- b."Liepe, Germany", marr. Maria Laura Auguste Muller at Berlin 20 July 1889/ No. 65595 (Vol. 5, p. 125).

10) HUTH, Gottlieb of Ripon (Fond du Lac Co.), Wisc.- b."Kolmer (Kolmar) Germany", marr. Emilie Lambrecht- b. "Kluestrien Germany"; at Brooklyn 16 November 1897/ Vol. 7 (1897-1900), p. 100.

11) HUTH, Gustav of Baldwin, St. Croix Co., Wisc.- b. "Lindenwerder Prov. Posen Germany", marr. Ida Voss at Warren township,
Waushara Co., Wisc. 11 April 1887/ No. 62930.

12) JABBUS(C)H, Herman of Town of Randolf (Randolph), Columbia Co.
(Wisc.)- b. "Radzin (Ratschin), Germany", marr. Wilhelmine
Dehl at Manchester 11 a.m.-4 March 1880/ No. 51723.

13) JAHNKE, Ludwig- b. "Budzin (Budsin), Provinz Pose(n), Germany",
marr. Ernestine Birkholz b(orn) o(f) Lemke- b. "Rackow (Co.
Arnswalde), Province Brandenburg, Germany"; at Town of Kingston
8 March 1887/ No. 62660 (Vol. 5, p. 111).

14) JAHNS, August- b. "Caodeszen (Chodziesen=Kolmar) (Prussia)",
marr. Wilhelmine Marrwitz at Manchester 15 January 1874.

15) KLATT, Gustav- b. "Cutshesen (Chodziesen=Kolmar), Provinz Posen, Preussen, Europa", marr. Ida Emilie Oelke at Town of
Princeton 4 p.m.-28 November 1895/ Vol. 6 (1893-1897), p. 333.

16) KLOTH, Julius of Fox Lake (Dodge Co., Wisc.)- b. "Lipin (Prussia)", marr. Juliane Krause at Manchester 28 October 1874.

17) KONIG, Johann- b. "Radervanke (Radwonke), Prussia, Germany",
marr. Wilhelmine Grassin at Shields, Marquette Co. 28 May
1855/ Early Vol. 3 (1852-1855), p. 175.

18) KOWOLOWSKI, Gustav of Scott (twp.), Columbia Co. (Wisc.)- b.
"Adolfsheim, Germany", marr. Amalie, Wilhelmine, Dietrich- b.
"Gotscheming (Gottschimm, Co. Friedeberg/Neumark, Prov. Bran-
denburg), Germany"; at Manchester 30 March 1891/ No. 67942
(Vol. 5, p. 135).

19) KRUEGER, Ernst Ludwig- b. "Borowokoland (Borowo-Hauland), Posen, Germany", marr. Gusta Emilie Dolgner- b. "Zadsdorf, Brandenburg, Germany"; at Manchester 16 January 1890/ No. 66357
(Vol. 5, p. 127).

20) KRUNN, Ottilie Auguste- b. "Lelgenan (Selgenau?) Germany",
marr. Julius Chas. Lud. Dreblow at Marquette 25 January 1898/
Vol. 7 (1897-1900), p. 126.

21) LINKE, Johann- b. "Heliodorowo (a.k.a. Helldorf) Prussia",
marr. Luise Sauermann (nee Marquardt) at Village of Manchester
6 June 1869.

22) LUECK, Gottlieb- b. "Stoewen, Circuit of Chodziesen (County
Kolmar), Province of Posen Prussia", marr. Anna Rosine Teske
at the house of Joh. Teske in the Town of Princeton 2 May 1858/
Early Vol. 3 (1856-1858), p. 128.

23) MACZOLEK, Albert of Metomen, Fond du Lac Co., Wisc.- b. "Szamoczin (Samotschin), Germany", marr. Minnie Meyer- b. "Cuertow
(Co. Arnswalde, Prov. Brandenburg) Germany"; at Brooklyn 6 February 1895/ Vol. 6 (1893-1897), p. 263.

24) MANTAIE (Manthey?), Joseph- b. "Adolfshine (Adolphsheim) Prussia", marr. Manee Krassin at Shields, Marquette Co. 5 February
1856/ Early Vol. 3 (1856-1858), p. 30.

25) MANTHEY, Pauline Josephina- b. "Adolph's heim (Adolphsheim),
Posen, Prussia", marr. Fridrich Hunt at Princeton 6 November
1886/ No. 62231 (Vol. 5, p. 110) (Rom. Cath.).

26) MARQUARDT, Gustav- b. "Sammotschin (Pr. Posen) Prussien",
marr. Wilhelmine Schimmel at Manchester 17 February 1878/ No.
48813.

27) MARTEN, Carl Julius of Alto, Fond du Lac Co., Wisc.- b. "Kusch-
esen (Chodziesen=Kolmar) Posen Preussen", marr. Maria Abendroth
at Mackford 20 October 1880/ No. 52656.

28) MATTHEY, Minna- b. "Milz (Milsch), Germany", marr. Emil Simon-
b."Nowen (Cos. Wongrowitz or Kolmar), Germany"; at Markesan 22
April 1888/ No. 64122 (Vol. 5, p. 117).

29) MEINKE, Ferdinand of Westfield, Marquette Co.- b. "Zachasberg
Germany", marr. Anna, Rosina Schneider- b. "Zachasberg Germany";
at Township of Princeton 9 June 1890/ No. 66768 (Vol. 5, p. 129).

30) MUELLER, Fredric of "Christal"(Crystal Lake),Marquette Co. - b.
"Orstdorfke (Ostrowke) Germany", marr. Tena Roode (Rohde?)- b.
"Nickelskower (Nikolskowo) Germany"; at Dartford 25 July 1899/
Vol. 7 (1897-1900), p. 327.

31) PAHL, John Samuel- b. "Margolin Chozinsen (Margonin, Co. Chodz-
iesen=Kolmar) Prussia", marr. Caralina F. Block at the Town of
Marquette 20 June 1872.

32) PLAGNS (PLAGENS or PLAGENZ?), Michael, Christoph of Picketts,
Wisc.- b. "Brodden, Posen, Germany", marr. Auguste, Alvine
Huebner- b. "Drudoff, Posen, Germany"; at Kingston 14 April
1899/ No. 65299 (Vol. 5, p. 124).

33) RADETZKY (REDETZKE?), Friedrich- b. "Radzin (Ratschin) Prussia",
marr.Ernestine Wilhelmine Nothnagle (Nothnagel) at Princeton
21 October 1866/ Early Vol. 3 (1858-1867), p. 259.

34) RADTKE, Martin Ludwig- b. "Marschewow (Morzewo), Circuit of Chodziesen (County Kolmar), Province of Posen, Prussia", marr.
Emilie Mathilde Doring at Town 15 (Marquette) Green Lake County
4 July 1859/ Early Vol. 3 (1858-1867), p. 22.

35) RATHKE, Bertha Emilie, aged 17 years- bride had consent of parents- b. "Kolmar Posen Germany", marr. John Schreiber of the Town of Randolph (Columbia Co., Wisc.); at Manchester 25 November 1897/ Vol. 7 (1897-1900), p. 111.

36) REDEL, Herman- b. "Jankendorf Prussia Germany", marr. Anna Helen Riese- b. "Liede Proc (Prov.?) Brandenburg Prussia Germany"; at Manchester 20 November 1898/ Vol. 7 (1897-1900), p. 256.

37) REIER (nee Wendland), Wilhelmine- b. "Margolin (Margonin) Germany", marr. Frederick John Silgmann- b. "Westphalia (Prussian province in western Germany) Germany"; at Manchester 28 December 1893/ Vol. 6 (1893-1897), p. 104.

38) ROESLER, Johann- b. Radwenke (Radwonke) Pruss.", marr. Rosina Koplin at Shield(s), Marquette Co. 11 November 1856/ Early Vol. 3 (1856-1858), p. 118.

39) SCHEEL, August- b. "Margoninsdorf (Prussia)", marr. Emilie Brandenburg at the Town of Brooklyn 28 September 1874.

40) SCHROEDER, Carl Ludwig- b. "Josephsruh Posen Germany", marr. Bertha Muller (father's surname Lehmann)- b. Konigsdorf (Co. Flatow), West Preussen"; at Berlin 8 September 1882/ No. 55547 (Vol. 5, p. 80) (Note: both had been married before).

41) SCHROEDER, Carl Ludwig (see above)- b. "Josephs Ruh (Josephsruh) Prussia Germ.", marr. Wilhelmine Jagoel- b. "Schubin (a county seat in Prov. Posen) Prussia Germ."; at Berlin 1 February 1899/ Vol. 7 (1897-1900), p. 277.

42) SEIDEL, Samuel Friedrich of "Meccane" (Mecan), Marquette Co.- b. "Brackwidz Haud (Braknitz-Hauland) Prussia", marr. Wilhelmine Bornick- b. "Stocben Prov. Posen Prussia"; at Berlin? 25 February 1866/ Early Vol. 3 (1858-1867), p. 235.

43) SOBIERAJSKA, Ladislava (no father?)- b. "Pruchnow (Prochnowo) Grand Duche (Duchy) of Posen Europe", marr. Nicolaus Gwitt- b. Rynaszewo (Rynarzewo) Co. Szubin (Schubin) Duche (Duchy) Posen"; at Princeton 9 November 1885/ No. 60664 (Vol. 5, p. 103) (Catholic ceremony, probably a Polish couple).

44) SOBIERAJSKI, Peter- b. "Prnchow? (Prochnowo)-Posen-Prussia", marr. Mary Skolarzyk- b. "Dombrowka-Posen Prussia"; at Princeton on the morning of 27 January 1885/ No. 59431 (Vol. 5, p. 98) (Catholic, probably a Polish couple).

45) STEINKE, Leopold Michael- b. "Neu-Strelitz Prussia Germ.",
marr. Ida Hulda Adeline Mielke- b. "Guntergost (Co. Wirsitz)
Prussia Germ."; at Berlin 13 May 1894/ Vol. 6 (1893-1897), p.
157.

46) WARNKE, Wilhelm- b. "Chodziesen (Prussien)", marr. Charlotte
Kelm at Manchester 14 November 1875.

47) WILKE, Hermann Emil- b. "Nalen(t)scha, Regier Bromberg (Regier-
ungsbezirk=Administrative District)", marr. Gusta Maria Kruger
nee Tessmer- b. "Brusenitz (Co. Saatzig, Prov. Pomerania),
Prussia"; at Markesan 21 August 1892/ No. 69977 (Vol. 5, p. 142).

48) ZECH, Carl- b. "Laskowo Reg. Bez. (Regierungsbezirk=Adminis-
trative District) Bromberg Preussen", marr. Johanna Zick at
the Town Manchester 31 December 1873.

49) ZIMPEL, Friedrich- b. "Neudorf Preussen", marr. Maria Zech geb.
(nee) Lack at Sacramento 10 February 1872.

Immigrants from County Wirsitz, Province Posen, Prussia:

1) BAHN, Luise- b. "Hermannsdorf, Province Posen, Germany", marr. Wilhelm Hund- b. "Bandin, Prov. Posen, Germany"; at Markesan 21 July 1883/ No. 57052 (Vol. 5, p. 87).

2) BEDKE, John August- b. "Lobsintz (Lobsens) Germany", marr. Emilie Bloch nee Sommerfeld- b. "Lindenwerder in (Co.) Kolmar Prussia"; at Utley 24 August 1892/ No. 69978 (Vol. 5, p. 142).

3) BELOW, August- b. "Anilla (Kol. Aniela), Prov. Posen, Germany", marr. Augusta Wudke- b. "Jacobsdorf (Jakobsdorf, Cos. Saatzig or Dramburg), Prov. Pommern (Pomerania), Germany"; at the Town of Manchester 31 August 1886/ No. 62143 (Vol. 5, p.109).

4) BEYER, William Fred- b. "Guenthergost (Güntergost), Germany", marr. Ida Hulda Bloch at Manchester 28 November 1889/ Vol. 5, p. 126).

5) BOETTCHER, Wilhelm- b. "Wirsitz (Prussian)", marr. Augusta Krueger at Manchester 19 November 1874.

6) BUTTER, Friedrich- b. "Wirsitz (Prussian)", marr. Mathilde Perske at Manchester 17 October 1875.

7) DIETRICH, Carl- b. "Nackel Germany", marr. Dorothea Sophie Salzwedel- b. "Pammin (Co. Arnswalde, Prov. Brandenburg) Germany"; at the Town of Mackford 4 January 1894/ Vol. 6 (1893-1897), p. 105.

8) DRETSKE (DREDSKE), Fred William- b. "Nauckl (Nakel) Germany", marr. Mary Lousie Yerk- b. "(Co.) Arnswalde (Prov. Brandenburg) Germany"; at Mackford 10 April 1888/ No. 64064 (Vol. 5, p. 117).

9) FALK, Eduard- b. "Nagel (Nakel), Prov. Posen, Germany", marr. Paulina Strauss- b. "Nagel (Nakel) Province Posen Germany"; at Kingston 22 August 1886/ No. 61806 (Vol. 5, p. 108).

10) HASSE, Ernestine- b. "Friedrichshorst, Germany", marr. August Julius Briese of Fairwater (Fond du Lac Co.), Wisc.- b. "Deutsch Krone (a county seat in Prov. West Prussia) Germany"; at Markesan 20 September 1885/ No. 60408 (Vol. 5, p. 102).

11) HOEFT, Emma Bertha- b. "Anilla (Kol. Aniela), Province Posen, Germany", marr. Albert Loose, a cigar maker from Waupun (Dodge & Fond du Lac Cos.), Wisc.- b. "Germany"; at Kingston 2 April 1888/ No. 64022 (Vol. 5, p. 117).

12) HOFT, Matilda Emilie- b. "Dreidorf (Administrative District of) Bromberg Kr. (Co.) Wirsitz Germany", marr. Fred Wm. Klinke of Springvale, Columbia Co. (Wisc.); at Kingston 16 December 1897/ Vol. 7 (1897-1900), p. 117.

13) KOBS, Ottilie Emily- b. "Retzthal (Netzthal) Prussia Germany", marr. Henry Gustavus Wendlandt of the Town of Randolph (Columbia Co., Wisc.); at Manchester 31 August 1898/ Vol. 7 (1897-1900), p. 201.

14) KRUBECK, Ottilie Pauline- b. "Walthershausen, Prussia Germany", marr. Heinrich Ahlers of the Town of Warren, Waushara Co.; at Berlin 30 April 1893/ Vol. 6 (1893-1897), p. 27.

15) LUEDTKE, Johann- b."Zatke (Sadke) Prussia", marr. Caroline Gehrke of the"Town of Neshkoro, Waushara Co." (actually Marquette Co.); at the Town og Green Lake 28 February 1883/ No. 56559 (Vol. 5, p. 85).

16) MIELKE, Ida Hulda Adeline- b. "Guentergost Prussia Germany", marr. Leopold Michael Steinke- b. "Neu-Strelitz (Co. Kolmar), Prussia Germ."; at Berlin 13 May 1894/ Vol. 6 (1893-1897), p. 157.

17) POKLOKTOWSKA (father Pokloktowski), Josephine- b. "Dembno- Europe-Prussia", marr. Joseph Philip- b. "Posen Europe Prussia"; at Princeton 19 January 1886/ No. 61002 (Vol. 5, p. 104) (Catholic ceremony, probably Polish couple).

18) RIECK, Ida Ottilie- b. Kreis (County) Wirsitz Baizette (Bezirk= District) Bromberg", marr. Heinrich Stelter-b. "Poetic Holland (Potulitz Hauland?)"; at Kingston 4 p.m.-26 November 1896/ Vol. 6 (1893-1897), p. 444.

19) SALZWEDEL, Wilhelmine Albertine- b. "Charlottenhof, Posen, Germany", marr. Wilhelm Gustav Puphal- b. "Town of Montello, Marquette Co."; at the Town of Marquette 28 October 1892/ No. 70358 (Vol. 5, p.143).

20) SCHAUER, Christian- b. "Osek (Oşiak or Netzthal) Prussia", marr. Caroline Kruiger at Shields, Marquette Co. 22 June 1856/ Early Vol. 3 (1855-1858), p. 75.

21) SOMERFELD, Friedrich Hermann- b. "Rudca b. Lobsins (Lubcza?* by Lobsens) Germany", marr. Auguste Wilhelmine Kelm at Princeton 30 March 1891/ No. 67904 (Vol. 5, p. 135)*(Note: Lubcza is actually in neighboring Co. Flatow, Prov. West Prussia).

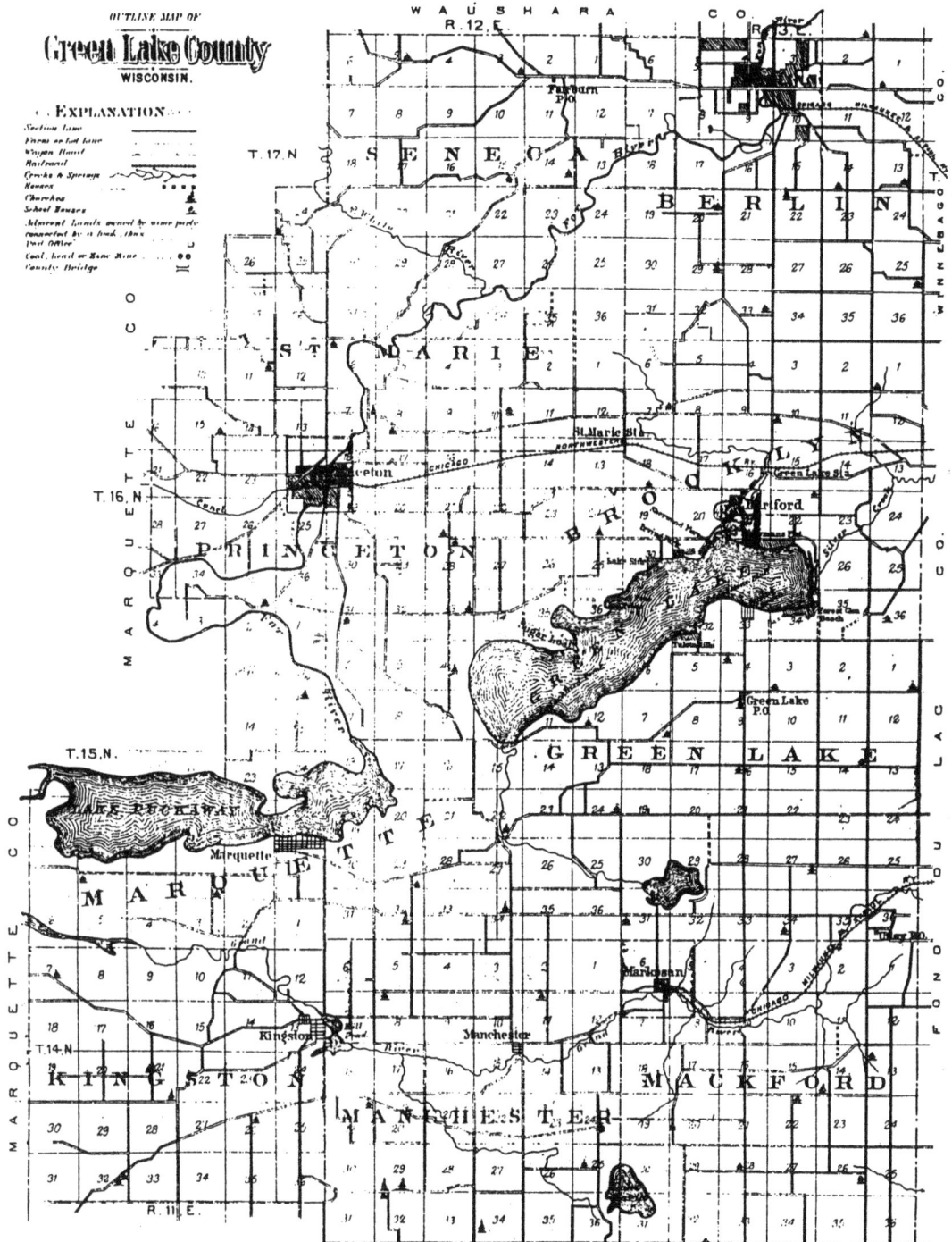

(From COME BACK IN TIME, Vol. I by Elaine Reetz)

22) STEUK, Michael Ernst- b. "Mroezen (Mrotschin), Posen Germany", marr. Auguste Henriette Stiller at Sacramento 9 March 1879/ No. 51737.

23) STILLERT, Gustav- b. "Nakel Province Posen", marr. Amalie Harske at Berlin 15 November 1870.

24) STILLERT, Reinhardt- b. "Near Nakel Posen", marr. Auguste Dumdei (also sometimes spelled Dumdey) at Berlin 25 February 1871.

25) WAIZ, Matilde- b. "Satke (Sadke) Germany", marr. Karl Albert Seemann of "Spring Dale", Columbia Co. (Wisc.)- b. "Ostrowith (Ostrowitte, Co. Konitz, Prov. West Prussia), Germany"; at Kingston Wed.-23 March 1892/ No. 69514 (Vol. 5, p. 142).

26) WOYDA, Carl- b. "Wirsitz Germany", marr. Anna L. Hannmann of Ripon (Fond du Lac Co.), Wisc.; at Berlin 22 September 1897/ Vol. 7 (1897-1900), p. 72.

27) ZERBEL, Ottilie- b. "Nagel (Nakel), Germany", marr. Charles Mueller- b. "Wulstrow, Germany"; at Kingston 2 January 1887/ No. 62397 (Vol. 5, p. 110).

Immigrants from County Wongrowitz, Province Posen, Prussia:

1) ALBRECHT, Nathanael Samuel (father Daniel)- b. "Kleinmerkowitz Prussia", marr. Emilie Albrecht (father Christoph) at Berlin city 19 April 1874.

2) ALBRECHT, Samuel Nathanael (see above)- b. "Klein Merkowitz (Mirkowitz). Posen, Prussia, Germ.", marr. Emma Adeline Wielengowski- b. "Bratien, Westpreussen (West Prussia), Prussia"; at Berlin 21 November 1888/ No. 64690 (Vol.5, p. 120).

3) BERENDTS, Friedrich August of Oshkosh (Winnebago Co.), Wisc.- b. "Buckowitz (Bukowitz) Prussia", marr. Theresa Zache at Berlin 23 October 1879/ No. 51155.

4) BUSSE (widow nee Hein), Louisa- b."Wrongowitz Germany", marr. Charles Thede- b. "Neu-Kloster, Germany"; at Manchester 22 April 1891/ No. 68055 (Vol. 5, p. 135).

5) CZAJKOWSKI, Thomas- b. "Czerzewo Gd. Duche (Czeszewo, Grand Duchy) Posen", marr. Joanna Duszynska at Princeton on the morning of 18 August 1884/ No. 58654 (Vol. 5, p. 95) (Catholic, probably Polish couple).

6) DYCH, Michel- b. "Tuniszewo Grand Duche (Duchy) of Posen Europe", marr. Balbina Komasa- b. "Czeszewo Gd. Duche of Posen-Europe"; at Princeton on the morning of 10 February 1885/ No. 59433 (Vol. 5, p. 98) (Catholic, likely Polish couple).

7) HAAK, Carl- b. "Grabowo Germany", marr. Wilhelmina Wendlandt- b. "Atlantic Ocean"; at Green Lake 21 October 1897/ Vol. 7 (1897-1900), p. 82.

8) HELLER, Emil Heinrich- b. "Slawiza (Slawica), Prov. Posen, Prussia, Germ.", marr. Emilie Gerlach- b. "Grosslubuwitz, Prov. Bromberg, Prussia, Germany"; at Berlin 8 "Dez." (December) 1889/ No. 66079 (Vol. 5, p. 126).

9) JACKOWSKI, Casimir- b. "Lekno Prussia", marr. Pauline Zuge at Berlin 12 May 1876 (Catholic, perhaps mixed Polish/German).

10) KEIM, Julius Hermann- b. "Wongrowitz (Prussian)", marr. Bertha Charlotte Otto at Manchester 12 November 1873.

11) KRENZ, Robert Carl- b. "Blumenfeld, Provinz Posen Germany", marr. Minna Bender- b. Randolph, Columbia Co. (Wisc.); at the Town of Mackford 15 December 1887/ No. 63671 (Vol. 5, p. 115).

12) LOHNING, Emilie- b. "Grabawow (Grabowo?), Posen Germany", marr. August Zellmer- b. "Pulzig Pommern Germany"; at Markesan 29 January 1890/ No. 66356 (Vol. 5, p. 127).

13) LOSINSKA (father Losinski), Apolonia- b. "Krzyzanka (Krzyzanki or Baltenkreuz) Europe Prussia", marr. John Czaja- b. "Gorczyn (Gorsin, Co. Bromberg?) Europe Prussia"; at Princeton on the morning of 18 January 1886/ No. 61001 (Vol. 5, p. 104) (Catholic, likely Polish couple).

14) MILBRATH, Emelina Paulina- b. "Noven (Nowen) Germany", marr. Edward Wurch- b. "Valinowka Russia"; at Manchester 16 April 1895/ Vol. 6 (1893-1897), p. 278.

15) MISSALL, Wilhelm- b. "Wongrowitz (Prussien)", marr. Wilhelmine Nehring at Marquette 11 January 1874.

16) MUELLER, Albert- b. "Wongrowetz Germany", marr. Theresa Pahl at Princeton 15 November 1899/ Vol. 7 (1897-1900), p. 377.

17) PALUGA, Anna- b. "Lekno Europe Prussia", marr. Martin Maslowski- b. "Owczs-Glowy?-Europe Prussia"; at Princeton 19 July 1885/ No. 60153 (Vol. 5, p. 102) (Catholic, likely Polish couple).

18) PETRIK, Martin- b. "Wongrowitz, Pommern (?), (Germani)", marr. Juliane Orth at Manchester 15 June 1873.

19) REDEL (wid.), Anna- b. "Nowen Germany", marr. Frederick William Tonn (wid.)- b. "Nowen, Germany"; at the Town of Manchester 15 May 1888/ No. 64182 (Vol. 5, p. 117).

20) SIMON, Emil- b. "Nowen, Germany", marr. Minna Matthey- b. "Milz (Milsch, Co. Kolmar) Germany"; at Markesan 22 April 1888/ No. 64122 (Vol. 5, p.   ).

21) SMARSZ, Jacob- b. "Tuniszewo Prussia Eruope", marr. Catharina Kendziora- b. "Goszyna Prussia Europe"; at Princeton 8 February 1886/ No. 61005 (Vol. 5, p. 104) (Catholic, likely Polish).

22) STEINKE, Emilie- b. "Nowen Wongrowitz Germany", marr. Georgey Kohn (his 2nd marriage) at Marquette 5 p.m.-19 November 1896/ Vol. 6 (1893-1897), p. 435.

23) TESSMER, Emma- b. "Ragolsk (Rgielsko), Germany", marr. Fred Pottmann of Chicago, Ill.- b. "Bielefeld (Prussian Prov. of Westphalia, in western Germany), Germany"; at Manchester 6 December 1891/ No. 68951 (Vol. 5, p. 138).

24) TONN, Johann Wilhelm- b. "Nowen Prussia", marr. Hanna Wilhelmine Krueger (widow by Wilhelm) at the Town of Manchester 2 July 1871.

25) WOPSCHALL (Wobschall?), Carl Ferdinand- b. "Stumbochowa (Stempu-chowo), Posen, Prussia, Germ.", marr. Julia Warnke-b. "Hammer (Co. Czarnikau?), Prussia, Germ."; at Berlin 30 April 1890/ No. 66652 (Vol. 5, p. 128).

26) ZIERKE, Emilie- b. "Deutschbriesen (Deutsch Briesen), Prussia", marr. Johan Julius Grieger of Casselton, Cass Co. "Dacota T(er-ritory)."- b. "Bracknitz Hauland (Co. Kolmar) Prussia"; at Man-chester 31 December/ No. 56169 (Vol. 5, p. 83).

Immigrants from the City, County, or Administrative District of
"Bromberg", Province Posen, Prussia:

1) ADAMCZAK, John- b. "Regiarung Berik (Regierungsbezirk=Adminis-
   trative District) Bromberg Prussia", marr. Mary Jaszezyk (nee
   "Berhardt"- b. "Marienworer (Marienwerder, a county and district seat) West Prussia"; at Princeton 27 August 1900/ Vol. 7
   (1897-1900), p. 471 (Catholic, likely Polish couple).

2) BOELTER, David Hermann, a peasant from the Town of "Banno",
   West Portage Co. (Wisc.)- b. "Hohenwalde, Prussia", marr. Wilhelmine Ernestine Scharlotte Piatraschke at Berlin 28 December
   1875.

3) BOELTER, Herman August- b. "Hohenwalde Prussia Germany", marr.
   Agnes Francisca Lungwitz of the Town of Warren (Waushara Co.);
   at Berlin 11 October 1898/ Vol. 7 (1897-1900), p. 225.

4) DRAGER, Mary T.- b. "Welno (Wielno) Germany", marr. George R.
   Passmore of Flushing, Genessee Co., Mich.; at the residence of
   the bride's parents, 5 p.m.-9 May 1895/ Vol. 6 (1893-1897), p.
   285.

5) FENNER, Julius- b. "Gromoden (Gromaden, Cos. Wirsitz or Schubin?) (Bromberg) Prussien", marr. Juliane Wilke at Manchester
   22 January 1876.

6) GERLACH, Emilie- b. "Grosslubuwitz, Prov. Bromberg, Prussia,
   Germany", marr. Emil Heinrich Heller- b. "Slawiza (Slawica, Co.
   Wongrowitz), Prov. Posen, Prussia, Germ."; at Berlin 8 "Dez."
   (December)1889/ No. 66079 (Vol. 5, p. 126).

7) GOSH, Anna- b. "Bromberg W.(?) Prussia", marr. Charles Nitz at
   Berlin 20 September 1898/ Vol. 7 (1897-1900), P. 208 (Catholic,
   probably Polish couple).

8) HELLA (nee Mroz), Rosalia- b. "Rgbezirk (Regierungsbezirk=Ad-
   ministrative District) Bromberg Germany", marr. Frank Wozcsinski (or Wrzesinski)- b. Kreis (County) Posen Germany"; at Princeton 3 January 1900/ Vol. 7 (1897-1900), p. 417 (Catholic, likely Polish couple).

9) JAHNS, Eduard- b. Winkon (or Winkow) by Bromberg (Prussian)",
   marr. Ernestine Marrwitz at Manchester 7 June 1875.

10) KASENMANN, Gustav Johann of the Town of Trenton (Dodge Co.,
    Wisc.)- b."Kreis (County) Bromberg Posen,Germany", marr. Mar-
    that Ladwig of the Town of Trenton Dodge Co.; at the Town of
    Manchester 28 April 1897/ Vol. 7 (1897-1900), p. 26.

11) KLAWITER, Frank- b. "Bromberg Province Posen", marr. Justine Fleming at Princeton 25 August 1900/ Vol. 7 (1897-1900), p. 472 (Rom. Cath.).

12) KOPP, Gottlob of Bevaer Dam (Dodge Co., Wisc.)- b. "Bromberg (Prussian)", marr. Ernestine Ratke at Manchester 22 September 1873.

13) LISKE, Julius Christoph- b. "Bromberg Prussia", marr. Rose Schmidt at Berlin 8 December 1872.

14) MATTWIG nee Ebert, Auguste- b. "Kreis (County) Bromberg Germany", marr. August Redmann- b. "Province Posen Germany"; at Green Lake County 5 p.m.-10 December 1896/ Vol. 6 (1893-1897), p. 453.

15) RADKE, Johann- b. "Bromberg Preussen", marr. Emilie Henslin at Manchester 4 p.m.-25 June 1879/ No. 52137.

16) REKOW, Anna- b. "Bromberg, Province of Posen German Empire" , marr. Wolfgang Vogel- b. "Lam, Bavaria, German Empire"; at Manchester 30 May 1886/ No. 61550 (Vol. 5, p. 106).

17) SCHRODER, Carl Ludwig- b. "Bromberg Prussia", marr. Wilhelmine Friederike Johanne Strubing at Berlin 5 December 1872.

18) SEMPF, Gustav of Lake City, Wabasha Co., Minn.- b. "Bromberg. Prussia", marr. Helene Frohlich- b. "Prussia"; at the residence of Mr. Stolp-Princeton, 9 January 1883/ No. 57008 (Vol. 5, p. 87).

19) STENTZEL, Julius- b. "Bromberg (Prussian)", marr. Wilhelmine Schewe at Manchester 14 September 1873.

20) TROCINSKA, Cecilia- b. "Bromberg W.(?) Prussia", marr. Joseph Dopke- b. "Neustadt (a county seat) West Prussia"; at Berlin 3 May 1898/ Vol. 7 (1897-1900), p. 200 (Catholic, perhaps mixed Polish/German).

21) WENDT, Friedrich- b. "Bromberg (Prussien)", marr. Ernestine Grams at Manchester 24 December 1877/ No. 48637.

22) WUSKE, John- b. "Hammermihle (Hammermühle) Germany", marr. Emilie Reck- b. "Berbenbraeck (Berkenbrügge, Co. Arnswalde, Prov. Brandenburg) Germany"; at the Town of Manchester 30 March 1893/ Vol. 6 (1893-1897), p. 21.

Immigrants from County Obernick, Province Posen, Prussia:

1) CHELA, Anna- b. "Gorzewo Grand Duche (Duchy) of Posen Europe",
   marr. Clemens Jaworski- b. "Zukow-Grand Duche of Posen-Europe";
   at Princeton the morning of 4 May 1886/ No. 61443 (Vol. 5, p.
   106) (Catholic, likely Polish couple).

2) ERDMANN, Thedor Julius- b. Kreis (County) Obornick Posen Germany", marr. Clara Ida Juade (Quade?) of the Town of Randolph
   (Columbia Co.); at Manchester 17 March 1896/ Vol. 6 (1893-1897),
   p. 367.

3) FRANKE, Gottlieb of "Randolf Grove", Columbia Co. (Wisc.)- b.
   "Gramsdorf (Prussien)", marr. Auguste Otto at Manchester 30 September 1875.

4) GORNY, Michel- b. "Chrustow (Chrostowo?)-Europe-Prussia", marr.
   Francis Sobieraj- b."Ludomia-Europe-Prussia"; at Princeton the
   morning of 26 January 1886/ No. 61004 (Vol. 5, p. 104) (Catholic,
   likely Polish couple).

5) JARZYNA, Catharina- b. "Gorzewo-Prussia-Europe", marr. Joseph
   Ziemianski- b. "Parkowo-Prussia-Europe"; at Princeton the morning of 23 February 1886/ No. 61165 (Vol. 5, p. 105) (Catholic,
   likely Polish couple, she was a widow).

6) KUHN, Michael August- b. "Obornick in Prussia", marr. Auguste
   Henriette Bugel at Princeton 26 December 1866/ Early Vol. 3
   (1858-1867), p. 270.

7) MI(E?)TZNER, Carl August- b. "Rogasen, Prussia", marr. Huldah,
   Alwine Loose- b. "Olganofka Colonie, Ruszland (Russia)"; at the
   Township of Princeton 20 August 1891/ No. 68425 (Vol. 5, p. 136).

8) POLENSKE, Emma Alvine- b. "Turnova (Tarnowo) Germany", marr.
   Herman Jul. Baumann of the Town of Spring(vale) Columbia Co.
   (Wisc.)- b. "Frechland Germany"; at Marquette 25 November 1897/
   Vol. 7 (1897-1900), p. 103.

9) RAU, Ernst Ludwig- b. "Ubernik (Obernick or Obornik) Germany",
   marr. Amilia Charlotte Hilger- b. "Germany"; at Mackford 15
   March 1893/ Vol. 6 (1893-1897), p. 17.

10) ROZEK, Joseph- b. "Ludom Prussia Europe", marr. Marianne Michal-
    ska (father Michalski)- b. "Gorzewo-Prussia-Europe"; at Princeton
    9 February 1886/ No. 61006 (Vol. 5, p. 104) (Catholic, likely
    Polish couple).

11) SOBIERAJ, Stanislava- b. "Ludomia Europe Prussia", marr. Stephen Siekierka of Neshkoro (Marquette Co.)- b. "Kukonia Europe Prussia"; at Princeton the morning of 26 January 1886/ No. 61003 (Vol. 5, p. 104) (Catholic, likely Polish couple).

12) SONNEBERG, John- b. "Ludoma-Prussia-Europe", marr. Rosalia Rozek of "McCane (Mecan)" Marquette Co. (Wisc.) ; at Princeton the morning 12 March 1886/ No. 61166 (Vol. 5, p. 105) (Catholic, perhaps mixed German/Polish?).

13) SWIDERSKA, Mariann (father Swiderski)- b. Colonie ludoma Duche (Duchy) Posen-Europe", marr. Stanislaus Rataiczak (Ratajczak?)- b. "Ludom-Duche Posen-Europe"; at Princeton 11 o'clack-8 June 1886/ No. 61589 (Vol. 5, p. 106) (Catholic, Polish couple).

14) WENDLAND, John Edward- b. "Obornek (Obernick) Prussia", marr. Adelene Mathilde Stellmacher at Manchester 11 a.m.-27 June 1880/ No. 52138.

15) WENDLAND, Peter August- b. "Beiersdorf (Beyersdorf) Prussia", marr. Karoline Otto at the Village of Manchester, 27 March 1870.

16) WERNER, Ernst- b. "Heidedombrowke, Circuit (County) of Obernik, Province of Posen Prussia", marr. Henriette Guse at Mecan, Marquette Co. 12 April 1858/ Early Vol. 3 (1856-1858), p. 122.

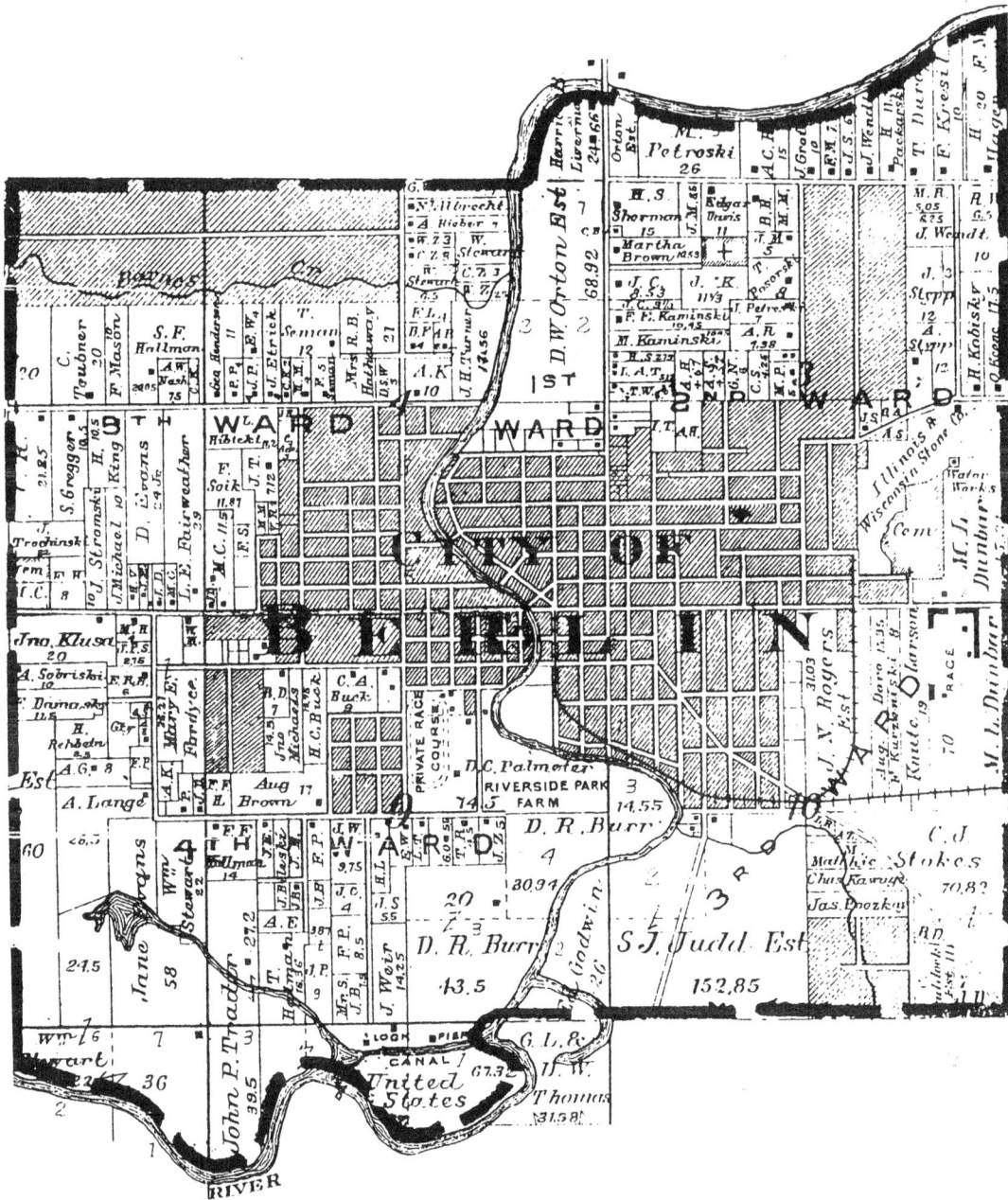

(From COME BACK IN TIME, Vol. I by Elaine Reetz)

Immigrants from County Czarnikau, Province Posen, Prussia:

1) BITTELMANN, Gottfried- b. "Proseke (Prossekel) in the Circuit (County) of Czarnekow (Czarnikau) in the Province of Posen in Kingdom of Prussia", marr. Ernestine Wilhelmine Breitenfeld at the Town of Crystal Lake (Marquette Co.) in the house of Aug. Breitenfeld 7 March 1858/ Early Vol. 3 (1856-1858), p. 108.

2) BOHN, Wilhelm- b. "Sokolowo (Prussian)", marr. Pauline Gehrke at Manchester 2 July 1873.

3) BORNICK, August- b. "Lemnitz Preussen Germany", marr. Maria Kelm in Princeton 11 December 1890/ No. 67573 (Vol. 5, p. 133).

4) BUSSE, Richard Robert- b. "Radalin (Radolin) Proving (Provinz or Province) Posen Europe", marr. Johannah Marie Reetz at the Town of Seneca 7 p.m.-6 February 1896/ Vol. 6 (1893-1897), p. 370.

5) DUNDEI (DUMDEY?), Julius- b. "Scharnikow (Scharnikau or Czarnikau), Posen Germany", marr. Wilhelmine Zimmermann at Berlin 18 February 1880/ No. 51663.

6) EHRHARD, Albert of Fairwater, Fond du Lac Co. (Wisc.)- b. "Broseka(Czharniko) (Prussian)--(Prossekel, Co. Czarnikau)", marr. Auguste Heller at Manchester 6 September 1874.

7) GRIESE, Friedrich Wilhelm- b. "Krauzin (Krutsen?) Prussia", marr. Johanna Luise Emilne Salzwedel at the Town of Princeton 29 August 1869.

8) HASS, Gustav Emil- b. "Romanshoff, Prov. of Posen, Germany", marr. Pauline Mary Silgmann- b. Lake Mills (Jefferson Co.), Wisc.; at Manchester 3 October 1886/ No. 62018 (Vol. 5, p. 109).

9) KRUEGER, Wilhelm- b. "Nikasken (Niekosken). Province Posen, Prussia", marr. Henriette Werth at Berlin 27 December 1869/ Vol. 5, p. 13.

10) LEHMANN, Frederike Albertine- b. "Butzighauland,*Polen (Putzig-Hauland, Poland), Germany", marr. Charles Stanke- b. "Augustwalde (Co. Arnswalde, Prov. Brandenburg), Germany"; at Ripon, Fond du Lac Co. (Wisc.) 19 February 1882/ No. 54850.

11) MARKERT, Gustus J. (Gustav J. Marquardt?)- b. "Lemnitz Province, Posen Prussia", marr. Matilda A. Dudley at Mackford 20 December 1877/ No. 48489.

12) SCIAEPRT(?), Amial (Emil Schubert or Szurpit?)- b. "near Schonlacke (Schönlanke) Germany", marr. Lizzie Lang- b. "Kungobirg (Königsberg?, East Prussia or Brandenburg?) Germany"; at Berlin 11 a.m.-29 July 1895/ Vol. 6 (1893-1897), p. 296.

(Note: Putzig-Hauland actually in neighboring County Filhene)

13) WARNKE, Johann Gottlieb- b. "Corda, Circuit (County) of Czarni-
    kow (Czarnikau), Province of Posen, Prussia", marr. Juliane
    Wilhelmine Nast at Princeton 12 November 1858/ Early Vol. 3
    (1858-1867), p. 1.

14) WARNKE, Julia- b. "Hammer, Prussia, Germ.", marr. Carl Ferdi-
    nand Wopschall (Wobschall?)- b. "Stumbochowa (Stempuchowo, Co.
    Wongrowitz), Posen, Prussia"; at Berlin 30 April 1890/ No.
    66652 (Vol. 5, p. 128).

Immigrants from County Schubin, Province Posen, Prussia:

1) FROEHLICH, Michael- b. "Wladislawono (Wladislawo) Germany",
    marr. Jozefa Marchewka at Berlin 8 May 1876 (Catholic, probab-
    ly German/Polish couple).

2) GWITT, Nicolaus- b. "Rynaszewo (Rynarzewo) Co. Szubin (Schubin)
    Duche (Duchy) Posen", marr. Ladislava Sobierajska- b. "Pruchnow
    (Prochnowo, Co. Kolmar?) Grand Duche of Posen Europe"; at Prince-
    ton 9 November 1885/ No. 60664 (Vol. 5, p. 103) (Catholic, pro-
    bably Polish couple).

3) HARSKE, Johann- b. "Labischen (Labischin), Posen, Prussia",
    marr. Pauline Steuk at Sacramento 28 December 1871.

4) JAGOEL, Wilhelmine- b. "Schubin Prussia Germ.", marr. Carl Lud-
    wig Schroeder- b. "Josephs Ruh (Josephsruh, Co. Kolmar) Prussia
    Germ."; at Berlin 1 February 1899/ Vol. 7 (1897-1900), p. 277.

5) NAGEL, Martin Georg- n. "Sobicjucho (Sobicjuchy) Posen Prussia",
    marr. Wilhelmine Justrow at Berlin 12 April 1868.

6) RADKE, Albertine- b. "Koppelin, Kreis (County) Schubin Germany",
    marr. Robert H. Williams at the Town of Manchester 26 December
    1890/ No. 67514 (Vol. 5, p. 133).

7) SCHERMER, Auguste Henriette- b. "Schubin, Prussia, Germ.",
    marr. Franklin O. Murdock- b. "New Orleans Co. New York"; at
    Berlin 26 November 1890/ No. 67399 (Vol. 5, p. 132).

8) S(CH?)WERSINSKE, Emil Herman- b. "Ludwig Kowa (Ludwikowo) Prus-
    sia Germany", marr. Emelie Anna Mueller at Berlin 2 May 1895/
    Vol. 6 (1893-1897), p. 281.

Immigrants from County Filhene, Province Posen, Prussia:

1) BAHR, Hermann- b. "Klein Dre(n)sen (Posen) Prussia", marr. Friderike Zastrow at Manchester 16 September 1877.

2) GELHAR (GEHLHAAR?), Gustav Adolf- b. "Grashuette (Glashütte) Germany", marr. Louise, Wilhelmina Tonn at Manchester 24 November 1891/ No. 68903 (Vol. 5, p. 138).

3) MACH, Friedrich Ferdinand- b. "Putzig, Prussia, Germ.", marr. Anna Maria Arnsdorff- b. "Zuchow (Co. Dramburg, Prov. Pomerania), Prussia Germ."; at Berlin 24 November 1892/ No. 70404 (Vol. 5, p. 143).

4) MARTWICH, Ludwig Friedrich- b. "Jaegersburg. Posen, Prussia", marr. Henriette Weinkauf at Princeton 27 December 1868/ Vol. 5, p. 9.

5) MUELLER, Samuel August- b. "Putzig Prussia", marr. Henriette Auguste Schmidt at the Town of Green Lake 11 October 1869.

6) QUAST, Wilhelm- b. "Neu Hofen (Neuhofen), Posen Prussia", marr. Rosalie Rimpler at Princeton 27 December 1868/ Vol. 5, p. 10.

7) REISEL, Emma Auguste- b. "Gornitz, Province Posen Germany", marr. Wilhelm Carl Friedrich Oesterreich- b. "Ravenstein (Revenstein, Co. Saatzig), Prov. Pommern (Pomerania), Germany"; at the Town of Green Lake 7 February 1884/ No. 58007 (Vol. 5, p. 91).

8) WESTRACK, Charles Julius, carsmith from Milwaukee- b. "Selchow, Germany", marr. Johanna Emily Schmidt- b. "Dobberphuhl (Co. Pyritz, Greifenhagen, or, Cammin, Prov. Pomerania) Germany"; at Manchester 12 December 1892/No. 7059 (Vol. 5, p. 144).

Immigrants from other locales in Province Posen, Prussia:

1) BOELTER, August Hermann- b. "Drawianowo Province Posen", marr. Auguste Wilhelmine Braun at Berlin 2 November 1870.

2) DENZIN, Friedrich- b. "Twenbuch (Ivenbusch, Co. Filehne?)., , Provinz Posen, Preussen ", marr. Wilhelmine Plagens at Kingston 2 p.m.-7 May 1881/ No. 53630.

3) GELHART (GEHLHAAR?), Rev. Ferdinand- b. "Schloppe (actually Co. Deutsch Krone, Prov. West Prussia) Province of Posen, Germany Europe", marr. Caroline Schroeder (nee Buck or Bouk)- b. "Wilonow (Wielno, Co. Bromberg?) Province of Posen, Germany Europe"; at Markesan 22 October 1899/ Vol. 7 (1897-1900),p. 367.

4) GERLACH, Albert Julius- b. "Welnau (Co. Gnesen). Prussia", marr. Ottilie Maria Rost at Berlin 1 January 1889/ No. 64901 (Vol. 5, p. 121).

5) HARTFIEL, Emilie- b. "Josephokow (perhaps Josefkowo, Co. Kolmar?), Polen (Poland)", marr. Charles Ladwig- b. "Altkow Germany"; at Berlin 3 February 1885/ No. 59502 (Vol. 5, p. 99).

6) HOUJER, Michael- b. "Craesnarsken, Province of Posen, Prussia", marr. Austena Janska at the Town of Crystal Lake (Marquette Co.) 16 January 1858/ Early Vol. 3 (1856-1858), p. 86.

7) HUEBNER, Auguste, Alvine- b. "Drudoff, Posen, Germany", marr. Michael, Christoph Plagns (Plagenz or Plagens) of "Picketts" (Fond du Lac Co.), Wis.- b. "Brodden (Co. Kolmar), Posen, Germany"; at Kingston 14 April 1889/ No. 65299 (Vol. 5, p. 124).

8) HUND, Wilhelm- b. "Bandin, Prov. Posen, Germany", marr. Luise Bahn- b. "Hermannsdorf (Co. Wirsitz), Prov. Posen, Germany"; at Markesan 21 July 1883/ No. 57052 (Vol. 5, p. 87).

9) JAWORSKI, Clemens- b. "Zukow (perhaps Zukowo, Co. Obernick?)- Grand Duche (Duchy) of Posen-Europe", marr. Anna Chela- b. "Gorzewo (Co. Obernick) Grand Duche of Posen Europe"; at Princeton the morning of 4 May 1886/ No. 61443 (Vol. 5, p. 106).

10) KLAWIKOWSKI, Pauline- b. "Ketrina (Co.)Gnesen Polonia (Poland)", marr. John Lipinski- b. "Korny (Co.)Gnesen Polonia (Poland)"; at Berlin 12 February 1900/ Vol. 7 (1897-1900), p. 421.

11) LINKE, Emilie- b. Schloppe (actually Co. Deutsch Krone, Prov. West Prussia), Prov. Posen Germany", marr. Gustav Braun-b. "(Co.) Kolmar Prov. Posen Germany"; at the Town of Mackford 19 November 1888/ No. 64732 (Vol. 5, p. 120).

12) LUTKE, Gottlieb (father Michael)- b. "Razmicrocwo, Province
Boscen (Posen) in Frus(s)ia", marr. Floretine Rosina Lutke
(father Christian) at Princeton 23 January 1866/ Early Vol. 3
(1858-1867), p. 225.

13) NIKODEM, Florian- b. "Sierdkowka (Sierpowko, Co. Samter?) Grand
Duche (Duchy) Posen Europe", marr. Cornelia Szurpict (Szurpit?)-
b. "Landing codie? New York"; at the Village of Princeton, the
morning of 12 January 1886/ No. 61000 (Vol. 5, p. 104) (Catholic,
likely Polish couple).

14) SCHRAMM, Gustav- b. "Nikiojene? Prov. Posen Germany", marr. Anna Fritz- b. "Liede, Province Brandenburg, Germany"; at Markesan
29 Setpember 1888/ No. 64505 (Vol. 5, p. 119).

15) SKOLARZYK, Mary- b. "Dombrowka (one of any half dozen places)-
Posen Prussia", marr. Peter Sobierajski- b. "Prnchow (Prochnowo,
Co. Kolmar?)-Posen-Prussia"; at Princeton, the morning of 27 January 1885/ No. 59431 (Vol. 5, p. 98) (Catholic, likely Polish
couple).

16) SPLIT(T)GERBER, Amalia Bertha- b. "Lodzer (perhaps Lodzia in Cos.
Wirsitz or Birnbaum?), Posen, Germany", marr. Joseph Schermer
at Berlin 20 April 1884/ No. 58325 (Vol. 5, p. 94).

17) STENZEL, Emma- b. "Samter (a county seat), Germany", marr. August Zuehlke- b. "Flatow (a county seat in West Prussia), Germany"; at Markesan 16 September 1888/ No. 64837 (Vol. 5, p. 121).

18) WARGULA, Francis- b. "Zukowo (Co. Obernick) Grand Duche (Duchy)
Posen Europe", marr. Justine Zielinska (father Zielinski)- b.
"Waldowka-Gd. Duche Posen-Europe"; at Princeton, the morning of
3 February 1885/ No. 59432 (Vol. 5, p. 98) (Catholic, likely Polish).

19) W(E)INKAUF, Christopher- b. "Vorsidge Provence of Posen, Kingdom
of Prussia", marr. Caroline Borger (*also Boerger and Berger) at
the Town of Mecan (Marquette Co.) 23 October 1856/ Early Vol. 3
(1855-1858), p. 116. (*note: Mrs. Gayle Marshall of Westfield,
Wisc. notes that her Weinkauf ancestor was from Debenke, Co. Wirsitz, apparently "Vorsedge"=Wirsitz, as well as supplying the
other spellings of the wife's name.)

Immigrants from the City, County, Administrative District,or Province of Posen, Prussia:

1) BORNICK, Wilhelmine- b. "(Stocbin Province Posen Prussia)" (perhaps Stobnica, Co. Samter?), marr. Samuel Friedrich Seidel of "Meccane (Mecan) Marquette Co."- b. Brackwidz Haud (Braknitz-Hauland, Co. Kolmar, Prov. Posen) Prussia"; at Berlin (?) 25 February 1866/ Early Vol. 3 (1858-1867), p. 235.

2) BRIESE, Wilhelmine- b. "Posen Prussia", marr. Theodor Ludwig Luethe- b. "Town Wildow Minn."; at Green Lake 9 "Marz (March)" 1882/ No. 54873 (Vol. 5, p. 78).

3) BROCK, Nickodan- b. "Regieringsbezirk (Regierungsbezirk=Administrative District) Posen Germany", marr. Matilda Gizella- b. "Coeln an Rhedupr (Köln=Cologne on Rhine Prussia?)"; at Berlin 18 January 1898/ Vol. 7 (1897-1900), p. 158 (Catholic, likely Polish couple).

4) BUBOLZ, Emilie Auguste- b. "Posen Germany", marr. Ludwig Johann Ferdinand Achterberg of Randolph (Columbia Co., Wisc.); at Manchester 21 February 1897/ Vol. 6 (1893-1897), p. 480.

5) BUCHHOLZ, August of Bloomfield township, Waushara Co.- b. "Prov. Posen Prussia", marr. Mathilde Harzke (no location given) 23 April 1885/ No. 59787.

6) CISZKE, Anton S. of Ripon (Fond du Lac Co., Wisc.) & Berlin Colonie (Green Lake Co.?)- b. "Posen i. Prussia", marr. Pauline Marinkowska at Berlin 11 June 1876 (Catholic, likely Polish couple).

7) CRAPA, Francis- b. "Posen Prussia", marr. Paulina Grota at Berlin 24 January 1878/ No. 49041 (Catholic, probably Polish).

8) CZAJKOWSKI, Valentin- b. "Posen Germany", marr. Marianna Reinke or Reginek (mother's name is Bucholz)- b."Posen, Germany"; at Princeton 22 November 1886/ No. 62232 (Vol. 5, p. 110) (Rom. Cath., probably Polish).

9) CZOLNECKI, Valentin- b. "Posen Germany", marr. Marianna Jankowiak- b. "Posen Germany"; at Princeton 23 November 1886/ No. 62233 (Vol. 5, p. 110) (Rom. Cath., probably Polish couple).

10) DEHL, Fredericke- b. "Posen, Prussia", marr. Wilhelm Buchholz of the Town of Randolph Center, Columbia Co.- b. "Schonfeld, Prussia"; at the Town of Manchester 8 March 1883/ No. 56560 (Vol. 5, p. 85).

11) DIETRICH, Auguste Emilie- b. "Posen, Prussia", marr. Gotthielf Stabs- b. "(Prov.) Brandenburg, Prussia"; at Manchester 29 December 1881/ No. 54563.

12) DURAWA, John-(wid.)-b. "Posen Prussia", marr. Susanna Machol (wid.) at Berlin 5 February 1878/ No. 49042 (Rom. Cath., likely Polish couple).

13) FENSKE, Theodor- b. "Germany Posen", marr. Dona Mason at Berlin 9 May 1880/ No. 51995.

14) GAIG, Anna Caroline-b. "Prussia (Prov. Posen)", marr. Gustav Wilhelm Ernst Hammer of T. Randolf (Columbia Co.), Wis.- b. "Prussia (Prov. Pommern)"; at Manchester 2 December 1882/ No. 55991 (Vol. 5, p. 82).

15) GENRICH, Gottlieb Frederich .of the Town of Scott, Columbia Co.- b. "Posen Prussia", marr. Anna Helena Spengler at Manchester 1 p.m.-3 April 1881/ No. 53348.

16) GOLHAAR (GEHLHAAR?), Gustav Adolf- b. "Posen Germany", marr. Emilie Ida Radke at the residence of Martin Radke, Town Marquette 19 April 1896/ Vol. 6 (1893-1897), p. 374.

17) GUDARIAN (GUDERIAN?), Gustav- b. "Herzothum (Herzogthum=Duchy) Posen Germany", marr. Alvine Kolb at Berlin 27 November 1880/ No. 52765.

18) HARMEL, Hermann- b. "Prov. Posen Prussia; Germany", marr. Juliane Barkowski at Berlin 5 April 1886/ No. 61475.

19) HEISER, Friderika- b. "Posen Prussia", marr. Andreas Gizella- b. "Reg. Bzg. (Regierungsbezirk=Administrative District) Danzig (also a county seat) West Prussia"; at Berlin 21 February 1898/ Vol.7 (1897-1900), p. 157 (Catholic, probably mixed German/Polish).

20) HELD, Carl Ludwig- b. Kingdom of Possen (Preussen?=Prussia) in Germany", marr. Fredericka Liska at "Marquette Co." 23 December 1854/ Early Vol. 3 (1852-1855), p. 127.

21) HINCA, Frank- b. "Prussia Posen", marr. Rose Czapa at Berlin 19 January 1880/ No. 51914 (Rom. Cath., probably Polish).

22) HINZ, Mary Poline (Pauline?)- b. "Posen Prussua", marr. Friedrich Ropcke, a blacksmith from Buffalo Grove, Iowa-b. "Pommern Prussia"; at Manchester 19 January 1882/ No. 54564 (Vol. 5, p. 76).

GREEN LAKE
AND SURROUNDINGS.

Scale: 1 mile 4 inches.

PRINCETON TOWNSHIP

BROOKLYN

GREEN

Jos. Paulus

Herm Verch

J. Schimmel

H. Hageman

K. Busse

26

Keine

Ferd

Ann Anderson

F. Krueger

F. Klatt

Chas Hoffman

Chas. Hoffman

W. J. & Mabel Boenning

25

Frank Krueger

Benjamin Haigh

Elizabeth Malcolm

W. Kraft

Kopernick

W. W. Davis. Est.

V. D. Owen 24

E. A. Parker

Robert Allen

SCHOOL NO 13

Robert Allen

E. Krueger

E. Boenning

W. S. Haigh

Lot 3

Lot 4

MALCOLM

J. Musolf

A. Krueger

E. Wastrack

F. & R. Welk

Ernest Page

F. W. Page

F. W. Page

A. West Point

Ferd. Keine

Aug Mahlzan

Chris Britsvold

E. A. Parker

Lot 1

Lot 2

PIGEON CREEK

Point

35

Aug Mahlzan

F. W. Page

NORWEGIAN BAY

DEPTH 50'

DEPTH 100'

DEPTH 200'

Henry Hoffman

A. Hoffman

Lot 2

J. A. Hamlin

Lot 4

Loaf Pennock

Uno Bueller

Frank Summerfelt

L. & Eva Wiser

J. Smith

J. F. Keene

Lot 1

QUIMBY'S BAY

DEPTH 230'

DEPTH 237'

DEPTH 230'

DICKINSON BAY

P. W.

Lot 1

Lot 2

Lot 2

C. B. Dickinson

SPRING

Blackbird Point

Fred

Snow

Lot 5

Lot 3

Frank Wilde

Chas. Salzwedel

H. Oelke

Robert Walter

Lot 3

K. Salzwedel

FAIRVIEW FARM

August Kuhl

SCHOOL

W. Shade

Fox River Improv't Co.

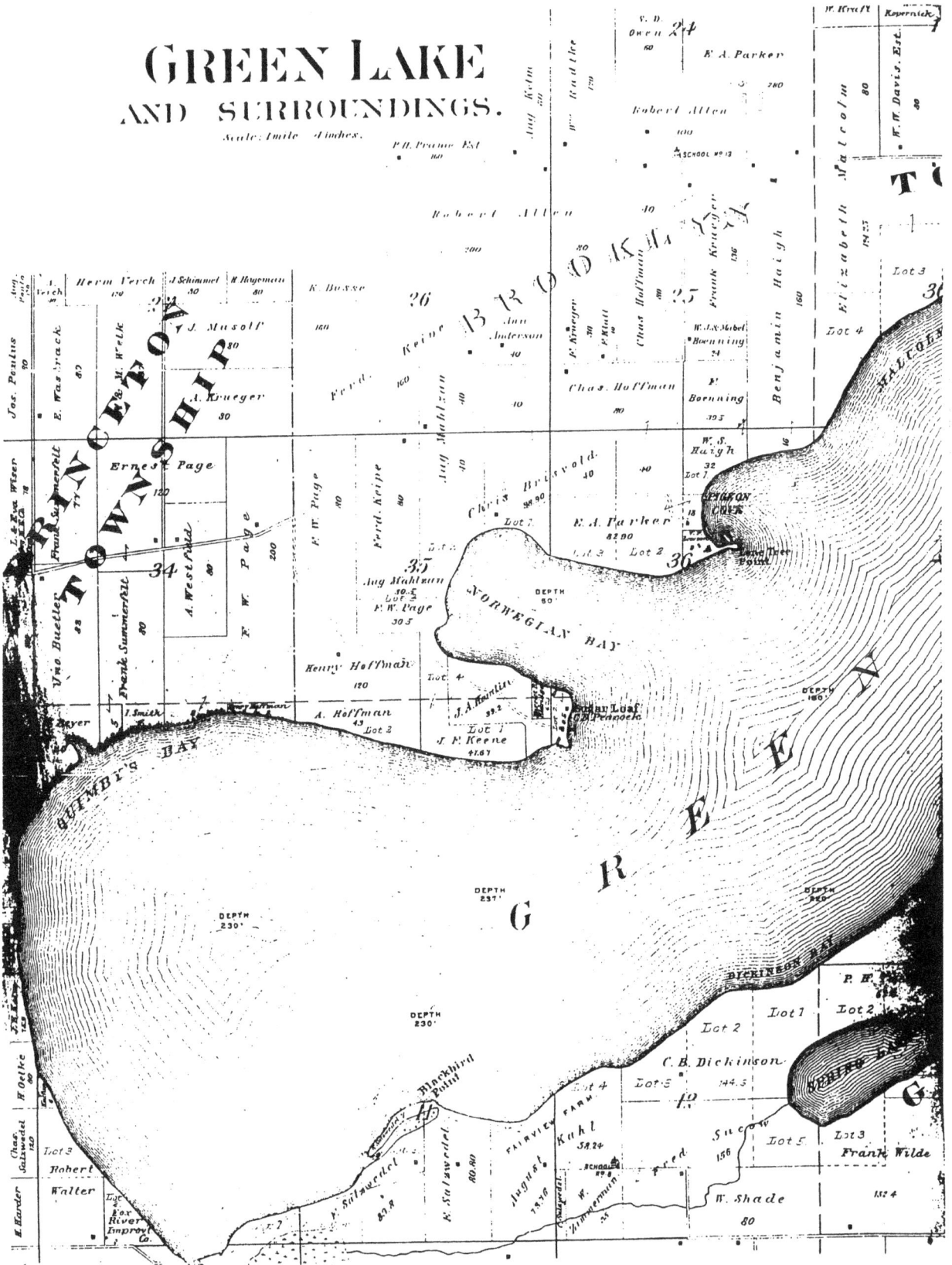

(From COME BAK IN TIME, Vol. I

L. D. Patterson 20   P.W. Locke   HARTFORD   J.C. Miles   Smith Walker   J.N. Smith   W.P. Smith   Fred Wiedman

T. J. Crabtree   El. Fery   W. I. Sherwood 100   Hattie S. Kutchin 126.25   DARTFORD BAY   Alice T. Mather   Mrs. T.T. Kutchin   N. E. Miller   C. S. Stinson

OWNSHIP   G. W. Greenway   M. BRAYMAN'S PLAT   J. W. Walker   C. M. Walker   O. Lewis

W. I. Sherwood 63.5   Zachow   Minnie Kutchin   Lot 2   40.9   Oakwood   J. W. Walker

Lot 2   Lot 1   Lot 3   Sherwood Forest   C. Beckwith   G.B.& W. R.R. Co.

BAY   St. Lorice   Hugo Wendler

L A K E   DEPTH 100' TO 180'   DEPTH 60'   Henry Creek

Length of Lake 14 miles   Area 115 square miles   DEPTH 180'

WOODS BAY   Lot 1   Lot 4   Lot 3   33   August Albrecht

Wm. Lucas 131.80   Lot 2   H. R. Hill   S. & G. Scott

P. L. Gibberd 40   Scot Horner 80   G. E. Horner 50   Mrs. Geo. Scott

Lot 1   H. Prelvitz 42.44   P. L. Gibberd 48.87   J. Crawford 41.04   David Crook 45.15   Alice Hazelwood   G. Hazelwood   Wm Crook   Crook 39.33

T. Hunale   SCHOOL NO 4   F. Unger   D. Williams   Wm Crook

C. Wendlandt   Mrs. H. Wood   S. Burdick   W. H. Welch

Lot 7   Wm Hunger   C. Prelvitz 102.1   Mrs. L. M. Hazeley 40   Amos Hazeley   P. King   M. B. Hutchins

Nursery Co.   Lot 2   TWIN LAKES   David Creek   Jno Bazeley   J. Kohler   Geo Currier

J. Cassiday   Lot 2   C. Burling Est.   SCHOOL NO 5

Kimble   Lot 3   Lot 2   C. Burling Est.   J. A. Kimble GREEN LAKE P.O.   Wm Bazeley   E. Jassen   G. Miller

Fortnum Sr.   Jno. Nichols Est. 102   H. M. Currier 80

Albert Unger   GREEN LAKE TOWNSHIP

Jno Fortnum Jr.   H. Gallert 30   Fred Nothnagel 128.5   Mrs. A. F. King   J. F. King   J. A. Kimble

Jno Fortnum Jr. 47   J Cassiday 40   H Burling   H. Kimble

by Elaine Reetz)

23) HOLZ, Ferdinand- b. "Posna Prussia", marr. Miss Bertha Schaetzke at Neshkoro (Marquette Co.) 4 February 1855/ Early Vol. 3
(1852-1855), p. 143.

24) HOPPA, Anthony- b. "Posen Germany Europe", marr. Marianna Klapa-
"Posen Germany Europe"; at Princeton 10 January 1887/ No. 62445
(Vol. 5, p. 111) (rom. cath., likely Polish couple).

25) JANKOWSKI, Wm.- b. "Posen Prussia", marr. Anna Jazdzewska (father Jazdzewski) at Berlin 9 February 1878/ No. 49043 (Rom.
Cath. probably Polish couple).

26) KASZUBOWSKI, Leo of the Town of Warren (Waushara Co.)- b. "Prussia, Posen", marr. Mary Mar(c?)hewka of the Town of Warren; at
Berlin 20 September 1899/ Vol. 7 (1897-1900), p. 338 (Rom. Cath.,
likely Polish couple).

27) KIRSCHBAUM, Julius- b. "Prov. Posen, Prussia. Germany", marr.
Julie Warneke at Berlin 28 August 1887/ No. 63331.

28) KOEBERNIK, William- b. "Prussia Provinz Posen", marr. Wilhelmine
Schmidt- b. "Provinz Posen"; at Berlin 29 April 1877/ No. 47543.

29) KOEPP, Augustus- b. "Posna Prussia", marr. Miss Ernestine Brech-
el at Princeton 28 January 1855/ Early Vol. 3 (1852-1855), p.
144.

30) KRUEGER, Wilhelm Friedr. of Poy Sippi, Waushara Co.- b. "Prov.
Posen, Prussia, Germany", marr. Marie, Martha, Elisabeth Ruske
at Berlin 12 October 1887/ No. 63558.

31) KRUSE, Louis Julius- b. "Posen Germany", marr. Barbara Baer at
Manchester 6 p.m.-28 May 1880/ No. 52131.

32) KUJAT(H?), Eleonora- b. "Germany province of Posen", marr. John
Janitzki- b. "Germany Westpreussen (West Prussia)"; at Kingston
11¼ a.m.-21 January 1889/ No. 64956 (Vol. 5, p. 122).

33) MACKOWSKI, Joseph M.- b. "Posen Germany", marr. Catherine T. Ca-
vanaugh at Princeton, Tues.-10 July 1900/ Vol. 7 (1897-1900),
p. 462 (Rom. Cath., likely Polish/Irish mixed).

34) MALEKKI, Michael- b. "Posen Germany", marr. Maria Smarzynska at
the City of Berlin 17 August 1875/ (Catholic, likely Polish).

35) MARTEN, Carl Julius- b. "Posen Preussen", marr. Christine Abendroth at Mackford 2 March 1882/ No. 54762.

36) MARZEJON, August- b. "Posen Prussia", marr. Cecylia Troczynska
at Berlin 15 February 1878/ No. 49045 (Rom. Cath., likely Polish).

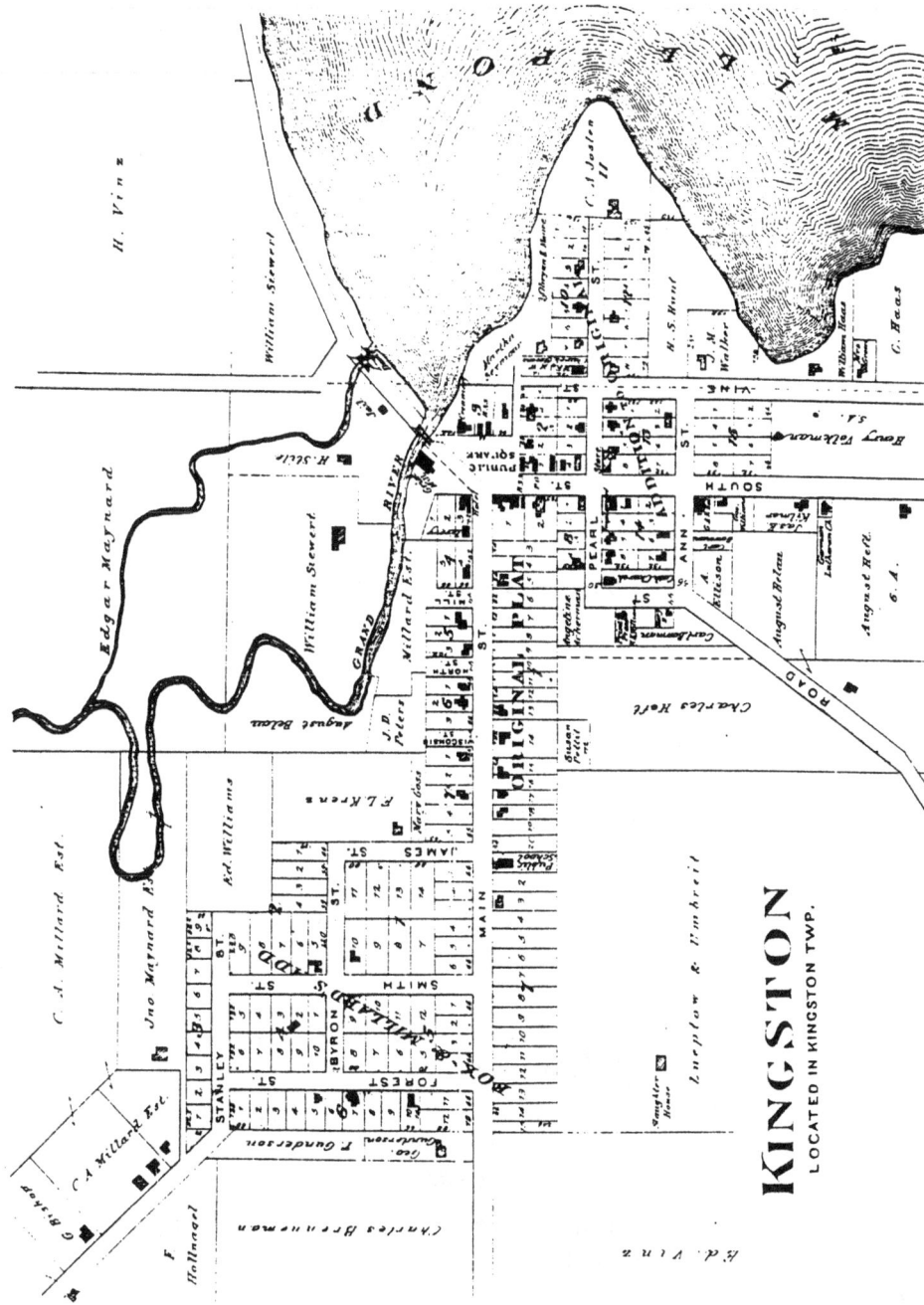

KINGSTON

LOCATED IN KINGSTON TWP.

(From COME BACK IN TIME, Vol. I by Elaine Reetz)

37) NEUMANN, Emma- b. "Posen Prussia", marr. Wm. Weisjahn- b. "Posen, Prussia"; at Manchester 8 p.m.-15 December 1883/ No. 57625 (Vol. 5, p. 89).

38) NIEMER, Peter G.-b. "Rgb. (Regierungsbezirk=Administrative District) Posen- Germany", marr. Anna Rozek at Princeton 27 April 1900/ Vol. 7 (1897-1900), p. 441 (Catholic, likely Polish or mixed couple).

39) NIGBUR, August- b. "Posen Prussia", marr. Julianna Grota at Berlin 19 February 1878/ No. 49046 (Rom. Cath., likely Polish).

40) PHILIP, Joseph- b. "Posen Europe Prussia", marr. Josephine Pokloktowska (father Pokloktowski)- b. "Dembno (Co. Wirsitz)-Europe-Prussia"; at Princeton 19 January 1886/ No. 61002 (Vol. 5, p. 104) (Cath., probably Polish couple).

41) PIESCHKE, August of Aberdeen, Brown Co. Dakota T.(erritory)-b. "Prov. Posen Germany", marr. Wilhelmine Dreblo(w?) at Marquette 30 March 1885/ No. 59726 (Vol. 5, p. 100).

42) REITER, Ludwig- b. "Poocen (Posen) in Germany", marr. Julia Keller at Markesan 16 October 1865/ Early Vol. 3 (1858-1867), p. 215.

43) SCHAETZKE, William- b. "Posna Prussia", marr. Miss Frederica Uiker (Uecker?) at Neshkoro (Marquette Co.) 4 February 1855/ Early Vol. 3 (1852-1855), p. 146.

44) SCHMIDT, Friedrich of Davenport (Scott Co.), Iowa- b. "Posen (Prussian)", marr. Henriette Abraham at Manchester 21 September 1873.

45) SCHROEDER, Gustav- b. "Province of Posen, Germany", marr. Mathilde Wuske at Manchester 5 p.m.-29 March 1885/ No. 59687 (Vol. 5, p. 99).

46) SIEBERT, Wilhelm- b. "Posen, Prussia", marr. Helene Wodtke at the Town of Manchester 2 p.m.-19 September 1883/ No. 57184 (Vol. 5, p. 88).

47) STUBBE, Aug.- b. "Prov. Posen, Prussia Germany", marr. Emilie Jann at Berlin 18 April 1886/ No. 61476.

48) TONN, William of Westfield, Marquette Co.- b. "Province Posen", marr. Emilie Gruse- b. "Province of Brandenburg"; at Manchester 12 noon-28 June 1885/ No. 60048 (Vol. 5, p. 101).

49) WENDTA, John- b. "Posen Germany", marr. Elizabeth Blazcjewska (father Blazcjewski) at Berlin 24 January 1876 (Catholic, likely Polish).

50) WENTA, Michael- b."Posen Prussia", marr. Mary Durava at Berlin 20 February 1878/ No. 49047 (Rom. Cath., probably Polish).

51) WICZLINSKI, Rudolph- b. "Posen Prussia", marr. Sophia Putz at Berlin 12 February 1878/ No. 49044 (Rom. Cath., perhaps Polish/ German mixed?).

52) WOJAHN, Rudolf Julius- b. "Posen, Prussia", marr. Fredericke Wilhelmine Mielke at Manchester 29 January 1881/ No. 53151.

53) WOZNIAK, Madaline- b. "Posen Prussia", marr. Frank Cieszynski- b. "Rgl. (Regierungsbezirk=Administrative District) Danzig Kries Benoz (County Berent?) West Prussia (note: Danzig was a county seat, itself)"; at Berlin City 3 October 1898/ Vol. 7 (1897-1900), p. 216 (Cath., surely Polish).

54) WOZCSINSKI (or WRZESINSKI), Frank- b. "Kreis (County) Posen Germany", marr. Rosalia Hella (nee Mroz)- b. "Rgbezirk (Regierunsbezirk=Administrative District) Bromberg Germany"; at Princeton 3 January 1900/ Vol. 7 (1897-1900), p. 417 (Rom. Cath., likely Polish couple).

55) ZANDER, August- b. "Posen,Prussia", marr. Pauline Albrecht at the Town of Green Lake 1 p.m.- 31 July 1881/ No. 53870.

56) ZBLEWSKI, John- b. "Posen Germany", marr. Marianna Glon at Berlin 14 November 1875 (Catholic, likely Polish couple).

57) ZI(E?)RKE, John- b. "Posen, Germany", marr. Henriette Bischoff at Manchester 2 p.m.-24 March 1881/ No. 53319.

Immigrants (Polish Catholics) from "Prussian Poland", "Polish Prussia", and other variants for Province Posen:

1) BARANOWSKA (father Baranowski), Anne- b. "Prussian Poland", marr. John Klasa- b. "Prussian Poland"; at Berlin 4 February 1890/ No. 66912 (Vol. 5, p. 129).

2) BARANOWSKI, Bronislawa- b. "Prussian Poland", marr. Michael Syberalski- b. "Prussian Poland"; at Berlin 22 July 1890/ No. 66913 (Vol. 5, p. 129).

3) BARANOWSKI, Joseph- b. "Poland Prussia", marr. Any Nigbur- b. "Poland Prussia" ; at Berlin 23 June 1881/ No. 53237.

4) BECZKALA, Mary- b. "Prussian Poland", marr. Adalbertus Krempa- b. "Prussian Poland"; at Berlin 27 July 1891/ Vol. 6 (1893-1897), p. 42.

5) BIEGANEK, Valentine- b. "prussian Poland", marr. Anne Gizela- b. "prussian Poland"; at Berlin 3 February 1891/ Vol. 6 (1893-1897), p. 38.

6) BIELINSKI, Veronica- b. "Prussian Poland", marr. Frank Kaminski at Berlin 10 January 1893/ Vol. 6 (1893-1897), p. 109.

7) BIEMKOWSKI, Adalbertus- b. "Prussian Poland", marr. Martha Pypka at Berlin 30 January 1894/ Vol. 6 (1893-1897), p. 243.

8) BLAZEJEWSKA (father Blazejewski), Elizabeth- b. "Prussian Poland", marr. Frank Brocki- b. "Prussian Poland"; at Berlin 28 January 1890/ No. 66909 (Vol. 5, p. 129).

9) BRILOWSKI, Peter- b. "Poland Prussia", marr. Rosalia Czapa at Berlin 27 January 1885/ No. 59588 (Vol. 5, p. 99).

10) BROMBEREK, Michael- b. "Polland Germany", marr. Helena Krzywiniewski- b. "Poland Germany"; at Princeton 30 October 1893/ Vol. 6 (1893-1897), p. 97.

11) BRYLOWSKI, Anne- b. "Prussian Poland", marr. Bernardus Drogosz- b. "pr. Poland"; at Berlin 21 January 1891/ Vol. 6 (1893-1897), p. 36.

12) BRYLOWSKI, Michael- b. "Prussian Poland", marr. Anne Cyman- b. "Prussian Poland"; at Berlin 19 October 1891/ Vol. 6 (1893-1897), p. 44.

13) BRYLOWSKI, Veronica- b. "Poland Prussia", marr. Antony Marzejon- b. "Poland Prussia"; at Berlin 31 January 1881/ No. 53239.

14) BRZESKI, Francis- b. "Poland Prussia", marr. Bertha Markowska at Berlin 25 November 1884/ No. 59583 (Vol. 5, p. 99).

15) BRZESKI, Franciszek- b. "Poland Prussia", marr. Susy Gutowska
(father Gutowski)- b. "Poland Prussia"; (no location given) 28
January 1885/ No. 59589 (Vol. 5, p. 99).

16) BUKOWSKI, Andreas- b. "Prussian Poland", marr. Anna Rosa (no
location given) 23 April 1882/ No. 55499 (Vol. 5, p. 80).

17) BURZYNSKA, Maryanna- b. "Prussian Poland", marr. Francis Wagner
of Ripon (Fond du Lac Co., Wisc.)- b. "Prussian Poland"; at
Berlin 13 February 1882/ No. 55496 (Vol. 5, p. 80).

18) CIERZMOWSKI, August- b. "Polish Prussia", marr. Clara Piechow-
ska (father Piechowski) at Berlin 8 February 1897/ Vol. 7
(1897-1900), p. 39.

19) CYMAN, Anna- b. "Prussian Poland", marr. Theophilus Olszewski-
b. "Prussian Poland"; at Berlin 16 May 1890/ No. 66909½ (Vol.
5, p. 129).

20) CYMAN, Mary- b. "Prussian Poland", marr. Felix Lukaszewicz- b.
"Prussian Poland"; at Berlin 9 June 1891/ Vol. 6 (1893-1897),
p. 39.

21) CYMANN, Martin- b. "Poland Prussia", marr. Barbara Kotlowska
(father Kotlowski)- b. "Poland Prussia"; at Berlin 31 January
1881/ No. 53240.

22) CZEIHOLINSKI, Valeria- b. "Prussian Poland", marr. Nicodemus
Strychalski- b. "Prussian Poland"; at Berlin 30 May 1893/ Vol.
6 (1893-1897), p. 119.

23) CZOSKA, Frank- b. "Poland Prussia", marr. Johanna Pawtowcha
(widow, father Marzejan)- b. "Prusah Poland"; at Berlin 7 February 1882/ No. 55495 (Vol. 5, p. 80).

24) CZYZAK, Sophia- b. "Polish Prussia", marr. Max Bulski of Milwaukee; at Berlin 26 September 1899/ Vol. 7 (1897-1900), p. 353.

25) DOMACHOWSKA, Josephina- b. "Prussia Poland", marr. Martin Guz-
man- b. "Prussia Poland"; at Berlin 14 February 1882/ No. 55497
(Vol. 5, p. 80).

26) DURAWA, August- b. "Prussian Polland", marr. Martha Leman- b.
"Prussian Polland"; at Berlin 25 November 1890/ Vol. 6 (1893-
1897), p. 33.

27) EKMANN, August- b. "Poland Prussia", marr. Josephina Walkosz
at Berlin 28 February 1879/ No. 52004.

28) EKMANN, John- b. "Poland Prussia", marr. Anny Munska (father
Munski)- b. "Poland Prussia"; at Berlin 24 January 1881/ No.
53238.

56

MANCHESTER

LOCATED IN MANCHESTER TP.

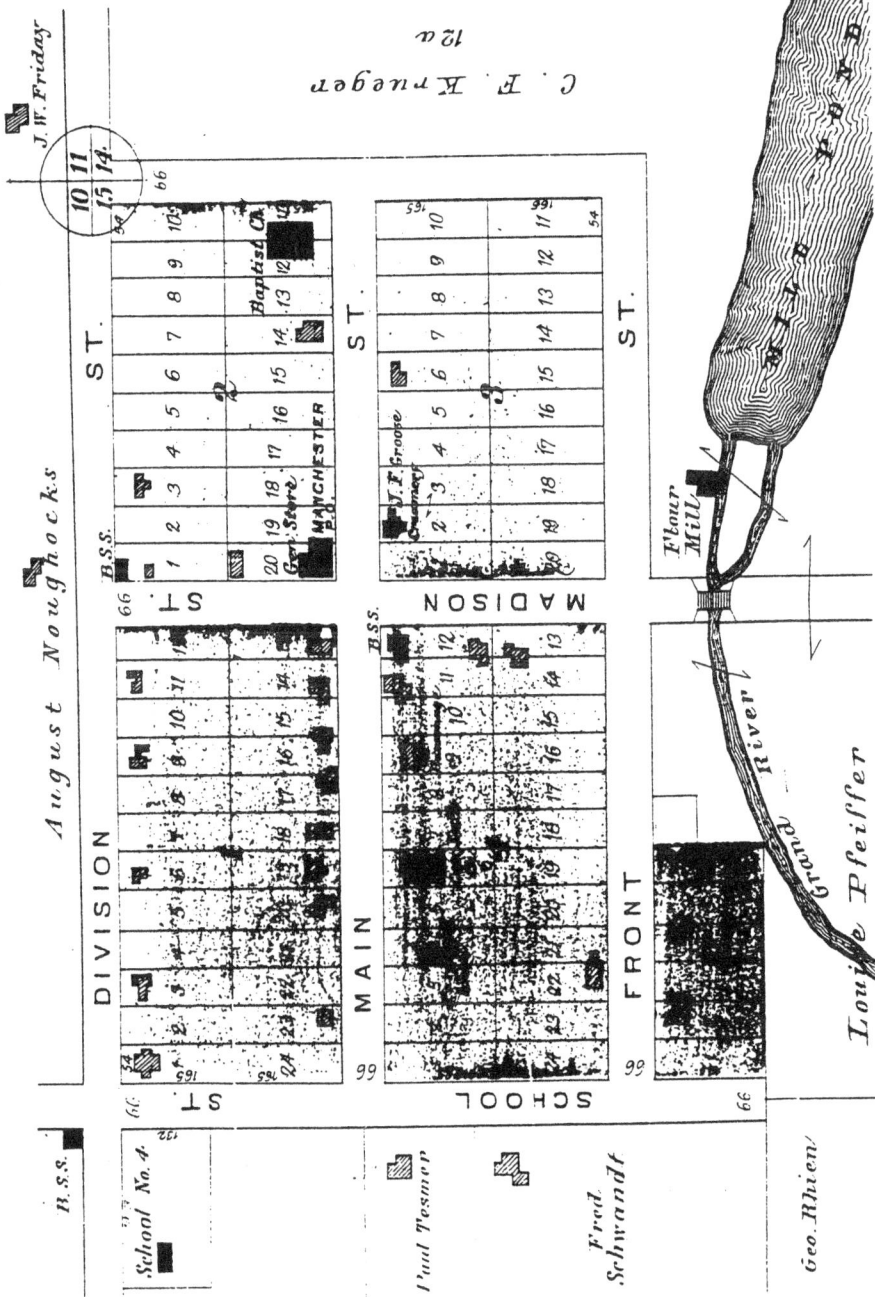

August Noughocks

J. W. Friday

C. F. Krueger

12a

DIVISION ST.

MAIN ST.

FRONT ST.

SCHOOL ST.

MADISON ST.

Mill Pond

Flour Mill

Grand River

Louie Pfeiffer

Geo. Rhien

School No. 4

Paul Vesmer

Fred. Schwandt

Baptist Ch.

Gen. Store

MANCHESTER P.O.

J. F. Groose Creamery

B.S.S.

(From COME BACK IN TIME, Vol. I by Elaine Reetz)

57

29) FABISZ, Anne- b. "Prussian Poland", marr. Casinious Muszynski-
b. "Prussian Poland"; at Berlin 9 January 1893/ Vol. 6 (1893-
1897), p. 108.

30) FABRIZAK, Mary- b. "Prussian Poland", marr. Xaverius Pawlowski-
"Prussian Poland"; at Berlin 3 May 1893/ Vol. 6 (1893-1897),
p. 118.

31) GEYGER, Julianna- b. "Prussia", marr. Antonius Majkrzak (perhaps
Majchrzak?)- b. "Polland"; at Princeton 11 April 1883/ No.
56568 (Vol. 5, p. 85) (perhaps German/Polish mixed?).

32) GIERSZEWSKI, Frank- b. "Polish Prussia", marr. Mary Dutak at
Berlin 18 January 1898/ Vol. 7 (1897-1900), p. 139.

33) GIZELA, Bertha- b. "Prussian Poland", marr. Frank Ryband- b.
"Prussian Poland"; at Berlin 7 February 1893/ Vol. 6 (1893-1897),
p. 114.

34) GOIK, Antom-b. "Poland i Prussia", marr. Stanislawa Podlewska
(father Podlewski)- b. "Poland (Prussia)"; at Berlin 28 April
1885/ No. 59991 (Vol. 5, p. 101).

35) GORKOWSKA, Mary- b. "Prussian Poland", marr. Valentine Nowak-
b. "Prussian Poland"; at Birlin 5 February 1894/ Vol. 6 (1893-
1897), p. 239.

36) GREGER, Albertina- b. "Prussian Poland", marr. Alexander Pawel-
ski- b. "Prussian Poland"; at Berlin 15 January 1894/ Vol. 6
(1893-1897), p. 245.

37) GREGER, Martin- b. "Prussian Poland", marr. Anne Bulizak at
Berlin 5 August 1890/ Vol. 6 (1893-1897), p. 32.

38) GREGIER, August- b. "Poland Prussia", marr. Julia Siuda- b.
"Poland Prussia"; at Berlin 11 January 1885/ No. 59585 (Vol.
5, p. 99).

39) GROTA, Albert- b. "Poland Prussia", marr. Ewe Klawikowski- b.
"Poland Prussia"; at Berlin 16 May 1882/ No. 55501 (Vol. 5,
p. 80).

40) GROTA (nee Domaszek), Anastasia- b. "Polish Prussia", marr.
Frank Knak- b. "Prussia"; at Berlin 17 January 1898/ Vol. 7
(1897-1900), p. 138.

41) GROTA, Joseph- b. "Polish Prussia", marr. Antonia Nowizka- b.
"Polish Prussia "; at Berlin 23 October 1899/ Vol.7 (1897-1900),
p. 369.

42) GRZEMIA, Joseph- b. "Poland (Prussia)", marr. Any Albertowska (father Albertowski) at Berlin 10 January 1881/ No. 53234.

43) GUTOWSKA, Euphemia (father Gutowski)- b. "Prussian Poland", marr. John Tyburski of Milwaukee- b. "Prussian Poland "; at Berlin 6 May 1890/ No. 66911 (Vol. 5, p. 129).

44) HAAS, Augustinus- b. "Prussian Poland", marr. Prasedes Meyer- b. "Prussian Poland "; at Belrin 9 June 1891/ Vol. 6 (1893-1897), p. 40.

45) HALMAN, Frank- b. "Prussian Poland", marr. Julia Zabrowska- b. "Prussian Poland"; at Berlin 13 July 1891/ Vol. 6 (1893-1897), p. 41.

46) JAGODZINSKA (father Jagodzinski), Theophila- b. "Polish Prussia", marr. Frank Goik at Berlin 14 November 1899/ Vol. 7 (1897-1900), p. 391.

47) JANICKA (father Janicki), Elisabeth- b. "Poland (Prussia)", marr. Andrew Piekarski- b. "Poland(Prussia)"; at Berlin 20 April 1885/ No. 59990 (Vol. 5, p. 101).

48) JANICKI, Anton- b. "Poland Germany", marr. Victoria Szpot- b. "Poland Germany"; at Princeton 16 October 1893/ Vol. 6 (1893-1897), p. 96.

49) JANKOWSKA (nee Jazdzewski), Anne- b. "Prussian Poland", marr. John Myszk- b. "Prussian Poland"; at Berlin 20 January 1891/ Vol. 6 (1893-1897), p. 35.

50) JUSIK, Martinus- b. "Prussian Poland", marr. Mary Dysterheft at Berlin 13 Novmeber 1893/ Vol. 6 (1893-1897), p. 123.

51) JUSIK, Mary- b. "Prussian Poland", marr. Martinus Nowicki- b. "Prussian Poland"; at Berlin 14 May 1894/ Vol. 6 (1893-1897), p. 237.

52) KALAS, Wenzeslaus- b. "Polish Prussia", marr. Michthildis Mezyk at Berlin 31 January 1898/ Vol. 7 (1897-1900), p. 140.

53) KAMINSKA (father Kaminski), Anny- b."Poland Prussia", marr. Alojzy Nigbur- b. "Poland Prussia"; at Berlin 21 February 1881/ No. 53236.

54) KAMINSKA, Julia- b. "Prussian Poland", marr. Adolphus Anthony Polaszek- b. "Bohemia"; at Berlin 31 July 1893/ Vol 6 (1893-1897), p. 122.

55) KASPROWICZ, Martinus- b. "Prussian Poland", marr. Veronica Krause- b. "Prussian Poland"; at Berlin 7 August 1894/ Vol. 6 (1893-1897), p. 236.

56) KESO(W?), Herman- b. "Poland", marr. Augusta Spiekman at Marquette 28 November 1868/ Vol. 5, p. 8 (Episcopal Church).

57) KIEWICZ, John- b. "Prussian Poland", marr. Lucia Walkusz- b. "Prussian Poland"; at Berlin 10 November 1891/ Vol. 6 (1893-1897), p. 45.

58) KIEWICZ, Mary- b. "Poland Prussia", marr. John Kierski- b. "Poland Russia"; at Berlin 19 January 1885/ No. 59586 (Vol. 5, p. 99).

59) KISIELEWSKI, Adam- b. "Polish Prussia", marr. Susanna Molus- b. "Polish Prussia"; at Berlin 3 May 1897/ Vol. 7 (1897-1900), p. 42.

60) KOMEDULSAN, Tosefo- b. "in Polonier Europe", marr. Martin Wachowiak- b. "in Prasia Europe"; at Princeton 1 October 1895/ Vol. 6 (1893-1897), p. 310.

61) KOTLOWSKA (father Kotlowski), Augusta- b. "Poland (Prussia)", marr. Joseph Stroinski- b. "Poland(Prussia)"; at Berlin 26 November 1884/ No. 59584 (Vol. 5, p. 99).

62) KRANZA, Theophil- b. "Poland Prussia", marr. Mary Kaminski at Berlin 24 November 1885/ No. 59582.

63) KREGIER, Pauline- b. "Poland Prussia", marr. August Sinda- b. "Poland Prussia"; at Berlin 9 October 1881/ No. 55303.

64) KREMPA, Theodorus- b. "Prussian Poland", marr. Anne Cyman at Berlin 17 January 1893/ Vol. 6 (1893-1897), p. 110.

65) KUPEL, Anastas- b. "Poland Germany", marr. Waleria Mlodzik- b. "Poland Germany"; at Princeton 8 November 1893/ Vol. 6 (1893-1897), p. 98.

66) KURKOWSKI, John- b. "Prussian Poland", marr. Mechtildes Miclewczyk- b. "Prussian Poland"; at Berlin 11 November 1891/ Vol. 6. (1893-1897), p. 46.

67) LATWOSKI, Martinus- b. "Prussian Poland", marr. Anne Lzweda (Szweda?) at Berlin 24 January 1893/ Vol. 6 (1893-1897), p. 112.

68) LIS, Thomas- b. "Prussian Poland", marr. Catherina Losinska (father Losinski)- b. "Prussian Poland"; at Berlin 2 August 1891/ Vol. 6 (1893-1897), p. 43.

69) MACHOL, Paulina- b. "Poland (Prussia)", marr. Joseph Munski-b. "Poland Prussia"; at Berlin 20 January 1885/ No. 59587 (Vol. 5, p. 99).

70) MACHOL, Theela- b. "Prussian Poland", marr. August Mlynski- b. "Prussian Poland"; at Berlin 15 December 1896/ Vol. 6 (1893-1897), p. 465.

71) MACIEJEWSKA (father Maciejewski), Joseph(a?)- b. "Polish Prussia", marr. John Leman at Berlin 11 January 1898/ Vol. 7 (1897-1900), p. 137.

72) MARCINKOWSKI, Romanus- b. "Prussian Poland", marr. Anie Kotlowska at Berlin 13 February 1893/ Vol. 6 (1893-1897), p. 116.

73) MARZEJON, Frank- b. "Poland (Prussia) Newtown", marr. Marianna Wysynska (father Wysynski)- b. "Poland Prussia"; at Berlin 18 January 1881/ No. 53235.

74) MATYA, Frank- b. "Polish Prussia", marr. Mary Machol at Berlin 22 November 1899/ Vol. 7 (1897-1900), p. 393.

75) MATYA, Joseph- b. "Prussian Poland", marr. Martha Kemnitz- b. "Prussia"; at Berlin 20 January 1897/ Vol. 7 (1897-1900), p. 38.

76) McKOSKIE, Katie (father Joseph McKoskie)- b. "Poland", marr. John Detmann of Walworth Co., Wisc.; at Marquette 10 February 1891/ No. 67711 (Vol. 5, p. 133).

77) MEDLEWSKI, Catharina- b. "Poland Prussia", marr. Theophile Ryszewski of Ripon (Fond du Lac Co., Wisc.)- b. "Poland (Prussia)"; at Berlin 3 February 1885/ No. 59591 (Vol. 5 p. 99).

78) MIELEWCZYK, Augusta- b. "Poland Prussia", marr. August Munski- b. "Poland Prussia"; at Berlin 23 February 1881/ No. 53241.

79) MIERA, Mary- b. "Germany Polen (Poland)", marr. William Pugh-b. "Welch (Welsh?)"; at Princeton 11 February 1888/ No. 63860 (Vol. 5, p. 116).

80) MYSZK, August- b. "Prussian Poland", marr. Anna Majer at Berlin 27 November 1894/ Vol. 6 (1893-1897), p. 247.

81) NASTALI, John of Chicago- b. "Poland Prussia", marr. Augusta Tibowska (father Tibowski) at Berlin 26 October 1884/ No. 58958.

82) OKONEK, Frank- b. "Prussia Poland", marr. Anna Parolewska (father Parolewski)- b. "Prussia Poland"; at Berlin 14 January 1884/ No. 58062 (Vol. 5, p. 92).

83) PAROLEWSKI, Paulus of Bessemer (Gogebic Co.), Mich.- b. "Prussian Poland", marr. Mary Lesniak at Berlin 3 May 1897/ Vol. 7 (1897-1900), p. 41.

84) PAWLOWSKA, Martha- b. "Polish Prussia", marr. John Cyman at Berlin 6 November 1899/ Vol. 7 (1897-1900), p. 372.

85) PIPKA, Frank- b. "Poland Prussia", marr. Mary Albertowska (father Albertowski) at Berlin 21 January 1879/ No. 52002.

86) REGINKA, Cecilia- b. "Poland", marr. Andrew Wiski of Montello (Marquette Co.)- b. "Germany"; at Princeton 22 October 1888/ No. 64856 (Vol. 5, p. 121).

87) ROSSA, Agnes- b. "Prussian Poland", marr. John Szymanski of Michigan- b. "Prussian Poland"; at Berlin 24 June 1890/ No. 66909 (Vol. 5, p. 129).

88) RYBAND, Joseph- b. "Prussian Poland", marr. Magdalen Stoychalski at Berlin 15 January 1894/ Vol. 6 (1893-1897), p. 234.

89) RYBAND, Mary- b. "Prussian Poland", marr. Maximilianus Splitt- b. "Prussian Poland"; at Berlin 27 January 1891/ Vol. 6 (1893-1897), p. 37.

90) RYZOP, Theophila- b. "Prussian Poland", marr. Valetnine Domaszek at Berlin 25 April 1893/ Vol. 6 (1893-1897), p. 117.

91) SCHURPIT (SZURPIT?), Frank- b. "Germ. Poland", marr. Mary Bartol at Prenceton 16 January 1888/ No. 63856 (Vol. 5, p. 116) (Pol. Cath.).

92) SIKORA, Julia- b. "Prussian Poland", marr. Otto Wendke- b. "Prussian Poland"; at Berlin 12 May 1890/ No. 66910 (Vol. 5, p. 129).

93) SOBCZIEWSKI, Joseph- b. "Poland Prussia", marr. Augusta Gosz at Berlin 3 February 1885/ No. 59590 (Vol. 5, p. 99).

94) STELMACH, Miss Anna- b. "Poland (Prussia)", marr. Mr. Joseph Greas- b. "Prussia"; at Kingston 15 January 1883/ No. 56127 (Vol. 5, p. 83).

95) STIP, August- b. "Poland (Prussia)", marr. Juliana Czaja at Berlin 8 January 1879/ No. 51911 (both signed certificates "Styp").

96) STRZEBIELINSKA (father Strzebielinski), Matilda- b. "Prussian Poland", marr. Conradus Zelewski- b. "Prussian Poland"; at Berlin 23 January 1894/ Vol. 6 (1893-1897), p. 246.

97) SZOSTEK, Julianus- b. "Prussian Poland", marr. Catherine Czyzak at Berlin 29 January 1894/ Vol. 6 (1893-1897), p. 244.

98) TOMASZEWSKA, Clara- b. "Prussian Poland", marr. Ignatz Smolinski of Oshkosh (Winnebago Co., Wisc.)- b. "Russian Poland"; at Berlin 5 February 1897/ Vol. 7 (1897-1900), p. 40.

99) TRAMP, Anna- b. "Polish Prussia", marr. Andrew Wiarek- b. "Polish Prussia"; at Berlin 19 November 1899/ Vol. 7 (1897-1900), p. 392.

100) TREDER, Sophia- b. "Prussian Poland", marr. Frank Markowski at Berlin 18 January 1893/ Vol. 6 (1893-1897), p. 111.

101) WAWRZYNIAK, Anna- b. "Polish Prussian", marr. Thomas D. Evans, jr. at Berlin 28 May 1897/ Vol. 7 (1897-1900), p. 43.

102) ZACHARIAS, Paul Gustav- b. "Polen (Poland) Prussia Germany", marr. Ida Francisca Draeger of Flint (Genesee Co.), Mich.; at Marquette 19 April 1900/ Vol. 7 (1897-1900), p. 439 (religious ceremony, not Catholic, probably a German couple).

Immigrants from Province Schlesien (Silesia), Prussia:

1) BARTSOP, Ernst. August of "Saxeville Green Lake Co. (actually Waushara Co.)"- b. Jacobscorp in Schlesien in Prussia", marr. Anna Henriette Tunun at Princeton 19 November 1865/ Early Vol. 3 (1858-1867), p. 220.

2) BURMANN, Karl- b. "Hirschberg (a county seat) (Schlesien) Prussien)", marr. Wilhelmine Steinkraus at Manchester 18 January 1878/ No. 48638.

3) HOFFMAN, J.C. Gottlieb of Amherst, Portage Co. (Wisc.)- b. "Schlesisch Hausdorf Province Schlesien Germania", marr. Miss Friedericke Exner at Princeton- in the house of Frederick Ellinger 11 May 1885/ No. 60506.

4) SCHOSCHNECK, Luise- b. "Schlesien Prussia", marr. John Ernst Conrad Vinz- b. "Erfurt (Prussian Province of Saxony in central Germany) Germany"; at Manchester 11 p.m.-12 August 1883/ No. 57039 (Vol. 5, p. 87).

5) ZOBEL, Hermann- b. "Birkickt Kreis (County) Hirs(c)hberg Provinz Schlesien Europa", marr. Pauline Kahl at the Town of Marquette 1 January 1878/ No. 48507.

Immigrants from County Flatow, Province West Prussia:

1) BEHNKE, Johann- b. "Large Wisnefke (Gross-Wisniewke) Prussia", marr. Caroline Boelter at Berlin 30 September 1873.

2) BRAUN, August- b. "Flatow Prussia Germany", marr. Juliane Bolter at Berlin 3 January 1873.

3) BRAUN, August (see above)- b. "Fladow (Flatow) Westpreussen (West Prussia)", marr. Elisabeth Stahlmann at Berlin 14 July 1880/ No. 52219.

4) HANSTER (or HAMLER?), August Wilhelm- b. "Pempersin, Prussia", marr. Auguste Luise Hennig at the Village of Manchester 26 December 1870.

5) JANZ, Hermann Albert- b. "Koenigsdorf, Prussia, Germany", marr. Minna Wilhelmine Schroder at Berlin 19 April 1892/ No. 69622 (Vol. 5, p. 140).

6) KEEHN (perhaps Kuehn?), Gust W. - b. "Illowa (Illowo) Germany", marr. Elma Durkee of Spring Lake (Waushara Co.); at Berlin 2 November 1898/ Vol. 7 (1897-1900), p. 285.

7) KUEHN, Lena Louise- b. "Ilovo (Illowo), West Prussia, Germany", marr. Wilhelm Ferdinand Bohn- b. "Schoenwerder, Germany (Cos. Wirsitz, Prov. Posen or Pyritz, Prov. Pomerania?)"; at the City of Berlin 18 November 1893/ Vol. 6 (1893-1897), p. 84.

8) LINK, Wilhelmine Maria- b. "Kreis Flats (County Flatow) (Administrative District of) Marienwerde(r), Prussia", marr. Edward August Radschweit- b. "East Prussia"; at Mackford 25 April 1897/ Vol. 7 (1897-1900), p. 23.

9) LIPINSKI, Eva- b. "Lubezin (Lubcza or Glubczun) West Prussia", marr. John Eikman at Berlin 12 June 1899/ Vol. 7 (1897-1900), p. 322 (Rom. Cath., likely Polish couple).

10) MARWAN, Wilhelm Eduard- b. "Koenigsdorff, Westprussia, Germany", marr. Anna Mathilde Grutzner- b. "Stettin (county & district seat in Prov. Pomerania), Prussia"; at Berlin 16 March 1890/ No. 66542 (Vol. 5, p. 128).

11) MULLER, Bertha (father's name Lehmann, perhaps previously married?)- b. "Konigsdorf, West Preussen", marr. Carl Ludwig Schroder- b. "Josephsruh (Co. Kolmar) Posen Germany"; at Berlin 8 September 1882/ No. 55547 (Vol. 5, p. 80) (both marr. one before).

12) PLAGENS, Heinrich- b. "Glubsin (Glubczun) (Prussia)", marr. Wilhelmine Pischke at the Town of Green Lake 30 October 1873.

13) PRAHL, Carl Albert Ludwig- b. "Glomen (Glumen) Prussia Germ.", Bertha Fredericke Quade at Berlin 19 April 1899/ Vol. 7 (1897-1900), p. 297.

14) PRAHL, Johann Edward- b. "Koenigsdorf Prussia Germany", marr. Ida Auguste Voss at Berlin 15 April 1895/ Vol. 6 (1893-1897), p. 280.

15) PRAWL (PRAHL?), Emma Mathilde- b. "Koenigsdorf Prussia Germany", marr. Stacy R. Angle (no location given) 11 November 1899/ Vol. 7 (1897-1900), p. 379.

16) SCHRANDT, Johann- b. "Flatow Prussia Germany", marr. Emilie Beltin at Berlin 16 March 1881/ No. 53290.

17) STOLP, Hulda Auguste- b. "Pitzewo (Petzewo), Prussia, Germany", marr. Frank August Ferdinand Zimmermann- b. "Steinberg (Co. Arnswalde, Prov. Brandenburg), Prussia, Germany"; at the Town of Brooklyn 18 December 1884/ No. 59307 (Vol. 5, p. 97).

18) ZUEHLKE, August- b. "Flatow, Germany", marr. Emma Stenzel- b. "Samter (county seat in Prov. Posen), Germany"; at Markesan 16 September 1888/ No. 64837 (Vol. 5, p. 121).

PLAT OF MARQUETTE

Townships 15&16 North. Ranges 11&12 East.

LAKE PUCKAWAY

(From COME BACK IN TIME, Vol. I by Elaine Reetz)

65

Immigrants from County Deutsch Krone, Province West Prussia:

1) ABENDROTH, Mary Louisa- b. "Schultzendorf Germany", marr. Anton Henry William Menke of Alto Fond du Lac Co. (Wisc.)- b. "Schleswig Manitowoc Co. Wisc."; at Mackford 10 January 1888/ No. 63763 (Vol. 5, p. 116).

2) BRIESE, August Julius of Fairwater (Fond du Lac Co., Wisc.)- b. "Deutsch Krone Germany", marr. Ernestine Hasse - b. "Friedrichshorst (Co. Wirsitz, Prov. Posen), Germany"; at Markesan 20 September 1885/ No. 60408 (Vol. 5, p. 102).

3) HEMPEL, Auguste Ernestine- b. "Werder Wess (West) Preussen Germany", marr. Emil Hermann Metzig of the Town of Wolf River Winnebago Co.; at Berlin 31 "Okt." (October) 1896/ Vol. 6 (1893-1897), p. 425.

4) PERLWITZ, Gustav Theodor- b. "Deutsch Krone Prussia", marr. Wilhelmine Albertine Sau (widow, nee Sommer) at the Town of Princeton 14 January 1871.

5) SCHULTZ, Johann Ludwig- b. "Schlop(p)e Prussia", marr. Marie Erlich at the Village of Princeton 28 September 1872.

6) STELIMACHER, Gustav William of Grd. Prairie, Wis.- b. "Deutsch Kron(e), Germany", marr. Magdalena Steil at Manchester 27 November 1888/ No. 64733 (Vol. 5, p. 120).

7) TEWS, Friedrich Christoph of Rush Lake Winnebago Co. (Wisc.)- b. "Langhof, Prussia, Germany", marr. Wilhelmine, Auguste, Louise Bausch- b. "Schwachenwalde Kreis (County) Arnswalde (Prov. Brandenburg) Germany"; at the Tshp. of Princeton 14 May 1891/ No. 68105 (Vol. 5, p. 135).

8) ZARBUCK, Mariha Louise Johanne (father Wilhelm)- b. "Lueben, Province (West) Preussen Germany", marr. Joahnn Friedrich Zarbuck (father Johann)- b. "Mecan (Marquette Co.)"; at the Town of Marquette 17 May 1896/ Vol. 6 (1893-1897), p. 383.

Immigrants from additional locales in Province West Prussia:

1) BARKOWSKI, Johann Julius of Chicago (Cook Co.), Ill.- b. "Wul-
   kow, Westpreussen, Germ.", marr. Anna Nessbauer-b. "New York,
   N.Y."; at Berlin 29 January 1892/ No. 69289 (Vol. 5, p. 139).

2) BOYK, Anna- b "Danzig W. Prussia", marr. Andrew Toba- b. "Danzig W. Prussia" (a county & district seat); at Berlin 24 October 1898/ Vol. 7 (1897-1900), p. 231 (Catholic, likely Polish).

3) CIESZYNSKI, Frank- b. "Rgl. (Regierungsbezirk=Administrative
   District) Danzig Kreis Benoz (County Berent?) West Prussia",
   marr. Madaline Wozniak- b. "Posen, Prussia"; at Berlin City 3
   October 1898/ Vol. 7 (1897-1900), p. 216 (Catholic, likely Polish couple).

4) DOPKE, Joseph- b. "Neustadt (a county seat) West Prussia", marr.
   Cecilia Trocinska- b. "Bromberg W. Prussia (actually a county &
   district seat in Prov. Posen)"; at Berlin 3 May 1898/ Vol. 7
   (1897-1900), p. 200 (Catholic, perhaps German/Polish mixed?).

5) GIZELLA, Andreas- b. "Reg. Bez. (Regierungsbezirk=Administrative
   District) Danzig (also a county seat) West Prussia", marr. Fri-
   derika Heiser- b. "Posen, Prussia"; at Berlin 21 February 1898/
   Vol. 7 (1897-1900), p. 157 (Catholic, perhaps Polish/German mixed?).

6) HERMANN, Wilhelm- b. "Seeheim West Preussen Germany" (there is
   a Seeheim in Co. Wirsitz, Prov. Posen), marr. Ernestine Steinke
   at Berlin 20 December 1885/ No. 60838.

7) JASZEZYK, Mary (nee Berhardt)- b. "Marienworer (Marienwerder,
   a county & district seat) West Prussia", marr. John Adamczak-
   "Regiarung Berik (Regierungsbezirk=Administrative District)
   Bromberg (Prov. Posen) Prussia"; at Princeton 27 August 1900/
   Vol. 7 (1897-1900), p. 471 (Rom. Cath., likely Polish couple).

8) MARWAN, Ferdinand- b. "Marienwerder (a county & district seat),
   Westpreussen", marr. Alvine Gruetzner- b. "Neulinden, Vorpom(m)-
   ern (Farther or western Pomerania), Germany"; at Berlin 14 May
   1888/ No. 64200 (Vol. 5, p. 117).

9) MUELLER, Alma, Emma, Clara- b. "City of Thorn (a county seat),
   Prussia, Germ.", marr. Louis Kolpin at the Town of Seneca 26
   "Dez." (December) 1892/ No. 70590 (Vol. 5, p. 145).

10) NEUBAUER, Emilie Juliane- b. "Hulta (Hutta, Co. Tuchel?) Prus-
    sia Germany", marr. Otto Valentin Lungroitz of the Town of
    "Lien" (Lind) Waupaca Co. (Wisc.); at Berlin 1 July 1894/ Vol.
    6 (1893-1897), p. 164.

11) NIMKE, August- b. "Grossbislaw (Co. Tuchel) Reg. Bez. (Regierungsbezirk=Administrative District) Marienwerder Westpreussen", marr. Marie Schroeder at Berlin 15 October 1870.

12) OLLMANN, John- b. "Dancig (Danzig, a county district seat) Germany", marr. Mrs. Anna Prebatoskie (nee Wire=Weier?)- b. "Carthaus (Karthaus, a county seat) Germany"; at Berlin 31 January 1898/ Vol. 7 (1897-1900), p. 135.

13) PRIEWE, Ernest, Henry- b. "Denzig (Danzig, a county & district seat), Germany", marr. Paulina, Mathilda Hanslin at the town of Marquette 26 November 1889/ No. 66026 (Vol. 5, p. 126).

14) REINKE, Ernst Friedrich- b. "Danzig (a county & district seat), Prussia Germany", marr. Wilhelmine Henriette Lucht at the Town of Bloomfield, Waushara Co. 25 April 1873.

15) SCHILLING, Karl- b. "Friedrichsbruchs. (Co. Konitz) Prussia Germany", marr. Mary Chappa- b. "Goranchien Prussia Germany"; at Berlin 22 July 1890/ No. 66897 (Vol. 5, p. 129).

16) SEEMANN, Karl Albert of Sring Dale (Springvale twp.) Columbia Co. (Wisc.)- b. "Ostrowith (either Ostrowitte, Co. Konitz or Ostrowitt, Cos.Lobau or Marienwerder?), Germany", marr. Matilde Walz- b. "Satke (Sadke, Co. Wirsitz, Prov. Posen) Germany"; at Kingston Wed.-23 March 1892/ No. 69514 (Vol. 5, p. 140).

17) THIEL, William of Berlin (twp.) Maratha (Marathon) Co. Wisc.- b. "Wit(t)stock Germany (Co. Tuchel)", marr. Winna Winland at the City of Berlin 30 July 1866/ Early Vol. 3 (1858-1867), p. 246.

18) THOM, Carl August- b. "Gastrow, Reg. Bez. (Regierungsbezirk= Administrative District) Marienwerder Province Westpreussen, Prussia", marr. Wilhelmine Caroline Nimke at Berlin 24 July 1878.

19) WARNKE, Julia- b. Hammer (perhaps Co. Schlochau, but more likely Co. Czarnikau, Prov. Posen), Prussia, Germ.", marr. Carl Ferdinand Wopschall (Wobschall?)- b. "Stumbochowa (Stempuchowo, Co. Wongrowitz, Prov.)Posen, Prussia, Germ."; at Berlin 30 April 1890/ No. 66652 (Vol. 5, p. 128).

20) WELINTZ, William Frederick Herman- b. "Silberstorf (Silbersdorf, Co. Briesen?), Germany", marr. Minnie Fredericka Lousia Bobholz of Fox Lake (Dodge Co., Wisc.); at Manchester 26 September 1895/ Vol. 6 (1893-1897), p. 313.

21) WIELENGOWSKI, Emma Adeline- b. "Bratien, Westpreussen, Prussia, Germ.", marr. Samuel Nathan Albrecht- b. "Klein Merkowitz (Mirkowitz, Co. Wongrowitz), Posen, Prussia, Germ."; at Berlin 21 November 1888/ No. 64690 (Vol. 5, p. 120).

22) ZANDER, Carl August Hermann- b. "Hammerstein (Co. Schlochau), Westprussian, Germ.", marr. Johanna Christina Rehwinkel at Berlin 17 July 1889/ No. 65570 (Vol. 5, p. 125).

Immigrants from the Province of "Westpreussen" or "West Prussia":

1) BETTIN, Gustav of "Wesley Faulk Co. Dakota Territory"- b. "West Preussen, Germany"; marr. Louise Wiederhoeft at Berlin 7 March 1886/ No. 61198.

2) BOEHM, Johann of Walworth Co. Dakota- b. "Prussia (West Preussen) Germany", marr. Ottilie Pomreinke at Berlin 25 March 1885/ No. 59786.

3) DERRA, John- b. "Westprice Prussia (Westpreussen?)", marr. Franciske Poklekowske- b. "Prussia"; at Princeton 16 August 1892/ No. 69963 (Vol. 5, p. 142).

4) EICHMANN, Joseph- b. "Westprussia Germany", marr. Regina Machol at Berlin 26 February 1876.

5) EICHMANN, Julius Ferdinand- b. "West Prussia,Germany", marr. Sophia Dietrich nee Salzwedel- b. "Panim (Pammin, Co.-) Arnswalde (Prov.) Brandenburg Germany"; at the Town of Manchester 31 March 1897/ Vol. 7 (1897-1900), p. 21.

6) EWALD, August Johann resident of South Dakota- b. "Westpreussen, Prussia, Germ.", marr. Emilie Ottilie Elisabeth Schlueter- b. "Baumgarten (Co. Dramburg, Prov. Pomerania?) Prussia Germany"; at Berlin 29 March 1893/ Vol. 6 (1893-1897), p. 20.

7) FUHDE, Emilie- b. "Germany W. Prussia", marr. Richard Schneider of Oshkosh (Winnebago Co., Wisc.) at the residence of Martin Fuhde in the Town of Princeton 27 April 1892/ No. 69852 (Vol. 5, p. 141).

8) GRAFF, Gustav- b. "Province of West Prussia Germany", marr. Ottillie Roedel at Manchester 2 December 1884/ No. 59113 (Vol. 5, p. 96).

9) JANITZKI, John- b. "Germany Westpreussen", marr. Eleonora Kujat(h?) - b. "Germany province of Posen"; at Kingston 11¼ a.m.-21 January 1889/ No. 64956 (Vol. 5, p. 122).

10) KRUEGER, Emil- b. "West Preussen. Prussia (Germany)", marr. Henriette Behnke at Berlin 24 February 1886/ No. 61196.

11) LOEFFLER, Julius- b. "Prov. West Preussen. Germany", marr. Hulda Retzlaff at Berlin 28 June 1885/ No. 60099.

12) MARKOWSKI, Jozef- b. "West Preuson (Preussen)", marr. Josephina Czapiewska (father Czapiewski) at Berlin 24 September 1876 (Catholic, likely Polish couple).

13) NIGBOR, John- b. "Westprussia Germany", marr. Katherine Derra at the City of Berlin 8 November 1875 (Catholic, likely Polish).

14) SOMMERFELD, Rudolf of Chicago- b. "Westpreussen Germany", marr. Wilhelmine Posorski of the Town of Auroraville, Waushara Co.; at Berlin 23 April 1888/ No. 64091 (Vol. 5, p. 117).

PRINCETON

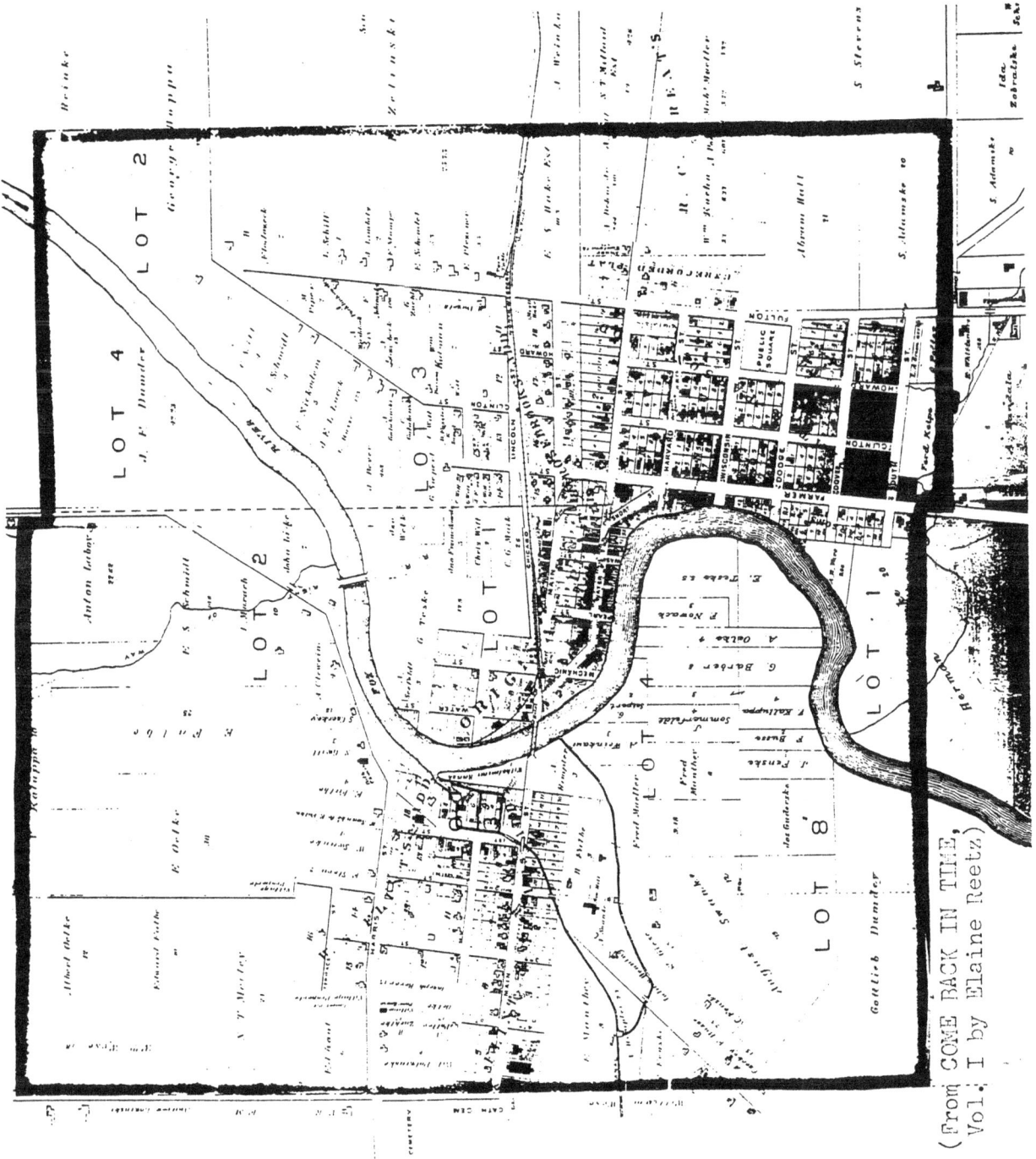

(From COME BACK IN TIME,
Vol. I by Elaine Reetz)

Immigrants from County Arnswalde, Province Brandenburg, Prussia:

1) ARNDT, August William- b. "Panmain (Pammin) near Arnswalde Reg. Bezirk (Administrative District) Frankfurt (an der Oder) Prussia Germany", marr. Clara Bertha Block at Brandon Fond du Lac Co., 3 p.m.-2 November 1899/ Vol. 7 (1897-1900), p. 374.

2) BAUSCH, Wilhelmine, Auguste, Louise- b. "Schwachenwalde Kreis (County) Arnswalde Germany", marr. Friedrich Christoph Tews of Rush Lake Winnebago Co., (Wisc.)- b. "Langhof (Co. Deutsch Krone, Prov. West Prussia), Prussia, Germany"; at the Tshp. of Princeton 14 May 1891/ No. 68105 (Vol. 5, p. 135).

3) BENZ, Bertha- b. "Silsdorf, Transwalde (Zuhlsdorf, Co. Arnswalde), Germany", marr. Wilhelm Neering (Nehring?)- b. "Riez (Reetz, Co. Arnswalde) Transwalde, Germany"; at Markesan 31 December 1892/ No. 70565 (Vol. 5, p. 144).

4) BIRKHOLZ b.o. (born of) LEMKE, Ernestine- b. "Rackow, Province Brandenburg Germany", marr. Ludwig Jahnke- b. "Budzin (Budsin, Co. Kolmar), Provniz (Province) Pose(n), Germany"; at the Town Kingston 8 March 1887/ No. 62660 (Vol. 5, p. 111).

5) BOEHNING, Ferdinand- b. "Arnswald(e) Germany", marr. Alice Birkholz at the Town of Dartford (Green Lake, itself, the county seat) 17 February 1881/ No. 53171.

6) BOELTER, Friedrich Wilhelm- b. "Neu Wedell (Neuwedell), Germany", marr. Mathilde Caroline Schmidt- b. "Neu Wedell (Neuwedell), Germany"; at the Town of Mackford 22 April 1889/ No. 65315 (Vol. 5, p. 124).

7) BORNHAGEN, John, Herman- b. "Radun, Germany", marr. Mary, Augusta Schmidt at Manchester 26 November 1891/ No. 68904 (Vol. 5, p. 138).

8) BRECHLIN, Herman Franz of the Town of Warren, Waushara Co.- b. "Marienhoff Prussia Germany", marr. Ida Wiese at Berlin 16 November 1897/ Vol. 7 (1897-1900), p. 99.

9) BRELAU, Henriette- b. "Rohrbeck, Kreis (County) Arnswalde, Germany", marr. Frank Ludwig Wilde- b. "Pammin, Kreis Arnswalde, Germany"; at the Town of Princeton 27 June 1890/ No. 66840 (Vol. 5, p. 129).

10) BUNDING, Wilhelm- b. "Arnswalde (Prussian)", marr. Karoline Reetz at Marquette 6 December 1874.

11) DOERRING, Franz Herman Gustav- b. "Sellnow Prussia Germ.", marr. Bertha Emilie Auguste Kerl- b. "Baumgarten (Co. Dramburg, Prov. Pomerania) Prussia Germ."; at Berlin 1 March 1897/ Vol. 7 (1897-1900), p. 2.

12) DOLGNER, Franz Ferdinand- b. "Zylsdorf (Zühlsdorf),Province Brandenburg, Germany", marr. Martha Ernestine Caroline Hollnagel of the Town of Wautoma (Waushara Co.); at Kingston 12 a.m.- 29 March 1894/ Vol. 6 (1893-1897), p. 133.

13) DR(A?)EGER, Rudolph (father Louis) of Fond du Lac (co. seat, Wisc.)- b. "Sel(l)now Germany", marr. Bertha Dr(a?)eger (father Charles)- b. "Sel(l)now Germany"; at Green Lake Co. 6 p.m.- 6 November 1895/ Vol. 6 (1893-1897), p. 322.

14) EHLERT, Caroline Hannah Charlotte, a widow (nee Bremer)- b. "Arnswalde Germany", marr. Ernst Henry Utke- b. "Certen (Zehrten, Co. Saatzig, Prov. Pomerania) Germany"; at Manchester 14 July 1895/ Vol. 6 (1893-1897), p. 293.

15) FELDT, Ernestine Wilhelmine- b. "Pam(m)in Germany Europe", marr. Herman A. Wegner at Mecan (Marquette Co.) 3 p.m.-19 April 1900/ Vol. 7 (1897-1900), p. 442.

16) FERCH, Christian Friedrich Hermann- b. "Arenswalde Prussia", marr. Julie Wolff at Princeton 21 October 1866/ Early Vol. 3 (1858-1867), p. 259.

17) FERCH, Johann Charles August- b. "Berkenbruegge, Pruessen, Germany", marr. Auguste Emma Lechelt at Dartforth (Dartford=Green Lake) 25 November 1880/ No. 52885.

18) FERG(E?), Eduard- b. "Berkenbrugge, Prussia, Germany", marr. Auguste Leistikow at Dartforth (Dartford=Green Lake) 14 December 1882/ No. 56128.

19) FRANZ, Anna Minnie Emilie- b. "Rohrbeck, Germany", marr. Fred William Zimmermann- b. "Klein-Silber, Germany"; at Ripon, Fond du Lac Co., Wisc.; 27 July 1884/ No. 58647 (Vol. 5, p. 94).

20) FRANZ, Hermann- b. "Zatten, Germany", marr. Bertha Kaufmann- b. "Sel(l)now, Germany"; at Markesan 13 March 1886/ No. 61231 (Vol. 5, p. 105).

21) FRITZ, Charles Ludwic (Ludwig?)- b. "Sel(l)now, Germany", marr. Louise, Mathilda, Augusta Uecker- b. "Geilenfelde (Co. Friedeberg/Neumark, Prov. Brandenburg) Germany"; at Manchester 3 November 1891/ No. 68853 (Vol. 5, p. 137).

22) FRITZ, Gustav Gottlieb- b. "Sel(l)now Kreis Senswalde (County Arnswalde) Germany", marr. Bertha Auguste Wilhelmina Kelm- b. "Kreis Senswalde (County Arnswalde) Germany"; at Manchester 13 February 1896/ Vol. 6 (1893-1897) p. 354.

23) FRITZ, Gustav Gottlieb (see previous listing)- b. "Sel(l)now Auswalde (Arnswalde) Brandenburg Germany", marr. Martha Maria Elisabeth Schade- b. "Ro(h)rbeck Auswalde (Arnswalde) Brandenburg Germany"; at Manchester 17 October 1896/ Vol. 6 (1893-1897), p. 423.

24) GEBHARDT, Franz Michael Helmuth- b. "Arnswalde Brandenburg Germany", marr. Bertha Franciska Lemke- b. "Kurtow Arnswalde Brandenburg Germany"; at Manchester 15 November 1896/ Vol. 6 (1893-1897), p. 448.

25) GRAMS (nee FRITZ), Ottilie Amelia Theresa- b. "Kreis (County) Arnswalde, Germany", marr. Charles Fredric Willie Giese- b. "Germany"; at the Town of Mackford 23 November 1893/ Vol. 6 (1893-1897), p. 89.

26) HELMER, Herman August- b. "Arnswalde Germany", marr. Johanna Mary Hollnagel- b. "New York(City)"; at Manchester 26 September 1886/ No. 62014 (Vol. 5, p. 108).

27) HOFFMAN, Franz Wilhelm Herman of Wausau Marathon Co. (Wisc.)- b. "Avenswalde (Arnswalde) in Prussia", marr. Johanna Henrich? Auguste Schultz at Princeton 6 September 1866/ Early Vol. 3 (1858-1867), p. 253.

28) JERK, Carl of Brandon. Fond du Lac Co. (Wisc.)- b. "Nardin (Wardin?) Prussia Europ(e)", marr. Mina Zillsdorf (Zühlsdorf?) at Mackford 22 December 1869/ Vol. 5, p. 13.

29) KLATT, Frank Ferd- b. "Stolzenflede, Province of Brandenburg, Germany", marr. Bertha Friederika Kurth at the residence of W. Kurth-Town of Green Lake 16 March 1893/ Vol. 6 (1893-1897), p. 14.

30) KLATT, Wilhelm- b. "Stolzenfelde Kr. (Co.) Arnswalde Reg. Bez. (Administrative District) Frankford (Frankfurt) an der Oder (a river) Preutsen (Preussen=Prussia) Germ. Europa", marr. Ernstine Krueger at the Town of Princeton 1"Januar" (German for January) 1879/ No. 50126.

31) KLINGBEIL, Ottilie Louise Antonia- b. "Eisenhammer (may be Co. Schlochau, Prov. West Prussia, but unlikely), Prussia, Germany", marr. Carl August Radnenzel(Raduenzel?) of the Town of Auroraville Waushara Co.;-married at same place 6 April 1893/ Vol. 6 (1893-1897), p. 23.

32) KOEPKE, Frank- b. "Langenfuhr, Province Brandenburg, Germany", marr. Emilie Ne(h?)ring- b. "Ri(e)tzig, Province Brandenburg, Germany"; at Markesan 7 September 1884/ No. 58726 (Vol. 5, p. 95).

33) KOPLIN, Friedrich Wilhelm- b. "Lang(en)fuhr Prussia", marr. Auguste Emilie Krause at the Town of Princeton 22 November 1868/ Vol. 5, p. 9.

34) KREBS, Henry, Otto Albert- b. "Nemischhoff, Prov. Brandenburg Germany", marr. Emma Perske at Manchester 27 January 1889/ No. 64991 (Vol. 5, p. 122).

35) KRUEGER, Alvine Wilhelmine Henriette- b. "Balkenbruegge (Berkenbruegge) Poussia (Prussia) Germ.", marr. August Edward Heinrich Kobischke at Berlin 8 April 1896/ Vol. 6 (18931-1897), p. 375.

36) KRUEGER, Karl Wilhelm- b. "Pommin (Pammin) Prussia", marr. Karoline Nehring at the Town of Manchester 20 December 1868/ Vol. 5, p. 9.

37) LENZ, August Hermann- b. "Kleinsilber (Klein-Silber) Provinz Brandenburg Germany", marr. Auguste Albertine Schulz- b. "Kleinsilber Germany"; at Manchester 2 January 1896/ Vol. 6 (1893-1897), p. 343.

38) LENZ, Wilhelmine Ernestine- b. "Klein Silber Neumark (region) Germany", marr. Fred William Lange at Green Lake Co. 21 April 1897/ Vol. 7 (1897-1900), p. 8.

39) LEASA, Anna or LIESE, Anna Maria Emilie- b. "Rostenburg Prussia Germany", marr. Albert Ziehl or Albert Carl Reinhard Ziehl of West Bloomfield Town Waushara Co.; at Berlin 17 May 1899/ Vol. 7 (1897-1900), p. 310.

40) MARTEN, Florentine Johanna Louise- b. "Springe, Prussia, Germany", marr. Carl August Timm of the Town of Poy Sippi (Waushara Co.)- at the same place 7 January 1890/ No. 66221 (Vol. 5, p. 127).

41) MARTENS, Ottilie Pauline Amalia- b. "Springe, Neu Mark (Neumark, a region), Prussia, Germ.", Johann Friedrich Bauernfeind of Jefferson (a county seat), Wis.; at the Town of Poy Sippi "Green Lake Co." (actually Waushara Co.) 22 November 1888/ No. 64691 (Vol. 5, p. 120).

42) MEYER, Anna- b. "Curtow Germany", marr. Samuel L. Kohnke at Ripon Fond du Lac Co. (Wisc.) 30 October 1899/ Vol. 7 (1897-1900), p. p. 365.

43) MEYER, Minnie- b. "Cuerton (Kürtow or Cürtow) Germany", marr. Albert Maczolek of Metomen Fond du Lac Co. (Wisc.)- b. "Szamoczin (Samotschin, Co. Kolmar, Prov. Posen), Germany"; at Brooklyn 6 February 1895/ Vol. 6 (1893-1897), p. 263.

44) MILLER, Martha Louise- b. "Arnswalde Kreis Lazig (?) Germany", marr. August Herman Born- b. "Jakobshagen Kreis Lazig (County Saatzig, Prov. Pomerania) Germany"; at Markesan 2 p.m.-22 October 1896/ Vol. 6 (1893-1897), p. 427.

45) OELKE, Herman- b. "Arnswalde Brandenburg Germany", marr. Wilhelmine Goldbeck (no location given 8 March 1889/ No. 65227 (Vol. 5, p. 123).

46) PETRICK, Julius Hermann August- b. "Rohrbeck, Prussia, Germany", marr. Bertha Elisabeth Heier at Berlin 18 February 1889/ No. 65108 (Vol. 5, p. 123).

47) PROCHNOW, Karl Robert- b. "Zuhlsdorf Abrnswalde (Zühlsdorf, Co. Arnswalde) Germany", marr. Wilhelmine Hubner- b. "Klein Dreidorf Germany"; at Kingston 2 p.m.-3 December 1895/ Vol. 6 (1893-1897), p. 331.

48) RABEHL, Friedrich Michael- b. "Koertow Kreis Arnswalde, Germany", marr. Bertha Auguste Mathilde Salzwedel- b. "Pommin (Pammin) Kreis (County) Arnswalde, Germany"; at Princeton 4 June 1891/ No. 68163 (Vol. 5, p. 136).

49) RABEHL, Karl Ludwig- b. "Schlagenthin, Prussia", marr. Johanne Emilie Bertha Mueller at the Village of Manchester 15 May 1870.

50) RA(D?)TKE, August of Salemville Columbia Co. (Wisc.)- b. "Arnswalde (Prussien)", marr. Friederike Lempke at Manchester 15 February 1878/ No. 48812.

51) REECK, Minna Martha- b. "Nemischhoff, Prussia, Germ.", marr. Conrad August Julius Raduenzel of the Town of Auroraville Waushara Co.- at the same place 10 August 1892/ No. 69955 (Vol. 5, p. 142).

52) REEK, Emilie- b. "Berbenbraeck (Berkenbrügge), Germany", marr. John Wuske- b. "Hammermihle (Hammermühle, Co. Bromberg, Prov. Posen) Germany"; at the Town of Manchester 30 March 1893/ Vol. 6 (1893-1897), p. 21.

53) RODER, Julius Hermann- b. "Pam(m)in Kreis (County) Arnswalde Prussia Germany", marr. August. Friederike Schroder at the Town of Princeton 12 "Mai" (May) 1878/ No. 49327.

54) ROESKE, Charles- b. "Marien Walde (Marienwalde) Prusia Europe", marr. Wilhelmina Schwandt at Princeton 1 January 1877.

55) RUENGER, Carl Wilhelm- b. "Gottberg, Province Brandenburg, Germany", marr. Martha Louida Grams at the Town of Fox Lake Dodge Co. (Wisc.) 4 October 1899/ Vol. 7 (1897-1900), p. 349.

56) SACK, Carl Friedrich- b. "Arnswalde, Provinz Brandenburg, Germany", marr. Wilhelmine Steinkraus- b. "Colberg (Kolberg, a county seat), Provinz Pommern (Pomerania), Germany"; at the township of Manchester 6 April 1891/ No. 67928 (Vol. 5, p. 135).

57) SACK, Johanna Louisa Carolina- b. "Pamine (Pammin), Kreis (County), Arnswalde, Germany", marr. Theron White of Farmington, Washington Co., Wisc.; at Mackford 2 October 1888/ No. 64517 (Vol. 5, p. 119).

58) SALZWEDEL, Dorothea Sophia- b. "Pammin Germany", marr. Carl Dietrich- b. "Nackel (Nakel, Co. Wirsitz, Prov. Posen), Germany"; at the Town of Mackford 4 January 1894/ Vol. 6 (1893-1897), p. 105.

59) SALZWEDEL, Ernst August Theodor- b. "Kleinsilber by Reetz, Kreis (County) Arnswalde Germany", marr. Wilhelmine Friederike Schulz (nee Nennemann)- b. "Reetz, Kreis Arnswalde, Germany"; at Princeton 28 March 1893/ Vol. 6 (1893-1897), p. 18.

60) SALZWEDEL, Herman August- b. "Pammin, Prussia, Germany", marr. Ida Aga(t)he Wegner of Newton (Marquette Co.); at Manchester 3 June 1900/ Vol. 7 (1897-1900), p. 453.

61) SALZWEDEL, Louise- b. "Kleinsilber (Klein-Silber) Germany", marr. August Maas, of the Town of Randolph, Columbia Co. (Wisc.)- b. "Gross silber (Co. Saatzig, Prov. Pomerania) Germany"; at Manchester 28 August 1887/ No. 63215 (Vol. 5, p. 113).

62) SCHALOW, Gottfried- b. "Kuertow Prussia", marr. Wilhelmine Ernestine Doege at the Town of Brooklyn 2 February 1868/ Vol. 5, p. 9.

63) SCHEEWE, Emiel- b. "Pam(m)in. Kreis (County) Arnswalde. Reg. Bez. (Administrative District) Frankfort (Frankfurt an der Oder) Preutsen (Preussen=Prussia) Germany Europa", marr. Louise Block at the Town of St. Marie 11 December 1878/ No. 50123.

64) SCHIMMEL, Augusta Louise- b. "Arnswalde, Germany", marr. Albert Fred Neid, resident of the Town of Randolph (Columbia Co., Wisc.); at Manchester 29 September 1886/ No. 62016 (Vol. 5, p. 109).

65) SCHMECK, August Robert- b. "Zue(h)lsdorf, Prussia, Germany", marr. Augustine Ernestine Plagens at the Town of Green Lake 14 April 1898/ Vol. 7 (1897-1900), p. 172.

66) SCHULZ, August Herman- b. "Schulzendorf Kreis (County) Arnswalde, Germany", marr. Mary Emilie Schwandt at the Town of Princeton 6 January 1892/ No. 69067 (Vol. 5, p. 139).

67) SELL, Albert Charles- b. "Kuertow Province Brandenburg Prussia", marr. Bertha Caroline Schmuhl of Manitowoc (a county seat; Wisc.); at Manchester 9 November 1899/ Vol. 7 (1897-1900), p. 375.

68) SELL, Charles, Gottlieb, Bernhard- b. "Kuertow, Povo (Prov.) Brandenburg, Germany", marr. Auguste, Ernestine, Friederike Rennpferd at Manchester 22 April 1889/ No. 65312 (Vol. 5, p. 124).

69) SELL, Karl Gottlob Bernhard (see above)- b. "Ku(e)rtow Arnswalde Germany", marr. Anna Maria Haas at Manchester September 1897/ Vol. 7 (1897-1900), p. 77.

70) SOMMER, Ferdinand Edward- b. "Glembeck Reg. Bez. (Administrative District) Frankfurt (an der Oder) Kr. (Co.) Arnswalde Preusen Europa", marr. Ottilie Wilhelmine Albertine Wilde at the Town of Manchester 6 "Marz" (March) 1879/ No. 50386.

71) STANKE, Charles- b. "Augustwalde, Germany", marr. Frederike Albertine Lehmann- b. "Butzighauland (Putzig-Hauland, Co. Filehne), Polen (Posen or Poland), Germany"; at Ripon Fond du Lac Co. (Wisc.) 19 February 1882/ No. 54850.

72) STANKE, Wilhelm Friedrich- b. "Sel(l)now, Kreis (County) Arnswalde, Preussen, Europa", marr. Auguste Bertha Lambrecht of Ripon (Fond du Lac Co., Wisc.); at Brooklin 11 May 1893/ Vol. 6 (1893-1897), p. 30.

73) STANKE, Wilhelm Friedrich Christian- b. "Marienhof, Prussia, Germany", marr. Maria Louise Therese Buelow at Berlin 6 March 1889/ No. 65109 (Vol. 5, p. 123).

74) STRUTZ, Robert Edward Johannes- b. "Schlagenthin Preussen Europe", marr. Emma Pauline Kahl at Green Lake 21 May 1896/ Vol. 6 (1893-1897), p. 382.

75) TABBERT, Hermann- b. "Arnswalde Prussia Germany", marr. Albertine Kepke at Berlin 2 December 1876.

76) TETZLAFF, Friedrich- b. "Chuertow (Kuertow), Prov. Brandenburg, Germany", marr. Auguste Wittschow- b. "Steinberg, Prov. Brandenburg Germany"; at Markesan 23 July 1887/ No. 63137 (Vol. 5, p. 113).

77) TORNOW, Anna- b. "Sel(l)now, Province Brandenburg, Germany", marr. Herman Wilhelm Giese- b. "Gross Mellen Province Brandenburg? (actually Co. Saatzig, Prov. Pomerania?) Germany"; at Marquette 7 February 1884/ No. 58006 (Vol. 5, p. 91).

78) WILDE, Ferdinand A.- b. "Pammin Prussia", marr. Matilda C. Thompson at Princeton 25 December 1866/ Early Vol. 3 (1858-1867), p. 270.

79) WILDE, Karl August- b. "Klein Silber Prussia", marr. Anna Juliane Kasemann at the Town of Princeton 26 September 1869.

80) WILDE, Leopold- b. "Stolzenfelde Reg. Bez. (Regierungsbezirk=
Administrative District) Frankford (Frankfurt an der Oder) Preus-
sen Europa", marr. Emma Marquartt (Marquardt?) at the Town of
Marquette 21 March 1878/ No. 49064.

81) WILKE, Carl Julius of West Bloomfield, Waushara Co.- b. "K(r)an-
zin, Neumark (region), Germany", marr. Anna Auguste Heier- b.
Freudenberg, Neumark, Germany"; at Berlin 3 April 1884/ No.
58247 (Vol. 5, p. 93).

82) WOBIG, Friedrich Wilhelm Erdmann- b. "Klein Silber, Prussia",
marr. Wilhelmine Zuehls at the Village of Manchester 27 March
1870.

83) YERK, Mary Louise- b. "Arnswalde Germany", marr. Fred William
Dretske (Dredske?)- b. "Nauckl (Nakel, Co. Wirsitz, Prov. Posen) Germany"; at Mackford 10 April 1888/ No. 64604 (Vol. 5,
p. 117).

84) ZADE, Christian- b. "Wardin Reg. Bez. (Regierungsbezirk=Admini-
strative District) Frankford (Frankfurt an der Oder). Preussen
Germany- Europa", marr. Friederika Hasse at the Town of "Bruk-
lien" (Brooklyn) 13 "Marz" (March) 1879/ No. 50387.

85) ZIMMERMANN, Frank August Ferdinand- b. "Steinberg, Prussia, Germany", marr. Hulda Auguste Stolp- b. "Pitzewo (Petzewo, Co. Flatow, Prov. West Prussia), Prussia, Germany"; at the Town of
Brooklyn 18 December 1884/ No. 59307 (Vol. 5, p. 97).

86) ZIMMERMANN, Johann Gottlieb- b. "Klein Silber, Germany", marr.
Wilhelmine Franz, a widow alias Schonrock; at the Town of Dartforth (Dartford=Green Lake) 25 October 1883/ No. 57573 (Vol. 5,
p. 89).

87) ZIMMERMAN, Wilhelm Erich- b. "Grossgut Arnswalde Germany", marr.
(Ella) Alice Auguste Gedanke at Mackford 23 "Dez."(December)
1896/ Vol. 6 (1893-1897), p. 456.

Immigrants from County Friedeberg/Neumark, Province Brandenburg, Prussia:

1) DIETRICH, Amalie, Wilhelmine- b. "Gotscheming (Gottschimm?), Germany", marr. Gustav Kowolowski of Scott (twp.) Columbia Co. (Wisc.)- b. "Adolfsheim (Co. Kolmar, Prov. Posen), Germany"; at Manchester 30 March 1891/ No. 67942 (Vol. 5, p. 135).

2) LINDEMANN, Bertha- b. "Schoenrode, Germany", marr. Fred, Wm. Aug. Ferdinand Pollack at Marquette 6 February 1892/ No. 69313 (Vol. 5, p. 140).

3) MEYER, Carl- b. "Lichtenow bei Friedeberg Germany", marr. Emma Lueptow at Markesan 3 December 1891/ No. 68931 (Vol. 5, p. 138).

4) UECKER, Louise, Mathilda, Augusta- b. "Geilenfelde Germany", marr. Charles Ludwic (Ludwig) Fritz- b. "Sel(l)now (Co. Arns-walde), Germany"; at Manchester 3 November 1891/ No. 68853 (Vol. 5, p. 137).

5) VOSS, Robert- b. "Schuttenberg, Prussia, Germany", marr. Johanne Dettmann (widow, nee Oeffner)- "Doebel, Prussia, Germany"; at the Town of Brooklin 7 October 1884/ No. 58951 (Vol. 5, p. 95).

PLAT OF
PRINCETON

Townships 15 & 16 North. Ranges 11 & 12 East

(From COME BACK IN TIME, Vol. I by Elaine Reetz)

Immigrants from additional locales in Province Brandenburg, Prussia:

1) DOLGNER, Gusta, Emilie- b. "Zadsdorf, Brandenburg, Germany",
   marr. Ernst Ludwig Krueger- b. "Borowokoland (Borowo-Hauland,
   Co. Kolmar), Posen Germany"; at Manchester 16 January 1890/
   No. 66357 (Vol. 5, p. 127).

2) EILERT, Franz Robert Theodor, a Minister of the Gospel from
   Ripon (Fond du Lac Co., Wisc.)- b. "Brandenburg, Prussia Germany", marr. Mathilde Wilhelmine Norton (nee Bringer) of Milwaukee; (no location given) 28 December 1893/ Vol. 6 (1893-
   1897), p. 102.

3) FRITZ, Anna- b. "Liede, Province Brandenburg, Germany", marr.
   Gustav Schramm- b. "Nikiojene Prov. Posen Germany"; at Markesan 29 September 1888/ No. 64505 (Vol. 5, p. 119).

4) GOSSFELDT, Marie Emilie Auguste (father Carl)- b. "Warbende
   Province Brandenburg Germany", marr. Carl Friedrick Wilhelm
   Gossfeldt (no father given)- b. "Goldenbaum, (Grand Duchy of)
   Mecklenburg, Strelitz (in central northern) Germany"; at the
   Town of Mackford 15 November 1898/ Vol. 7 (1897-1900), p. 243.

5) GRAEPLER, Friderich August- b. "Bergcolonie Neumark (region)
   Germany", marr. Augusta Minna Arnsdorf- b. "Wangerin (Co. Regenwalde, Prov.-) Pom(m)ern Germany"; at Berlin 6 March 1884/ No.
   58133 (Vol. 5, p. 93).

6) GRAMS, Gusta Lena- b. "Brandenburg Neumark (region) Germany",
   marr. John Frederick Olsen at "Mackford Prairy" 4 July 1897/
   Vol. 7 (1897-1900), p. 52.

7) GRUSE, Emilie- b. "Province of Brandenburg", marr. William Tonn
   of Westfield, Marquette Co.- b. "Province Posen"; at Manchester
   12 noon-28 June 1885/ No. 60048 (Vol. 5, p. 101).

8) HEIER, Anna Auguste- b. "Freudenberg, Neumark (region), Germany", marr. Carl Julius Wilke of West Bloomfield, Waushara Co.-
   b. "K(r)anzin (Co. Arnswalde), Neumark, Germany"; at Berlin
   3 April 1884/ No. 58247 (Vol. 5, p. 93).

9) JUNG, Aurel Michael of Milwaukee- b. "Neudam(m?) Kr.(Co.) Koe-
   nigsberg(/Neumark) Brandenburg Preussen", marr. Henriette Caroline Emilie Blodorn at Berlin 4 August 1870/ Vol. 5, p. 16.

10) KOLITZ, Albert George Ludwig- b. "Berlin Germany", marr. Ida
    Minna Helen Schade- b. "Unfliess Germany"; at Manchester 15
    September 1898/ Vol. 7 (1897-1900), p. 207.

11) KOLPIN, William (race: "German color")- b. "Kyritz, Brandenburg Europa", marr. Wilhelmina Hadel at "Dacota, dacota town Waushara Co. Wisc." 1 January 1889/ No. 69404 (Vol. 5, p. 124).

12) KOWALD, Helne- b. "Landsberg (an der Warte, a county seat), Brandenburg, Prussia", marr. David Evans- b. "Wells Co. England"; at Manchester 15 November 1893/ Vol. 6 (1893-1897), p. 88.

13) KRANC (perhaps Krank or Kranz?), Wm.- b. "Berlin, Germany", marr. Mary Ute at the Village of Markesan 27 December 1877/ No. 48497 ("these parties both had their birthplace in the German Empire on the Continent of Europe").

14) MANTEUFEL, Carl Friedrich August of Big Plain "Schawonow" (Shawano) Co. Wisc.- b. "Amatienhop (Amalienhof?) Province Brandcub (Brandenburg) Prusia", marr. Lousie Restock at Princeton 31 January 1866/ Early Vol. 3 (1858-1867), p. 228.

15) MANTHEI, Friedrich August- b. "Kelpin, Frankfurth (an der Oder) Co. (Prussian)", marr. Mathilde Zimmerman at Manchester 9 February 1874.

16) NAUGOCKS (NAUJOCKS?), Maria Anna- b. "Magdeburg Prussia", marr. Emil Robert Rad(t?)ke- b. "Luezdorf (Zuehlsdorf, Co. Arnswalde?) Peor (Prov.?) Brandenburg Prussia"; at Manchester 3 April 1898/ Vol. 7 (1897-1900), p. 163.

17) PETRUSCHKE, Richard, owner of laundry- b. "Berlin Germany", marr. Louisa Kobis(ch?)ke at Berlin 31 August 1896/ Vol. 6 (1893-1897), p. 408.

18) RENNPFERD, August Fred- b. "Karlshoff, Prov. Brandenburg, Germany", marr. Emma Rosetta Stainke at Manchester 27 March 1889/ No. 65199 (Vol. 5, p. 123).

19) RENNPFERD, Wilhelmine- b. "Neumark (region) Prussia", marr. Wilhelm Tettenborn- b. "Prov. Pommern (Pomerania), Prussia"; at Manchester 8 p.m.-4 December 1883/ No. 57624 (Vol. 5, p. 89).

20) RIESE, Anna Helen- b. "Liede Proc (Prov.?) Brandenburg Prussia Germany", marr. Herman Redel- b. "Jankendorf (Co. Kolmar, Prov. Posen) Prussia Germany"; at Manchester 30 November 1898/ Vol. 7 (1897-1900), p. 256.

21) ROCHWITE (Radschweit?), August, a watch maker- b. "Berlin Germany", marr. Kate Reamer at Kingston 11 August 1896/ Vol. 6 (1893-1897), p. 406.

22) STABS, Gotthielf- b. "Brandenburg, Prussia", marr. Auguste Emilie Dietrich- b. "Posen Prussia"; at Manchester 29 December 1881/ No. 54563.

Immigrants from County Dramburg, Province Pomerania, Prussia:

1) ABEL, Carl Hermann Leopold- b. "Baumgarten Prussia Germany",
    marr. Martha Elisabeth Wiese at Berlin 7 February 1899/ Vol. 7
    (1897-1900), p. 276.

2) ARNSDORFF, Anna Maria- b. "Zuchow, Prussia Germ.", marr. Fried-
    rich Ferdinand Mach- b. "Putzig (Co. Filehne, Prov. Posen),
    Prussia, Germ."; (no location given) 24 November 1892/ No. 70404
    (Vol. 5, p. 143).

3) BUSSIAN, Albert- b. "Neu-Laatzig Prussia", marr. Henriette Red-
    man(n?) in Berlin City 12 April 1874.

4) KERL, Anna Maria Louise- b. "Baumgarten Prussia Germany", marr.
    Johann August Schroark (Schwark?) in Berlin 16 November 1897/
    Vol. 7 (1897-1900), p. 97.

5) KERL, Bertha Emilie Auguste- b. "Baumgarten Prussia Germ.", marr.
    Franz Hermann Gustav Doerring- b. "Sellnow (Co. Arnswalde, Prov.
    Brandenburg) Prussia Germ."; at Berlin 1 March 1897/ Vol. 7
    (1897-1900), p. 2.

6) KERL, Maria Ida- b. "Baumgarten Prussia Germany", marr. Martin
    Martin Ferdinand Schwark at Berlin 16 October 1898/ Vol. 7
    (1897-1900), p. 226.

7) KOPP, Gottlieb August Julius- b. "Cetzien (Zetzin) Prussia",
    marr. Auguste Schlender at Berlin 30 January 1874.

8) LOEK (perhaps Lueck?), Hermann August Theodor- b. "Gersdorf.
    Pommern. Prussia", marr. Auguste Albertine Fischer in Berlin
    25 June 1871.

9) LUEBKE, August- b. "Gersdorf Pomern Prussia", marr. Wilhelmine
    Krueger- b. "Altdamerow (Co. Saatzig) Pomern, Prussia"; at Man-
    chester 6 April 1883/ No. 56616 (Vol. 5, p. 86).

10) RAMOW, Ernst Fredrick- b. "Guentershagen, Prussia, Germany",
    marr. Emilie Wilhelmine Katherine Jamm- b. "Baltimore Maryland";
    at Berlin 20 March 1894/ Vol. 6 (1893-1897), p. 131.

11) SCHLUETER, Emilie Ottilie Elisabeth- b. "Baumgarten Prussia Ger-
    many", marr. August Johann Ewald, a resident of South Dakota-
    b. "Westpreussen, Prussia, Germ."; at Berlin 29 March 1893/
    Vol. 6 (1893-1897), p. 20.

12) SCHMIDT, Gustav Theodor- b. "Gross Gruenow Prussia", marr. Mary
    Ellen Jordan at Berlin 10 November 1879/ No. 51293.

13) SCHMIDT, Johann August- b. "Gross Grunow", marr. Emilie Friede-
    rike Wru(c?)k at the City of Berlin 22 December 1874.

14) SCHMIDT, Johann Gottfried Julius- b. "Zetzin Prussia", marr. Au-
    gust Tine Stoeck at Berlin 10 November 1879/ No. 51294.

15) SCHWANDT, Herman Leopold- b. "Giesen (Co.) Dramburg Pommerania
    Germany", marr. Emma Hein- b. "Pommerania Germany"; at the Town
    of Manchester 25 February 1897/ Vol. 6 (1893-1897), p. 479.

16) STUF, Charles of Minnesota- b. "Gross-Spiegel (Stettin) (Prus-
    sian)--(Administrative District of Stettin?), marr. Auguste Ab-
    raham at Manchester 7 April 1874.

17) ZIMMERMANN, Anna (illegitimate child- her mother, Louise Bene-
    dix)- b. "Kallies, Pommerania", marr. Gustav Fr. Wm. Zimmermann
    (father Henry)- b. "Germany"; at Manchester 16 October 1892/
    No. 70272 (Vol. 5, p. 143).

18) ZIMMERMANN, Minnie, Louise, Bertha- b. "Giesen, Germany", marr.
    Frederick Stern- b. "Germany"; at Manchester 1 February 1886/
    No. 60987 (Vol. 5, p. 105).

19) ZUETLOW, Bertha Maria Therese- b. "Baumgarten Germany", marr.
    Friedrich Wilhelm Ludwig Buelow at Berlin 22 February 1898/
    Vol. 7 (1897-1900), p. 146.

Immigrants from County Saatzig, Province Pomerania, Prussia:

1) BAUMAN(N?), Emilie- b. "Stargart (Stargard, Saatzig's county seat), Germany", marr. Albert Polensky of Cambria Town of Scott (Columbia Co., Wisc.); at the Town of Marquette 15 October 1898/ Vol. 7 (1897-1900), p. 224.

2) BOESE, Wilhelm- b. "Falkenwalde Prussia", marr. Emilie Beyer at the Town of Princeton 18 July 1869.

3) BORN, August Herman- b. "Jakobshagen Kreis Lazig (County Saatzig) Germany", marr. Martha Louise Miller- b. "Arnswalde (county seat in Prov. Brandenburg) Kreis Lazig?Germany"; at Markesan 2 p.m.-22 October 1896/ Vol. 6 (1893-1897), p. 427.

4) BUBLITZ, August F. of Merrill (Lincoln Co.), Wisc.- b. "Langenhagen Prussia", marr. Sepha U. Borham- b. "Norton England"; at Berlin 8 July 1885/ No. 60092 (Vol. 5, p. 101).

5) DAHLMANN, Charles William- b. "Ziegenhagen (Prussia)", marr. Auguste Wilhelmine Miehlke at the Town of Green Lake 18 September 1873.

6) FRITZ, Maria Auguste Louise- b. "Rahmverder (Rahnwerder) Prussia Germ.", marr. Johann Hermann Gallert at Berlin 16 November 1898/ Vol. 7 (1897-1900), p. 246.

7) GIESE, William Fred, a "saloonist"- b. "Grossmellen, Germany", marr. Mary Theresa Tessmer- b. "Tonawanda, N.Y."; at the town of Manchester 14 January 1892/ No. 69195 (Vol. 5, p. 139).

8) GRIESE, Herman Wilhelm- b. "Gross Mellen Province Brandenburg (?) Germany", marr. Anna Tornow- b. "Sel(l)now, (Co. Arnswalde) Province Brandenburg, Germany"; at Marquette 7 February 1884/ No. 58006 (Vol. 5, p. 91).

9) KRUGER nee TESSMER, Gusta Maria- b. "Brusenitz Prussia", marr. Herman Emil Wilke- b. "Nalen(t)scha (Co. Kolmar) Regier (Regierungsbezirk=Administrative District) Bromberg (Prov. Posen)"; at Markesan 21 August 1892/ No. 69977 (Vol. 5, p. 142).

10) KRUEGER, Wilhelmine- b. "Altdamerow Pom(m)ern, Prussia", marr. August Luebke- b. "Gersdorf (Co. Dramburg) Pom(m)ern Prussia"; at Manchester 6 April 1883/ No. 56616 (Vol. 5, p. 86).

11) LUCK, Bertha Mene L.- b. "Refenstein (Revenstein) Ger.", marr. Fred Jam(e)s Williams of Spring Lake Waushara Co.; at the "T. Spincelton (Princeton?)" Green Lake Co. 15 July 1897/ Vol. 7 (1897-1900), p. 55.

12) LUEPTOW, Franz, Friedrich- b. "Altdamerow, Kreis (County) Sa(a)tzig, Germany", marr. Hanna, Louise Janke at Princeton 13 October 1892/ No. 70246 (Vol. 5, p. 143).

13) MAAS, August of the Town of Randolph, Columbia Co. (Wisc.)- b. "Gross silber Germany", marr. Louise Salzwedel- b. "Kleinsilber (Co. Arnswalde, Prov. Brandenburg) Germany"; at Manchester 28 August 1887/ No. 63215 (Vol. 5, p. 113).

14) OESTERREICH, Wilhelm Carl Friedrich- b. "Ravenstein (Revenstein), Province Pommern, Germany", marr. Emma Augusta Reisel- b. "Gornitz (Co. Filehne) Province Posen Germany"; at the Town of Green Lake 7 February 1884/ No. 58007 (Vol. 5, p. 91).

15) OSTREICH, Ferdinant August- b. "Rafenstein (Revenstein) Kreis Sazig (County Saatzig) Konigr(e)ich Preussen (Kingdom of Prussia) Germany Europe"; marr Ella Marquartt (Marquardt?) at the Town of Marquette 19 December 1877/ No. 48506.

16) PUST, Christlieb Wilhelm Aug.- b. "Rahnwerder, Kr. (Co.) Saatzig, Prov. Pommern. Germany", marr. Bertha Ernestine Frohloff at Berlin 3 November 1887/ No. 63557.

17) SCHLIEP, Julius- b. "Stargard (county seat), Prussian", marr. Ernestine Milke at Manchester 11 December 1873.

18) STEINKRAUSS, Freidrich- b. "Stargard (county seat) Prussia", marr. Bertha Gross at Manchester 1 p.m.-17 October 1880/ No. 52720.

19) UTKE, Ernst Henry- b. "Certen(Zehrten) Germany", marr. Caroline Hannah Charlotte Ehlert (widow, nee Bremer)- b. "(Co.) Arnswalde (Prov. Brandenburg) Germany"; at Manchester 14 July 1895/ Vol. 6 (1893-1897), p. 293.

20) ZASTROW, Emily- b. "AltDam(e)row, Germany", marr. William, Fred Link- b. "(Co.) Franzburg (-Barth, Prov. Pomerania), Germany"; at Manchester 26 December 1892/ No. 70578 (Vol. 5, p. 144).

Immigrants from County Neustettin, Province Pomerania, Prussia:

1) HELLER, Auguste Friedericke Louise- b. "Neblin Prussia Germany", marr. Edward Kechn (perhaps Kuehn?) at Berlin 6 December 1899/ Vol. 7 (1897-1900), p. 399.

2) KRATZKE, August of Eureka Winnebago Co. (Wisc.)- b. "Persanzig. Pommern", marr. Caroline Krause at Berlin 1 May 1869/ Vol. 5, p. 10.

3) KRUEGER, Mathilda Johanna Maria- b. "Flederborn Prussia Germany", marr. Johann Carl Krause at Berlin 9 November 1897/ Vol. 7 (1897-1900), p. 98.

4) SEELIGER, Heinrich- b. "Neustettin, Province Pommern, Germany", marr. Luise Ziemer- b. "Klaushagen, Prov. Pommern Germany"; at Markesan 2 September 1883/ No. 57086 (Vol. 5, p. 87).

5) SEELIGER, Wilhelm-b "Steinfurt (Steinforth) Prov. Pommern", marr. Emilie Elies- b. "Turofken, Preussen"; at Markesan 14 "Okt." (October) 1888/ No. 64539 (Vol. 5, p. 119).

6) WACHHOLZ, Wilhelmine Caroline Albertine- b. "Barken, Prussia, Germ.", marr. Samuel Edward Mueller of "Christ Lake" Washington Co. (Wisc.); at Berlin 23 April 1897/ Vol. 7 (1897-1900), p. 18.

7) ZICK, Friedrich Herman- b. "Wolflatzke (Wulflatzke) Germany", marr. Minna Klatt at Markesan 20 September 1885/ No. 60409 (Vol. 5, p. 102).

Immigrants from County Pyritz, Province Pomerania, Prussia:

1) FRIEDRICH, Franz Heinrich- b. "Pyritz in Germany", marr. Pauline Louise Polinske- b. "Potolitzhauland (Potulice-Hauland, Co. Wongrowitz, Prov. Posen) in Germany"; at Markesan 15 September 1889/ No. 65807 (Vol. 5, p. 125).

2) HOEFT, Maria, Louise- b. "Fuerstensee, Kreis Pieritz (County Pyritz), Germany", marr. Friedrich Wilhelm Adler of Ripon (Fond du Lac Co.), Wisc.- b. "Ruehlow, (Grand Duchy of) Mecklenburg Strelitz, Germany"; at Markesan 21 September 1892/ No. 70065 (Vol. 5, p. 142).

3) LEISTIKOW, Fred August- b. "(T or) Jago (Jagow?), Preussen, Germany", marr. Emma Bratsch (Braetsch) at Dartforth (Dartford= Green Lake) 27 January 1884/ No. 57933 (Vol. 5, p. 90).

4) LEISTEKOW, Fred Wm.(see above)- b. "Javo (Jagow?), Germany", marr. Emma Louise Mueller at Town:Lake Maria (St. Marie?) 27 October 1887/ No. 63461 (Vol. 5, p. 114).

5) SCHMIDT, Johanna Emily- b. "Dobberphuhl, Germany", marr. Charles Julius Westrack, a carsmith from Milwaukee- b. "Selchow (Co. Filhene, Prov. Posen), Germany"; at Manchester 12 December 1892/ No. 7059 (Vol. 5, p. 144).

Immigrants from other locales in Province Pomerania, Prussia:

1) ARNSDORF, August Julius Eduard- b. "Wannerin (perhaps Wangerin, Co. Regenwalde?), Pommern Germany", marr. Auguste Friederike Arndt at Berlin 22 "Okt." (October) 1882/ No. 55733 (Vol. 5, p. 81).

2) ARNSDORF, Auguste Minna- b. "Wangerin (Co. Regenwalde) Pom(m)ern Germany", marr. Friedrich August Graepler- b. "Bergcolonie Neumark (region, Prov. Brandenburg) Germany"; at Berlin 6 March 1884/ No. 58133 (Vol. 5, p. 93).

3) BARKOW, Hermann Carl Julius- b. "Margow (Co. Cammin), Prussia, Germany", marr. Emilie Bertha Louise Steinke at Berlin 27 November 1884/ No. 59156.

4) BARNETT, Ferdinand of Eureka Winnebago Co. (Wisc.)- b. "Fitzig Pommern Prussia", marr. Eveline Kaufmann at Berlin 22 August 1873.

5) BEJICK, Carl Eduard of Eureka Winnebago Co. (Wisc.)- b. "Lauenberg (a county seat) Prussia", marr. Johanne Kassien at Berlin 13 April 1873.

6) BRAUN, Bertha- b. "Silligsdorf (Co. Regenwalde) Pom(m)ern Germany", marr. Louis Deichtgreber- b. "Missouri" -a resident of Oshkosh (Winnebago Co., Wisc. county seat); at Berlin 7 October 1883/ No. 57230 (Vol. 5, p. 88).

7) BUSCH, Ferdinand of the Town of Scott Columbia Co. (Wisc.)- b. "Katschenke (Pommern) Prussien", marr. Emilie Fennrich (widow, nee Froehlich) at Manchester 4 October 1877/ No. 48128.

8) BUTOW, Elnoald? Gustav Wilhelm- b. "Technow Kreis (County) Schiefelbein Germany", marr. Emilie Domke- b. "Germany"; at Markesan 1 p.m.-4 April 1896/ Vol. 6 (1893-1897), p. 371.

9) DETTMANN (nee OEFFNER), Johanne- b. "Doebel (Co. Belgard), Prussia, Germany", marr. Robert Voss- b. "Schuttenburg (Co. Friedeberg/Neumark, Prov. Brandenburg), Prussia, Germany"; at the Town of Brooklin 7 October 1884/ No. 58951 (Vol. 5, p. 95).

10) DRESCHNER, Carl Friedrich- b. "Siehlingsdorf Reg. Bez. (Regierungsbezirk=Administrative District) Stettin Pommern", marr. Eva Rosina Zabel at Berlin 8 February 1871.

11) FRANK, Herman- b. "Zernin (Co. Kolberg-Körlin) Pomern, Germany", marr. Johanna Platz- b. "Benzin (Co. Köslin) Pommern"; at Berlin 6 May 1884/ No. 58396 (Vol. 5, p. 94).

12) GARBER, Friedrich Johann- b. "Gr. Tuchau (or Tuchan--Gross-Tu-chen, Co. Butow?) Prussia", marr. Friederike Albertine Zuge at Berlin 18 April 1875.

13) GEHRKE, Mathilde- b. "Puesto(w, Co. Rummelsberg) Prussia", marr. Wilhelm Bettin- b. "Coloni Prussia"; at Berlin 12 December 1881/ No. 54359.

14) GLAMM, Carl Friedrich Hermann- b. "Greifenberg (a county seat), Prussia", marr. Auguste Henriette Belding (nee Jelchmann)- b. "Leznick, Prussia"; at Princeton Sunday-12 April 1885/ No. 61794 (Vol. 5, p. 107).

15) GRUETZNER, Alvine- b. "Neulinden Vorpomern (Farther or western Pomerania), Germany", marr. Ferdinand Marwan- b. "Marienwerder (county & district seat), Westpreussen (Prov. West Prussia)"; at Berlin 14 May 1888/ No. 64200 (Vol. 5, p. 117).

16) HEIN, August- b. "Friedwalden, Pommern, Europe", marr. Elrisa-beth Feldt of Beaver Dam (Dodge Co., Wisc.); at Markesan 10 May 1894/ Vol. 6 (1893-1897), p. 150.

17) KATH, Ida Wilhelmine Ernestine- b. "Kl(e)in-Wachlin Pomerania", marr. Albert Wilhelm Froehlick of the Town of Scott, Columbia Co. (Wisc.); 8 July 1897/ Vol. 7 (1897-1900), p. 76.

18) KNITT, Johann Friedrich- b. "Glawitz (Glewitz, Co. Cammin) Prussia", marr. Henriette Brandt at Berlin 6 February 1874.

19) LADEWIG, Johann Wilhelm Gottfried- b. "Dusterbeck (Co. Naugard), Prussia", marr. Charlotte Friederike Wilhelmine Porad (Porath?) at the Village of Manchester 21 August 1870.

20) LAMBRECHT, Frederick Herman- b. "Kolberg (-Körlin, a county seat) Prussia Germany", marr. Wilhelmine Winne at the Tp. of Manchester 14 January 1900/ Vol. 7 (1897-1900), p. 412.

21) LAMPKE, Wilhelm- b. "Pamin (?) by Koeslin (a county seat) (Prussien)", marr. Charlotte Karow at Kingston 29 August 1875.

22) LENZ, Wilhelmine Friedericke- b. "Zuersdorf Pomern Germany", marr. William Schmieg- b. "Milwaukee"; at Berlin 26 January 1884/ No. 57843 (Vol. 5, p. 90).

23) LINK, William, Fred- b. (Co.)Franzburg (-Barth), Germany", marr. Emily Zastrow- b. "AltDam(e)row (Co. Saatzig), Germany"; at Manchester 26 December 1892/ No. 70578 (Vol. 5, p. 144).

24) MOEDE, Hermann- b. "Plathe, Circuit (County) of Regenwalde, Province of Pommer(n), Prussia", marr. Catharina Baumgaertner at Manchester 4 November 1858/ Early Vol. 3 (1858-1867), p. 2.

25) NICKEL, William Albert Gotthilf of Oshkosh (Winnebago Co.,
Wisc. county seat)- b. "(T or) Pollnow (Co. Schlawe), Prussia",
marr. Auguste Harske at Sakramento 13 September 1874.

26) PAGEL, Johann Friedrich Bernhard of the Town of Bloomfield,
Waushara Co.- b. "Trieglaff (Co. Regenwalde) Pommern Prussia",
marr. Wilhelmine Johanne Friederike Vogt at the Town of Bloomfield Waushara Co. 27 July 1873.

27) PIOTRASCHKE, Friedrich Richard Otto- b. "(Usedom-)Wollin (a
county seat), Prussia", marr. Auguste Behnke at Berlin 1 May
1889/ No. 65333 (Vol. 5, p. 124).

28) POOCH, Heinrich Wilhelm August- b. "Rummelsburg (a county seat)
Prussia Germany", marr. Caroline Pauline Weidman(n?)- b. "Wol-
lynien (Volhynia, a region) Russia"; at the Town of Dartford
(Green Lake) 12 March 1895/ Vol. 6 (1893-1897), p. 272.

29) PRISKE, Johann- b. "Lauenberg (a county seat) Prussia", marr.
Emilie Glaser at Berlin 10 April 1874.

30) SCHMIDT, August of the Town of Bloomfield (Waushara Co.)- b.
"Barkow Pommern Prussia", marr. Bertha Timm at the Town of
Bloomfield (Waushara Co.) 6 July 1873.

31) SCHMIDT, Johann Heinrich Hermann- b. "Garrin (Co. Kolberg-Körlin) Prussia", marr. Anna Friederike Arndt at Berlin City 8
May 1874.

32) STEINKRAUSS, Otto- b. "Kolberg(-Körlin, a county seat), Germany", marr. Hulda Busse- b. "Germany"; at Manchester 14 September 1888/ No. 64462 (Vol. 5, p. 119).

33) STEINKRAUS(S?), Wilhelmine- b. "Colberg (Kolberg-Körlin, a county seat), Provinz Pommern, Germany", marr. Carl Friedrich Sack-
b. "Arnswalde (a county seat), Provinz Brandenburg, Germany";
at the township of Manchester 6 April 1891/ No. 67928 (Vol. 5,
p. 135).

34) WENDT, Emil Theodor- b. "Tezow (Tietzow, Co. Belgard?) Prussia",
marr. Louise Kraning at Berlin City 17 April 1874.

35) WENDT, Rudolph Johann Richard- b. "Paraschin Reg. Bez. (Regier-
ungsbezirk=Administrative District) Koslin (?, a county seat)
Pommern Germany", marr. Caroline Zech at Berlin 13 November
1870.

36) WUDKE, Augusta- b. "Jacobsdorf (Cos. Dramburg or Saatzig?),
Prov. Pommern, Germany", marr. August Below- b. "Anilla (Kol.
Aniela, Co. Wirsitz) Prov. Posen, Germany"; at the Town of Man-
chester 31 October 1886/ No. 62143 (Vol. 5, p. 109).

37) ZELLMER, August- b. "Pulzig Pommern Germany", marr. Emilie
Lohning- b. "Grabowow (Grabowo, Co. Wongrowitz, Prov.) Posen
Germany"; at Markesan 29 January 1890/ No. 66356 (Vol. 5, p.
127).

Immigrants from "Province Pommern" or "Pomerania", Prussia:

1) ALBRIGHT (Albrecht?), Hermann Martin of Poy Sippi Waushara Co.-
"Pommern in Germany", marr. Pauline Louise Lichtenberg at the
Town of Seneca 18 January 1888/No. 63835 (Vol. 5, p. 116).

2) BARNETT, Johann Carl of Rushford, Winnebago Co.(Wisc.)- b.
"Pommern, Preussen, Germany", marr. Wilhelmine Nest at Berlin
15 March 1886/ No. 61474.

3) BAUMAN(N?), Karl Fredrich Ernst- "Pommern Germany", marr. Ida
Lena Bausch at Markesan 4 p.m.-3 April 1895/ Vol. 6 (1893-1897),
p. 277.

4) BE(C?)KMANN, Friederich August- b. "Bommern Preussen Germanien",
marr. Wilhelmine Ernztina Degner at Manchester 15 December 1871.

5) BUCHHOLZ, August- b. "Pommern Prussia", marr. Elisabeth Sauer-
brei at Manchester 21 November 1880/ No. 52739.

6) EHLERT, Ernstine Mary Louise- b. Pommerania, Germany",marr.
Julius Frederick Ferdinand Steinich- b. "Pommerania", Germany";
at the Town of Randolph (Columbia Co., Wisc.) 12 April 1894/
Vol. 6 (1893-1897), p. 138.

7) HAMMER, Gustav Wilhelm Ernst of T. Randolf (Columbia Co.),
Wisc.- b."Prussia (Prov. Pommern)", marr. Anna Caroline Gaig-
b. "Prussia (Prov. Posen)"; at Manchester 2 December 1882/ No.
55991 (Vol. 5, p. 82).

8) HEIN, Emma- b. "Pommerania Germany", marr. Herman Leopold
Schwandt- b. "Giesen (Co.) Dramburg Pommerania Germany"; at
the Town of Manchester 25 February 1897/ Vol. 6 (18931897), p.
479.

9) HERZFELD, August - b. "Prov. Pommern Prussia Germany", marr.
Hulda Pomerenke at Berlin 4 October 1886/ No. 62153.

10) KLOSSOWKSI, Wilhelm- b. Pommerania Germany", marr. Marianne
Ebel at Berlin 4 May 1876 (Catholic, likely Polish).

11) LECHELT, Samuel- b. "Pomorania, Prussia in Europe", marr. Wilhelmine Zech- b. "(Prov.) Brandenburg, Prussia in Europe"; at
Princeton 6 May 1886/ No. 61491 (Vol. 5, p. 106).

12) MAAS, Charley of the Town of Randolph, Columbia Co.(Wisc.)- b.
"Pommern Prussia", marr. Elise Hecker at Manchester 16 November 1880/ No. 52738.

13) NITZKE, Carl of Poygan Winnebago Co. (Wisc.)- b. "Pommerania
    Prussia Germany", marr. Bertha Herzberg at Berlin 11 March
    1885/ No. 59785.

14) ROPCKE, Johann Friedrich a blacksmith from Buffalo Grove, Iowa-
    b. "Pommern Prussia", marr. Mary Poline Hinz- b. "(Prov.) Po-
    sen Prussia"; at Manchester 1 p.m.-19 January 1882/ No. 54564
    (Vol. 5, p.76).

15) SALZWEDEL, Mary Frederika- b. "Pammia Germany", marr. William
    Frederick Schimmel at Manchester 29 November 1894/ Vol. 6
    (1893-1897), p. 222.

16) SCHWANDT, Ferdinand- b. "Pommern, Prussia", marr. Wilhelmine
    Schmuhl at Manchester 5 p.m.-19 September 1883/ No. 57183 (Vol.
    5, p. 87).

17) TETTENBORN, Wilhelm- b. "Prov. Pommern, Prussia", marr. Wilhel-
    mine Rennpferd- b. "Neumark (region of Prov. Brandenburg) Prus-
    sia"; at Manchester 8 p.m.-4 December 1883/ No. 57624 (Vol. 5,
    p. 89).

Immigrants from Province East Prussia:

1) GOLAND, Emma Ida- b. "Osterode (a county seat), Prussia, Germ.",
   marr. Johann Friedrich Lenz at Berlin 6 May 1897/ Vol. 7 (1897-
   1900), p. 28.

2) KOEPKE, Leopold Frederick August- b. "Rossol (Rossel?, a county
   seat), Germany", marr. Augusta Bertha Wegner of Crystal Lake
   (Marquette Co.); at Kingston 12 October 1898/ Vol. 7 (1897-1900),
   p. 223.

3) LINK, Charles William- b. "Grunau near Friedland (a county & district court town within same), Prussia (East)", marr. Ida Ernestine Kleinert at the Tp. of Marquette 28 May 1899/ Vol. 7 (1897-
   1900), p. 319.

4) RADSCHWEIT, Edward August- b. "East Prussia", marr. Wilhelmine
   Maria Link- b. "Kreis Flats (County Flatow, Administrative District of) Marienwerde(r), (West) Prussia"; at Mackford 25 April
   1897/ Vol. 7 (1897-1900), p. 23.

Immigrants with German names from "Russia" (Lutheran unless noted):

1) HERMANN widow (nee KORTMANN), Ottilia- b. "Russia", marr.
    Frederick Albert Kinar- b. "Russia"; at Princeton 7 November
    1897/ Vol. 7 (1897-1900), p. 112.

2) KLINGBEIL, Emma Wilhelmine- b. "Russia", marr. Ludwig Wallner
    of the Town Mecan Marquette Co.- b. "Germany"; at the residence
    of Carl Klingbeil, Town of St. Marie 30 October 1891/ No. 69004
    (Vol. 5, p. 138).

3) KORDMANN, Alvine- b. "Russia", marr. Ferdinand Wirch- b. "Ger-
    many"; at Princeton 3 June 1895/ Vol. 7 (1897-1900), p. 16.

4) LOOSE, Huldah, Alwine- b. "Olganofka Colonie, Ruszland (Russ-
    land in German=Russia)", marr. Carl August Mi(e?)tzner- b.
    "Rogasen (Co. Obernick, Prov. Posen), Prussia, Germany"; at
    the Twp. of Princeton 20 August 1891/ No. 68425 (Vol. 5, p.
    136) (rel.).

5) OEHLKE, Albert Emil- b. "Russia", marr. Mary Elisabeth Manthey
    at Princeton 8 October 1889/ No. 65832 (Vol. 5, p. 125).

6) PFEIFER, Ferd- b. "Warnburg Russia", marr. Bartha Klingbeil
    at St. Marie 8 November (1899)/ Vol. 7 (1897-1900), p. 378
    ("reglus"=religious).

7) PFEIFER, Johann Heinrich- b. "Wannburg Russland Europa", marr.
    Ottilie Auguste Kuehl at Dartford (Green Lake) 16 November
    1893/ Vol. 6 (1893-1897), p. 82 (Evangelical Association).

8) PFEIFER, Maria- b. "Nasurenburg Russland (Russia)", marr. Ed-
    ward Boyk at Princeton 30 November 1894/ Vol. 6 (1893-1897),
    p. 230 (religious protestant).

9) WEIDMAN(N?), Caroline Pauline- b. "Wollynien (Wolhynien=Vol-
    hynia, a region) Russia", marr.Heinrich Wilhelm August Pooch-
    b. "Rummelsburg (a county seat in Pomerania) Prussia Germany";
    at the Town of Dartford (Green Lake) 12 March 1895/ Vol. 6
    (1893-1897), p. 272.

10) WIRCH, Bertha- b. "Russia", marr. Charles Julius Schwanke at
    Princeton 31 May 1891/ No. 68284 (Vol. 5, p. 136).

11) WURCH, Edward- b. "Valinonowka Russia", marr. Emelina Paulina
    Milbrath- b. "Noven (Co. Wongrowitz, or Kolmar, Prov. Posen)
    Germany"; at Manchester 16 April 1895/ Vol. 6 (1893-1897),
    p. 278.

Immigrants from the Grand Duchies of Mecklenburg-Schwerin and Mecklenburg-Strelitz, in north central Germany:

1) ADLER, Friedrich Wilhelm of Ripon (Fond du Lac Co.), Wisc.- b. "Ruehlow, Mecklenburg Strelitz, Germany", marr. Maria, Louise Hoeft- b. "Fuerstensee, Kreis Pieritz (Co. Pyritz, Prov. Pomerania, Prussia), Germany"; at Markesan 21 September 1892/ No. 70065 (Vol. 5, p. 142).

2) FLEGEL, Wilhelm- b. "Mecklenburg Germany", marr. Luise Marquardt at Manchester 11 a.m.-1 January 1881/ No. 52962.

3) GOSSFELDT, Carl Friedrick Wilhelm (no father given)- b. "Goldenbaum, Mecklenburg, Strelitz, Germany", marr. Marie Emilie Auguste Gossfeldt (father Carl)- b. "Warbende Province Brandenburg (Prussia) Germany"; at the Town of Mackford 15 November 1898/ Vol. 7 (1897-1900), p. 243.

4) LUEDERS, Heinrich Hanz George, a.hotel keeper from Milwaukee- b. "Bodelsdorff Mecklenburg Schwerin Germany", marr. Anna Katherine Maria Kavelmacher at Berlin 30 December 1888/ No. 64899 (Vol. 5, p. 121).

5) MASCH, Carl Friedrich- b. "Worlin Mecklenburg Strelitz Germany", marr. Henriette Mathilde Grulke at the Town of Marquette 2 November 1877/ No. 48356.

6) NICKEL, Theodor A.F.W.G.G., a pastor from Shawano (county seat), Wisc.- b. "Guestrow, Mecklenburg (Schwerin), Germ.", marr. Lydia Maria Rosine Ebert at Berlin 19 October 1890/ No. 67267 (Vol. 5, p. 132).

7) SCHRODER, Ludwig- b. "Mecklenburg Germany", marr. Louise Grams at Berlin 17 May 1880/ No. 52022.

8) SPRINGBORN, Charles- b. "Me(c)klenburg Strelitz (Germany)", marr. Mary Vinz at Manchester 22 April 1877/ No. 49304.

9) THEDE, Ludwig Karl Theodor- b. "Klein Neuenhagen Mecklenburg Schwerin', marr. Karoline Thiel at the Town of Manchester 16 October 1870.

Immigrants from the Prussian Province of or independent Kingdom of
Saxony, in central Germany:

1) FERGE, Christoph- b. "Eisenach (Prussian Prov. Saxony?) Germany",
marr. Mary Catherine Vinz- b. "Geilsdorf, Germany"; at Manchester
9 July 1888/ No. 64317 (Vol. 5, p. 118).

2) KEDANEE, John P.- b. "Saxony Germany", marr. Christian Keiser at
Brooklyn 22 September 1877/ No. 48008.

3) MULLER, Gustav Gottlob Ferdinand- b. "Laucha Saxony Germany",
marr. Maria Amalia Brugger at Berlin 11 May 1879/ No. 50797.

4) SCHERMER, Wilhelmine- b. "Harp Province Sachsen (Saxony, Prussia), Germany", marr. Julius Birkholz- b. "Millshaland (Milsch-
Hauland, Co. Kolmar, Prov. Posen) Prussia Germany"; at Berlin
23 May 1882/ No. 55203 (Vol. 5, p. 79).

5) SCHIRLAND, Joachim- b. "Fielbaum Provinz Saxonia (Saxony,Prus-
sia)", marr. Wilhelmine Steinke at Berlin 10 March 1878/ No.
48996.

6) SchucherT, Charles of Beaver Dam Dodge Co.(Wisc.)- b. "Walters-
hausen (Coburg-Gotha)* Prussia", marr. Dorothea Schatz at Manchester 26 December 1875*(see No. 7).

7) THIEL, August- b. "Saxen Gotha (part of the Thuringian States)
Germana", marr. Henriette Louisa Luitha at Mekan (Marquette Co.)
1 June 1856/ Early Vol. 3 (1855-1858), p. 77.

8) UMBREIT, Traugott- b. "Saxon-Weimar (part of the Thuringian
States) in the Kingdom of Prussia in Europa", marr. Catharina
Blockwitz at the Town of Manchester 2 March 1860/ Early Vol.
3 (1858-1867), p. 48.

9) VINZ, John Ernst Conrad- b. "Erfurt (Prussian Prov. Saxony)
Germany", marr. Luise Schoschneck- b. "Schlesien (Prussian
Prov. of Silesia) Prussia"; at Manchester 11 p.m.-12 August
1883/ No. 57039 (Vol. 5, p. 87).

10) von BERG, Andreas- b. "Sachsen Coburg (part of the Thuringian
States)", marr. Magdalena Buhrmann at Manchester 1 April 1872.

<u>Immigrants from the Grand Duchy of Hessen-Darmstadt or the Prussian Province of Hessen & Hessen-Nassau, in central Germany</u>:

1) GEISS, Franz D.- b. "Meisenheim, Hessen Homburg (Prussian Prov. Hessen-Nassau)", marr. "Renettnt"? (Henriette) Timm at Ripon (Fond du Lac Co.) 18 March 1876. (no pagation)

2) LANGSDORF, Anton- b. "Friedberg (Hessen) Prussian", marr. Johanna Ferge at Manchester 28 December 1873 (no pagation).

3) PORT, Kaspar- b. "Ober Pessingen (Hessen) (Prussien)", marr. Emilie Walther at Manchester 14 June 1875.

4) POST, John Henry- b. "Oberbessinger in the Grand Dukedom of (Hessen-) Darmstadt, Germany", marr. Justine Wilhelmine Hein at the Town of Manchester in the house of Johannes Post 20 February 1861/ Early Vol. 3 (1858-1867), p. 93.

5) WEISEL, Conrad- b. "Muenzenberg, Hessen Darmstadt" (father-Wilhelm), marr. Anna Margaretha Weisel (father Conrad) in the house of Conrad Weisel, Green Lake Co. 20 October 1861/ Early Vol. 3 (1858-1867), p. 112.

6) WEISEL, Conrad of Austin, Minn.- b. "Hessen-Darmstadt, Germany", marr. Mary Miller-b. "Waterloo, Wisc."; at Manchester 4 p.m.- 2 April 1882/ No. 55011 (Vol. 5, p. 78).

7) WENZEL, Mathias- b. "Hainstadt, Offenbach Hessen (Darmstadt)", marr. Louise Seidel at the Town of Shields (Marquette Co.) 18 April 1857/ Early Vol. 3 (1856-1858), p. 45.

8) ZIMMER, Johann of "Stitelspoint (Stevens Point?)"- b. "(Hessen-) Darmstadt (Germany", marr. Dorothea Geisler at Manchester 18 May 1873.

Immigrants from the Kingdom of Bavaria:

1) BLOCKWITZ, Peter of Harden, Marquette Co.- b. "Germany or Kingdom of Bauern (Bayern=Bavaria)", marr. Elisabeth Sauer at Harden,
Marquette Co. 15 March 1855/ Early Vol. 3 (1852-1855), p. 158.

2) CHUMMER, Eugen of the Town of Wolf River Waupaca Co.- b. "Bamberg
Bavaria", marr. Auguste Zander at Berlin 9 May 1869 (no pagation).

3) HAGER, Conrad- b. "Germany or Kingdom of Boiern (Bayern=Bavaria)",
marr. Ernestine Rose at "Marquette Co." 5 January 1855/ Early Vol.
3 (1852-1855), p. 136.

4) LINHART, John Adam of Marquette, "Marquette Co."- b. "Bavaran in
Germany", marr. Mrs. Mary Inman (nee Couly) at Marquette 24 March
1855/ Early Vol. 3 (1852-1855), p. 160.

5) RHEIN, Magdalena- b. "Kaiser(s)lautern, Rheinbayern (Rhine Bavaria, Palatinate region) Germany", marr. Paul Julius Reinoehl of Token Creek, Dane Co. (Wisc.)- b. "Rubgarten (Kingdom of) Wurt(t)em-
berg"; at Manchester 8 p.m.-28 December 1882/ No. 55992 (Vol. 5,
p. 82).

6) SEDLINGER, Otto of Sheboygan (Wisc.)- b. "Muenchen (Munich) Bavaria Germany", marr. Emma Lizzie Reunpferd at Manchester 17 February 1895/ Vol. 6 (1893-1897), p. 266.

7) STRASSER, John of Oshkosh (county seat of Winnebago Co., Wisc.),
marr. Mary Smich at Berlin 20 April 1880/ No. 51917 (Rom. Cath.).

8) VOGEL, Wolfgang- b. "Lam, Bavaria, German Empire", marr. Anna Re-
kow- b. "Bromberg (county & district seat), Province of Posen
(Prussia) German Empire"; at Manchester 30 May 1886/ No. 61550
(Vol. 5, p. 106).

Immigrants from the Grand Duchy of Baden & Kingdom of Württemberg
(now the State of Baden-Württemberg in southwest Germany):

1) BECK, J. David of Eureka Winnebago Co. (Wisc.)- b."Weiler, Kingdom of Wuertenberg (Württemberg)", marr. Rosina Sophia Klink at
   Berlin 13 April 1872 (no pagation).

2) DURBAN, Jakob of St. Joseph (Berrien Co.) Mich.- b. "Baden Europe",
   Merry Hahn at Marquette 31 May 1873 (no pagation).

3) FREI, Ferdinand of Ripon Fond du Lac Co.- b. "Holzschlag in the
   Grand Duchy of Baden, Germany", marr. Auguste Soefer at the house
   of Christian Soefer-Mecan, Marquette Co. 6 April 1858/ Early Vol.
   3 (1856-1858), p. 115.

4) FREY, Frank of Ripon (Fond du Lac Co.),- b. "Wurtenberg (Kingdom
   of Württemberg), Germany", marr. Annie Garlo at Princeton 9 June
   1885/ No. 59969 (Vol. 5, p. 100) ("as the statute provides--The
   husband being charged by the wife of being and obligated to marry").

5) KAISER, Friedrich- b. "Waldhausen Wurtenberg (Württemberg)", marr.
   Ernestine Boese at the Town of Brooklin, 12 March 1873 (no pagation).

6) KLEIBER, Gabriel- b. "Durlach Baden Germany", marr. Mary Hecht-
   b. "Strassburgh Lancaster Co. Pa."; at Berlin 8 p.m.-16 August
   1892/ No. 69968 (Vol. 5, p. 142).

7) MAYER, Georg- b. "Kingdom of Wuert(t)emberg", marr. Caroline
   Behnke at Berlin 4 May 1886/ No. 61477.

8) MESSING, Georg of Almond Portage Co. (Wisc.)- b. "Baden Germany",
   marr. Henriette Erdmann (widow) nee Zimmermann- b. "Germany"; at
   the residence of Jacob Messing-Princeton 1 November 1884/ No.
   59363 (Vol. 5, p. 97).

9) REINOEHL, Paul Julius of Token Creek, Dane Co. (Wisc.)- b. "Rubgarten Wurt(t)emberg", marr. Magdalena Rhein- b. "Kaiser(s)lau-
   tern, Rheinbayern (Rhine Bavaria in Palatinate region) Germany";
   at Manchester 8 p.m.- 28 December 1882/ No. 55992 (Vol. 5, p. 82).

10) RITTER, Rudolph- b. "Wurttenberg (Württemberg) Europh", marr.
    Rosa Gewetzki at Berlin 18 July 1876 (no pagation).

Immigrants with German names from Switzerland & Austria:

1) BAEBLER, Oswald of Black Wolf (twp.) Winnebago Co.- b. "Glarus
    Schweitz (Schweiz=Switzerland, Glarus a canton seat)", marr.
    Maria Koch at Marquette 8 November 1875 (no pagation).

2) BEYL, Paul J.-b."Rorschach (canton of St. Gallen), Switzerland",
    marr. Marie Schepp at the T. of Manchester 16 July 1900/ Vol. 7
    (1897-1900), p. 459.

3) CHRISTIAN, Fred- b. "Berne, Switzerland (a canton seat)", marr.
    Lenona Coomer- b. "Delaware Ohio"; at Berlin 30 March 1885/ No.
    59690 (Vol. 5, p. 100).

4) FISCHER, Philipp- b. "Arnitzgreu Austria", marr. Auguste Nieba
    at the City of Berlin 4 June 1874 (no pagation).

5) KNETZING, Francis- b. "Burns (Bern, a canton seat) Switzerland",
    marr. Cora Harrington at Berlin 19 November 1873.

6) WILHELM, Jacob- b. "Lafenwil, Canton A(a)rgau. Schweitz (Switzer-
    land)", marr. Johanna Wilhelmine Krueger at Berlin 1 March 1868/
    Vol. 5, p. 6.

7) WOHLWEND, John- b. "Rute (Ruti, Canton Zurich), Switzerland",
    marr. Wilhelmina Fink of Metomen Fond du Lac Co.; at Berlin 10
    June 1897/ Vol. 7 (1897-1900), p. 47.

Immigrants from Prussia's Rhine Province and Alsace-Lorraine territory, in western and southwestern Germany:

1) GIZELLA, Matilda- b. "Coeln an Rhedupr (Köln or Cologne an Rhein-
    preussen=Rhine Prussia?)", marr. Nickodem Brock- b. "Regierung(s)-
    bezirk (Administrative District, Prov.) Posen Germany"; at Berlin
    18 January 1898/ Vol. 7 (1897-1900), p. 158 (Cath.)

2) GRUNDER, Michael- b. "Strassburg Elsatia (Elsass=Alsace) Europe",
    marr. Wilhelmine Henriette Kobiske at Berlin 21 September 1893/
    Vol. 6 (1893-1897), p. 62.

3) HECKES, Hermann of West Rosendale (Fond du Lac Co.)- b. "Circu-
    it (County) of Gelden, Prove/Rheinland Prussia", marr. Auguste
    Butzin at Brooklyn 4 April 1859/ Early Vol. 3 (1858-1867), p. 17.

4) KIELWASSER, Carolina- b. "Elsass (Alsace)", marr. Andreas Land-
    mann- b. "Elsass (Alsace)"; at Kingston 6 October 1897/ Vol. 7
    (1897-1900), p. 73 (Cath.).

5) MOHR, Carl- b. "Braunfels in Rhine Province, Prussia", marr. Mar-
    tha Catharina Arch at the residence of William Carl Arch-Town of
    Randolph Columbia Co. 28 October 1860/ Early Vol. 3 (1858-1867),
    p. 79.

Immigrants from the former independent Kingdom and later Prussian Province of Hannover:

1) FABEL, Fridrich- b. "Schmasau, Hannover", marr. Wilhelmine Beyer at Berlin 25 April 1869/ Vol. 5, p. 10.

2) KOPPLIN, Julius of Columbus, Columbia Co. (Wisc.)- b. "Han(n)over Europh", marr. Wilhelmina Weiser at Princeton 17 March 1874 (no pagation).

3) LESCOW, Charles Wm. Godfrey Bernhard, a clergyman from Kohlsville Washington Co. Wis.- b. "Osnabruck Germany", marr. Bertha, Alvine Schmidt at Manchester 9 September 1891/ No. 68517 (Vol. 5, p. 136).

4) SCHONKE, Anna Sophia- b. "Hannover in Prussia", marr. Carl Adolph David Querfurth of Reedsburg Sauk Co. (Wisc.)- b. "Braunschweig (a Duchy in western Germany) in Germany", at Reedsburg Sauk Co. 1 March 1868/ Vol. 5,p. 5.

5) WARNICKE, Frederick Cheistof (Christoph?)- b. "Germany Han(n)over", marr. Hattie "gune (geb.=born)?" Friday at Manchester 28 May 1884/ No. 58514 (Vol. 5, p. 94).

6) WARNS, Peter- b. "Sogobrium, Ost (East) Friesland (a district), Prussia Germany", marr. Emilie Auguste Fisher at Princeton 3 September 1869/ Vol. 5, p. 11.

Immigrants from other locales in northwestern Germany:

1) FOERSTER, Wilhelm, a brewer from Portage City Columbia Co.- b.
"Helmstaedt (in Duchy Braunschweig?) Germany", marr. Philippine
Rhein- b. "Germany"; at Marquette 26 April 1868 (no pagation).

2) HOYER, Adolf G.W.- b."Hamburg (independent city-state), Germany",
marr. Calra Henriette Thiel at Princeton 3 p.m.-19 May 1881/ No.
53698.

3) LEUCKE, Carl Wilhelm Friedrich- b. "Lippe Detmold (a duchy) in
Germany", marr. Wilhelmine Sophia Dorothea Ballbaum at Ripon (Fond
du Lac Co.), Wisc. 26 August 1866/ Early Vol. 3 (1858-1867), p.
252.

4) MATHIZEN, Jacob (Danish?), a sailor from Chicago- b. "Husum (in
Schleswig-Holstein) (Prussian)", marr. Juliane Bloch at Manchester 29 July 1874 (no pagation).

5) NEHLSEN, Max (Danish?) of Chicago- b. "Holstein Germany", marr.
Grace Mathews Cragoe at Markesan 5:15 a.m.-8 October 1895/ Vol.
6 (1893-1897), p. 314.

6) POTTMAN, Fred of Chicago- b. "Bielefeld (Prussian Prov. Westfalen),
Germany", marr. Emma Tessmer- b. "Ragolsk (Rgielsko, Co. Wongrowitz, Prov. Posen, Prussia?), Germany"; at Manchester 6 December
1891/ No. 68951 (Vol. 5, p. 138).

7) QUERFURTH, Carl Adolph David of Reedsburg Sauk Co. (Wisc.)- b.
"(Duchy of) Braunschweig in Germany", marr. Anna Sophia Schonke
b."(Prov.) Hannover in Prussia"; at Reedsburg Sauk Co. 1 March
1868/ Vol. 5, p. 5.

8) SILGMANN, Frederick John- b. "Westphalia (Prussian Prov. Westfalen)
Germany", marr. Wilhelmine Reier (nee Wendland)- b. "Margolin
(Margonin?, Co. Kolmar, Prov. Posen, Prussia), Germany"; at Man-
chester 28 December 1893/ Vol. 6 (1893-1897), p. 104.

9) SKOW, Emil (Danish?)- b. "Lion-Kloster, Schlesswig", marr. Helle-
borg Bjerre- b. "Skanneborg, Denmark"; at Ripon Fond du Lac Co.
(Wisc.) 12 September 1885/ No. 60407 (Vol. 5, p. 102).

Immigrants from other locales, not readily identifiable, throughout "Germany":

1) BARGSTED, Christiana (possibly Danish?)- "Hardelen Germany" (possibly Harlingen or Harsleben in Prussian Province of Saxony-Anhalt, or Hardisleben in Saxe-Weimar), marr. Christian Winter- b. "Horsens, Denmark"; at Berlin, 21 February 1889/ No. 67044 (Vol. 5, p. 130).

2) BAUMANN, Herman Jul. of the Town of Spring(vale) Columbia Co.- b. "Frechland Germany" (perhaps Frechen by Köln=Cologne, Rhineland Province, Prussia?), marr. Emma Alvina Polenske- b. "Turnova (Tarnowo, Co. Obernick, Prov. Posen, Prussia) Germany"; at Marquette 25 November 1899/ Vol. 7 (1897-1900), p. 103.

3) BOHM, Wilhelm Ferdinand- b. "Schoenwerder (Co. Wirsitz, Prov. Posen or Co. Pyritz, Prov. Pomerania?), Germany", marr. Lena Louise Kuehn- b. "Ilovo (Illowo, Co. Flatow, Prov.) West Prussia, Germany"; at the City of Berlin 18 November 1893/ Vol. 6 (1893-1897), p. 84.

4) BROSE, Wm.- b."Ibenburg, Germany" (perhaps Ivenbusch, Co. Filehne, Prov. Posen or Ibbenbüren, Prussian Prov. Westfalen=Westphalia?), marr. Anna Giese, widow (nee Thornow)- b. "Germany"; at Manchester 30 March 1891/ No. 67941 (Vol. 5, p. 135).

5) BUSSE, Emma, Alvine, Martha- b. "Steinach, Germany" (city in the Oberfranken district of Bayern=Bavaria and 5 places in that area), marr. Christian Mueller- b. "Watertown (Jefferson Co.), Wisc."; at Manchester 4 November 1888/ No. 64615 (Vol. 5, p. 121).

6) CHESKEY, Addie Bertha- b. "Neusted Germany" (could be any of many variations of Neustadt, like New Town or Newton), marr. John Michael Wiesenthal- b. "Ussel-Germany" (could be town of Usseln by Arolsen in the Principality of Waldeck, or the Ussel River by Wemding, in the Schwaben district of Bavaria); at Berlin 30 July 1881/ No. 53861.

7) CONRAD, Clark Willem - b. "Tinoplemau? Germany", marr. Bertha Bohn of Mecan (Marquette Co.) ; at Mackford 26 November 1896/ Vol. 6 (1893-1897), p. 443.

8) DEICH, Gustav Herman Hugo- b. "Perleberg Germany" (perhaps in Co. Prignitz, Prov. Brandenburg or Grand Duchy of Mecklenburg-Schwerin?), marr. Albertina Augusta Schuenke (nee Marquardt)- b. "Hamlong, Germany" (perhaps Hameln, near Hannover?); at Manchester 16 September 1894 (1893-1897), p. 180.

9) FITZKE, Henry Chr.- b. "Bovain Germany", marr. Emilie Caroline Schmidt- b. "Germany"; at the residence of Aug. Wirth-Princeton 2 February 1896/ Vol. 6 (1893-1897), p. 357.

10) GANGER, Bertha Minnie Augusta- b. "Frinke Germany", marr. Frederick William Stroschein at Manchester 1 October 1895/ Vol. 6 (1893-1897), p.311.

11) GERRITS, William of Waupun (Fond du Lac Co.)- b. "Holland Germany", marr. Polly Poole at the hotel of J.R. McCrakin; Village of Markesan 27 April 1873 (no pagation).

12) GRANSCHOW, Friedrich of Oshkosh (Winnebago Co.)- b. "Schwinkendorf Germany" (near Malchin in the Grand Duchy of Mecklenburg-Schwerin), marr. Christiana Thiel at Brooklyn 5 May 1896/ Vol. 6 (1893-1897), p. 378.

13) HELMER, August Ferdinand- b. "Samtin, Germany" (Perhaps Samtens an Rügen Island, Prov. Pomerania?), marr. Anna Pauline Hollnagel of the Town of Ripon (Fond du Lac Co.), Wis.; at Manchester 15 October 1886/ No. 63422 (Vol. 5, p. 114).

14) HUBNER, Wilhelmine- b. "Klein Dreidorf Germany" (Co. Wirsitz, Prov. Posen, Prussia), marr. Karl Robert Prochnow- b. "Zühlsdorf Abrnswalde (Co. Arnswalde, Prov. Brandenburg, Prussia) Germany"; at Kingston 2 p.m.-3 December 1895/ Vol. 6 (1893-1897), p. 331.

15) KOLB, Johann- b. "Weilen, Germany"(many places names Weiler in southwestern Germany), marr. Anna Louise (nee Leu) Jeske at the Town of Berlin 28 May 1881/ No. 53604.

16) KRENTZ, Emma- b. "Schobingen, Germany" (Maybe Schoppingen, Co. Steinfurt, Prov. Westfalen, Prussia?), marr. Wilhelm Harms of Fairwater (Fond du Lac Co.)- b. "Wisconsin, Toma(h, Monroe Co.)"; at Markesan 22 November 1892/ No. 70412 (Vol. 5, p. 143).

17) KUSS, Emilie- b. "Gastrow, Germany" (probably Güstrow, Grand Duchy of Mecklenburg-Schwerin), marr. William Klingbeil at the Town of Brooklyn 11 October 1899/ Vol. 7 (1897-1900), p. 357.

18) LADWIG, Charles- b. "Altkow, Germany", marr. Emilie Hartfiel- b. "Josephokow, Polen" (probably Josephkowo,Co. Kolmar, colony a.k.a. Bergheim, Prov. Posen, Prussia); at Berlin 3 February 1885/ No. 59502 (Vol. 5, p. 99).

19) LAMBRECHT, Emilie- b. "Kluestrien Germany"; marr. Gottlieb Huth of Ripon (Fond du Lac Co.); at Brooklyn 16 November 1897/ Vol. 7 (1897-1900), p. 100.

20) LANGE, Emma Emilie- b. "Luzernhof Kreis (County) Kornmark Germany", marr. Julius Ferdinand Tagatz- b. "Crystal Lake (Marquette Co.)"; (no location given) 4 p.m.-18 January 1897/ Vol. 6 (1893-1897), p. 467.

21) LIESNER, Wm. of Scott Columbia Co.- b. "Buchtenhagen, Germany", marr. Clara Zerbel- b. "Kuwelitkow, Germany"; at Kingston 25 March 1891/ No. 67833 (Vol. 5, p. 134).

22) LUDWIG, Carl Otto- b. "Webenheim Germany" (west of Zweibrücken, in the Pfalz=Palatiate, southwestern Germany), marr. Pauline Anna Agnes Zimmer- b. "Spandau (by Berlin, Prov. Brandenburg, Prussia) Germany"; at Berlin 3 March 1898/ Vol. 7 (1897-1900), p. 147.

23) MARQUARDT, Louis Fred of Randolph (Columbia Co.& Dodge Co.), Wisc.- b. "Worochowo, Germany", marr. Dorothea Bischoff- b. "Long Island, N.Y."; at Manchester 28 November 1889/ No. 66028 (Vol. 5, p. 126).

24) MUELLER, Charles- b. "Wulstrow, Germany", marr. Ottilie Zerbel- b. "Nagel (Nakel, Co. Wirsitz, Prov. Posen, Prussia), Germany"; at Kingston 2 January 1885/ No. 62397 (Vol. 5, p. 110).

25) POLINSKE, Pauline Louise- b. "Potolitzhauland in Germany" (either Potulitz-Hauland in Cos. Wongrowitz or Bromberg, Prov. Posen, Prussia), marr. Franz Heinrich Friedrich- b. "Pyritz (a county seat in Prov. Pomerania, Prussia) in Germany"; at Markesan 15 September 1889/ No. 65807 (Vol. 5, p. 125).

26) QUARTE, Theodor- b. "Lamedzin, Germany" (possibly Lamerden between Warburg and Höxter in the Principality of Lippe-Detmold?), marr. Pauline Grams at Manchester 5 p.m.-6 April 1880/ No. 51906.

27) RADKE, August- b. "Grunia, Germany" (perhaps Grüne, Co. Lisse, Prov. Posen, Prussia?), marr. Bertha Jahns at Princeton 26 April 1881/ No. 53476.

28) RUPNOW, August of Waupun (Fond du Lac Co.)- b. "Lamin Germany", marr. Friedericka Krueger at the residence of W. Krueger- Manchester 9 February 1882/ No. 54716.

29) SCHADE, Ida Minna Helen- b. "Unfliess Germany", marr. Albert George Ludwig Kolitz- b. "Berlin (Prov. Brandenburg) Germany"; at Manchester 15 September 1898/ Vol. 7 (1897-1900), p. 207.

30) SILGMANN, Minnie- b. "Recke, Germany" (near Osnabrück, Co. Tecklenburg, Prov. Westfalen, Prussia), marr. William Frank Lueck at Manchester 12 October 1898/ Vol. 7 (1897-1900), p. 222.

31) SMITH, Herman- b. "Brusch, Germany" (a brook near Saarburg in Lothringen=Lorraine, now France), marr. Louise Wisenborn of Waupaca (a county seat in Wisc.); at Berlin 8 June 1882/ No. 55292 (Vol. 5, p. 79).

32) SOMME(R)FELDT, Auguste Alvine- b. "Groshauland Germany", marr. John Huellmann of the Town of Randolph (Columbia Co.); at Manchester 28 April 1895/ Vol. 6 (1893-1897), p. 284.

33) STELTER, Julius, a sailor from Montello Marquette Co.- b. "Jacobowa Germany" (possibly Jakubowo, Co. Wongrowitz, Prov. Posen, Prussia), marr. Ida Wessner(or Wepner)- b. "Klemm Germany" (perhaps Klemmen, Co. Kammin, Prov. Pomerania, Prussia?); at Manchester 17 April 1891/ No. 63054 (Vol. 5, p. 135).

34) THEDE, Charles- b. "Neu-Kloster, Germany" (in Wismar district and lake by same name in Grand Duchy of Mecklenburg-Schwerin or in Stade district of Province Hannover, Prussia), marr. Louisa Busse (widow, nee Hein)- b. "Wrongowitz (a county seat in Prov. Posen, Prussia) Germany"; at Manchester 22 April 1891/ No. 68055 (Vol. 5, p. 135).

35) THIEL, Wilhelmine A.- "Steilitz Germany" (possibly Steglitz, Co. Czarnikau, Prov. Posen, Prussia?), marr. Grant Thomas- b. "Aurora Waushara Co."; at the City of Berlin 18 Sep. 1892/ No. 70184 (Vol. 5, p. 143).

36) VINZ, Mary Catherine- b. "Geilsdorf, Germany" (in Rudolstadt district of Thuringia, central Germany), marr. Christoph Ferge- b. "Eisenach (Saxe-Gotha in Thuringian States of central) Germany"; at Manchester 9 July 1888/No. 64317 (Vol. 5, p. 118).

37) WAGSTUFF, Ludwig of Nepeuaskin Winnebago Co.- b. "Poman Germany" (either Prov. Pommern=Pomerania, Prussia or Pammin, Co. Arnswalde, Prov. Brandenburg or Co. Dramburg, Prov. Pomerania?); marr. Alwaene Shevee (Alwine Schewe?) at Dartford (Green Lake) 16 July 1874. (no pagation)

38) WENDT, Rudolf, John, Richard- b. "Nieder-Lowitz (Co. Lauenburg in Prov. Pomerania, Prussia), Germany", marr. Auguste Henriette Schirmer at Berlin 22 October 1879/ No. 51134.

39) WERNER, Daniel- b. "Rasitz (Radzicz=Hermannsdorf, Co. Wirsitz, Prov. Posen, Prussia) Germanie", marr. Louise Krueger at Marquette 20 April 1869/ Vol. 5, p. 10.

40) WINNE, Christian- b. "Ottroff (Ottrott, Molsheim district of Elass=Alsace, near Strassburg?) Germany", marr. Christiane Burbach at the Town of Manchester 4 April 1880/ No. 51905.

COUNTY KOLMAR,
PROVINCE POSEN

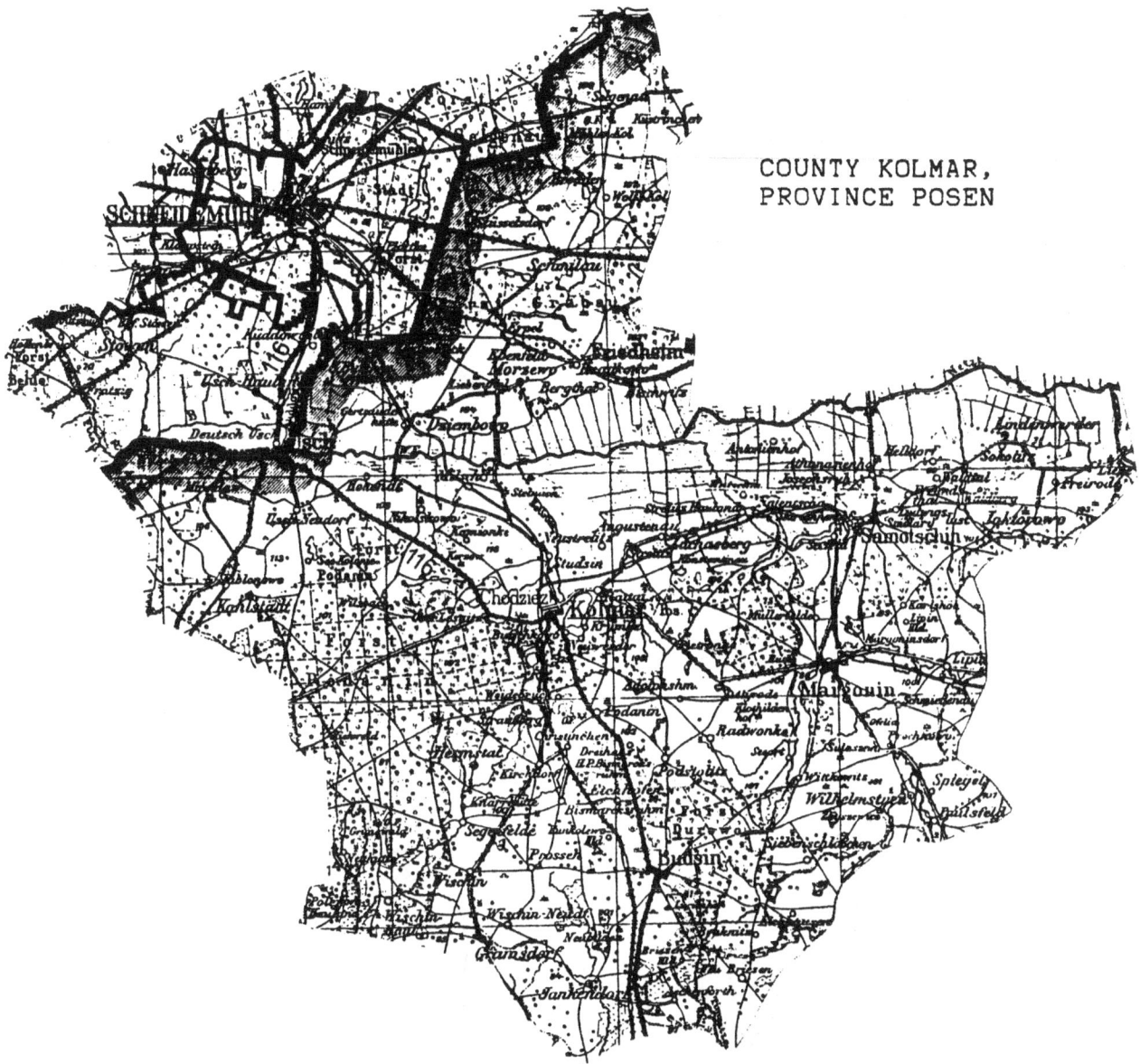

Sonderkarte Pommern 1 : 300,000
Mit Genehmigung des Instituts für Angewandte Geodäsie -
Aussenstelle Berlin - Nr. 211/92 vom 12.02.1992

COUNTY ARNSWALDE,
PROVINCE BRANDENBURG

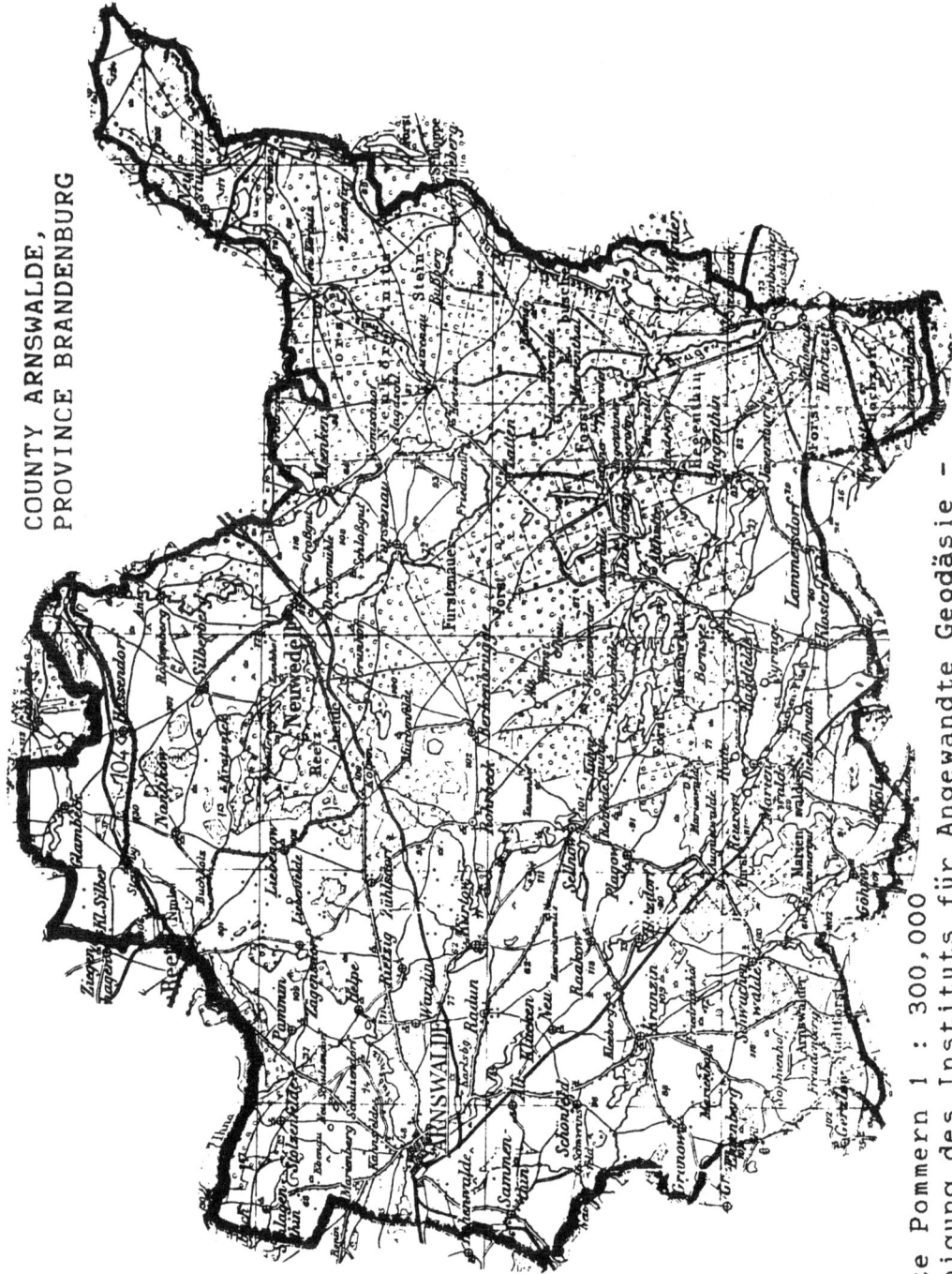

Sonderkarte Pommern 1 : 300,000
Mit Genehmigung des Instituts für Angewandte Geodäsie –
Aussenstelle Berlin – Nr. 211/92 vom 12.02.1992

COUNTY CZARNIKAU,
PROVINCE POSEN

Sonderkarte Pommern 1 : 300,000
Mit Genehmigung des Instituts für Angewandte Geodäsie -
Aussenstelle Berlin - Nr. 211/92 vom 12.02.1992

COUNTY WIRSITZ,
PROVINCE POSEN

Sonderkarte Pommern 1 : 300,000
Mit Genehmigung des Instituts für Angewandte Geodäsie –
Aussenstelle Berlin – Nr. 211/92 vom 12.02.1992

COUNTY FILEHNE,
PROVINCE POSEN

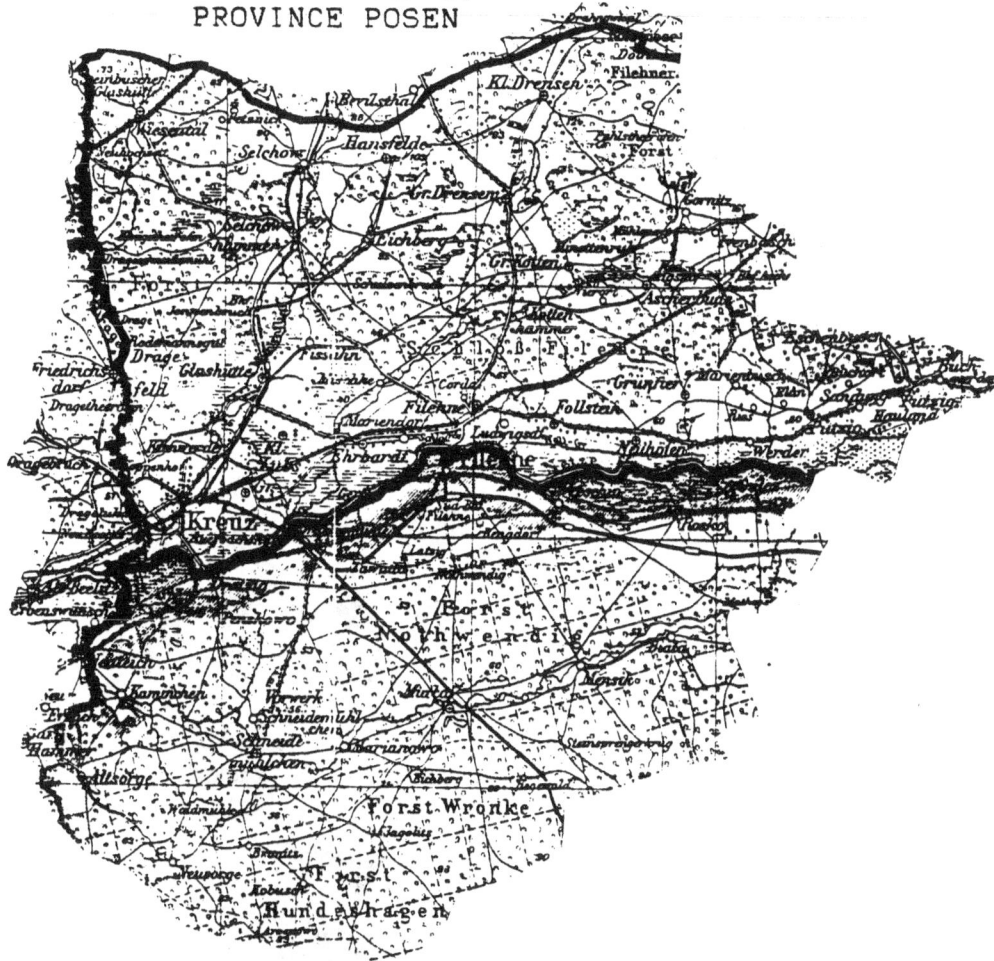

Sonderkarte Pommern 1 : 300,000
Mit Genehmigung des Instituts für Angewandte Geodäsie -
Aussenstelle Berlin - Nr. 211/92 vom 12.02.1992

COUNTY BROMBERG,
PROVINCE POSEN

Sonderkarte Pommern 1 : 300,000
Mit Genehmigung des Instituts
für Angewandte Geodäsie -
Aussenstelle Berlin -
Nr. 211/92 vom 12.02.1992

MARQUETTE COUNTY MARRIAGES

Immigrants from County Kolmar, Province Posen, Prussia:

1) BERNDT, Rudolph Heinrich- b."Strelitz Holland (-Hauland), Posen", marr. Wilhelmine Nickoley at Neshkoro, 4 April 1893/Vol. 2a,p.35.

2) BORNICKE, August- b. "Stoewen, Prussia", marr. Pauline Dahlke at Newton, 29 October 1876/Vol. 2, p. 28.

3) BUCHHOLTZ, Hermann Rudolf- b. "Zachelberg (Zachasberg), Germany", marr. Bertha Emilie Kohn at Newton, 12 October 1905/Vol. 3,p.220.

4) BUCHHOLZ, Carl Robert- b. "Zathesberg (Zachasberg) Colmar (Kolmar), Posen, Germany", marr. Ida Henriette Kohn at Newton, 28 April 1907/ Vol. 3, p. 241.

5) BUCHHOLZ, Josephine Hulda (father's name Carl)- b. "Kolmar, Germany", marr. Robert Ernest Mueller of Fox Lake (Dodge Co., Wisc.), at Westfield, 25 September 1907/ Vol. 3, p. 248.

6) BUNDT, Herman Friedrich- b. "Strelitz, Germany", marr. Ernestine Wilhelmine Kroll at Crystal Lake, 6 April 1896/ Vol. 3, p. 76.

7) BUSCHKE, Friedrich- b. "Joseph(s)ruh, Posen, Germany", marr. Caroline Wilhelmine Brose (previously married, parents' name Winkelman)- b. "Klein-Drensen (Co. Czarnikau), Posen, Germany", at Crystal Lake, 6 July 1898/ Vol. 3, p. 107.

8) BUSCHKE, Hulda- b. "Lindenwerter (Lindenwerder), Prov. Posen", marr. Gustav Eichstedt- b. "Deutsch Krone (county seat in Prov. West Prussia), Germany", at Newton, 6 April 1893/ Vol. 3, p. 34.

9) DUESTERHOEFT, Gustav Julius- b. "Siebenschloess(ch)en, Posen, Germany", marr. Ernestine Alwine Puphal- b. "Posen, Germany", at Mecan, 29 November 1894/ Vol. 3, p. 55.

10) ERDMANN, Emil- b. "Strosewa (Strozewo), Germany", marr. Emma Wendtland- b. "Prov. Posen, Germany", at Harrisville, 19 April 1896/ Vol. 3, p. 79.

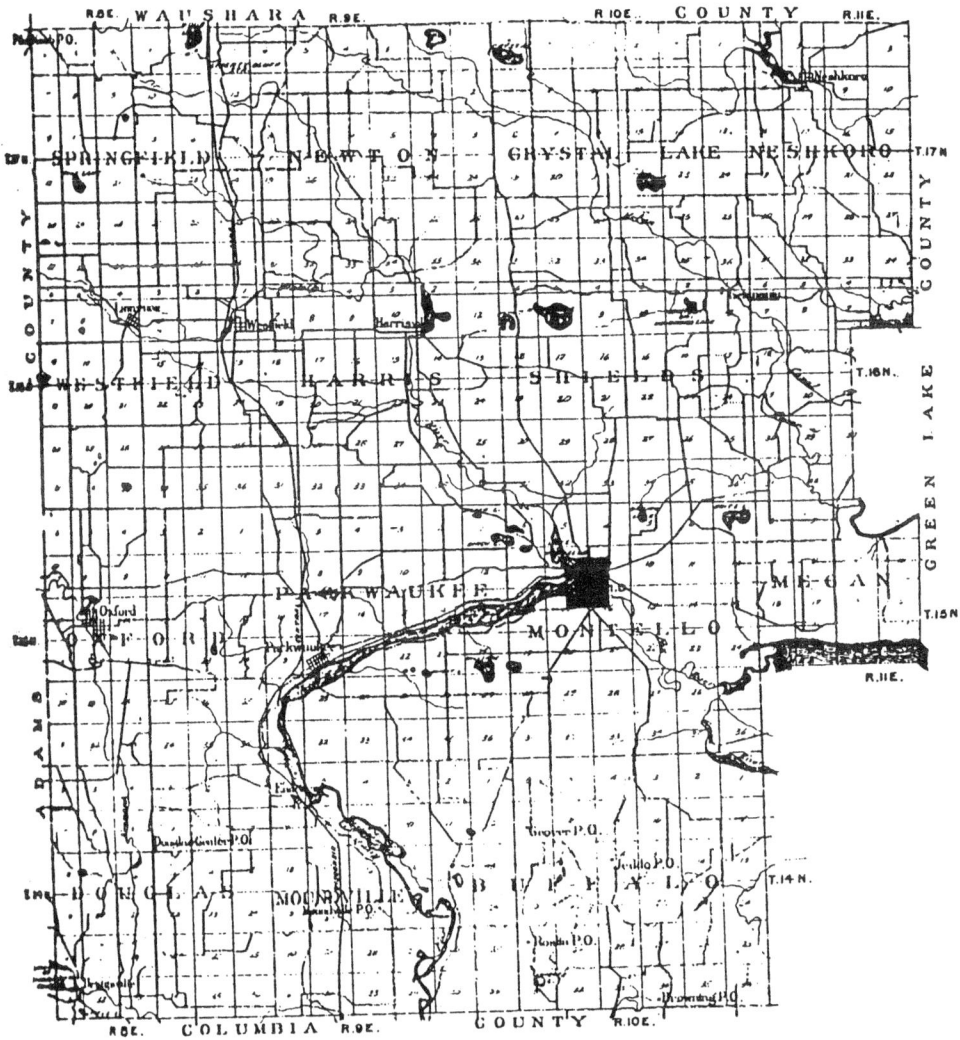

Marquette Co.
WISCONSIN

(Courtesy 1900 Marquette County Plat Book & *Come Back in Time*, Volume I, by Elaine Reetz)

11) FENNER, Johann Ludwig- b. "Kolmar, Provinz Posen, Polen (German name for Poland)", marr. Charlotte Gohlke- b."Brenkenhofsburg Frankfort a.d. Warte (Prov. Brandenburg)", at Germania, 17 November 1893/ Vol. 3, p. 43.

12) GUTSCHE, Emil of Dakota, Waushara Co.- b. "Lindenwerder, Prussia", marr. Auguste Pripke- b. "Prussia", at Harrisville, 25 December 1885/ Vol. 2a, p. 62.

13) GUTSCH(E?), Julius of Grand Forks, N. Dak.- b. "Lindenwerda (Lindenwerder), Germany", marr. Marie Priepke- b. "Svdien (Znin?), Germany", at Westfield, 3 March 1892/ Vol. 3, p. 20.

14) HEOFT (HOEFT?), Anthony of Oshkosh (Winnebago Co.), Wisc. (Catholic- mother's maiden name "Pierjock"=Pierdzioch? Polish for "old fart")- b."Schneidemulle (Schneidemühl), Prussia", marr. Agnes Pierjock at Montello, 17 April 1883/ Vol. 2a, p. 52.

15) JENNERMAN, Christoph- b. "Podonin (Podanin), Prussia", marr. Louise Eckert at Crystal Lake, 19 January 1874/ Vol. 2a, p. 19.

16) KOSLOWSKY, August H. of Dakota, Waushara Co.- b. "Radzin (Ratschin), Posen, Germany", marr. Bertha Clara Zuelke- b. "Coceczien (Chodziesen=Kolmar), Germany",at Crystal Lake, 24 January 1888/ Vol. 2a, p. 70.

17) KRAUSE, Emma- b. "Lipin, Germany", marr. Carl Julius Krueger- b. "Wirsitz (a county seat in Posen), Germ.", at Mecan, 10 February 1887/ Vol. 2a, p. 66.

18) KRUEGER, August Friedrich- b. "Borowoholland (Borowo-Hauland), Germany", marr. Auguste Wilhelmine Berg at Crystal Lake, 10 December 1896/ Vol. 3, p. 86.

19). KRUEGER, Herman August of Randolph (Columbia/Dodge Cos.),Wisc.- b. "Strehlitz (Strelitz), Posen, Germany", marr. Augusta O. Krueger at Crystal Lake, 7 December 1887/Vol. 2a, p. 68.

20) MILLER, Louise (father's surname Jachek)- b. "Josephsruh, Germany", marr. Herman Robert Traeger at Harrisville, 10 June 1903/ Vol. 3, p. 186.

21) MUELLER, Augusta Bertha- b. "Siebenschlos (Siebenschlösschen), Germany", marr. Julius F. Breitenfeldt at Crystal Lake, 5 December 1894/ Vol. 3, p. 56.

22) MUELLER, Emil Friderich- b. "Siehenschiessee (Siebenschlösschen), Germany", marr. Ida Maria Breitenfeld(t?) at Crystal Lake, 10 October 1897/ Vol. 3, p. 97.

23) NEST, Emil Theodor- b. "Augustinu (Augustenau), Posen, Germany", marr. Hulda Albertine S(ch?)wersinske- b. "Ludeoskowe (Ludwikowo, Co. Schubin), Posen, Germany", at Neshkoro, 28 May 1896/ Vol. 3, p. 79.

24) NEST, Gustav Julius- b. "Augustenow (Augustenau), Germany", Eva Blanch Ralph at Nehskoro, 5 March 1888/Vol. 2a, p. 70.

25) NICKOLAI, Wilhelm August- b. "Jankendorf, Germany", marr. Hulda Maria Fratzke at Neshkoro, 2 November 1893/ Vol. 3, p. 41.

26) PODOLL, Ernest Otto of New Chester, Adams Co. (Wisc., author's great-grandfather, his second marriage)- b. Radwonkee (Radwonke) Kriez Cochesen (Kreis Chodziesen= County Kolmar)", marr. Maria Werner at Westfield, 4 January 1899/ Vol. 3, p. 9.

27) PODOLL, Otto of Richford, Waushara Co.- b. "Radwinke (Radwonke), Prussia", marr. Emilie Malzahn- b. "Wiesenthal, Prussia", at Newton, 17 December 1886/ Vol. 2a, p. 66.

28) "OWADE" (QUADE?), Wilhelm- b. "Lindenwerder, Germany", marr. Emma Kluth at Packwaukee, 8 March 1899/ Vol. 3, p. 117.

29) RADSCH, Gustav- b. "Chodziesson (Chodziesen=Kolmar), Prussia", marr. Auguste W. Prochel at Neshkoro, 14 February 1871/ Vol. 2a, p. 10.

30) SCHEIN, Johann August- b. "Strelitz, Prussia, Germ.", marr. Pauline Auguste Krueger at Crystal Lake, 25 April 1869/ Vol. 2a, p. 4.

31) SCHEVE, Fredrick- b. "Strelitz in K. of Pruchen (Kingdom of Preussen-"proys-sen"=Prussia)", marr. Emi(l?)ge Tesner at Shields, 25 February 1871/ Vol. 2a, p. 10.

32) SCHILLERT, Julius- b. "Kolmar, Prussia", marr. Anna Wenzel- b. "Wesitz (Wirsitz?), Prussia", at Springfield, 9 March 1889/ Vol. 2a, p. 74.

33) SCHILLERT, Wilhelmine- b. "Ostrowke, Kreis Colmar, (Administrative District of) Bromberg", marr. John Bahn- b. "Josephine, Bromberg", at Germania, 10 March 1892/ Vol. 3, p. 20.

34) SCHONROCK, John Gottlieb of Alto, Fond du Lac Co. (Wisc.)- b. "Ostropke (Ostrowke), Prussia", marr. Wilhelmine Pauline Myers at Crystal Lake, 22 May 1873/ Vol. 2a, p. 16.

35) STELTER, Augusta (author's grand-aunt)- b. "Golmar (Kolmar), Germany", marr. Emil Schuls (Schulz) of Phillips (Price Co.) Wisc.- b. "Galice (Kallies?), Pommern (Pomerania), Germany", at Springfield, 22 January 1902/ Vol. 3, p. 161.

36) WARNKE, Emil Robert- b. "Colmar, Germany", marr. Wilhelmine Henriette Krueger at Crystal Lake, 1 December 1887/ Vol. 2a, p. 68

37) WARNKE, Maria Wilhelmine of Eau Claire (co. seat), Wisc.- b. "Colmar, Germany", marr. Heinrich Pehlke of Fall Creek (Eau Claire Co.), Wisc.; at Crystal Lake, 13 January 1885/ Vol. 2a, p. 59.

38) WISKI, John- b. "Schneidemuell (Schneidemühl), Posen, Prussia", marr. Amilia Brasel at Montello, 13 January 1883/ Vol. 2a, p. 51.

39) ZECH, Carl Friedrich- b. "Laskowa (Laskowo), Germany", marr. Auguste Fischer (nee Meyer)- b. "Straghts Howland (Strozewo-Hauland), Germany", at Westfield, 9 February 1904/ Vol. 3, p. 196.

40) ZUELKE, August Friedrick- b. "Borrows Holland (Borowo-Hauland), Germany", marr. Martha Matilda Krueger- b. "Borrow Holland (Borowo-Hauland), Germany", at Crystal Lake, 31 January 1893 (note: last residence of Rev. E. Theel also given as "Borrow Holland")/ Vol. 3, p. 30.

Immigrants from County Filehne, Province Posen, Prussia:

1) BOEKER, Herman F.- b. "Gross Drensen, Germany", marr. Wilhelmine P. Tagatz at Crystal Lake, 14 August 1892/ Vol. 3, p. 24.

2) BROSE, Caroline Wilhelmine (parents' name Winkelman)- b. "Klein-Drensen, Posen, Germany", marr. Friedrich Buschke- b. "Josephsruh (Co. Kolmar), Posen, Germany", at Crystal Lake, 6 July 1898/ Vol. 3, p. 107.

3) DREWITZ, Gottlieb (father John)- b. "Putzig, Prussia", marr. Juli Drewitz (father Michael) at Harrisville, 6 February 1873/ Vol. 2a, p. 15.

4) FLOETER, Ernestine- b. "Gross Drensen, Germany", marr. Herman Julius Matthias at Crystal Lake, 14 March 1899/ Vol. 3, p. 117.

5) FLOETER, Louise Henriette- b. "Gross Drensen, Germany", marr. Ernst Adolph C. Buelow- b. "Bredow, Germany" of Seneca, Green Lake Co.; at Crystal Lake, 15 January 1884/ Vol. 2a, p. 59.

6) FLOETER, Wilhelm- b. "Gross Drensen, Germany", marr. Auguste Wilhelmine Salzwedel- b. "Pamin (Co. Arnswalde, Prov. Brandenburg), Germany"; at Crystal Lake, 5 January 1888/ Vol. 2a, p. 70.

7) FLOETER, Wilhelmine - b."Gross Drensen, Germany", marr. Julius Manthei of Rosendale (Fond du Lac Co., Wisc.)- b. "Louisendorf, Germany"; at Crystal Lake, 1 May 1887/ Vol. 2a, p. 67.

8) GOHRKE, Anna Louise- b. "Neuhofen Philena (Filhene) Germany", marr. Friedrich August Nickel- b. "Radolin Scharnikow (Co. Czarnikau), Germany"; at Westfield, 14 July 1892/ Vol. 3, p. 23.

9) HENKE, Carl- b. "Selchow, Germany", marr. Minnie Arndt- b. "Dratzig, Germany"; at Harrisville, 14 May 1903/ Vol. 3, p. 181.

10) HENKE, Louise Bertha- b. "Selchow, Germany", marr. Wilhelm Zellmer at Newton, 15 November 1894/ Vol. 2a, p. 56.

11) KAATZ, Friedrich Herman of Richford, Waushara Co.- b. "Gross Drensen, Germany", marr. Emma Louise Boelter at Newton, 8 April 1883/ Vol. 2a, p. 53.

CRYSTAL LAKE TOWNSHIP (1900 Marquette County Plat Book)

12) KAATZ, Gottlob- b. "Gross Drensen, Prussia", marr. Pauline Bölter at Crystal Lake, 17 April 1874/ Vol. 2a, p. 20.

13) KRUESEL, Wilhelm of Fond du Lac (Wisc. county seat)- b. "Ichberg (Eichberg), Prussia", marr. Henriette Kaatz (a widow) at Newton, 13 December 1871/ Vol. 2a, p. 12.

14) LAUMER, Emma Auguste- b. "Gross Lubss (Lubs), Germany", marr. Otto Johann Robert Boesemann at Mecan, 4 October 1899/ Vol. 3, p. 124.

15) LAUMER, Martha Anna- b. "Gross Lups (Lubs)/Germany", marr. Karl Friedrich Guenther of Bruno, Nebraska- b. "Prov. Saxen (Sachsen or Saxony), Germany"; at Mecan, 3 May 1898/ Vol. 3, p. 105.

16) LUTHER, Johann August- b. "Putzig, Prussia, Germany", marr. Caroline Augusta Beutler at Newton, 1 May 1868/ Vol. 1, p. 206.

17) SCHULTZ, Wilhelmine E.- b."Gornitz, Germany", marr. Friedrich Wm. Meyer at Crystal Lake, 14 March 1888/ Vol. 2a, p. 71.

18) SCHUTZ, Herman Emil- b. "Gornitz, Germany", marr. Lyda Marie Wagner at Crystal Lake, 24 June 1896/ Vol. 3, p. 81.

19) SEIDLITZ, Lina- b. "Gross Lubs bei Kreuz, Posen, Germany", marr. Gottlieb Seehafer- b. "Nichorsz, West Preussen (Nichors, Co. Flatow, West Prussia), Germany"; at Germania, 20 February 1894/ Vol. 3, p. 48.

20) "FETZLAF" (TETZLAFF?), Bertha Emilie- b. "Gross Drensen, Germany", marr. Edmund Edward Sell at Crystal Lake, 8 March 1898/ Vol. 3, p. 103.

21) TETZLAFF, Herman Martin of Dakota, Waushara Co.- b. "Gross Drensen, Germany", marr. Pauline Bertha Brose- b. "Ibenbush (Ivenbusch), Germany"; at Crystal Lake, 8 May 1885/ Vol. 2a, p. 60.

Immigrants from County Czarnikau, Province Posen, Prussia:

1) BROSE, Pauline Bertha, b. "Ibenbush*(Ivenbusch), Germany", marr. Herman Martin Tetzlaff of Dakota, Waushara Co.- b. "Gross Drensen (Co. Filehne, Prov. Posen), Germany"; at Crystal Lake, 8 May 1885/ Vol. 2a, p. 60. (Note: Ivenbusch actually in Co. Filehne)

2) CONRAD, Johann August- b. "Czarnikau, Prov. of Posen, Germany", marr. Amelea Auguste "Johanke" at Newton, 26 January 1870/ Vol. 2a, p. 5.

3) DUMKE, Auguste E.- b. "Schönlanke, Prussia", marr. Julius August Krueger- b. "Guntergust (Güntergost, Co. Wirsitz, Prov. Posen), Prussia"; at Harrisville, 9 January 1885/ Vol. 2a, p. 59.

4) FLOETER, Adolf. Rudolf- b. "Theresia, Germany", marr. Albertine Wilh. Drewitz at Springfield, 17 March 1887/ Vol. 2a, p. 67.

5) FLOETER, August- b. "Theresia, Prussia", marr. Henriette Ernestine Chemnitz (perhpas Kemnitz?) at Newton, 25 April 1869/ Vol. 2a, p. 4.

6) FRANK, August- b. "Stradhun (Straduhn), Germany", marr. Auguste Fabert* at Newton, 8 April 1869/ Vol. 2a, p. 2.
*(Note: Henriette Auguste Fabert was born at Zachasberg, County Kolmar. This information and more complete information in this couple's parrentage and children supplied by Mr. Wayne Fabert of San Diego, California and is available thru him.)

7) GARDOW, Emil-,b. "Schon Langen (Schönlanke), Germany", marr. Emilie Abraham at Westfield, 4 January 1898/ Vol. 3, p. 101.

8) HALLMAN, H.J.- b. "Behle, Germany", marr. Augusta E. Wenzel at Newton, 27 November 1895/ Vol. 3, p. 71.

9) HARDER, Johann August- b. "Czarnithau (Czarnikau), Prussia", marr. Pauline Reetz at Neshkora (Neshkoro), 14 February 1871/ Vol. 2a, p. 9.

10) HENKE, Frederick Wm.- b. "Czarn(i)kau, Prussia", marr. Susana Beier at Crystal Lake, 15 February 1869/ Vol. 2a, p. 1.

11) KUEHN, Christoph- b. "Beli (Behle), Prov. of Posen", marr. Wilhelmine Lentz at Mecan, 27 September 1868/ Vol. 1, p. 187.

12) MITTELSTAEDT, Eduard Friede- b. "Schoenlanke, Germany", marr. Louise Albertine Brehmer at Springfield, 27 April 1905/ Vol. 3, p. 215.

13) MODROW, Martin- b. "Raudoline (Radolin), Posen", marr. Pauline Koepp at Neshkoro, 7 January 1892/ Vol. 3, p. 18.

14) NICKEL, Friedrich August- b. "Radolin, Scharnikow (Czarnikau), Germany", marr. Anna Louise Gohrke- b. "Neuhofen Philena (Co. Filehne), Germany"; at Westfield, 14 July 1892/ Vol. 3, p. 23.

15) OTTO, August Julius of Quincy, Adams Co. (Wisc.)- b. "Lemnitz, Germany", marr. Effie Elnira Foss at Mecan, 30 June 1897/ Vol. 3, p. 94.

16) ROHDE, Gustav- b. "Strungelitz (Stieglitz?), Kreis Schunko (Co. Czarnikau)", marr. Emilge S. Miller at Crystal Lake, 19 April 1897/ Vol. 3, p. 90.

17) SCHOENFELD, Adolf- b. "Caroline (Kolonie Carolina) Posen, Germany", marr. Auguste Henke- b. "Liebenwerder (Lindenwerder, Co. Kolmar?), Posen, Germany"; at Harrisville, 14 April 1898/ Vol. 3, p. 103.

18) STELTER, Alvine Pauline- b. "Gembitz, Posen, Germany", marr. August Ferdinand Milbrandt- b. Segensdorf, Circuit (Kreis= Circuit=County, a literal translation) Arnswalde (Prov. Brandenburg), Germany"; at Mecan, 14 February 1900/ Vol. 3, p. 132.

19) STELTER, August (author's great-grand-uncle)- b. "Baele (Behle), Germany", marr. Emilie Ferg(e?) at Springfield, 28 November 1894/ Vol. 3, p. 55.

20) STELTER, Auguste Amalie- b. "Gembitz, Europe", marr. Julius Bloch at Mecan, 16 May 1906/ Vol. 3, p. 226.

21) ZABEL, August Fredrick Wilhelm- b. "Schonelck (Schönlanke), Prussia, Germany", marr. Caroline W.R. Hollander at Crystal Lake, 23 December 1870/ Vol. 2a, p. 9.

22) ZORN, Emilie Hulda- b. "Radolin, Prussia", marr. Friedrich Fierke- b. "Dninbrnok (Obernick?), Prussia"; at Newton, 27 January 1885/ Vol. 2a, p. 59.

Immigrants from the City, County, or Administrative District? of
"Bromberg", Province Posen, Prussia:

1) ALTENBURG, Michael- b. "Bromberg, Prussia", marr. Justine Pauline Urban at Newton, 26 January 1869/ Vol. 2a, p. 1.

2) BAHN, John- b. "Jospehine, Bromberg", marr.Wilhelmine Schillert-
   b. "Ostrowke, Kreis Colmar, Bromberg"; at Germania, 10 March
   1892/ Vol. 3, p. 20.

3) BUCKHOLZ, Albert L. of Rochester, Minnesota- b. "Bromberg, Germany", marr. Justina P. Henke at Nehskoro, 14 February 1895/
   Vol. 3, p. 59.

4) DRAGER, Wm. Frederick- b. "Bromberg in Prussia", marr. Henrietta Junke(n?)berg at Shields, 8 March 1870/ Vol. 2a, p. 7.

5) GLENZ, August of Princeton, Green Lake Co.- b. "Bromberg, Prussia", marr. Mathilde Zellmer at Crystal Lake, 2 January 1873/
   Vol. 2a, p. 15.

6) KALINSKI, Christoph- b. "Zramberg (Bromberg?), Germany", marr.
   Marie Krenz at Springfield, 16 April 1895/ Vol. 3, p. 60.

7) KATZ, Carl -b. "Bromberg, Prussia", marr. Auguste Ernestine
   Feldman, 16 January 1870 (no location given, perhaps a Jewish
   couple?)/ Vol. 2a, p. 5.

8) KIRST, Emilie- b. "Ksezaly (Dzlaly, Bromberg?), Germany", marr.
   Fritz Dickow of Chicago, Illinois- b. "Nashow, Germany"; at
   Westfield, 16 January 1895/ Vol. 3, p. 58.

9) KLETKE, Frederick Martin- b. "Bromberg, Prussia", marr. Auguste
   Puhl at Mecan, 23 February 1869/ Vol. 2a, p. 1.

10) KRUGER, Fredrick- b."Brimberg (Bromberg), Prussia", marr. Emi-
    lie F. Zimmermann at Crystal Lake, 10 March 1871/ Vol. 2a, p.
    10.

11) LANGE, Bertha- b. "Grunberg, Germany", marr. Rudolf Schrank at
    Harrisville, 24 April 1896/ Vol. 3, p. 76.

12) LIESKE, Friedrich of Berlin, Green Lake Co.- b. "Bromberg, Prus-
    sian", marr. Wilhelmine Grehn at Harrisville, 1 February 1875/
    Vol. 2a, p. 22.

HARRIS TOWNSHIP (1900 Marquette County Plat Book)

13) MIDDLESTADT, Johan Frederick- b. "Bromberg, Prussia", marr. Caroline Henke at Mecan, 23 February 1869/ Vol. 2a, p. 1.

14) NICKEL, Fredrick- b. "Bromberg, Prussia", marr. Bertha Zellmer at Crystal Lake, 24 February 1871/ Vol. 2a, p. 10.

15) REETZ, Gustav- b. "Bromberg, Prussia", marr. Auguste Louise Kenzel at Crystal Lake, 6 June 1870/ Vol. 2a, p. 7.

16) SEMRO(W?), August (father Paul)- b."Sidno (Dzidno, Bromberg?), Prussia", marr. Emilie Semro(w?) (father Martin); at Newton, 29 November 1873/ Vol. 2a, p. 17.

17) TONN, August- b. "Bromberg, Germany", marr. Hellene Plath at Montello, 11 Novmeber 1894/ Vol. 2a, p. 98.

18) VOLL, Gustav Carl of Oshkosh (Winnebago Co.), Wisc.- b. "Michlaw (Michalin or Mecheln, Bromberg?), Germany", marr. Lina Sophia John at Harrisville, 26 December 1883/ Vol. 2a, p. 55.

19) ZELLMER, Wilhelm- b. "Bromberg, Prussia", marr. Bertha A.D. Wilde at Crystal Lake, 8 February 1871/ Vol. 2a, p. 9.

Immigrants from County Wirsitz, Province Posen, Prussia:

1) BACHMANN, August Herman- b. "Wirsitz, Prussia", marr. Mathilde
   Bertha Schmolter- b. "Prussia"; at Westfield, 22 December 1884/
   Vol. 2a, p. 59.

2) DAHMS, Bertha- b. "Karlsbach, Germ.", marr. Herbert Pearson at
   Westfield, 25 October 1899/ Vol. 3, p. 125.

3) ELSNER, John- b. "Weritz (Wirsitz?), Germany", marr. Emilie
   Schinalofski- b. "Phomirk, Germany"; at Westfield, 15 April
   1885/ Vol. 3, p. 68.

4) FREIHEIT, Wilhelm- b. "Wirsitz, Prussia", marr. Emilie Timm-
   b. "Landsberg (a.d. Warte, Prov. Brandenburg), Prussia"; at
   Newton, 8 December 1887/ Vol. 2a, p. 69.

5) GILGAN(N?), John Jacob- b."Virsitz (Wirsitz), Prussia, Germany",
   marr. Emilie Pauline Raw (Rau?) at Shields, 4 February 1874/
   Vol. 2a, p. 19.

6) KRINKIE (perhaps KROENKE?), Fred- b. "Wesick (Wissek), Germany",
   marr. Gustinia Belter (parents' name 'Stetler'?) at Packwaukee,
   21 January 1895/ Vol. 3, p. 58.

7) KRUEGER, Carl Julius- b. "Wirsitz, Germany", marr. Emma Krause-
   b. "Lipin (Co. Kolmar), Germany"; at Mecan, 10 February 1887/
   Vol. 2a, p. 66.

8) KRUEGER, Julius August- b. "Guntergust (Güntergost), Prussia",
   marr. Auguste E. Dumke- b. "Schönlanke (Co. Czarnikau), Prussia"; at Harrisville, 9 January 1885/ Vol. 2a, p. 59.

9) LUEDTKE, Friedrich- b. "Katzke (Kraczke), Posen, Germany",
   marr. An. Juste. Kremin at Mecan, 10 July 1893/ Vol. 3, p. 38.

10) MORATZ, Carl- b. "Königstreu, Germany", marr. Henriette Wilhel-
    mine Thom at Harrisville, 6 January 1884/ Vol. 2a, p. 56.

11) REIER (nee Hark), Lina- b. "Nackel (Nakel), Germany", marr.
    Carl Petrick- b. "Landsberg a/Warte (Prov. Brandenburg) Ger-
    many"; at Wautoma, Waushara Co., 23 June 1907/ Vol. 3, p. 243.

12) RIEK, Friedrich- b. "Dreidorf", marr. Emielie Guelcow (Guelzow?)- b. "Stolp (co. seat in Pomerania)"; at Neshkoro, 24
September 1894/ Vol. 3,p. 52.

13) SCHWANKE, Johann J.- b. "Gersiwitz (Wirsitz?), Prussia", marr.
Wilhelmine Wagner at Marquette Co., 19 May 1874/ Vol. 2a, p.
20.

14) SEMRO(W?), Julius Carl- b. "Kreis Wirsitz, Posen", marr. Aug.
Emilie Fliegner at Newton, 17 February 1891/ Vol. 3, p. 2.

15) STOENZEL, Gottfried of "Mekan"- b. "Josephkowo (Josephowo)",
marr. Wilhelmine Kochel at "Chrestall Lake", 26 "Mai" 1861/
(no volume and page given).

16) TOBOLT, Wilhelm of Ripon (Fond du Lac Co.), Wisc.- b. "Circuit
Virsity (County Wirsitz), Posen, Germany", marr. Amanda Emma
Meyer at Crystal Lake, 24 May 1900/ Vol. 3, p. 136.

17) WENZEL, Anna- b. "Wesitz (Wirsitz), Prussia", marr. Julius
Schillert- b. "Kolmar, Prussia"; at Springfield, 9 March
1889/ Vol. 2a, p. 74.

18) WENZEL, Emilie H.- b. "Dreidorf, Germany", marr. Herman Rudolph Berndt- b. "Prussia"; at Newton, 23 March 1886/ Vol.
2a, p. 63.

Immigrants from County Obernick, Province Posen, Prussia:

1) ABRAHAM, Gustav Friedrich Albert- b. "Trunaw (Tarnowo?), Germany", marr. Pauline Ida Warnke at Packwaukee, 6 May 1903/ Vol. 3, p. 182.

2) BETHKE, Emma- b. "Taugenthin (?), Kreis Obornisk (County Obernick or Obornik), Herzogthum (Duchy) Posen", marr. Wilhelm Groth at Harrisville, 19 October 1971/ Vol. 3, p. 96.

3) FIERKE, Friedrich- b. Dninbrnok (Obernick?), Prussia", marr. Emilie Hulda Zorn- b. "Radolin (Co. Czarnikau), Prussia"; at Newton, 27 January 1885/ Vol. 2a, p. 59.

4) GRAMS, August- b. "Gramsdorf (village named after family?), Germany", marr. Henriette Auguste Wegner at Crystal Lake, 2 January 1870/ Vol. 2a, p. 5.

5) GRAMSE, Augusta- b. "Radum (Radom), Posen, Germany", marr. Gusstav Wilhelm Zülke (Zuehlke)- b. "Wersk (Co. Flatow, Prov.-) West Prussia, Germany"; at Neshkoro, 23 March 1896/ Vol. 3, p. 77.

6) KRAFKZAK (KRAFTCZAK or KRAWCZYK?), Katie- b. "Gorceino Rogasen, Kreis Obernuk (County Obernick), Pronnill Paren (Province Posen)"; marr, Martin Kirkowski at Montello, 7 January 1902/ Vol. 3, p. 160. (Catholic, probably Polish couple)

7) MENGE (nee KRAUSE), Anna- b. "Kreis Obornic (County Obernick), provinz Posen, Germany", marr. Theo. Karl Teske- b. "Pozen, Germany"; at Crystal Lake, 27 April 1895/ Vol. 3, p. 62.

8) SAGER, August- b. b. "Obernick, Prussia", marr. Pauline Zacharias at Montello, 16 August 1884/ Vol. 2a, p. 57.

9) TODARD, Joseph- b. "Orkernik (Obernick), Germany", marr. Francis Kanerski- b. "Ludom, Germany"; at Princeton, Green Lake Co., 5 January 1901/ Vol. 3, p. 147. (Catholic, probably Polish)

10) WIELGURZ, Francis b. "Obrinsk (Obernick), Posen, Germany", marr. Berth Bartol at Princeton, 5 February 1900/ Vol. 3, p. 130.(Catholic, probably Polish)

MEGAN TOWNSHIP
(1900 Marquette
County Plat Book)

Immigrants from County Schubin, Province Posen, Prussia:

1) FLEMMING, August of Fond du Lac (a county seat), Wisc.- b. "Circuit Schobin (County Schubin), Posen, Germany", marr. Auguste Schmudlach (widow of Daniel Schmudlach, widow of Mr. Hinz, "a-born" Schultz)- b. "Demmau, Posen, Germany"; at Mecan, 11 April 1898/ Vol. 3, p. 104.

2) FOLSKE, Bertha- b. "Salzdorf, Germany", marr. Frantz Fr. W. Ohm-b. "Griebow, Germany"; at Westfield, 21 November 1893/ Vol. 3, p. 43.

3) HARCK, Julius- b. "Veroneka (Veronika), Germany", marr. Hulda Bolke at Neshkoro, 7 November 1899/ Vol. 3, p. 126.

4) HARK, Bertha- b. "Veronika, Posen, Germany", marr. Gustav Ferdinand Bruch- b. "Ischinbowo (Ascherbude or Ivenbusch, Co. Filehne?), Posen, Germany"; at Neshkoro, 5 July 1895/ Vol. 3, p. 66.

5) HAZINSKI, Anna- b. "Exin, Germany, Europe"; marr. Francis Budnick of Milwaukee, Wisc.; at Montello, 10 September 1907/ Vol. 3, p. 245. (Catholic, probably Polish)

6) SCHWANKE, Auguste Ida- b. "Salzdorf, Germany", marr. Emil Robert Hollender at Crystal Lake, 27 December 1888/ Vol. 2a, p. 73.

7) S(CH?)WERSINSKE, Hulda Albertine- b. "Ludeoskowe (Luwikowo), Posen, Germany", marr. Emil Theodor Nest- b. "Augustinu (Augustenau), Co. Kolmar), Posen, Germany"; at Neshkoro, 28 May 1896/ Vol. 3, p. 79.

Immigrants from County Wongrowitz, Province Posen, Prussia:

1) ABRAHAM, Julius Wilhelm- b. "Sar(b)ka, Posen, Germany", marr.
   Ida Rosalie Polinske at Crystal Lake, 13 April 1893/ Vol. 3,
   p. 34.

2) ABRAHAM, Pauline O.- b. "Sar(b)ka, Posen, Germany", marr. Gustav F. Karnath- b. "Danzig (county seat in West Prussia), Germany"; at Newton, 23 February 1888/ Vol. 2a, p. 71.

3) GUST, Gustav Emil- b. "Briesen Holland (-Hauland), Germany",
   marr. Emma Louise Kreuger (father's name Krueger) at Green
   Lake (that county's seat), Wisc., 22 February 1902/ Vol. 3,
   p. 162.

4) HEBBE, Julius- b. "Gallange (Gollantsch or Gollancz), Posen,
   Germany", marr. Emilie Schrank at Newton, 13 October 1897/ Vol.
   3, p. 96.

5) SCHEDLER, Herman Emil- b. "Lukowo, Germany", marr. Ernestine
   Wilhelmine Bundt (nee Kroll) at Mecan, 20 August 1899/ Vol.
   3, p. 123.

6) TONN, Emil Johann- b. "Croposhin (Kopaschin), Germany", marr.
   Hulda Amanda Buchholz at Springfield, 11 March 1900/ Vol. 3,
   p. 133.

7) TONN, Theodor Ed.- b. "Nowen, Posen", marr. Auguste Emilie Sauer at Springfield, 8 April 1890/ Vol. 2a, p. 78.

Immigrants from additional locales in Province Posen, Prussia:

1) BATT, Joseph of Marathon Co., Wisc.- b. "Klulrum, Posen, Prussia", marr. Wilhelmine Wiski- b. "Posen, Prussia"; at Montello, 25 October 1884/ Vol. 2a, p. 58.

2) BRUSTMANN, Adolf- b. "Pczependowo (Szczepanowo, Co. Hohensalza?), Posen, Germany", marr. Alwine Adeline Katzer at Westfield, 26 December 1902/ Vol. 3, p. 174.

3) DAHLKE, Herman Reinhold- b. "Jakobowa (Co. Wongrowitz?), Posen, Germany", marr. Leontine Sophie Baler- b. "Jakowa, Posen, Germany"; at Mecan, 17 March 1894/ Vol. 3, p. 46.

4) GLASKE, Auguste Julia- b. "Harfschewtz (Scharfesort, Co. Samter?), Germany", marr. Gustav Leopold Werner at Westfield, 26 September 1893/ Vol. 3, p. 39.

5) HENKE, Emil- b. "Springberge, Prov. Po, Germ.", marr. Wilhelmine Radke at Harrisville, 2 March 1897/ Vol. 3, p. 88.

6) KLAWITTER, Emil Ludwig- b. "near Friedland, Prov. Posen, Germany", marr. Bertha Pauline Zarbuch at Packwaukee, 21 May 1900/ Vol. 3, p. 137.

7) MALLACH, Albert- b. "Lebinke, Prov. Posen (in actuality, probably Lebehnke, Co. Deutsch Krone, Prov. West Prussia), Germany", marr. Ida Lippert at Harrisville, 28 May 1896/ Vol. 3, p. 78.

8) MATHES, Emma Pauline- b. "Krisherbush, Posen", marr. John Theo. Fred Gley of Rosendale (Fond du Lac Co.), Wisc.- b. "Cremmin, Mecklenburg"; at Neshkoro, 17 November 1892/ Vol. 3, p. 25.

9) MI(E?)TZNER, Wilhelmine- b. "Grabewske, Posen, Germany", marr. Julius Schliepp- b. "Jacobsdorf (co. Saatzig), Pommern (Prov. Pomerania), Germany"; at Neshkoro, 3 July 1896/ (no pagation).

10) PRIEPKE, Bertha- b. "Salin (Zalin, Co. Znin), Germany", marr. August Herman Ebert at Westfield, 11 January 1899/ Vol. 3, p. 115.

11) PRIEPKE, Marie- b. "Svdien (Znin?), Germany", marr. Julius Gutsch(e?) of Grand Forks, North Dakota- b. "Lindenwerda (Lindenwerder, Co. Kolmar), Germany"; at Westfield, 3 March 1892/ Vol. 3, p. 20.

12) REVERS, Anthony- b. "Rogozno, Price (Rogozno the Polish name Rogasen, Kreis=County Obernick) Posen, Germany", marr. Heonrig Pralet- b. "Kreis (County) Posen, Germany"; at Princeton, (Green Lake Co.), 6 February 1900/ Vol. 3, p. 130. (Catholic, probably Polish couple)

13) SCHMIDT, Wilhelm- b. "Netzbruch, Posen", marr. Ottilie Zierke at Montello, 13 April 1887/ Vol. 2a, p. 67.

14) SCHMUDLACH, Auguste (widow of Daniel Schmudlach, widow of Mr. Hinz, "aborn" Schultz)- b. "Demmau, Posen, Germany", marr. August Flemming of Fond du Lac (a county seat), Wisc.- b. "Circuit (County) Schobin (Schubin), Posen, Germany"; at Mecan, 11 April 1898/ Vol. 3, p. 104.

15) SEIDLITZ, Emil K.- b. "Papiermuehle (name of one of at least three places in Counties Birnbaum, Filehne, or Meseritz), Prov. Posen, Germany", marr. Marie Emilie Schulz at Mecan, 30 January 1896/ Vol. 3, p. 74.

16) TESKE, Matilde- b. "Obersitzko (Co. Samter), Germany", marr. Paul A.A. Kenzel at Crystal Lake, 15 January 1893/ Vol. 3, p. 29.

17) WERNER, Daniel (parents- "none", invalid soldier)- b."Radsitz (perhaps Radzicz=Hermannsdorf, County Wirsitz?), Posen, Europe", marr. Charlotte Fenner (nee Gohlke)- b. "Brenkenhaus, Posen, Europe"; at Germania, 22 April 1902/ Vol. 3, p. 164.

18) WERNER, Daniel- b."Raditz, Germany" (see No. 17 above), marr. Rosine Sommerfeld at Montello, 25 March 1898/ Vol. 3, p. 103.

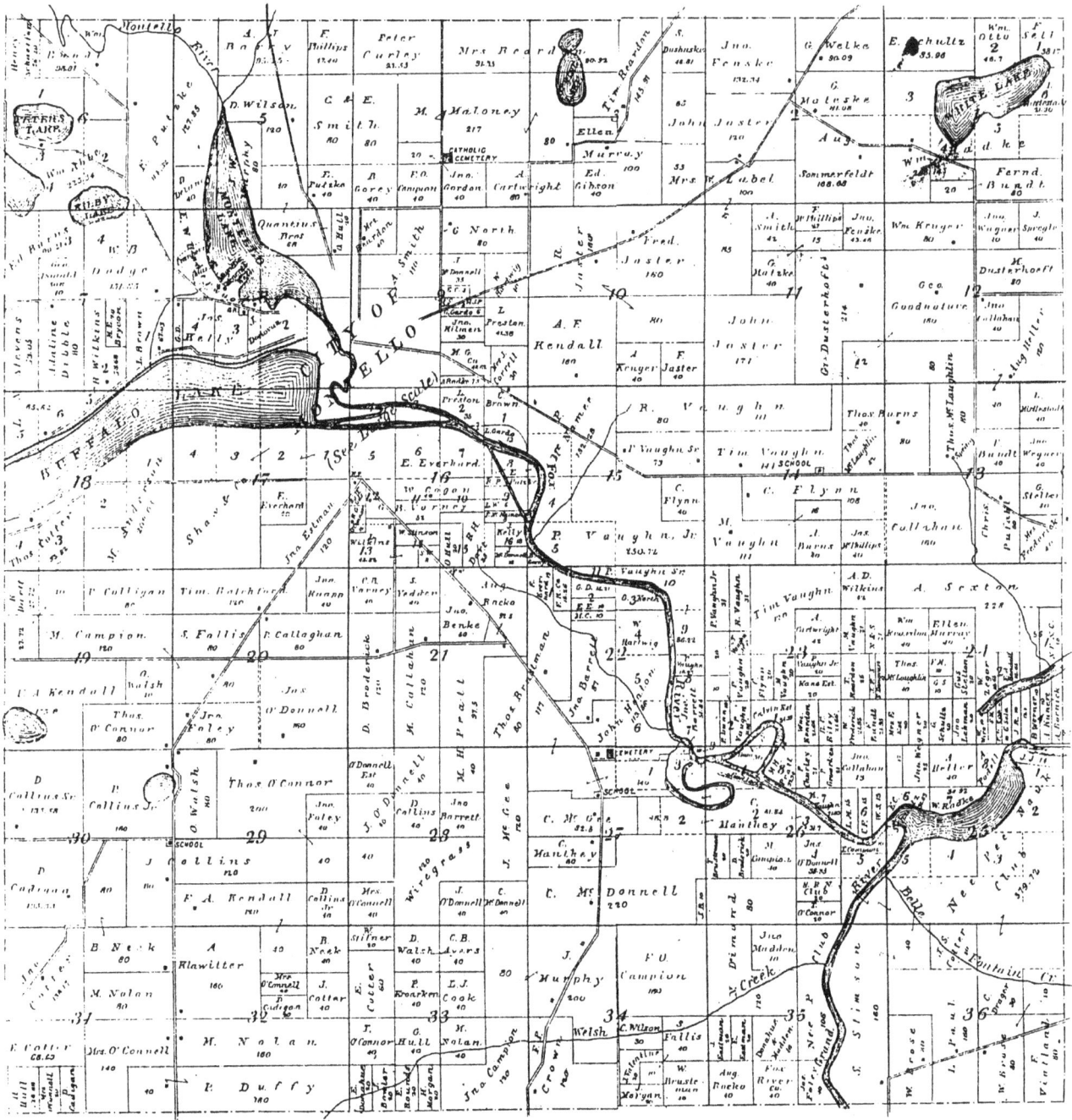

MONTELLO TOWNSHIP (1900 Marquette County Plat Book)

Immigrants from the City, County, Administrative District, or Province of "Posen", Prussia:

1) BOELTER, Adeline Ernestine- b. "Prov. Posen, Germany", marr. Karl Harzbury (?) Puphal- b. "Prov. of Posen, Germany"; at Mecan, 9 January 1895/ Vol. 3, p. 57.

2) BOELTER, August Carl- b. "Prov. of Posen", marr. Albertine Juliane Witt at Crystal Lake, 8 October 1868/ Vol. 1, p. 221.

3) BOELTER, Franz Edward of Oshkosh (Winnebago Co.), Wisc.- b. "Provinze Posen, Germany", marr. Ida Therese Puphal at Montello, 1 September 1900/ Vol. 3, p. 140.

4) BOETTCHER, Agathe Anna- b. "Prov. Posen, Germany", marr. Karl, Robert Walter at Mecan, 14 May 1899/ Vol. 3, p. 120.

5) BORKOSKI, Gabrala- b. "Prussia,Posen", marr. Jos. Dushinske at Montello, 27 January 1886/ Vol. 2a, p. 62.

6) BRUSTMANN, Theodor- b. "Posen, Germ. Europe", marr. Emilie Wilhemine Sager (nee Steifner)- b. "Posen, Germany"; at Mecan, 8 May 1904/ Vol. 3, p. 199.

7) BUCKHOLZ, Wilhem- b. "Province of Posen, Prussia", marr. Henriette Lieske at Shields, 29 December 1858/ Vol. 1, p. 2.

8) BURHARDT, Anthony of Princeton, Green Lake Co.- b. "Posen, Germany"; marr. Magdalena Barankowski at Princeton, 27 January 1903/ Vol. 3, p. 178.

9) CHANNITZ, Johann Aug.- b. "Province of Posen", marr. Dorothea Sophie Schmidt at Crystal Lake, 2 October 1868/ Vol. 1, p. 186.

10) DAHER, Gustav L.- b. "Posen", marr. Bertha Ki(e?)tzman(n?) at Newton, 18 April 1891/ (no pagation).

11) DEGENER, Christian Friedrich- b. "posen, Prussia", marr. An. Ros. Koenig at Shields, 11 March 1859/ Vol. 1, p. 32.

12) DUESTERHOEFT, Wilhelmine- b. "Posen, Germany", marr. William Radke- b. "Posen, Germany" ; at Mecan, 23 April 1885/ Vol. 2a, p. 68.

13) FRITZ, Emil- b. "Provinz Posen", marr. Mary Lippert at Lawrence, 10 October 1889/ Vol. 2a, p. 75.

14) GIESER, John- b. "Posen, Prussia", marr. Mary Magdalena Slavinsky at Neshkoro, 18 April 1893/ Vol. 3, p. 35.

15) GRAHN, Gustav Wilhelm (Sheriff of Marquette Co.)- b. "Province Posen, Germany", marr. Adeline Pauline Marten at Montello, 20 January 1895/ Vol. 3, p. 57.

16) GRIESE, Johann Ludwig- b. "Province Posen, Prussia", marr. Justi Wilmi Bethka at Mecan, 26 December 1858/ Vol. 1, p. 19.

17) HADON, Elvina- b. "Posen, Germany", marr. Joseph Greis of Kingston, Green Lake Co.; at Montello, 29 June 1884/ Vol. 2a, p. 57.

18) HARK, Bertha- b. "Posen", marr. Eduard Kruger of Coloma Station, Waushara Co.- b."West Prussia"; at Neshkoro, 9 April 1890/ Vol. 2a, p. 78.

19) HENNIG, John Ernest- b. "Posen i. Prussia", marr. Wilhelmin_ Krueger at Newton, 15 May 1870/ Vol. 2a, p. 7.

20) JAHNKE,"Giitlieb" (Gottlieb?)- b. "Posen, Prussia", marr. Mariah Eliz. Freitag at Mecan, 12 February 1859/ Vol. 1, p. 27.

21) JAHNS, Samuel of St. Marie, Green Lake Co.- b. "Province of Posen", marr. Auguste Ernestine "Neundorf"? at Crystal Lake, 5 April 1869/ Vol. 2a, p. 2.

22) JOHNKE, Frederick- b. "Posen, Prussia", marr. Emilie Hain at Crystal Lake, 23 March 1869/ Vol. 2a, p. 2.

23) KAEWSKE, Michael- b. "Posen", marr. Anna Binke at Montello, 23 Nov. 1882/ Vol. 2a, p. 50.(Catholic, probably Polish couple)

24) KAJEWSKE, John- b. "Poland in Posen, Germany", marr. Martha Renspies Pufahl- b. "Lobenke, Denchcrone (Lebehnke, Co. Deutsch Krone, Prov. West Prussia), Germany"; at Montello, 21 January 1902/ (no pagation).

25) KEEN (perhaps Kuehn?), Julius- b. "Posen, Prussia", marr. Annae Hillie at Nehskoro, 21 January 1867/ Vol. 1 , p. 146.

26) KIENITZ, Friedrich of Minnesota- b. "Posen", marr. Wilhelmine
Wiederhoeft- b. "Posen"; at Shields, 22 November 1885/ Vol.
2a, p. 62.

27) KLAWITTER, Emil Edward- b. "Posen, Germany", marr. Bertha Laura Zellmer at Mecan, 6 April 1896/ Vol. 3, p. 77.

28) KLAWITTER, Gustav Theodore- b. "Posen, Germany", marr. Ottilie
Therese Blech at Mecan, 21 February 1892/ Vol. 3, p. 19.

29) KOSLOWSKE, Gustav Carl of Richford, Waushara Co.- b. "Provinz
Posen", marr. Emilie Ottilie Schwirsinzki (Schwersenske?)- b.
"Provinz Posen"; at Newton, 13 January 1888/ Vol. 2a, p. 71.

30) KRENTZ, Albert Wilhelm- b. "Prov. Posen, Germany", marr. Clara
Therese Stubbe at Mecan, 2 June 1895/ Vol. 3, p. 65.

31) KRIENKE, Edward- b. "Posen i. Prus.", marr. Augusta Paulin_
Henslin at Mecan, 24 May 1870/ Vol. 2a, p. 7.

32) KRUGER, Rosana- b. "Posen, Prussia", marr. August Winette- b.
"Posen, Prussia"; at Montello, 21 October 1895/ Vol. 3, p. 69.

33) LABRENZ, Johann Gustav of the Town of Marquette, Green Lake Co.-
b. "Posen, Germany", marr. Auguste Wilhelmine Fredrich- b.
"Neu Wesel, Kreis Arnswalde (Neuwedell, Co. Arnswalde, Prov.
Brandenburg), Germany"; at Montello, 23 March 1893/ Vol. 3,
p. 33.

34) LAU, Carl Ludwig- b. "Posen, Prussia", marr. Henriette Warnke
at Crystal Lake, 25 March 1859/ Vol.1, p. 35.

35) LAU, Johann Gottfried- b. "Posen, Prussia", marr. Luise Warnke
at Crystal Lake, 25 March 1859/ Vol. 1, p. 34.

36) MANTEI, Ernst Gotthilf- b. "Posen, Prussia", marr. Emilie W.
Griese at Princeton (now Green Lake Co.), 25 July 1858/ Vol.
1, p. 4.

37) MANTHIE (probably MANTHEY, same as above), Friedrich- b. "Posen, Germany", marr. Wilhelmine Lippert at Harrisville, 15
July 1875/ Vol. 2a, p. 23.

38) MIESKE, Wilhelmine- b. "Posen", marr. Adolph Radke of Neills-
ville (Clark Co.), Wisc.; at Mecan, 25 October 1885/ Vol. 2a,
p. 61.

39) MUELLER, Martin- b. "Prov. of Posen", marr. Emilie Mathilde
Krueger at Crystal Lake, 23 February 1868/ Vol. 1, p. 218.

40) NAHARA, Stanislaus of Green Lake Co.- b. "Posen", marr. Rosa
Borkoski at Montello, 12 January 1879/ Vol. 2a, p. 36. (Catholic, probably Polish couple)

41) NICKEL, Otto Friedrich- b. "Posen, Germany", marr. Myrta Emilie Huntsinger at Montello, 27 March 1900/ Vol. 3, p 133.

42) NICOLAI, Ferdinand- b. "Posen i. Prussia",marr. Ernestine Caroline Weissfenny (Weisspfennig?) at Montello, 1 June 1869/
Vol. 2a, p. 21.

43) PUPHAL, Ernestine Alwine- b. "Posen, Germany", marr. Gustav
Julius Duesterhoeft- b. "Siebenschloess(ch)en (Co. Kolmar),
Posen, Germany"; at Mecan, 29 November 1894/ Vol. 3, p. 55.

44) RICK, Christian- b. "Posen, Prussia", marr. Charoline "Burmund"?
at Princeton (now Green Lake Co.), 31 January 1860/ Vol. 1, p.
79.

45) ROESLER, Wilhelm Heinrich- b. "Posen, Prussia", marr. Wilhel-
mini Caroline Kaeting at Shields, 25 February 1859/ Vol. 1,
p. 30.

46) ROSANSKE, Ewald- b. "Prov. Posen", marr. Emma Frank at Harrisville, 3 April 1893/ Vol. 3, p. 33.

47) SALZWEDEL, Emma Auguste- b. "Posen, Germany", marr. Karl Friedrich Albert Hafeman(n?)- b. "Rege(n)walde, Pommern (Prov. Pomerania), Germany"; at Mecan, 25 August 1894/ Vol. 3, p. 51.

48) SCHEDLER, Auguste Julia- b. "Provinz Posen, Germany", marr.
Friedrich Menge- b. "Provinz Brandenburg, Germany"; at Montello,
24 April 1898/ Vol. 3, p. 105.

49) SCHMIDT, Carl (widowed)- b. "Posen, Germany", marr. Mrs. Elisabeth Koegel (also widowed)- b. "Germany"; at Montello, 4 March
1903/ Vol. 3, p. 179.

NESHKORO

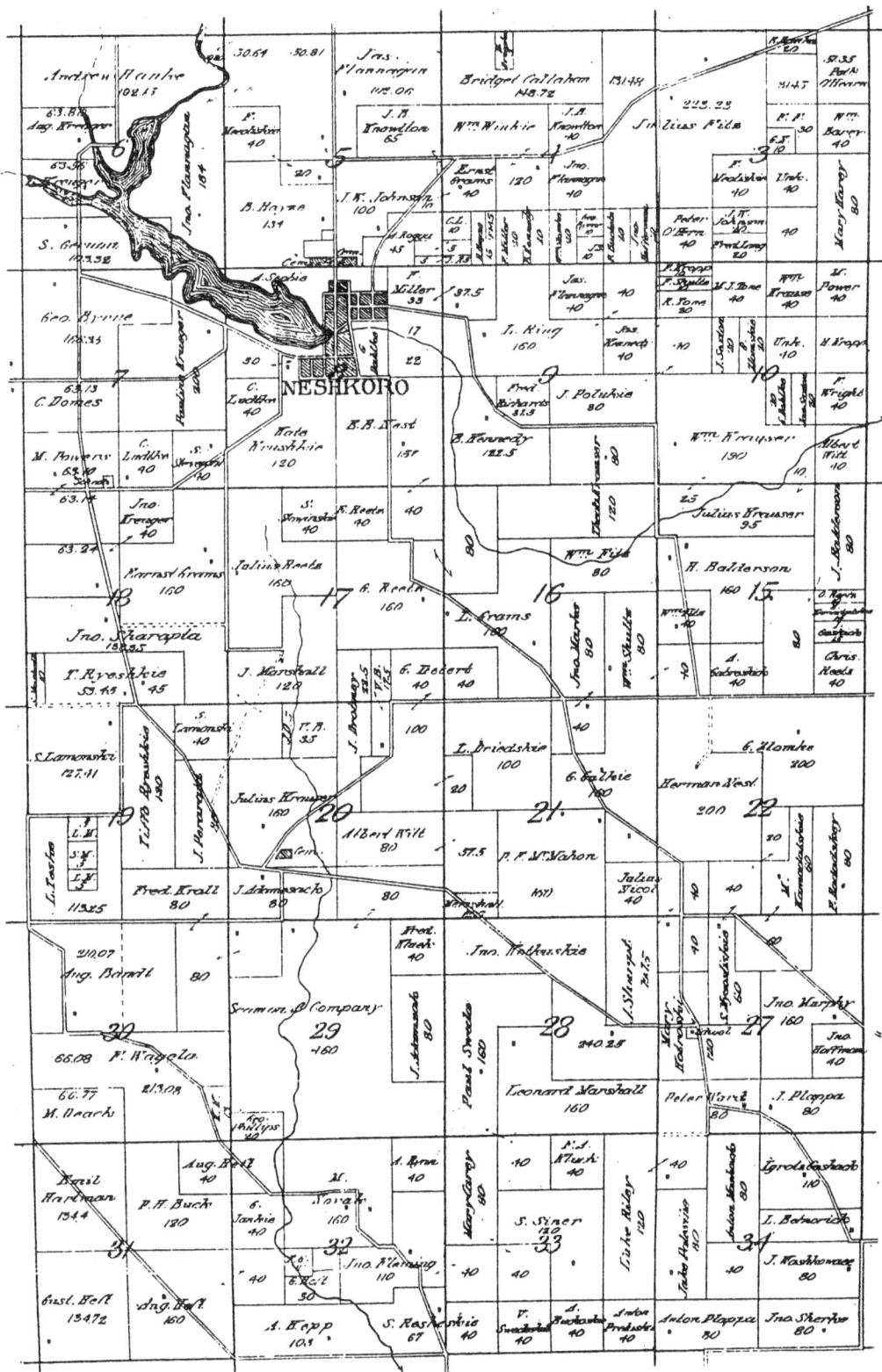

NESHKORO TOWNSHIP (1900 Marquette County Plat Book)

50) SCHMIDT, Maria- b. "Posen, Germ.", marr. Karl Ludwig Stibb-
b. "Pozen, Germany"; at Mecan, 15 April 1895/ Vol. 3, p. 62.

51) SCHULTZ, Ernst Gustav- b. "Posen, Germany", marr. Augusta Alwine Klingbeil at Mecan, 3 January 1893/ Vol. 3, p. 28.

52) SEIDLITZ, Emil Herman- b. "Prov. Posen, Germany", marr. Ida
Wilhelmine Nehring at Mecan, 18 February 1896/ Vol. 3, p. 75.

53) SEIDLITZ, Emma Alvine- b. "Provinz Posen, Germany", marr. Emil
Julius Zuge of West Rosendale (Fond du Lac Co.), Wisc.; at Mecan, 13 December 1893/ Vol. 3, p. 43.

54) SIEWERT, Julius- b. "Prov. of Posen, Prussia, Germania", marr.
Henrietta Wilhelmina Hammerschmidt at Mecan, 26 April 1868/
Vol. 1, p. 205.

55) SOMMERFELD, Christoph Edward- b. "Posen, Prussia", marr. Henrietta Schwark at Crystal Lake, 29 March 1869/ Vol. 2a, p. 2.

56) SOMMERFELDT, Rudolph H.- b. "Prov. Posen", marr. Emma Doege-
b. "Neumark (Prov. Brandenburg?)"; at Newton, 29 April 1891/
(no pagation)

57) STANKIE, Minnie- b. "Posen, Prussian Poland", marr. Chas. Shar-
lan of Berlin, Green Lake Co.; at Berlin, Green Lake Co., 14
January 1898/ Vol. 3, p. 102. (Catholic, probably Polish)

58) STAPEL, Ernst Johann of Springville, Columbia Co. (Wisc.)-
b. "Posen, Germany"; marr. Anna Margaretha Zellmer at Mecan,
3 May 1903/ Vol. 3, p. 182.

59) STELTER, Johann Gottlieb- b. "Prussia, Posen", marr. Ernestine
Wilhelmin_ Grahn at Mecan, 5 September 1869/ Vol. 2a, p. 4.

60) STUBBE, Gottfried- b. "Prov. Posen, Prussia", marr. Henr(i)ette
W. Vandrey (Wandrey?) at Crystal Lake, 22 September 1858/ Vol.
1, p. 5.

61) TESKE, Theo. Karl- b. "Pozen, Germany", marr. Anna Menge (nee
Krause)- b. "Kreis Obornic (County Obernick), provinz Posen,
Germany"; at Crystal Lake, 27 April 1895/ Vol. 3, p. 62.

62) VOGE, Johann G.- b. "Prov. Posen, Prussia", marr. Wilhelmine Streich at Mecan, 18 October 1858/ Vol. 1, p. 6.

63) WENDTLAND, Emma- b. "Prov. Posen, Germany", marr. Emil Erdmann- b. "Strosewa (Strozewo, Co. Kolmar), Germany"; at Harrisville, 19 April 1896/ Vol. 3, p. 79.

64) WENTLAND, Fred'k Aug.- b. "Posen, Germany", marr. Maria Magdalena Dretke at Neshkoro, 18 March 1896/ Vol. 3, p. 79.

65) WERNER (or WESNER?), Frederick August- b. "Posen i. Prussia", marr. Bertha Auguste Zellmer at Crystal Lake, 25 February 1870/ Vol. 2a, p. 6.

66) WILKE, Gottfried Samuel- b. "Posen, Prussia", marr. Wilhelmina Menge at Shields, 19 November 1858/ Vol. 1, p. 1.

67) WISKI, Wilhelmine- b. "Posen, Prussia", marr. Joseph Batt- b. "Klulrum, Posen, Prussia", of Marathon Co., Wisc.; at Montello, 25 October 1884/ Vol. 2a, p. 58.

68) WITT, Johann Aug.- b. "Posen, Germany", marr. Auguste Otto (widow, nee Lenz) at Mecan, 28 July 1885/ Vol. 2a, p. 61.

69) WORM (or WONN?), Johann Wilhelm- b. "Posen i. Prussia", marr. Ittilie Wilhelmine Wett at Princeton (now Green Lake Co.), 29 August 1869/ Vol. 2a, p. 4.

70) ZACHERIAS, H.F.- b."Posen, Germany", marr. Bertha Mittelstadt at Mecan, 5 December 1895/ Vol. 3, p. 71.

71) ZELLMER, Martin- b. "Posen-Prussia", marr. Emilie Horent. Auguste Bartz at Neshkoro, 2 March 1859/ Vol. 1, p. 31.

72) ZEMPEL, Reinhold of Minnesota- b. "Posen, Germany", marr. Henriette Petrich at Mecan, 20 October 1884/ Vol. 2a, p. 58.

Immigrants from County Deutsch Krone, Province West Prussia:

1) BRIESE, Caroline H.- b. "Lebehnke, Prussia", marr. Thomas J.C. Lackein- b. "Burangen, England"; at Harrisville, 26 February 1888/ Vol. 2a, p. 70.

2) EICHSTEDT, Gustav- b. "Deutsch Krone, Germany", marr. Hulda Buschke- b. "Lindenwerter (Lindenwerder, Co. Kolmar), Posen, Germany"; at Newton, 6 April 1893/ Vol. 3, p. 34.

3) MUSKE, August- b. "Dentosch Rione (Deutsch Krone), Germany", marr. Emma Schmudlack at Newton, 25 June 1901/ Vol. 3, p. 150.

4) MUSKE, Fred- b. "Salem (Salm), Germany", marr. Minnie Kottke at Neshkoro, 5 October 1905/ Vol. 3, p. 220.

5) MUSKE, Ida- b. "Salemshuette (Salmer Glashütte), Germany", marr. Adolf Schrank at Newton, 14 April 1898/ Vol. 3, p. 103.

6) MUSKE, Martha- b. "Lamische Hiebbe (Salmer Glashütte), Germany", marr. Herman Emil Schrank at Springfield, 1 October 1901/ Vol. 3, p. 156.

7) MUSKE, Minna- b. "Deutsch Krone, Germany", marr. Gustav Schumann at Newton, 29 December 1897/ Vol. 3, p. 100.

8) PUFAHL, Martha Renspies (previously married?)- b. "Lobenke, Denchcrone (Lebehnke, Deutsch Krone), Germany", marr. John Kajewske- b. "Poland in Posen, Germany"; at Montello, 21 January 1902/ Vol. 3, p. 160.

9) SCHMIDT, Emil- b. "New Lebenge (Neu-Lebehnke), Germany", marr. Lydia Amanda Pockrandt at Springfield, 30 August 1899/ Vol. 3, p. 123.

Immigrants from County Flatow, Province West Prussia:

1) HOLLANDER, Gustav T.- b. "Flatho (Flatow), Prussia", marr. Carolin_ A. Just at Crystal Lake, 6 January 1871/ Vol. 2a, p. 9.

2) KLAWITTER, Albert Gustav- b. "Batrowo (Battrow), Germany", marr. Therese Louise Weyer at Montello, 15 March 1899/ Vol. 3, p. 117.

3) KLAWITTER, August- b. "Lobza (Lubcza), Prussia", marr. Auguste Schonfeld at Harrisville, 31 January 1888/ Vol. 2, p. 70.

4) SEEHAFER, Gottlieb- b. "Nichorsz, West Preussen (Nichors, West Prussia), Germany", marr. Lina Seidlitz- b. "Gross Lubs bei Kreuz (Co. Filehne), Posen, Germany"; at Germania, 20 February 1894/ Vol.3, p. 48.

5) WEINKAUF, Auguste- b. "Greunhinde (Grünlinde), Westpreussen (West Prussia), Germany", marr. August Becker at Crystal Lake, 6 May 1893/ Vol. 3, p. 36.

6) ZUEHLKE, Gustav- b. "Werks (Wersk), Kr. Flatow, Germany", marr. Bertha Alwine Podoll- b. "Jacherjewski?, Germany"; at Newton, 9 January 1894/ Vol. 3, p. 45.

7) ZÜLKE, Gustav Wilhelm (same as above)- b. "Wersk, West Prussia, Germany", marr. Auguste Gramse- b. "Radum (Radom, Co. Obernick), Posen, Germany"; at Neshkoro, 23 March 1896/ Vol. 3, p. 77.

NEWTON TOWNSHIP (1900 Marquette County Plat Book)

Immigrants from additional locales in Province West Prussia:

1) BOY, Emil Carl Leopold- b. "Danzig (a county seat), Prussia, Germany", marr. Justine Zellmer at Crystal Lake, 19 November 1869/ Vol. 2a, p. 5.

2) DOBRINSKE, Friedrich- b. "Budziszewa, West Prussia", marr. Auguste Thim (probably Timm?) at Crystal Lake, 18 January 1883/ Vol. 2a, p. 52.

3) DOBRINSKI, Hermann Leopold- b. "Hohenkirch (Co. Briesen in Wpr.), Germany", marr. Adeline Wilhelmine Conrad at Springfield, 28 February 1901/ Vol. 3, p. 147.

4) HORNBURG, Mrs. Pauline "a"(nee) Mielke- b. "Westpreussen, Germany", marr. Friedrich Wilhelm Malinowsky- b. "Westpreussen, Germany"; at Mecan, 10 October 1903/ Vol. 3, p. 189.

5) KARNATH, Gustav F.- b. "Danzig, Germany", marr. Pauline O. Abraham- b. "Sar(b)ka (Co. Wongrowitz), Posen, Germany"; at Newton, 23 February 1888/ Vol. 2a, p. 71.

6) KRUGER, Eduard of Coloma Station, Waushara Co.- b. "West Prussia", marr. Bertha Hark- b. "Posen"; at Neshkoro, 9 April 1890/ Vol. 2a, p. 78.

7) MARCHEL, Catherine- b."Kreiss Wjnnysk (?), West Prussia", marr. Anton Polus at Princeton, Green Lake Co., 9 Janaury 1900/ Vol. 3, p. 130. (Catholic, probably Polish couple)

8) SEEHAWER, Gustav of Princeton, Green Lake Co.- b. "West Prussia", marr. Adaline Baethke- b. "Germany"; at Mecan, 7 December 1887/ Vol. 2a, p. 68.

9) STROHSCHEIN, Emil Hermann- b. "Kolun- or Kohenkirche (probably Hohenkirche, Co. Briesen?), Germany", marr. Alwine Bertha Schubert at Westfield, 21 August 1906/ Vol. 3, p. 231.

10) WEILAND, Albert August Luis- b. "Katzibur, West Prussia, Europe" (perhaps Ratzebuhr, Co. Neustettin, Prov. Pomerania?), marr. Minna Ida Meyer at Germania, 14 March 1899/ Vol. 3, p. 118.

11) WEISHAAR, Friedrich Herman- b. "Bloden (Bladau, Co. Tuchel?), Prussia", marr. Minna Wras(s)e- b. "New Stettin (Prov. Pomerania), Prussia"; at Harrisville, 29 December 1885/ (no pagation).

Immigrants from County Arnswalde, Province Brandenburg, Prussia:

1) ABIL (ABEL?), Albert Herm. Edward- b. "Arnswalde, Germany",
marr. Alvine Ida Dahlke at Neshkoro, 15 April 1895/ Vol. 3, p.
62.

2) BENZ, Wilhelm- b. "Zuelsdorf, Germany", marr. Otelie (Ottilie?)
Block at Harrisville, 16 January 1895/ Vol. 3, p. 57.

3) FREDRICH, Auguste Wilhelmine Bertha- b. "Neu Wesel (Neuwedell),
Kreis (County) Arnswalde, Germany", marr. Johann Gustav Labrenz
of the Town(ship) of Marquette, Green Lake Co.- b. "Posen, Germany"; at Montello, 23 March 1893/ Vol. 3, p. 33.

4) MILBRANDT, August Ferdinand- b. "Segensdorf (Zagendorf), Circuit
(Kreis=County, a literal translation) Arnswalde, Germany", marr.
Alvine Pauline Stelter- b. "Gembitz (Co. Czarnikau), Posen, Ger-
many"; at Mecan, 14 February 1900/ Vol. 3, p. 132.

5) MUELLER, Wiiliam- b. "Rohrbeck, Germany", marr. Emilie Kirst at
Springfield, 27 December 1899/ Vol. 3, p. 128.

6) PESCHEL, Johann Karl August- b. "Klein Kurtesenau (Fürstenau),
Germany", marr. Martha Maria Elis. Nehring- b. "Arnswalde, Germany"; at Springfield, 19 February 1894/ Vol. 3, p. 47.

7) PETRICK, Karl Fredrick- b. "Curtow (Kürtow), Brandenburg, Germany", marr. Bertha Auguste Bölke- b. "Veronika (Co. Schubin),
Posen, Germany"; at Neshkoro, 19 April 1897/ Vol. 3, p. 90.

8) SALZWEDEL, Auguste Wilhelmine- b. "Pamin (Pammin), Germany",
marr. Wilhelm Floeter- b. "Gross Drensen (Co. Czarnikau, Prov.
Posen), Germany"; at Crystal Lake, 5 January 1888/ Vol. 2a, p.
70.

9) SCHULTZ, Wilhelmine- b. "Pratznick (Kratznik), Germany", marr.
Carl F. Dee- b. "Amt-Kartz, Germany"; at Marion, Waushara Co.,
18 April 1907/ Vol. 3, p. 42.

10) SMITH, Christian- b. "Reichenbach, Germany", marr. Minnie Kohn-
b. "Germany"; at Oxford, 19 December 1906/ Vol. 3, p. 235.

11) WEBER, Johann Gottlieb Fried. of Princeton, Green Lake Co.- b.
"Sellnow, Germany", marr. Auguste Wilhelmine Mietzner- b. "Germany"; at Germania, 14 April 1887/ Vol. 2a, p. 67.

Immigrants from additional locales in Province Brandenburg, Prussia:

1) BILLING, Ellick- b. "Berlin, Germany", marr. Bertha Louisa
   Kropp at Marion, Waushara Co., 19 November 1903/ Vol. 3, p. 189.

2) BUCKHOLE (BUCHHOLZ?), Fredrick- b. Frankfort (Frankfurt), Prussia", marr. Austeni (Ernestine?) Wilhelmina Patenick (Petrich?)
   at Mecan, 30 June 1859/ Vol. 1, p. 26.

3) DOEGE, Emma- b."Neumark", marr. Rudolph H. Sommerfeldt- b.
   "Prov. Posen"; at Newton, 29 April 1891/ (no pagation).

4) H(E?)YER, Helena Auguste Pauline- b. "Berlin, Prussia", marr.
   Ernst Gottlob Henke at Neshkoro, 15 December 1892/ Vol. 3, p.
   27.

5) KAMP, Friedrich- b. "Kreuzdorf, Brandenburg, Germany", marr.
   Ernestine Streich at Harrisville, 26 December 1897/ Vol. 3, p.
   100.

6) KURZBEIN, Julius Edward- b. "Frankfort (Frankfurt), Prussia",
   marr. Ottilie L. Albrecht at Newton, 9 February 1870/ Vol. 2a,
   p. 6.

7) MEIER, Ernst of Marquette, Green Lake Co.- b. "Friedeberg(Co.
   Friedeberg/Neumark?), Germany", marr. Auguste E. Bohn at Mecan,
   15 November 1888/ Vol. 2a, p. 73.

8) MENGE, Friedrich- b. "Provinz Brandenburg, Germany", marr. Auguste Julia Schedler- b. "Provinz Posen, Germany"; at Montello,
   24 April 1898/ Vol. 3, p. 105.

9) OTTO, Wilhelm F. of Abbotsford (Marathon Co.), Wisc.- b.
   "Schwedt Ander Over (an der Oder river, Prov. Brandenburg),
   Germania", marr. Ida A. Meinke at Westfield, 11 July 1904/ Vol.
   3, p. 203.

10) PETRICK, Carl of Wautoma, Waushara Co.- b. "Landsberg a/Warte
    Germany", marr. Lina Reier (nee Hark)- b. "Nackel (Nakel, Co.
    Wirsitz, Prov. Posen), Germany"; at Wautoma, 23 June 1907/(no
    pagation).

11) POST, Ernst Wilhelm- b. "Neue Sping, Brandenburg, Germany", marr. Minna Streich at Harrisville, 1 December 1896/ Vol. 3, p. 83.

12) ROHDE, Ottilie Mathilde- b. "Driesen (Co. Friedeberg/Neumark), Germany", marr. Gottfried August Alff of Seneca, Green Lake Co.- b. "Cornosinan (?), Germany"; at Crystal Lake, 29 November 1896/ Vol. 3, p. 86.

13) SALZWEDEL, Friedrich William- b. "Prov. of Brandenburg, Germany", marr. Johanna Wilhelmina Zimmermann at Crystal Lake, 27 February 1868/ Vol. 1, p. 219.

14) SMITH, Feidor(?) Martha- b. "Europe, Berlin", marr. John Smith at Oxford, 22 April 1894/ Vol. 3, p. 49.

15) VERTH, Wilhelm H. of Princeton, Green Lake Co.- b. "Neumark, Germany", marr. Pauline O. Reetz at Neshkoro, 9 February 1888/ Vol. 2a, p. 70.

16) WIENKE, Anna Maria Louise- b. "Breitenstein, Brandenburg, Prussia", marr. John Ernst Emil Schulz of Marion, Waushara Co.; at Neshkoro, 30 August 1897/ Vol. 3, p. 94.

17) WIENKE, Ernestine Wilhelmine- b. "Braunziehn, Brandenburg, Prussia, Germany", marr. Otto Edward Schulz of Marion, Waushara Co.; at Neshkoro, 23 August 1897/ Vol. 3, p. 94.

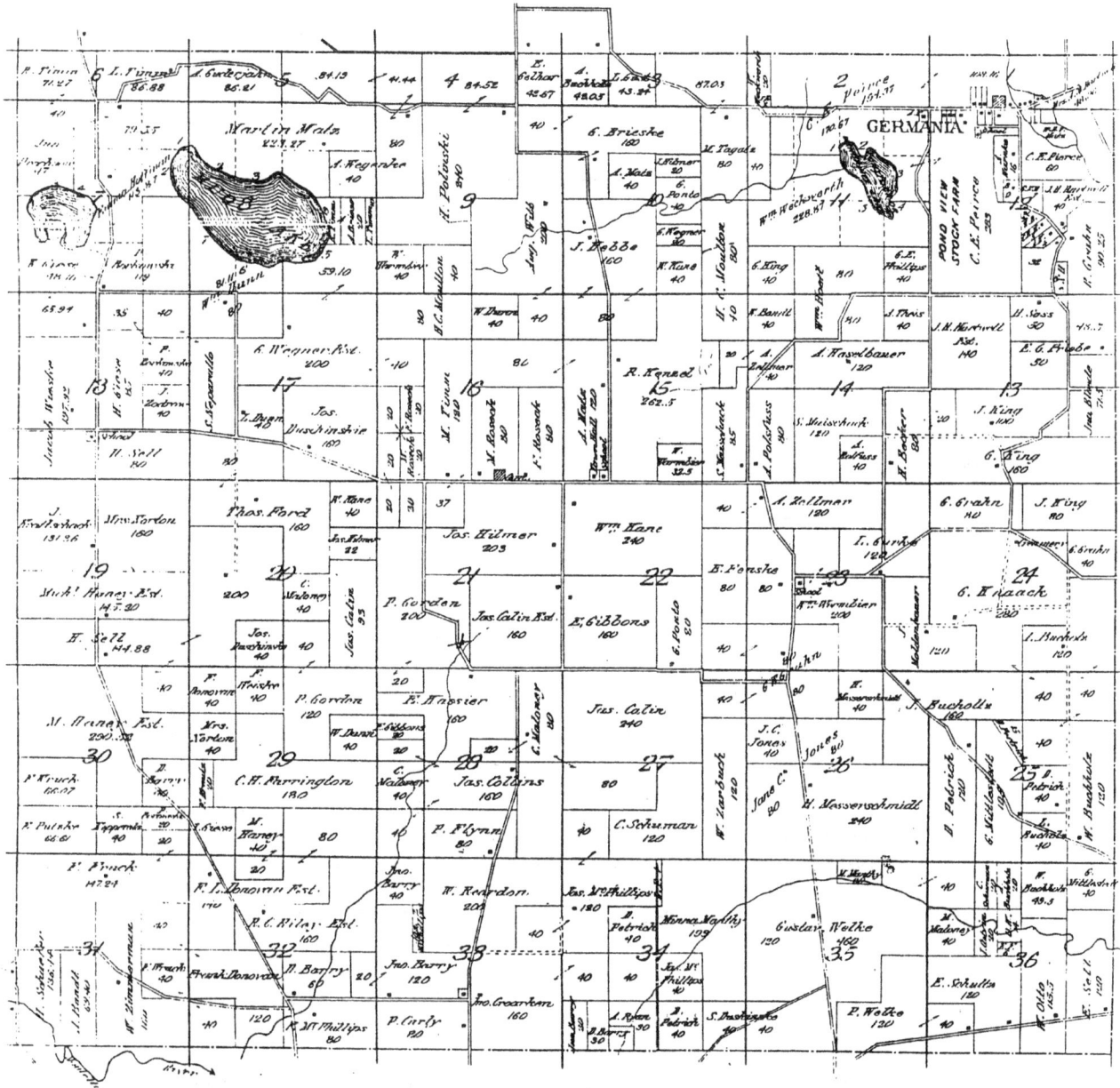

SHIELDS TOWNSHIP (1900 Marquette County Plat Book)

GERMANIA

Immigrants from Province Pomerania, Prussia:

1) BLEDOW, August Ferdinand Franz- b. "New Stettin (Neustettin, a a county seat), Prussia", marr. Bertha Emilie (a widow, nee-) Wegner at Crystal Lake, 27 January 1869/ (no pagation).

2) BRAUN, Wilhelm Carl F. of Hancock, Waushara Co.- b. "Pommern (Pomerania)", marr. Karoline Louise Schleif- b. "Pommern"; at Crystal Lake/Newton, 30 January 1889/ Vol. 2a, p. 75.

3) EHLERT, Gustav Emil Richard- b. "Pasenalk (Pasewalk, Co. Ueck-ermunde), Germany", marr. Bertha Lena (?) at Mecan, 26 June 1901/ Vol. 3, p. 151.

4) FRIEDRICH, Karl August Friedrich of Scott (Township), Columbia Co. (Wisc.)- b. "Pommern, Germany", marr. Ella Delilia Jepson at Mecan, 31 August 1904/ Vol. 3, p. 204.

5) GAELCOW (Guelzow?), Emielie- b. "Stolp (a county seat)", marr. Friedrich Riek- b. "Dreidorf (Co. Wirsitz, Prov. Posen)"; at Neshkoro, 24 September 1894/ (No pagation).

6) GUEGE, John Frederick William of Berlin, Green Lake Co.- b. "Stettin (a county seat), Prussia", marr. Albertine Brose at Crystal Lake, 21 December 1871/ Vol. 2a, p. 12.

7) GULZOW (see No. 5 above), Emilie- b. "Stolp, Pommern, Germany", marr. Friedrich Schmode of P$_0$y Sippi, Waushara Co.- b. "Stolp, Pommern, Germany"; at Neshkoro, 1 March 1894/ Vol. 3, p. 47.

8) HAFEMAN(N?), Karl Friedrich Albert- b. "Rege(n)walde (a county seat), Pommern, Germany", marr. Emma Auguste Salzwedel- b. "Posen, Germany"; at Mecan, 25 August 1894/ Vol. 3, p. 51.

9) HARTWIG, Friedrich Wm. F.- b. "Pommern", marr. Pauline Al. Imm at Newton, 28 March 1890/ Vol. 2a, p. 78.

10) KRUEGER, Bernhard- b. "Zehnin bei Stettin, Germany", marr. Ida Brisch at Germania, 29 January 1893/ Vol. 3, p. 30.

11) MUELLER, Friedrick- b. "New Buckow (Neu-Buckow, Co. Bublitz, Adm. Dist. Köslin), Germany", marr. Maria Briese at Packwaukee, 13 July 1898/ Vol. 3, p. 107.

12) PLOETZ, Wilhelm- b. "Pommern, Germany", marr. Lina Kuhn at Montello, 27 October 1897/ Vol. 3, p. 96.

13) POMPLUN, Emil Friedrich- b. "Wussow (either Co. Rummelsburg or Co. Lauenberg), Germany", marr. Ida Amalie Maik at Newton, 20 April 1898/ Vol. 3, p. 64.

14) POMPLUN, Otto- b. Wus(s)ow (Co. Lauenberg or Co. Rummelsburg), Germany", marr. Alwina Zieske at Springfield, 8 March 1892/ Vol. 3, p. 20.

15) POOCH, Henry J.- b. "Krus Rummelsbary (Kreis=County Rummelsburg), Germany", marr. Wilhelmine H. Schwinger at St. Marie (Township), Green Lake Co., 1 January 1874/ (No pagation).

16) REIMANN, Paul Hermann- b. "Stargard (seat of Co. Saatzig), Germany", marr. Alvine Emilie Hallman at Newton, 19 April 1892/ Vol. 3, p. 22.

17) RIEMER, Mr. Gottlieb Christian, a rag peddler from Princeton, Green Lake Co.- b. "Grossgestin, Pommern, Germany", marr. Henrietta Friederike Schram- b. "Germany, Europe"; at Mecan, 31 December 1904/ Vol. 3, p. 210.

18) RUTZ, Herman- b. "Cose Muehl, Pommern, Germany", marr. Emilie Pauline Warmbier at Mecan, 28 December 1893/ Vol. 3, p. 44.

19) SCHMIDT, Ferdinand Emil-of Milwaukee (county seat), Wisc.- b. "Pommern in Europe", marr. Juliana Wurch- b. "Russia in Europe"; at Germania, 12 April 1903/ Vol. 3, p. 180.

20) SCHULS (SCHULZ), Emil of Phillips (Price Co.), Wisc.- b. "Galice (Kallies, Co. Dramburg), Pommern, Germany", marr. Augusta Stelter (author's grand-aunt)- b. "Golmar (Kolmar, Prov. Posen), Germany"; at Springfield, 22 January 1902/ Vol. 3, p. 161.

21) TETZLAFF, Ernst- b. "Trilesow, Pommern, Germany", marr. Anna Christine Buchholz at Neshkoro, 14 April 1898/ Vol. 3, p. 104.

22) WACH(H?)OLTZ, Tielka Louise- b. "Lolten (Lottin), Neu, Stetten (Co. Neustettin), Prussia", marr. Wilhelm F. Miller at Crystal Lake, 18 March 1897/ (No pagation).

23) *WARGOWSKY, Julius Erdman(n?) of Quincy (Township), Adams Co. (Wisc.)- b. "Pommern", marr. Emma Pauline Ki(e?)tzmann at Newton, 18 April 1892/ Vol. 3, p. 21.

24) WRAS(S?)E, Minna- b. "New Stettin (Neustettin), Prussia", marr. Friedrich Herman Weishaar- b. "Bloden (Bladau, Co. Tuchel, Prov. West Prussia?), Prussia"; at Harrisville, 29 December 1885/ (No pagation).

25) ZEL(L?)MER, Wilhelm Ferd.- b. "Pommern, Germany", marr. Clara Amalie Weis(s?)haar at Newton, 10 January 1899/ Vol. 3, p. 115.

(*Note: In Adams Co. marriage record for Julius Erdmann Wargwosky and Hattie Louisa (Podoll) "Hagemann" (Hockerman), 22 August 1886/ Vol. 3, p. 31; his hometown is given as "Gohren, Pommern".)

Immigrants from not readily identifiable locales in "Prussia":

1) FRANK, Carl A.- b. "Demberg, Prussia" (perhaps Dembogora, Co. Schubin, Prov. Posen?), marr. Ernestine W. Krueger at Crystal Lake, 24 March 1871/ Vol. 2a, p. 10.

2) JAHNKE, Johann Friedrick of Minnesota- b. "Antonia, Prussia" (perhaps Antonienhof, Co. Kolmar, Prov. Posen?), marr. Ernestine Maria Kenzel at Shields, 23 May 1873/ Vol. 2a, p. 16.

3) KIERSKI, Walter- b. "Malawa, Prussia" (perhaps any number of places named Malachowo?), marr. Catharina Nolan- b. "Minneapolis, Minn."; at Montello, 14 February 1906/ Vol. 3, p. 224.

4) KIETZMANN, Michael- b. "Rositz, Prussia" (perhaps Rusiec, Co. Znin, Prov. Posen? or more likely, Rositz, Altenburg district, Prov. Sachsen=Saxony), marr. Auguste Reinke at Mecan, 21 January 1862/ (No pagation).

5) KROPP, Hermann Eduard- b. "Langwitz, Prussia, Europe" (perhaps a Haltestelle=stopping place between Erfurt & Thüringer Wald in central Germany?), marr. Auguste Wilhelmine Krause at Neshkoro, 13 December 1905/ Vol. 3, p. 228.

6) KRUEGER, August- b. "Snomadnow, Prussia", marr. Auguste Ebend at Mecan/Princeton, 24 November 1858/ Vol. 1, p. 2.

7) LIPPERT, Wilhelm- b. "Rilzig, Prussia", marr. Auguste Ottilie Berndt at Crystal Lake, 14 January 1874/ Vol. 2a, p. 19.

8) MATZ, John Julius- b. "Holland in Prussia" (a Hauland or Co. Prussian Holland, Prov. East Prussia?), marr. Wilhelmene Suchol at Crystal Lake, 3 December 1869/ Vol. 2a, p. 5.

9) SCHALK, Johanne Louise- b. "Loneberg, Prussia" (perhaps Lüneberg, a county seat in Prov. Hannover, or Lohnberg, a district town in Prov. Hessen-Nassau or Alt-Lüneberg by Bremerhaven?), marr. Gustav Friedrich Busse at Springfield, 26 March 1894/ Vol. 3, p. 47.

10) TIMM, Emilie- b. "Landsberg, Prussia" (perhaps Landsberg a/Warte, Prov. Brandenburg or Landsberg i. Preussen, Co. Preussisch Eylau, Prov. East Prussia?), marr. Wilhelm Freiheit- b. "Wirsitz (co. seat in Prov. Posen), Prussia"; at Newton, 8 December 1887/ Vol. 2a, p. 69.

11) WITTHUHN, Carl of Elmore (Fairbault Co.), Minn.- b. "Rutsberg, Prussia" (perhaps Ratzebuhr, Co. Neustettin, Prov. Pomerania, or Ratzeburg, near Lauenburg south of Lübeck in Mecklenburg?), marr. Auguste Meyer at Springfield, 23 December 1887/ Vol. 2a, p. 69.

Immigrants from the Grand Duchies of Mecklenburg (-Schwerin & -Stre-
litz):

1)   BEHRENS, Konrad, a clergyman- b. "Wismar, Mecklenburg (-Schwerin),
     Germany", marr. Emma Krentz at Newton, 3 July 1895/ Vol. 3, p.
     65.

2)   BELOW, Joe of Byron twp., Fond du Lac Co. (Wisc.)- b. "Mecklen-
     burg, Schwerin, Germany", marr. Emilie Fitzke (nee Pohl)- b.
     Constantine, Russia"; at Harrisville, 23 November 1904/ Vol. 3,
     208.

3)   GLEY, John Theo. Fred. of Rosendale (Fond du Lac Co.), Wisc.-
     b. "Cremmin, Mecklenburg", marr. Emma Pauline Mathes- b. "Krish-
     erbush, Posen"; at Neshkoro, 17 November 1892/ Vol. 3, p. 25.

4)   HOPPNER, Heinrich- b. "Schiserim, Mecklenburg", marr. Hulda Aug.
     Messersmith at Westfield, 16 April "1865" (1895?)/ Vol. 3, p.
     66.

5)   SCHAUENBERG, Carl Christian Frederick- b. "Baimkow, Mecklenburg-
     Schwerin, Germany", marr. Anna Elisa Marquar(d?)t at Crystal
     Lake, 12 July 1868/ (No pagation).

PILOT KNOB P. O.

C. Werner 103.78
B. Allen 94
L. Brooks 12.37
J. Ayers 14.79
Wm. Sohr 80
E. Church
Wm. Sohr 207.02
J. Noble 40
J.S. Phelps 40
C. Sonnenberg 78.38
J.H. Maynard 143.13
H. Sonnenberg 40
F. Leiske 80
C. Leiske 80

W. J. Miller 146.46
F.C.C. Miller 133.81
Van Slyke 153.57
A. Sanford 120
H. Weiskaar 130
G. Chensebro
C. Knitter 120
Chas. Knitter
Chas. Wachholtz
Henry Clocksin 160
S. Pond 110
C. Lebell 80
A.H. Nickell 160
A.H. Nickell 10
Horace Gibbs 160
A. Pekoskey

Lud. Press 100
Tagatz 140

C. Hohenweiler 88.30
A. Rosanske 80
A. Rosanske 63.63
Fred. Frank 63.78
Rosanske 120
Gus. Pockrandt 200
C. Wachholtz
O. Wachholtz
H. Pockrandt 80
A. Wruck 320
Fred. Baugch 160
A. Schrank 40
A. Duesterhoeft 280

Fred. Frank 1421
F. Rau 64.42
F. Rau 79.45
Liberty Bluff Sta.
W. Jennerman 95.51
A. Janke
Gust. Prill 80
C. Schalle 80
Carl Schalle 140
Mary Johnston 80
G. A. & B. F. Crawford 120
G. A. & B. F. Crawford 160

Fred. Large
Jul. Wachholtz 134.33
Ristan 44.10
J.W. Curran 53.32
Ole Mortenson 103.14
Liberty Bluff P.O.
A. Zorn 80
C. Penkesky 110
Augusta Stolp
G. Bertine 119.5
J.W. Curran
J.B. Crawford

J. B. Crawford 160
James Hamilton 240
L. Botker 240
A. Wachschall 80
E.L. Caldwell
C. Helke
A. Henke 77
Zimmerman 120
G.
E.L. Perry
A. Manweiler 160
W. Weishahn 280
Jul. Krueger
A. Schrank 80
Harry Weir
Wm. Weir
A.H. Nickell

John Ferch 117.91
F.E. Maynard 80
C. Maynard 80
G. Stalter 80
Deering Binder Co. 80
John Duesterhoeft 140
Fred. Ferch 140
G. Hause 120
Wm. Weir 280
H. Blaske
A. Schrank 40
Jno. Ullrich
John Gibson 240
L.S. Guptil
A. Schrank
I. Gibson
Thos. Gibson 160
Thos. Hamilton 120
Wm. H. Hamilton 160
Jno. Rahr 80
F.W. Bartz
R. Busse 120
Chas. Caldwell
Wm. Birkholtz
N.W. Bultes 140
J. Schrank
Jos. Corey
Gust. Birkholtz 187
Julius Berndt
E. Schlueder

Mary Smith
Jas. McCathie
Ernst Sonnenberg
F. Buchholtz
Twin Lakes
Sommerfeldt 40
C. Zebell 120
U.S. 40
J. Gibson 40
Geo. Miller 80
F. Long 40
F. Dobrinski 80
A. Campbell 80
O. Runnemann 80
E. McGraw 40
Jas. Long
F. McGraw 80
Busewith 80
Aug. Heyst 120
Jno. Smith
McCathie 160
N. McCathie
Fred. Bohnser
Carl Buchholtz 55
Dave Smith
A. Schorter
Jas. Long
Frank Long 40
Hamilton
F. Tann 40
E. Tann 40
W. Miller

Jos. McCathie
Goehlitz
L. J. Jahnke 120
Wm. Fritz
John Fuhrman 147
G. Bishop
L. & A. Maynard 80
C. Whitney
J. Whitney 198.5
Gibson
H. Alexander 160
Jas. Long
A. Miller 160
Aug. Herst 120
Wm. Phillips 200
Aug. Felbe 120
A. Jahnke 61.92
L.M. Jahnke 103.19
Werner
Jas. Jones 81
A. Vaughn 120
E. Cooper 383
Jno. Douglas
A. Doege
H. Roney
A. Paulrendes

SPRINGFIELD TOWNSHIP (1900 Marquette County Plat Book)

Immigrants from central Germany:

1) FRANKHANEL, Arthur Paul of Barnesville, Clay Co. (Minn.)- b. "Saxony, Germany", marr. Clara Maria Hartwig at Montello, 22 June 1902/ Vol. 3, p. 67.

2) GUENTHER, Karl Friedrich of Bruno (Butler Co.), Nebr.- b. "Prov. Saxen (Sachsen=Saxony, Prussia), Germany", marr. Martha Anna Laumer- b. "Gross Lups (-Lubs, Co. Filehne, Prov. Posen), Germany"; at Mecan, 3 May 1898/ Vol. 3, p. 105.

3) SCHROTH, Rudolf- b. "Dresden (Kingdom of Saxony), Germany", marr. Minna Wachholtz at Springfield, 23 September 1898/ Vol. 3, p. 111.

4) WESTPHAL, Christian Friedrich- b. "Mogenhai, Prov. Saxon(y, Prussia), Germany", marr. Mahtilda Emilie Doepke at Mecan, 20 August 1896/ Vol. 3, p. 82.

Immigrants from western Germany:

1) BLOEDEL, Anton of Rolfe (Pocahontas Co.), Iowa- b. "Muenchen, Bayern (Munich, Bavaria), Germany", marr. Pauline Therese Mittlesteadt at Mecan, 6 December 1899/ Vol. 3, p. 128.

2) BRAKEBUSH, Heinrich- b. "Salter, Brusiswig (Salder, Braunschweig or Brunswick), Germany", marr. Augusta Ella Peschel at Springfield, 14 January 1903/ Vol. 3, p. 176.

3) DEYHLE, Gottlieb Charles of Baraboo (Sauk Co.), Wisc.- b. "Stuttgart, Wuestemberg (Kingdom of Wuerttemberg), Germany", marr. Emma Clocksin (Glockzien or Klockzin?) at Crystal Lake, 26 December 1901/ Vol. 3, p. 158.

4) HENNE, Aug. Heinrich Christian- b. "Hanover, Germany", marr. Henrietta Schanfeld (Schoenfeld?) at Crystal Lake, 30 June 1871/ Vol. 1, p. 161.

5) HERNDOBLER, Mary- b. "Bavaria, Europe", marr. Frank Giese at Montello, 23 February 1897/ Vol. 3, p. 88.

6) HILLMER, Martha Maria Christine- b. "Hannover, Germany", marr. Julius Edward Klettke at Montello, 15 September 1901/ Vol. 3, p. 154.

7) JAEGER, Valentin of Milwaukee (co. seat), Wisc.-"(Grand Duchy of) Hessen Darmstadt, Germany", marr. Emma Emilie Gardo(w?) at Montello, 30 March 1895/ Vol. 3, p. 60.

8) MEYER, Heinrich- b. "Hanover", marr. Rose Weinkauf (no location given), 1 July 1861/ (No pagation).

9) STEINHAUS, Auguste Maria Magdalena- b. "Bremern (Bremen?), Germany", marr. Michael Frank Newland at Packwaukee, 13 March 1895/ Vol. 3, p. 60.

10) THALACKER, H.A.L.- b. "Hanover, Germany", marr. An. Ros. Zierke at Harrisville, 17 July 1867/ Vol. 1, p. 160.

11) von KETTLER, Heinrich- b. "Haat Korn, Minden (Prov. Westfalen or Westphalia, Prussia), Germany", marr. Henriette Zellmer at Crystal Lake, 22 March 1888/ Vol. 2a, p. 71.

Immigrants of German descent from "Russia":

1.) FITZKE (nee POHL), Emilie- b. "Constantine, Russia", marr. Ferdinand Reetz- b. "Prussia, Germany"; at Harrisville, 13 October 1904/ Vol. 3, p. 205.

2) GREH? or GUCH, Friedrich Wilhelm- b. "Kreis Lutzkie, Russia"; marr. Lina Linda Draeger at Mecan, 14 Dec. 1900/ Vol. 3, p. 143.

3) KIERSKI, John Joseph- b. "Prov. of Vistula, Russia"; marr. Eliz. Agnes Mondry at Montello, 16 April 1907/ Vol. 3, p. 243.

4) MISSAE, Johann Ludwig- b. "Kodletz, Russian Poland", marr. Aug. Friederike Werner at Neshkoro, 22 November 1858/ Vol. 1, p. 3.

5) WURCH, Juliana- b. "Russia in Europe", marr. Ferdinand Emil Schmidt of Milwaukee (county seat, Wisc.)- b. "Pommern" (Pomerania) in Europe"; at Germania, 12 April 1903/ Vol. 3, p. 180.

Immigrants from not readily identifiable locales in "Germany":

1) ALFF, Gottfried August of Seneca (Township), Green Lake Co. -
   b. "Cornosinan, Germany" (perhaps Konarschin, Co. Berent, Prov.
   West Prussia or Konarzin, Klein-, Gross-, & -Glashütte, Co.
   Schlochau, Prov. West Prussia?), marr. Ottilie Mathilde Rohde-
   b. "Driesen (Co. Friedeberg/Neumark, Prov. Brandenburg), Germany";
   at Crystal Lake, 29 November 1896/ Vol. 3, p. 86.

2) BREHMER or BREMNER?, Wilhelmine- b. "Wecso, Germany" (perhaps
   Wieczno-See (lake), Co. Briesen, Prov. West Prussia, or Weichsel
   River, or Wissoka, Co. Tuchel, Prov. West Prussia???), marr.
   Friedrich Aug. Krenz at Springfield, 30 April 1893/ Vol. 3,
   p. 36.

3) BRODERDORF, Ernst Wilhelm of Fountain Prairie, Columbia Co.
   (Wisc.)- b. "Jordandorf, Germany" (perhaps Jordenstorf Neu-Ka-
   len, Malchin district, Mecklenburg-Schwerin, west of Demmin?),
   marr. Etta Rosina Petrich at Newton, 7 April 1896/ Vol. 3, p.
   76.

4) BRUSTMANN, Gustav- b. "Schunendonow, Germany" (could be corrup-
   tion of any one of a half dozen names: Czekanowko, Szymanowo,
   Szkaradowo, Szemborowo, Szczepanowo, or Szczepankowo?), marr.
   Ernestine Wegner at Newton, 23 September 1898/ Vol. 3, p. 109.

5) BUELOW, Ernst Adolph C. of Seneca (Township), Green Lake Co. -
   b. "Bredow, Germany" (probably at Co. Stettin, Prov. Pomerania),
   marr. Louise Henriette Floeter- b. "Gross Drensen (Co. Filehne,
   Prov. Posen), Germany"; at Crystal Lake, 15 January 1884/ Vol.
   2a, p. 59.

6) BUNDE, Carl of Grand Rapids, Wisc.- b. "Altmarien, Germany"
   (perhaps Alt-Marrin, Co. Kolberg-Körlin, Prov. Pomerania, a
    knights landed estate community?), marr. Alwine Brosinske at
   Newton, 6 November 1883/ Vol. 2a, p. 55.

7) DAHMS, Auguste- b. "Wersike, Germany" (perhaps Wirsitz, a Posen county seat, or its Polish name Wierzyce?), marr. Fred.
   Cartwright at Westfield, 22 May 1893/ Vol. 3, p. 36.

8) DEE, Carl F.- b. "Amt-Kartz, Germany" (perhaps Karze, Co. Blec-
   kede, Prov. Hannover, near Lüneburg?), marr. Wilhelmine Schultz-
   b. "Pratznick (Kratznick, Co. Arnswalde, Prov. Brandenburg),
   Germany"; at Marion, Waushara Co., 8 April 1907/ Vol. 3, p.
   242.

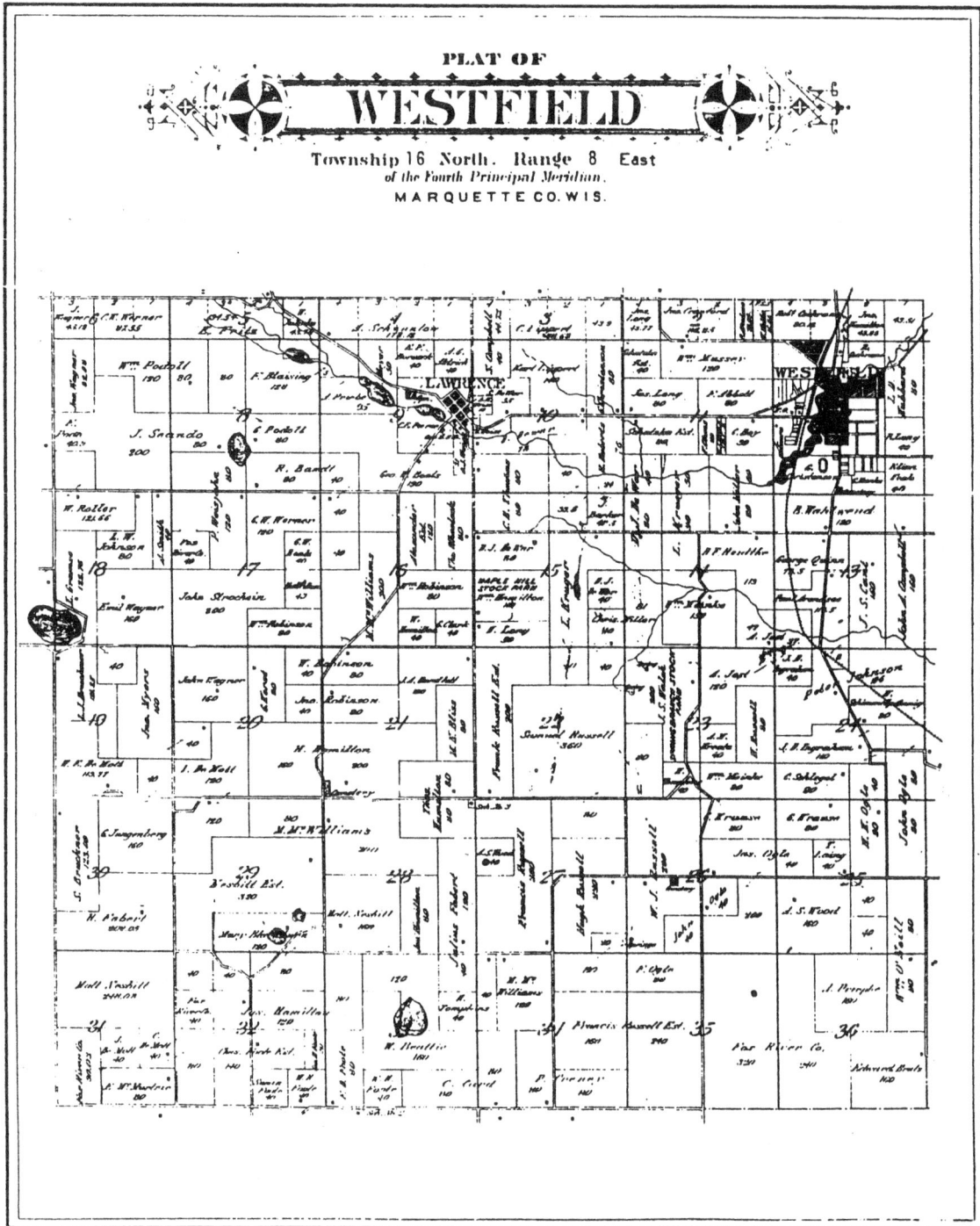

PLAT OF
WESTFIELD

Township 16 North. Range 8 East
of the Fourth Principal Meridian.
MARQUETTE CO. WIS.

(From 1900 Marquette County Plat Book and COME BACK IN TIME
Vol. I by Elaine Reetz. Note in Sec. 7 -upper left-"E. Podo
40.9", property of author's great-grandfather, Ernest Podoll,
homestead over the Adams County border.)

9) DICKOW, Fritz of Chicago (Cook Co.), Ill.- b. "Nashow, Germany" (perhaps Nassow, Co. Köslin, Prov. Pomerania?), marr. Emilie Kirst- b. "Ksezaly (Dzlaly, Co. Bromberg, Prov. Posen), Germany"; at Westfield, 16 January 1895/ Vol. 3, p. 58.

10) EIZENMANN, Fred. of Mazomanie (Dane Co.), Wisc.- b. "Helingen, Germany" (perhaps Rieth Hellingen, Romhild district near Coburg, Thuringia-central Germany), marr. Wilhelmina Mueller at Harrisville, 17 November 1895/ Vol. 3, p. 71.

11) FIERKE, Friedrich- b. "Greenhap, Germany" (could be one of 3 locales named Grünhof?), marr. Ernestine Schoenfeld at Harrisville, 26 April 1897/ Vol. 3, p. 91.

12) GOLDSCHMIDT, August Carl- b. "Twenbusch, Germany" (probably Ivenbusch, Co. Filehne , Prov. Posen), marr. Bertha Mathilde Zuelke at Newton, 14 August 1902/ Vol. 3, p. 169.

13) GOLDSCHMIDT, Auguste Hulda- b. "Twenbush (same as above), Germany", marr. August Herman Klingbeil at Newton, 14 December 1893/ Vol. 3, p. 44.

14) HUEBNER, Karl- b. "Cristine, Germany" (could be place with prefix Christinen-, such as Christinenfeld or Christinenberg?), marr. Emma Kottke at Westfield, 15 November 1896/ Vol. 3, p. 85.

15) KRUEGER, Emma Bertha- b. "Muellerspelde, Germany", marr. Edward Krueger at Springfield, 3 January 1907/ Vol. 3, p. 258.

16) KRUEGER, Ida Auguste- b. "Muellersfelde, Germany" (surely the correct name, perhaps Müllenfelde, Göttingen district of Prov. Hannover?), marr. Adolf Ferdinand Weishaar at Springfield, 1 June 1903/ Vol. 3, p. 183.

17) ?LEIDNER, Hulda E.- b. "Germania, Germany", marr. Joseph A. Luger at Douglas, 30 June 1904/ Vol. 3, p. 202.

18) MANS, Edward- b. "Zuchowmohre, Germany" (perhaps Zuchow, Co. Dramburg, Prov. Pomerania?), marr. Auguste Reckow at Newton, 9 April 1899/ Vol. 3, p. 119.

19) MANTHEI, Julius of Rosendale (Fond du Lac Co.), Wisc.- b. "Louisendorf, Germany" (perhaps Louisendorf, near Kleve, Düsseldorf district, Rhine Province, Prussia?), marr. Wilhelmine Floeter- b. "Gross Drensen (Co. Filehne, Prov. Posen), Germany"; at Crystal Lake, 1 May 1887/ Vol. 2a, p. 67.

20) MANTHEY, Julius Johann (same as No. 19)- b. "Louisendorf, Germany", marr. Mrs. Jennie May C. Drake- b. "State of Missouri"; at Buffalo, 31 May 1906/ Vol. 3, p. 228. (Louisendorf could also be Kassel district of Prov. Hessen-Nassau, near Marburg)

21) MILLER, Daniel of "Mekan"- b. "Schamlowa (Slembowo, Co. Znin, Prov. Posen?), Europa", marr. Elizabeth Wegener at "Nescora" (Neshkoro), 23 "Mai" 1861/ (No pagation).

22) MULLER, Friedrich- b. "Shlorozentin (Schlagenthin, Co. Arnswalde, Prov. Brandenburg?)", marr. Ottilie Drewitz at Newton, 15 February 1876/ Vol. 2a, p. 26.

23) OHM, Frantz Fr. W.- b. "Griebow, Germany" (perhaps Griebo, Zerbst district, Prov. Sachsen-Anhalt, Prussia, near Wittenberg?), marr. Bertha Folske- b. "Salzdorf (Co. Schubin, Prov. Posen), Germany"; at Westfield, 21 November 1893/ Vol. 3, p. 43.

24) POHLKE, Otto- b. "Solowen, Germany", marr. Ernestine Wilhelmine Stolp at Springfield, 25 January 1898/ Vol. 3, p. 102.

25) SCHAENFELD, Frederick- b. "Nendorf, Germany" (probably Nendorf, Stolzenau district, Prov. Hannover, Prussia), marr. Rosina Schwark (nee Elftman?)- b. "Neindorf, Germany" (perhaps Neindorf, Co. Gifhorn, Prov. Hannover?); no location of marriage given, 22 January 1900/ Vol. 3, p. 130.

26) SCHAFER, Theodora A.M.- b. "Peterfelt, Germany" (perhaps Peterswalde, Marienwerder dist., Co. Schlochau, Prov. West Prussia?), marr. John Smith at Oxford, 17 January 1892/ Vol. 3, p. 19.

27) SCHINALOFSKI, Emilie- b. "Phomirk , Germany", marr. John Elsner- b. "Weritz (Wirsitz, Posen?), Germany"; at Westfield, 15 April "1885" (1895?)/ (No pagation).

28) SOMERFELT, Christopher- b. "Ashingfen, Germany", marr. Henriette Krentz at Westfield, 27 November 1886/ (No pagation).

29) WACHHOLZ, Emil Leopold- b. "Saben, Germany" (Klein- or Gross-Sabin, Co. Dramburg, Prov. Pomerania, Prussia?), marr. Laura A.A. Schwanke at Newton, 1 February 1877/ Vol. 2a, p. 29.

30) WENDLAND, Ernst- b. "Kafsliewo Kauland, Germany" (perhaps a corruption of Chociszewo-Hauland, Co. Wongrowitz, Prov. Posen?), marr. Anna Emiline Bertha Schulz at Springfield, 28 May 1901/ Vol. 3, p. 150.

31) WOBSCHA(L?), Helena- b. "Frieseneck, Germany", marr. Ernst Martin Doege at Springfield, 13 December 1893/ Vol. 3, p. 43.

(Note: As you will see in Green Lake County listings, Province Posen was also sometimes referred to as Prussian Poland or Polish Prussia. That being the case, we decided to include this listing here:)

DUSHINSKI, Anna- b. "Germany, Prussia Poland"; marr. Francis Donovan at Montello, 7 January 1903/ Vol. 3, p. 175 (Catholic, she is probably Polish, he may be Irish).

MARQUETTE COUNTY NATURALIZATIONS

Immigrants from County Kolmar, Province Posen, Prussia:

1) BORN, Otto Julius- b. "Freirode, Germany", from Buffalo twp., decl. 27 July 1914- nat. 28 August 1916/ Vol. 2, p. 93.

2) BUCHHOLTZ, Charles Robert- b. "Sachesberg (Zachasberg), Germany", from Newton twp., decl. 20 August 1913- nat. 23 August 1915/ Vol. 2, p.76.

3) DUESTERHOEFT, Charles Robert- b. "Ratty (Rattai), Germany", from Springfield twp., decl. 20 May 1910- nat. 9 July 1913/ Vol. 2, p. 16.

4) DUESTERHOEFT, John Gottlieb (author's great-grand-uncle)- b. "Petronke (Pietronke), Germany", from Springfield twp.; his wife Julianna was b. "Zachasberg, Germany" and first son, Charles Robert b. "Rattay, Germany" (see above); decl. in Green Lake Co. 3 November 1882- nat. 9 July 1913/ Vol. 2, p. 17.

5) GAY, Carl- b. "Colmar (Kolmar), Germany", from Westfield, decl. in Green Lake Co. 3 November 1882- nat. 23 January 1912/ Vol. 1, p. 35.

6) HAASE, Rudolph- b. "Zachasburg (Zachasberg),Prussia", from Springfield twp., decl. 24 October 1906- nat. 15 December 1910/ Vol. 1, p. 15.

7) HAASE, Rudolph Herman- b. "Zachasberg, Germany", from Springfield twp., decl. 11 April 1911- nat. 9 July 1913/ Vol. 2, p. 15.

8) JANKE, Louis Martin- b. "Prosen (Prossen), Germany", from Westfield; his wife Odelia b. "Germany"; decl. 30 November 1884- nat. 26 March 1914/ Vol. 2, p. 45.

9) KRUEGER, August Frederick- b. "Narova Holland (Strozewo- or Borowo-Hauland?), Prussia", from Crystal twp., decl. 3 November 1884- nat. 29 August 1914/ Vol. 2, p. 52.

10) KRUEGER, Otto William- b. "Morganeen (Margonin), Germany", from Westfield; decl. 27 October 1910- nat. 12 June 1913/ Vol. 2, p. 5.

11) KRUGER, August- b. "Samotgin (Samotschin), Germany", from Springfield twp.; his wife Joanna and first son both b. "Samotgin, Germany"; decl. 23 October 1888- nat. 28 February 1913/ Vol. 1, p. 46.

12) KUJATH, Emil Robert- b."(Co.) Kolmar, Podanin, Germany", from Harris twp.; his wife Emilie b. "Kemnitz (Kamnitz, Co. Wongrowitz?), Germany"; decl. in Wabasha Co., Minn. 31 October 1892- nat. 28 November 1913/ Vol. 2, p. 38.

13) MONDRY, Peter- b. "Rownopole b. Friedheim (Ebenfeld, Co. Kolmar) Germany", from Montello; his wife Agnes b. "Arnsfelde (Co. Deutsch Krone, Prov. West Prussia) Germany"; decl. under provisions of 1910- nat. 8 October 1914/ Vol. 2, p. 56.

14) NICKEL, Otto Ferdinand- b. "Lippen (Lipin), Germany", from Montello, decl. 27 December 1910- nat. 27 December 1912/ Vol. 1, p. 44.

15) NICKEL, Paul Robert- b. "Lippinn (Lipin) Kreis (County) Kolmar Germany", from Montello, decl. 28 November 1910- nat. 20 December 1912/ Vol. 1, p. 43.

16) SCHWOCHERT, John E.- "Kolma(r) Germany", from Montello; his wife b. "Kolma(r)" and 3 sons b. "Zimbowo at Kolma (Dziembowo, Co. Kolmar)"; decl. 2 November 1888- nat. 6 July 1909/ Vol. 1, p. 5.

17) SCHWOCHERT, Joseph- b. "Jimbovo (Dziembowo), Germany", from Pakcwaukee twp., decl. 11 July 1912- nat. 14 December 1915/ Vol. 2, p. 84.

18) SONNENBERG, Herman August- b. "Wimbowo (Dziembowo?) Germany", from Springfield twp., decl. 19 August 1914- nat. 8 December 1916/ Vol. 2, p. 99.

19) STELTER, (Friedrich) Gustav- b. "(Jablonowo) Kolmar, Germany", from Springfield twp.; his wife "Delia" (Ottilie Duesterhoeft, they are author's great-grandparents) and first daughter b. "Kolmar, Germany" (mother actually b. at Pietronke); decl. at at St. Joseph Co., Ind. 30 May 1884- nat. 14 September 1914/ Vol. 2, p. 54.

20) WISKE, John- b. "Pladke (Plöttke) Germany", from Montello; his wife Amelia b. "Arpel (Erpel) Germany"; decl. 3 November 1882- nat. 10 January 1911/ Vol. 1, p. 23.

Immigrants from County Czarnikau, Province Posen, Prussia:

1) FRANK, Ferdinand- b. "Strandun (Straduhn) Germany"; decl. in
Ripon, Fond du Lac Co. (Wisc.) 31 October 1876- nat. 20 June
1914/ Vol. 2, p. 50.

2) FREITAG, Heinrich August- b. "Radalien (Radolin) Germany", from
Montello; decl. 28 July 1910- nat. 12 July 1913/ Vol. 2, p. 25.

3) GARDOW, Alfred- b. "Schönlanke, Germany", from Westfield; decl.
24 February 1910- nat. 9 April 1912/ Vol. 1, p. 37.

4) HALLMAN, Herman Julius- b. "Shalanke (Schönlanke) Germany", from
Newton twp.; decl. 20 August 1913- nat. 23 August 1915/ Vol. 2,
p. 75.

5) JUST, August Karl- b. "Schulanka Nudorf (Schönlanke Neudorf) Germany", from Montello; decl. 26 March 1881- nat. 9 April 1914/
Vol. 2, p. 46.

Immigrants from County Wirsitz, Province Posen, Prussia:

1) BOETTCHER, Robert Otto- b. "Netzthal Germany", from Packwaukee;
decl. in Green Lake Co. 2 November 1896- nat. 10 July 1913/ Vol.
2, p. 23.

2) BUCHHOLZ, Carl- b. "Friedheim Germany", from Westfield; his deceased wife Christine Wilhelmine and first 3 children all b.
"Cojazin (Chodziesen=Kolmar) Germany"; decl. in Green Lake Co.
3 November 1882- nat. 22 September 1913/ Vol. 2, p. 30.

3) DAHLKE, Julius- b. "Kustriechan (Küstrinchen) Germany", from
Westfield; decl. 2 September 1911- nat. 20 December 1913/ Vol.
2, p. 42.

4) DAHMS, Gustav Ferdinand- b. "Carlsbach (Karlsbach) Germany", from
Westfield; his wife Erna b."Germany"; decl. 27 December 1913-
nat. 9 June 1916/ Vol. 2, p. 87.

Immigrants from County Filehne, Province Posen, Prussia:

1) HENKE, August Ferdinand -b. "Pruhsacle (Prossekel) Germany",
last residence- "Selnow (Co. Arnswalde, Prov. Brandenburg?) Germany", from Springfield; his wife Bertha b. "Germany"; decl. 21
November 1913- nat. 23 November 1915/ Vol. 2, p. 82.

2) HENKE, Charles Ludwig- b. "Selchow Germany (see above)", from
Newton twp.; his wife Minnie b. "Germany"; decl. 21 November
1913- nat. 23 November 1915/ Vol. 2, p. 83.

3) MEYER, August- b. "Eichberg Prussia Germany", from Crystal Lake;
his wife Julia b. "Germany"; decl. 31 October 1914- nat. 31 October 1916/ Vol. 2, p. 96.

4) SCHULTZ, Herman Amiel- b. "Gornitz Posen Germany", from Crystal
Lake; his wife Leda b. "Germany"; decl. 12 September 1914- nat.
3 October 1916/ Vol. 2, p. 94.

Immigrants from additional locales in Province Posen, Prussia:

1) BORN, August Julius- b. "Mitzkowo (Mieczkowo, Co. Schubin) Germany", from Buffalo twp.; his wife Anna b. "Germany" and first child b. "Parkowo, Germany" and next 2 children b. "Colmar, Germany"; decl. 28 October 1886- nat. 28 April 1916/ Vol. 2, p. 85.

2) DAHLKE, August William- b. "Jakubowo (Cos. Wongrowitz or Obernick?) Germany", from Montello; his wife Justina b. "Jakubowo, Germany"; decl. 1 November 1880- nat. 7 March 1914/ Vol. 2, p. 44.

3) DAHLKE, Herman- b. "Jakubowo (see above) Germany", from Montello; his wife Lena b. "Jakubowo, Germany"; decl. in Mason Co., Ill., 5 October 1892- nat. 20 December 1910/ Vol. 1, p. 16.

4) DUESTERHOEFT, August- b. "Posen, Germany", from Springfield twp.; his wife Wilhelmina b. "Atlantic Ocean"; decl. 20 March 1913- nat. 23 March 1915/ Vol. 2, p. 64.

5) GIESE, John- b. "Posen, Germany", from Shields; his wife Maggie b. "Posen, Germany"; decl. 30 March 1886- nat. 31 December 1910/ Vol. 1, p. 22.

6) HADOW, John- b. "Mosnetz (Mosnitz, Co. Konitz, Prov. West Prussia?) Germany", from Harrisville; his wife Caroline b. "Zipenewow, Pozen" and first 2 children b. "Walkowitz (Co. Czarnikau), Pozen"; decl. 5 November 1881- nat. 26 September 1913/ Vol. 2, p. 32.

7) HELL, Christoph- b. "Provinz Posen Germany", from Newton; his wife Minnie b. "Provinz Pozen"; decl. 1 November 1886- nat. 7 January 1914/ Vol. 2, p. 43.

8) KRENTZ, Alexander Fritz- b. "Schobein (Schubin, a county seat) Germany"; from Shields; decl. 23 June 1911- nat. 8 July 1913/ Vol. 2, p. 13.

9) KRUGER, Rhynie- b. "Posen Germany", from Springfield; decl. 20 March 1913- nat. 23 March 1915/ Vol. 2, p. 65.

10) LABRENZ, Gust- b. "Obornik (Obernick, a county seat) Germany", from Oxford; his wife Agusta b. "Germany"; decl. 30 October 1886- nat. 5 July 1913/ Vol. 2, p. 12.

11) LANGE, Friedrich Wilhelm- b. "Shtobnicahauland (Stobnica-Hauland, a.k.a. Treuenheim, Co. Obernick) Germany", from Harris twp.; his wife Emma b. "Germany"; decl. 9 July 1913- nat. 2 November 1915/ Vol. 2, p. 80.

12) MIKESCHAK, Stanislaus- b. "Lippekolonia (Lippe-Kolonie, Co. Obernick), Germany", from Shields; his wife Paulina b. "Lippekolonia, Germany"; decl. in Green Lake Co., 25 October 1884- nat.
24 October 1911/ Vol. 1,p. 34.

13) MILLER, Emil Friedrich- b. "Bromberg, Germany", from Crystal
Lake; decl. 28 October 1892- nat. 11 Octber 1911/ Vol. 2, p. 33.

14) PRUST, Carl Henry William- b. "Lovin Germany", from Shields;
his wife Emma b. "Province Pozen"; decl. in Jefferson Co., Wisc.,
3 November 1888- nat. 30 December 1910/ Vol. 1, p. 20.

15) SCHMIDT, Carl- b. "Province Pozen Germany", from Montello; his
first son b. "Westpozen Germany"; decl. 6 November 1882- nat.
8 December 1913/ Vol. 2, p. 41.

16) TONN, Emil- b. "Posen Germany", from Springfield; decl. 28 February 1913- nat. 26 March 1915/ Vol. 2, p. 66.

(*Note: "Lovin" is probably Lowin, Co. Meseritz, Prov. Posen)

Immigrants from County Deutsch Krone, Province West Prussia:

1) ARNDT, Gustav- b. "Tribiene (Trebbin), Germany", from Neshkoro; decl. 29 October 1890 in Green Lake Co.- nat. 16 June 1911/ Vol. 1, p. 28.

2) BRIESE, August- b. "Lebehnke Germany", from Harris; his wife Lizzie b. "Germany"; decl. 24 March 1914- nat. 10 October 1916/ Vol. 2, p. 95.

3) KLAPOETKE, August- b. "Lebehnke, Germany", from Harris; decl. 24 October 1906- nat. 21 July 1911/ Vol. 1, p. 33.

4) KLAPOETKE, Christoph- b. "Lebehnke, Germany", from Harris; his wife Appolena b. "Lebehnke, Germany" and also first son; decl. 1 April 1882- nat. 21 July 1911/ Vol. 1, p.32.

5) LIESKE, Robert Amiel (believed to be author's half-great-grand-uncle)- b. "Schloep (Schloppe?)", from Westfield; his wife Tina Weddie (Wedde?) Lieske b. "Pumeron (Pommern or Pomerania?)"; decl. 17 June 1913- nat. 23 November 1914/ Vol. 2, p. 60.

6) MALLACH, Albert August- b. "Lehbenke (Lebehnke) Germany", from Westfield; decl. 29 October 1894- nat. 6 December 1913/ Vol. 2, p. 40.

7) PUFAHL, Leo Paul- b. "Labenke (Lebehnke) Germany", from Harris twp.; decl. 3 April 1913- nat. 9 June 1915/ Vol. 2, p. 70.

8) THIEDE, Frank- b. "Lehbehnke (Lebehnke), Germany", from Harris twp.; decl. 17 April 1913- nat. 17 June 1914/ Vol. 2, p. 49.

Immigrants from additional locales in Province West Prussia:

1) DOBRINSKE, Herman- b. "Hohan Kirch (Hohenkirche, Co. Briesen) Germany", from Newton; decl. 5 November 1892- nat. 24 May 1915/ Vol. 2, p. 68.

2) EICHMANN, Julius Ferdinand- b. "Derschau (Dirschau, a county seat), Germany", from Town Newton; his wife Sofie b. "Germany"; decl. 4 November 1882- nat. 9 July 1913/ Vol. 2, p. 14.

3) KLAWITTER, Albert Gustav- b. "Schiskov (Cziskowo, Co. Flatow) Germany", from Montello; decl. in Green Lake Co. 2 November 1898- nat. 5 December 1913/ Vol. 2, p. 39.

4) MANTZEL, Frederick- b. "Dantzic (Danzig, a city and county seat) Germany", from Mecan twp.; his wife Pauline b. Marienburg (a county seat), Germany"; decl. 31 October 1892- nat. 1 September 1915/ Vol. 2, p. 78.

5) ROSS, Ludwig- b. "Flotow (Flatow, a county seat) Germany", from Montello; his wife Adelina b. "Germany"; decl. 2 March 1889- nat. 16 May 1916/ Vol. 2, p. 86.

Immigrants from Province Brandenburg, Prussia:

1) BAKER, August- b. "Richts, Province of Brandenburg, Prussia", from Newton; his wife Augusta Lizzie b. "West Prussia" (see previous page); decl. 1 November 1886- nat. 20 April 1911/ Vol. 1, p. 26.

2) HERNKIND, August- b. "near Berlin, Germany", from Buffalo twp.; decl. in Ripon, Fond du Lac Co. (Wisc.) 4 November 1878- nat. 24 June 1916/ Vol. 2, p. 88.

3) KLINGBEIL, Carl- b. "Pommine (Pammin, Co. Arnswalde?) Germany", from Westfield; his wife Augusta b. "Gros(s)spiegel (Co. Arnswalde?), Germany" and 5 children b. "Forrest House, Pommine, Germany" (note: "Pommine" could also be Pommern or Pomerania) between 1870-1876; decl. 31 October 1884- nat. 8 January 1910/ Vol. 1, p. 7.

4) LIESKE, Fred William (believed to be author's half-great-grand-uncle)- b. "Kreis Freidberg (Co. Friedeberg/Neumark) Germany", from Westfield; decl. 13 April 1911- nat. 23 November 1914/ Vol. 2, p. 59.

5) MILLER, Herman August- b. "Rohrbe(c)k (Co. Arnswalde?) Germany", from Harris; his wife Tenna b. "Crevitz, Germany"; decl. 1 November 1884- nat. 5 July 1913/ Vol. 2, p. 11.

6) SCHULTZ, Oscar Otto Friedrich- b. "Driesen (Co. Friedeberg/Neumark) Germany", from Harrisville; his wife Mary Elizabeth b. "Setehour Germany" and first child b. "Driesen Germany"; decl. 25 October 1888- nat. 21 November 1913/ Vol. 2, p. 37.

Immigrants from Province Pomerania, Prussia:

1) BAKER, Christian- b. "Dopperphuhl (Dobberphul, Co. Pyritz?, Co. Greifenhagen?, or Co. Cammin?) Germany", from Packwaukee; his wife Anna b. "Regensbusch Germany"; decl. in Merrill, Lincoln Co. ,Wisc. 17 December 1890- nat. 11 June 1913/ Vol. 2, p. 4.

2) BAKER, William- b. "Dobberful (Dobberphul) Germany", from Pack- waukee; his wife Minnie b. "Wassen Germany"; decl. as honorably discharged soldier, 1864- nat. 21 May 1913/ Vol. 2, p. 1.

3) BAUMANN, Herman- b. "Stargard (seat of Co. Saatzig) Germany", from Buffalo twp.; his wife Emma b. "Germany"; decl. in Colum- bia Co. (Wisc.) 29 October 1892- nat. 15 July 1916/ Vol. 2, p. 90.

4) HAFEMAN, Albert- b. "Regenwalde (a county seat) Germany", from Montello; his wife Emma b. "Lobsens (Co. Wirsitz, Prov. Posen) Germany"; decl. in Ripon, Fond du Lac Co. (Wisc.) 8 November 1892- nat. 28 January 1915/ Vol. 2, p. 63.

5) HAMMER, Gustav- b. "Hinter Pommern (eastern Pomerania) Germany", from Westfield; his wife Lena b. "Posen"; decl. Fond du Lac Co., 6 April 1874- nat. 3 September 1914/ Vol. 2, p. 53.

6) HAYES, George- b. "Reischanbach (Reichenbach, Co. Pyritz?) Ger- many", from Westfield; decl. 3 July 1906- nat. 10 July 1913/ Vol. 2, p. 22.

7) KLINGBEIL, Frank Otto- b. "Pomeraine Germany", from Oxford; decl. 10 July 1911- nat. 10 July 1913/ Vol. 2, p. 24.

8) LEMKE, Charles Frederick- b. "Stettin (a county & district seat) Germany", from Buffalo twp.; decl. 17 July 1914- nat. 4 August 1916/ Vol. 2, p. 91.

9) POMPLUN, Otto- b. "Wussow (Co. Lauenberg or Co. Rummelsburg?) Germany", from Springfield; decl. in Waushara Co. 3 April 1896- nat. 24 May 1915/ Vol. 2, p. 69.

10) REIMANN, Paul Herman- b. "Borzichow Germany" (note: marr. record gives "Stargard", a county seat), from town of Newton; decl. 17 October 1884- nat. 20 August 1913/ Vol. 2, p. 28.

11) STEINHAUS, Fredrick Ferdinand- b. "Pomerania Germany", from Packwaukee twp.; decl. 5 June 1913- nat. 6 July 1915/ Vol. 2, p. 73.

12) ZELLMER, William Ferdinand- b. "Pomerian Germany", from Harris; decl. 7 November 1912- nat. 14 November 1914/ Vol. 2, p. 58.

Immigrants from western Germany:

1) BRAKEBUSCH, Gustav- b. "Haverloh (Co. Marienburg, Prov. Hanno-
    ver, Prussia) Germany", last residence- "Neferlingen, Germany",
    from Montello; decl. in Milwaukee, Wisc. 30 April 1910- nat.
    7 July 1915/ Vol. 2, p. 74.

2) GEBLER, Joseph- b. "Bavaria Germany", from Endeavor; his wife
    Bertha b. "Germany"; decl. 2 October 1913- nat. 13 October 1915/
    Vol. 2, p. 79.

3) HERZ, Frederick William- b. "Hadem Westfalia (Prov. Westfalen
    or Westphalia, Prussia) Germany", from Harrisville; decl. in
    Franklin Co., Nebr. 29 September 1890- nat. 26 September 1913/
    Vol. 2, p. 31.

4) HILLMER, John- b. "Hanover Germany", from Montello; decl. 29
    March 1890- nat. 24 April 1911/ Vol. 1, p. 27.

5) SCHMIDT, Fredrick William- b. "Hamburg Germany", from Montel-
    lo; his wife Francis b. "Germany"; decl. 12 July 1913- nat.
    16 November 1915/ Vol. 2, p. 81.

Immigrants from not readily identifiable locales in "Germany":

1) DEE, Julius- b. "Kerceich (Kircheich?) Germany", from Newton;
   decl. 26 November 1912- nat. 28 November 1914/ Vol. 2, p. 61.

2) FALK, Edward- b. "Boudetz Germany", from Douglas twp.; his wife
   Minnie b. "Germany" and first daughter b. "Schinefeld Germany";
   decl. 28 October 1887- nat. 12 August 1916/ Vol. 2, p. 92.

3) GERBITZ, Wilhelm (Willie) Franz- b. "Schanwenbeck Germany"; decl.
   in Columbia Co. (Wisc.) 27 October 1888- nat. 12 July 1913/ Vol.
   2, p. 26.

4) GRUBB, Frank- b. "Resken, Germany", from Douglas; his wife Anna
   b. "Schenwald, Germany"; decl. 15 May 1905- nat. 10 July 1913/
   Vol. 2, p. 19.

5) KLIMKE, Albert Hermann- b. "Grabotke, Prussia", from Newton;
   his wife Matilda Augusta b. "Dreidorf (Co. Wirsitz, Prov. Posen?),
   Germany"; decl. 4 October 1888- nat. 3 January 1913/ Vol. 1, p.
   45.

6) KLOSS, Friedrich- b. "Nieder Miesau, Germany", from Westfield;
   his wife Ida b. "Schoeno (Schönow, Co. Deutsch Krone, Prov.
   West Prussia?); decl. in Dane Co., Wisc. 31 October 1904- nat.
   4 March 1912/ Vol. 1, p. 36.

7) KRATZ, Ferdinand- b. "Gross Joletz Germany", from Montello; decl.
   under provisions of 1910, June 25th- nat. 21 June 1915/ Vol. 2,
   p. 71.

8) KROLL, Gustaf- b. "Kalinka, Germany" (Prussia), from Montello;
   his wife Amelia b. "Germany"; decl. 6 November 1876- nat. 15
   March 1913/ Vol. 1, p. 47.

9) LANGE, Gustav Herman- b. "Gringberg Germany", from Harrisville;
   his wife Emma b. "Strobnefehauland (Strozewo-Hauland, Co. Kolmar, Prov. Posen, Prussia?), Germany"; decl. 6 April 1886- nat.
   29 April 1913/ Vol. 1, p. 50.

10) LAVZOW, Jospeh- b. "(Grand Duchy of) Mecklenburg, Germany", from
    Buffalo; decl. in Rock Co., Wisc. 27 March 1877- nat. 5 October
    1914/ Vol. 2, p. 55.

11) MANTHEY, Julius- b. "Luisendorf Germany", from Montello; decl.
    24 October 1884- nat. 5 July 1916/ Vol. 2, p. 89.

12) PESCHEL, August- b. "KateNau Germany", from Springfield; his
    deceased wife Elizabeth b. "Germany"; decl. in Milwaukee, Wisc.
    6 November 1882- nat. 12 November 1915/ Vol. 2, p. 36.

MARQUETTE COUNTY DEATHS

<u>Immigrants from County Kolmar, Province Posen, Prussia:</u>

1) BLOCH, Johann- b. "Laskowo, Prussia, Europe"; d. in Mecan 22 September 1895/ Vol. 2, p. 41.

2) BONAS, Michael- b. "Coserson (Chodizesen=Kolmar) Germany"; d. in Oxford 11 August 1901/ Vol. 3, p. 71.

3) GILLHAR (Gehlhaar?), Anna Elizabeth- b. "Chodizesen, Germany"; d. in Neshkoro 19 January 1897 (bur. from St. Peter's Germania, at Mecan)/ Vol. 2, p. 49.

4) HOFFMAN (nee Buettner), Justine- b. "Stroblnzo (Strozewo-?) Hauland Germ."; d. in Shields 14 August 1901/ Vol. 3, p. 71.

5) SCHAEFER KEINITZ, Louise- b. "Strelitz Kolmer (Kolmar) Germany"; d. in Crystal Lake 11 December 1903 (bur. Richford, Waushara Co.)/ Vol. 3, p. 112.

6) SCHULZ, Anna Wilhelmine- b. "Chodziesen, Posen, Europe"; d. in T. Mecan 17 March 1897 (bur. Neshkoro)/ Vol. 2, p. 50.

7) STIBB, Gottlieb- b. "Neulsragonowo (Nikolskowo or Rzadkowo?) Keis (Kreis=County) Kolmar, Europe"; d. in Mecan 15 May 1897/ Vol. 2, p. 50.

8) STUBBE (Fiedeke?), Wilhelmine- b. "Czamoschien (Samotschin) Germany"; d. in Montello 12 October 1904/ Vol. 3, p. 130.

Immigrants from additional locales in Province Posen, Prussia:

1) DAHMS, Alvina E.- "Carlsbach (Karlsbach, Co. Wirsitz?) Ger.";
   d. in Westfield 19 December 1905/ Vol. 3, p. 154.

2) DOEPKE, Daniel- b. (he & both his parents) "Radsitz (probably
   Radzicz a.k.a. Hermannsdorf, Co. Wirsitz) Posen Germany"; d. in
   Mecan 29 May 1907 (bur. Princeton, Green Lake Co.)/ Vol. 3, p.
   100.

3) DREVITZ (DREWITZ), Gottlieb- b. "Germane, Schuentanke (Schönlanke, Co. Czarnikau)"; d. in Newton 17 March 1899/ Vol. 3, p.
   25.

4) FLUTER (FLOETER), August- b. "Tresa (Theresia, Co. Czarnikau)
   Germany"; d. in Newton 1 May 1906 (bur. East Side-Westfield)/
   Vol. 3, p. 160.

5) GRAMSE (Traling), Rosina- b. "Province Posen Germany"; d. in
   Westfield, 19 May 1904 (a New Chester, Adams Co. resident)/
   Vol. 3, p. 124.

6) HOLLENDER (Werner), Anna Stena- b. "Lubsius (Lobsens, Co. Wirsitz?) Germany"; d. in Oxford 17 December 1911 (bur. Budsin)/
   Vol. 4, p. 559.

7) HOLLMAN, August W.- b. "Lammetz (Lemnitz, Co. Czarnikau?) Ger.";
   d. in Newton 23 April 1906/ Vol. 3, p. 161.

8) JANKE (Lubitz), Henriette- b. "Lucast (Lukatz, Co. Filehne)
   Europe"; d. in Mecan 2 a.m.- 17 January 1907 (bur. Germania)/
   Vol. 3, p. 172.

9) MATZ, Frederick Wilhelm- b. Mecan, but both parents from "Bromberg Germany Europe"; d. in Montello 20 March 1901 (bur. St.
   Peter's Mecan)/ Vol. 3, p. 63.

10) RATHMANN (Stelter), Mrs. D.- b. "Prov. of Pozen, Germany"; d.
    in Westfield 18 February 1899/ Vol. 3, p. 26.

11) SCHATZKE, Frederica- b. "Posen, Germany"; d. in Westfield 29 Au-
    gust 1903/ Vol. 3, p. 107.

12) SEIDLITZ, Carl Friedrich- b. "Kreis Lubr (Lubs, Co. Filhene?),
    Posen Europe"; d. in West Rosendale (Fond du Lac Co.), Wisc.
    25 January 1897 (bur. Mecan)/ Vol. 2, p. 49.

13) STANDKE, Christian Friedrich Wm.- b. *"Nugarten, Posen, Europe";
    d. in Marion (twp.), Waushara Co. 23 May 1896 (bur. Neshkoro
    Ev. Luth. Cem.)/ Vol. 2, p. 42.

14) STIBB, Gustine- b. "Provinz Posen Europe"; d. in Mecan 20 Oc-
    tober 1894/ Vol. 2, p. 23.

(*Note: There was a Wugarten, but it was in Co. Friedeberg/Neumark,
  Prov. Brandenburg.)

15) TESKE, Caroline- b."Posen, Germany"; d. in Crystal Lake 14 March 1895/ Vol. 2, p. 28.

16), TESKE, Theodor- b. "Schobin (Schubin, a county seat), Posin (Posen)"; d. in Germania, p.m. 17 September 1900/ Vol. 3, p. 52.

17) VEHRMANN, August- b. "Gornitz (Co. Filehne), Germany"; d. in Newton 9 April 1898/ Vol. 3, p. 11.

<u>Immigrants from Province Brandenburg, Prussia</u>:

1) BEHM, Albert R. of Princeton, Green Lake Co., his parents from "Berlin, Germany"; d. in Westfield, 13 September 1904/ Vol. 3, p. 128.

2) BEHM, August- b. "Berlin, Germany"; d. in Westfield 20 September 1897/ Vol. 3, p. 1.

3) KRENTZ, William F.- b. "Voldenburg (Woldenburg, Co. Friedeberg/ Neumark), Germany"; d. in Westfield 23 March 1905/ Vol. 3, p. 139.

4) LANGE, Ottilie Wilhelmine- b. "Prov. Brandenburg, Schmar Jendorf, Nekermark"; d. in Neshkoro 15 December 1896/ Vol. 2, p. 46.

5) WRUCK, Daniel J.- b. "Lugentorfh (Langenfuhr, Co. Arnswalde?) Germany"; d. in Newton 30 November 1905 (bur. Harrisville)/ Vol. 3, p. 165.

Immigrants from additional locales throughout "Germany":

1) DAVIDSON, John- b. "Hamburger, Germany"; d. in Lawrence 3 March 1899/ Vol. 3, p. 26.

2) GOLDSMITH (GOLDSCHMIDT?), August C. "Eitenbush (possibly Iven-busch, Co. Filehne , Prov. Posen?) Germany"; d. in Newton 3 June 1907/ Vol. 3, p. 181.

3) HALLMAN, Amelia- b. "Henwitz, Germany"; d. in Montello 4 February 1892/ Vol. 2, p. 9.

4) HARKE, Louise- b. "Prussia"; d. in Crystal Lake from "strangulation by hanging"- aged 6 years, 3 September 1899 (bur. Neshkoro)/ Vol. 3, p. 33.

5) HOLTZ (Saxtatter), Mary- b. "Munich Bavaria"; d. in Westfield 9 May 1906 (bur. Richford, Waushara Co.)/ Vol. 3, p. 161.

6) JACOB, Henry- b. "Oderheim Germany"; d. in Westfield 1 May 1905/ Vol. 3, p. 141.

7) JOST, August W.- b. "Chranzui (?) Prussia Ger."; d. in Westfield 12 August 1906/ Vol. 3, p. 167.

8) KELLER, Wilhelm Frederick- b. "Schonefeldt Germany"; d. in Town Princeton, Green Lake Co. 21 December 1901 (bur. Princeton)/ Vol. 3, p. 77.

9) MARX (Kocker), Annie- b. "Berry Dane Co. (Wisc.), parents from "Prov. Pummer (Pommern or Pomerania) Ger."; d. in Buffalo 6 July 1907/ Vol. 3, p. 1841.

10) PAGEL (Voigt), Mrs. Scharlotte-b. "Conborg Germany"; d. in Westfield 25 March 1903/ Vol. 3, p. 98.

11) POLINSKE, Ludwig F.- b. "Putzland (perhaps Putzig-Hauland, Co. Filehne, Prov. Posen?) Ger."; d. in Newton 1 April 1907 (bur. Westfield)/ Vol. 3, p. 178.

12) QUANTIUS, Anthony- b. "Northern France, which has since been joined to Prussia (Alsace-Lorraine?)"; d. in Montello 8 July 1883/ Vol. 1, p. 55.

13) TAGATZ (Schertzke), Louise- b. "Bitzeyhanham (?) Germany"; d. in Montello 5 June 1903/ Vol. 3, p. 102.

14) VINZ (nee Lunking), Mrs. Amelia Louise- b. "Scharlobenburg (Charlottenburg?) Germany"; d. in Westfield 31 January 1899/ Vol. 3, p. 27.

15) WESSING, Edward Joseph- b. "Duelmen Germany"; d. in Packwaukee 5 December 1901/ Vol. 3, p. 76.

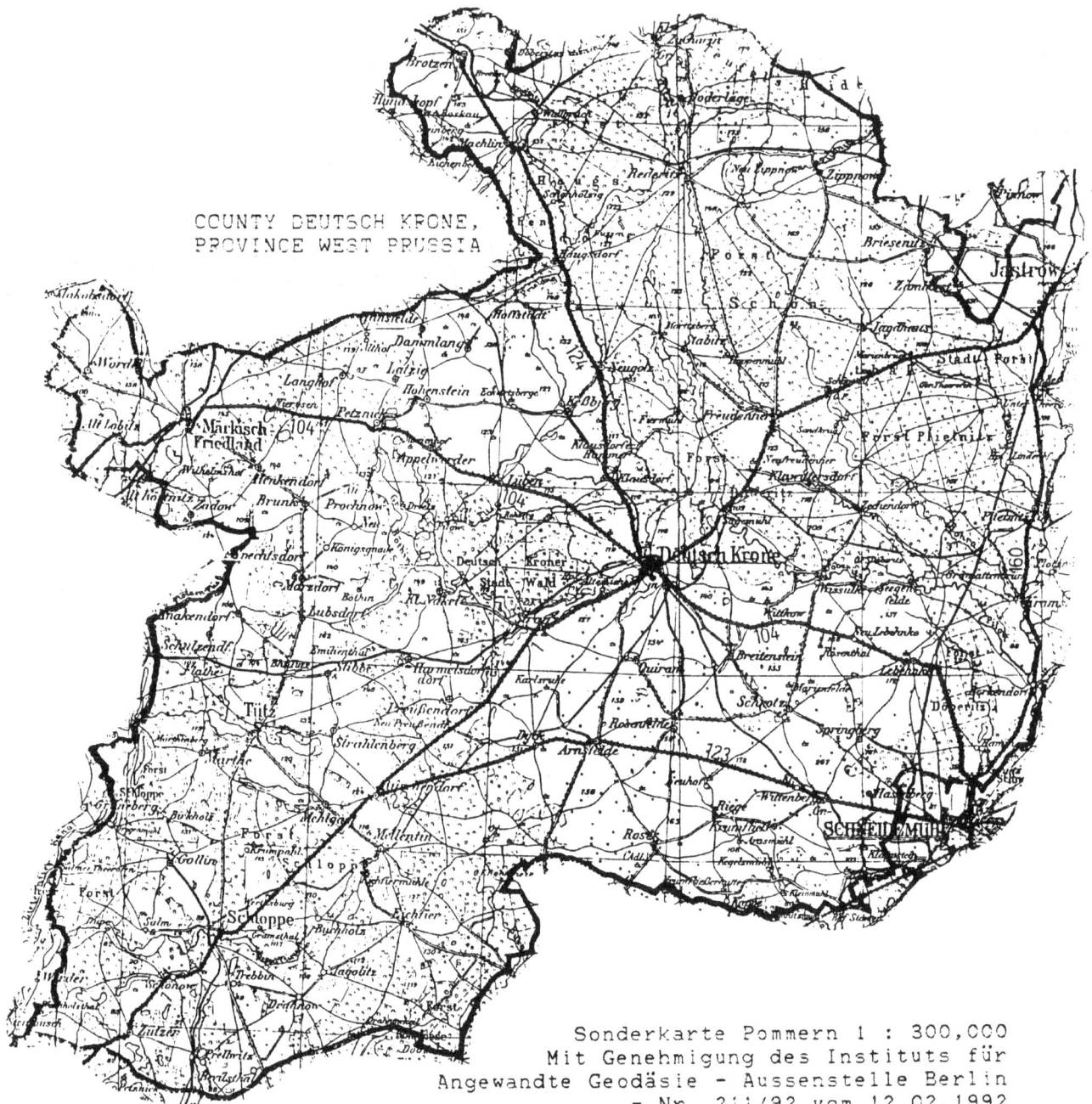

COUNTY DEUTSCH KRONE,
PROVINCE WEST PRUSSIA

Sonderkarte Pommern 1 : 300,000
Mit Genehmigung des Instituts für
Angewandte Geodäsie - Aussenstelle Berlin
- Nr. 211/92 vom 12.02.1992

COUNTY FLATOW,
PROVINCE WEST PRUSSIA

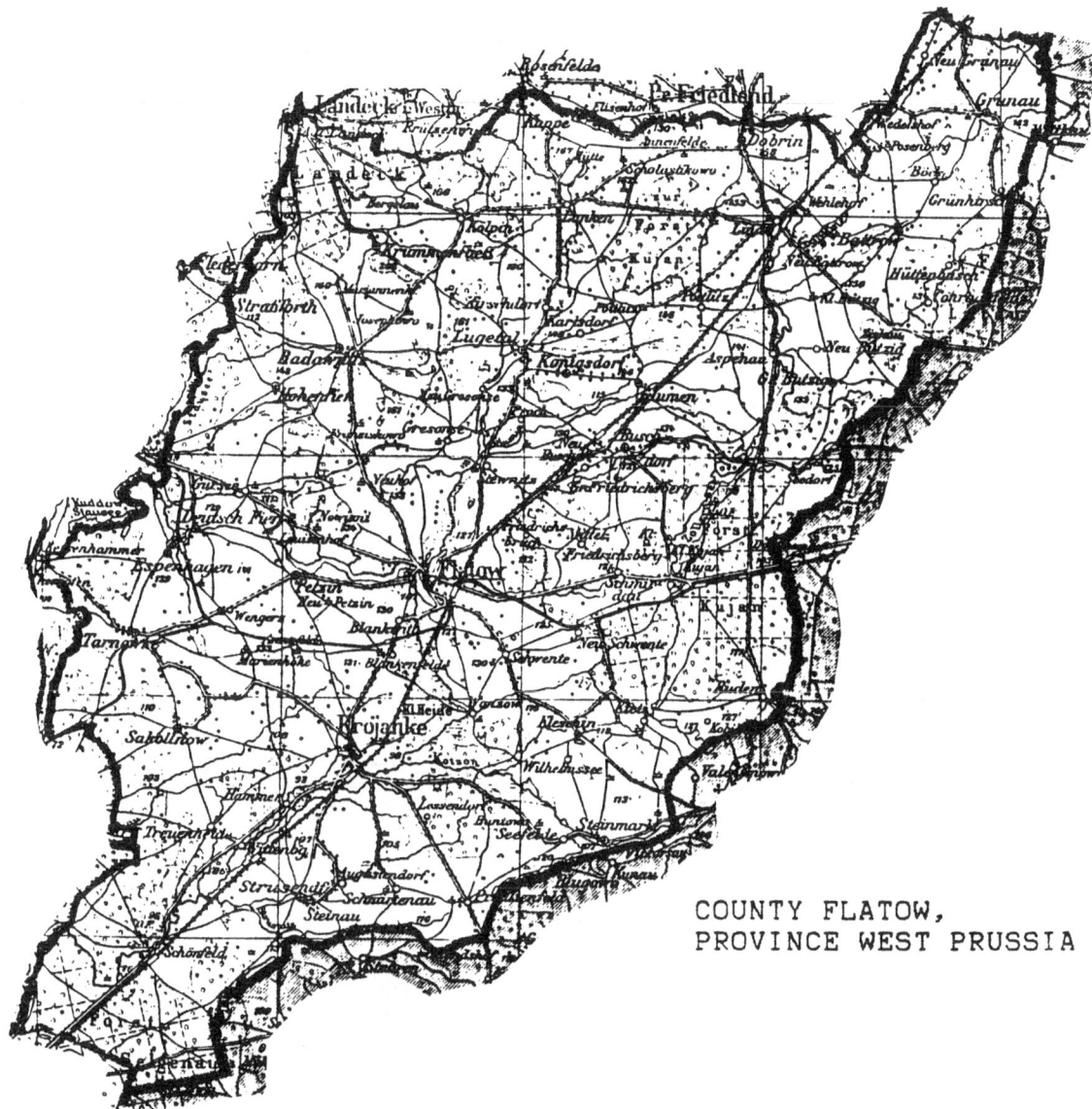

Sonderkarte Pommern 1 : 300,000
Mit Genehmigung des Instituts für Angewandte Geodäsie -
Aussenstelle Berlin - Nr. 211/92 vom 12.02.1992

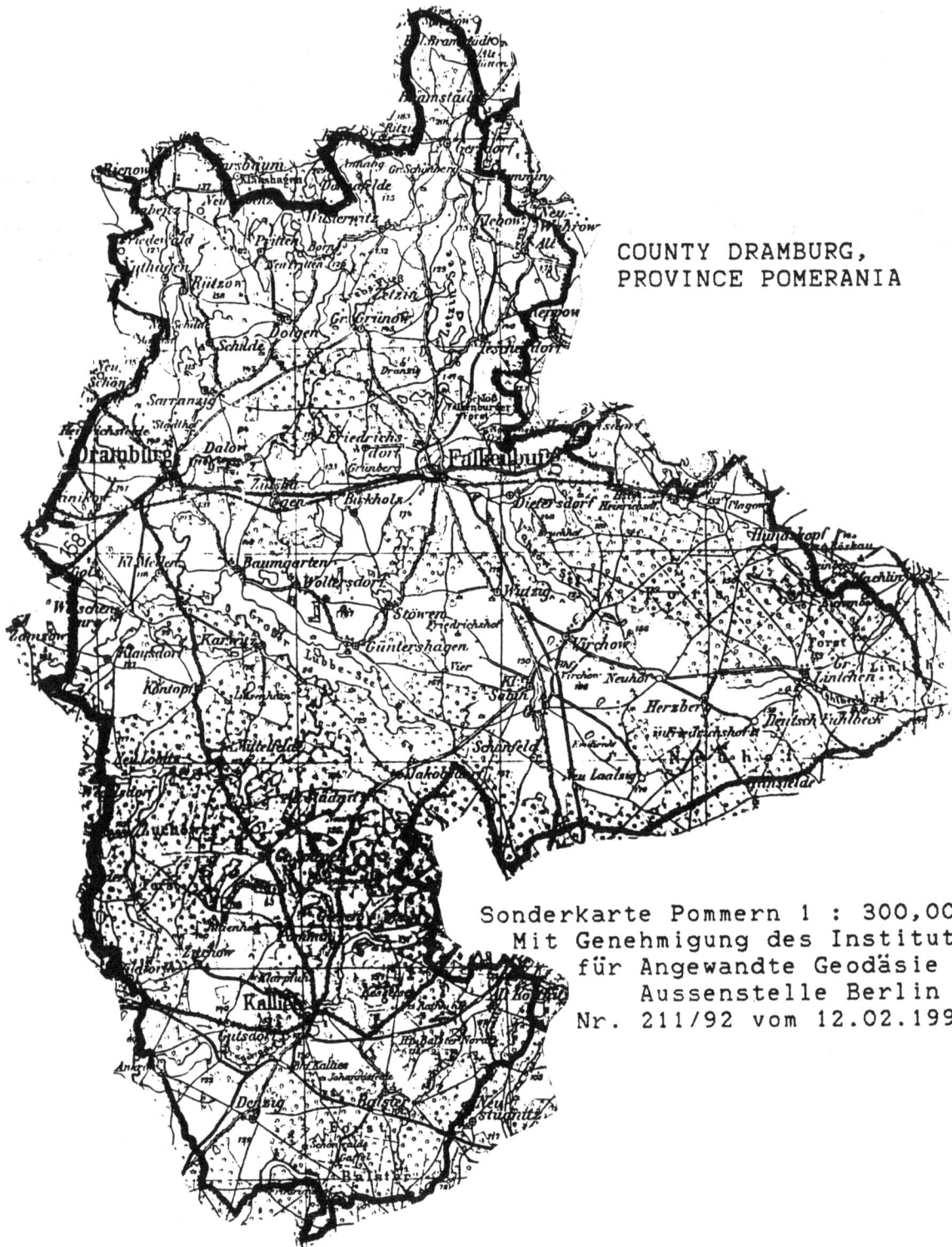

COUNTY DRAMBURG,
PROVINCE POMERANIA

Sonderkarte Pommern 1 : 300,000
Mit Genehmigung des Instituts
für Angewandte Geodäsie -
Aussenstelle Berlin -
Nr. 211/92 vom 12.02.1992

COUNTY SAATZIG
AND STARGARD,
PROVINCE POMERANIA

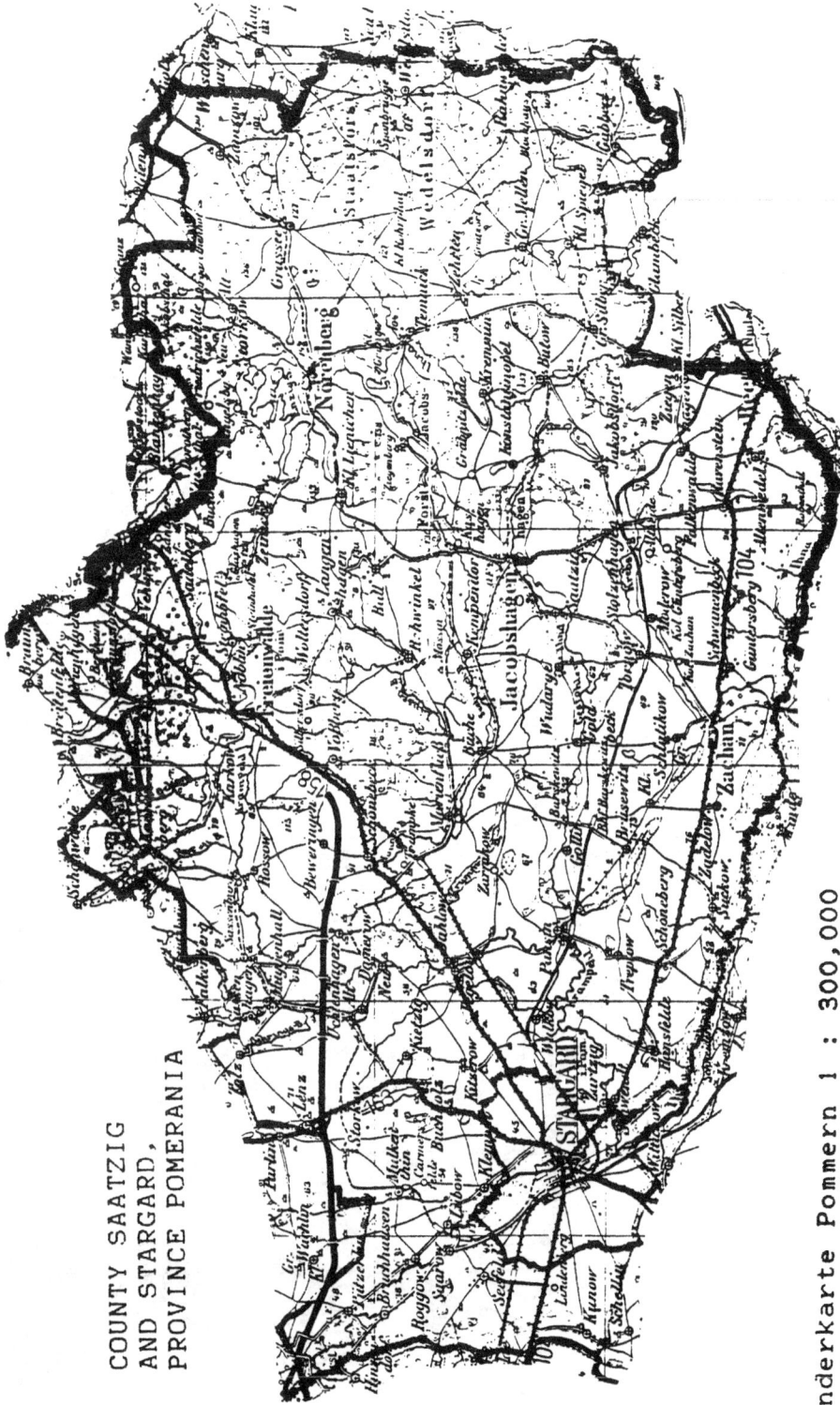

Sonderkarte Pommern 1 : 300.000
Mit Genehmigung des Instituts für Angewandte Geodäsie –
Aussenstelle Berlin – Nr. 211/92 vom 12.02.1992

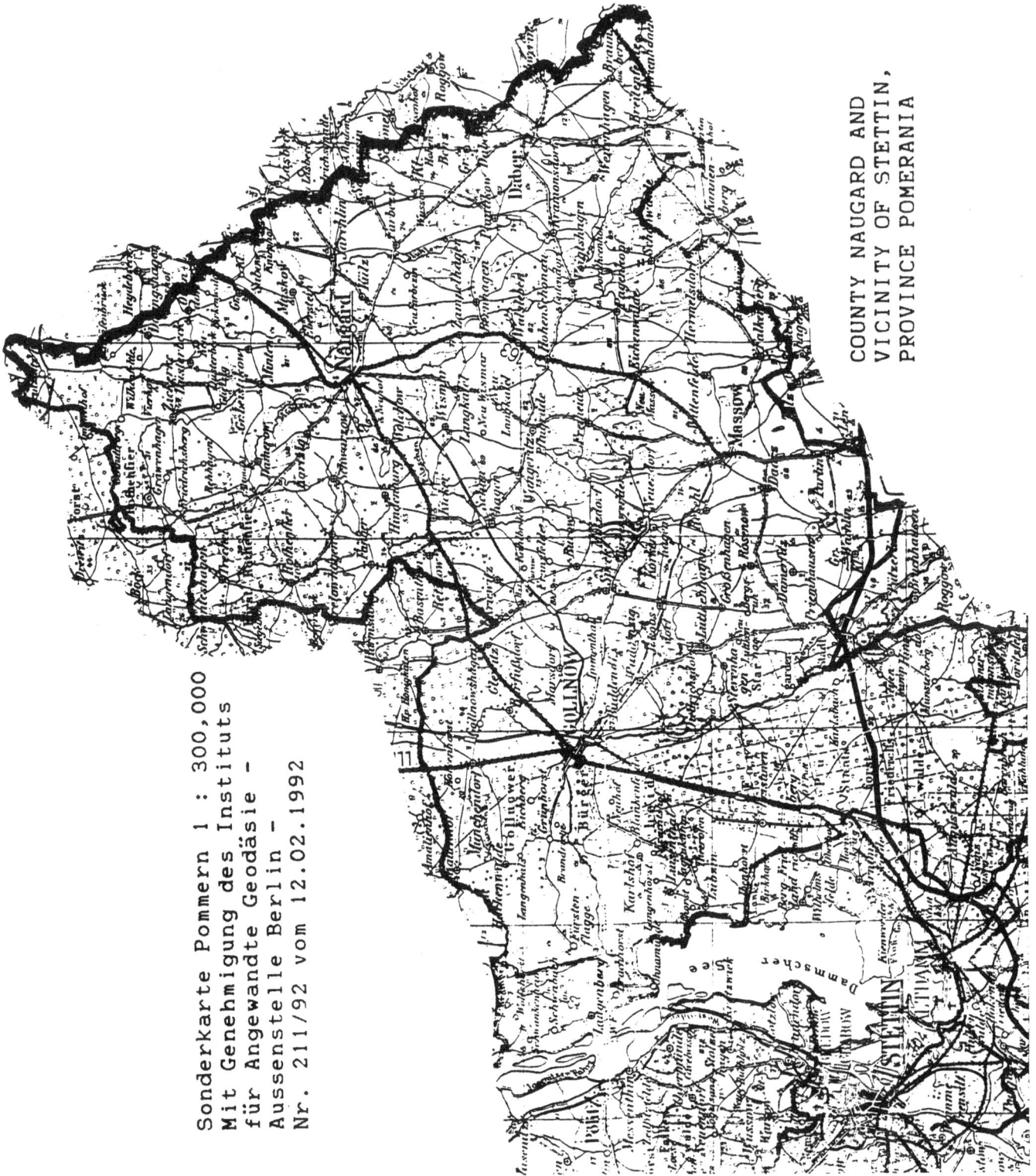

COUNTY NAUGARD AND
VICINITY OF STETTIN,
PROVINCE POMERANIA

Sonderkarte Pommern 1 : 300,000
Mit Genehmigung des Instituts
für Angewandte Geodäsie -
Aussenstelle Berlin -
Nr. 211/92 vom 12.02.1992

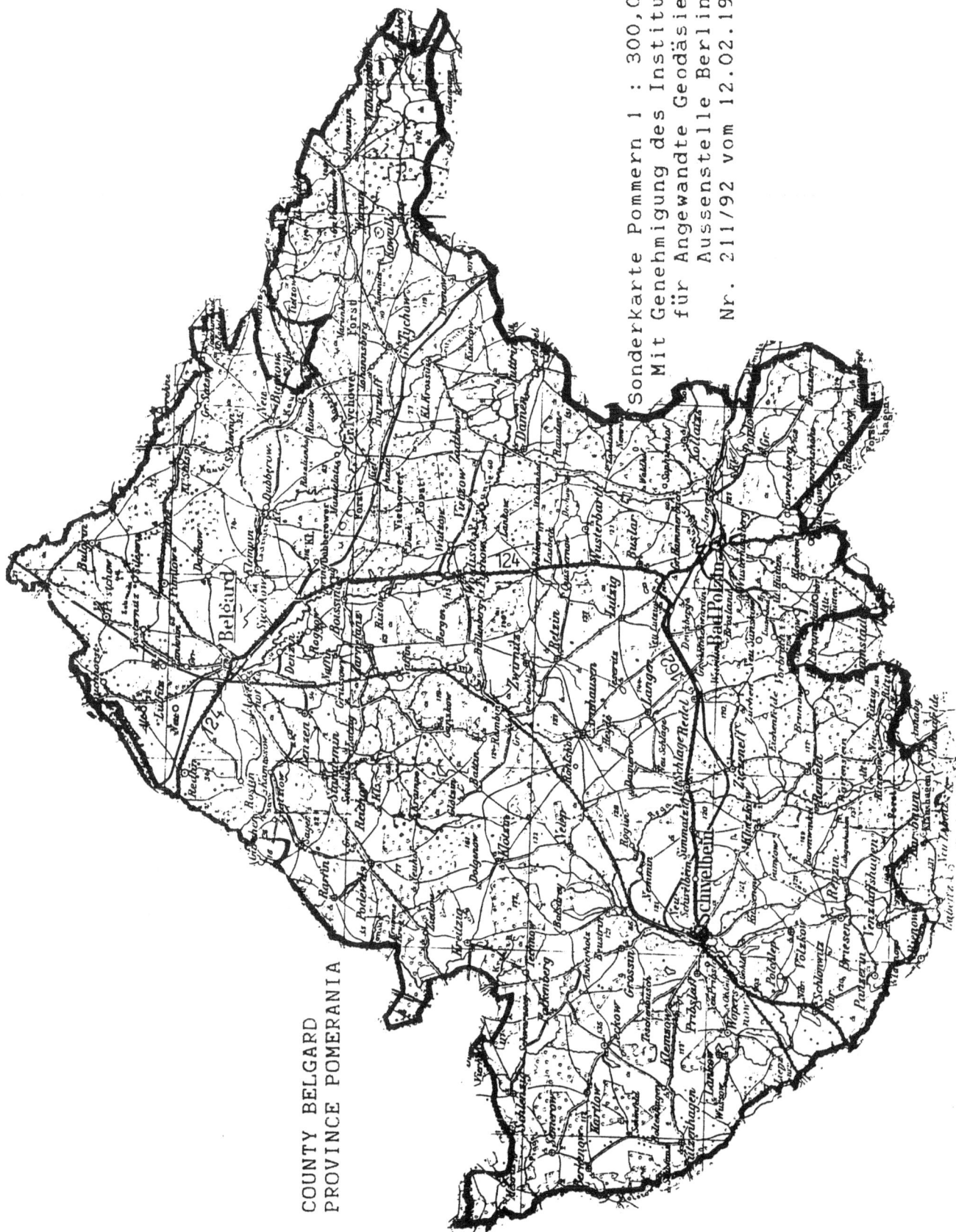

COUNTY BELGARD
PROVINCE POMERANIA

Sonderkarte Pommern 1 : 300,000
Mit Genehmigung des Instituts
für Angewandte Geodäsie –
Aussenstelle Berlin –
Nr. 211/92 vom 12.02.1992

WAUSHARA COUNTY MARRIAGES

<u>Immigrants from County Kolmar, Province Posen, Prussia:</u>

1) JAHNS, Auguste (Bölter)- b. "Ratschin Germany", marr. Friedrich Wilhelm Lang- b. "Lipehne Germany" (<u>Lipin</u>, Co. Kolmar?); at Richford 18 April 1897/ Vol. D, p. 142, no. 32.

2) JERICK, Emelie Amelia- b. "Laskowo Prussia Germ.", marr. Franz Richard Toews- b. "Hohenstein Germany" (could be one of 11 places); at Berlin, Green Lake Co. 11 September 1901/ Vol. D, p. 227, no. 70.

3) JOHNKE, August Friedrich of Marquette Co.- b. "Calmar (Kolmar) Posen", marr. Auguste Johanna Kruger- b. "Pommeran" (Province Pomerania); at Coloma 7 April 1893/ Vol. D, p. 62, no. 41.

4) KIENITZ, Christoph Ludwig of Rushford "Waushara Co." (Winnebago Co.)- b. "Strelitz Prov. Pozen Prussia", marr. Anna Justine Jahns at Richford 22 "Feby" 1887/ Vol. 3 (1870-1890), p. 71, no. 11.

5) KOEPP, August- b. "Gutsieschen Germany" (maybe Chodziesen=Kolmar or Küstrinchen, Co. Wirsitz?), marr. Bertha Wilhelmine Schrank (Chemnitz)- b. "Zschornika" (Czarnikau, a Posen county seat); at the Town of Coloma 4 April (1895)/ Vol. D, p. 107, no. 49.

6) MITTELSTEDT, Edward of Oshkosh (Winnebago Co.)- b. Lippe Prussia" (maybe Liepe, Co. Kolmar?), marr. Othilee Thews at Bloomfield 29 March 1869/ Vol. 2 (1863-1870), p. 152.

7) NOACK, Julius- b. "Sippe (Lippe?) Posen Pruesen" (Liepe?), marr. Ottilie Mueller at Bloomfield 28 June 1882/ Vol. 3 (1870-1890), p. 47, no. 54.

8) PRAHL, Frederick Augustus of Lebanon, Waupaca Co. (Wisc.)- b. "Brotten (Brodden) Prussia", marr. Florentine Schoneck at Bloomfield 16 November 1862/ Vol. 1 (1852-1863), p. 144.

9) WEHSNER, August- b. "Zachersberg (Zachasberg) Germany", marr. Minnie Haensel- b. "Putzig (Co. Filhene, Prov. Posen, Prussia) Germany"; at the Town of Richford 13 January 1894/ Vol. D, p. 78, no. 6.

Waushara County

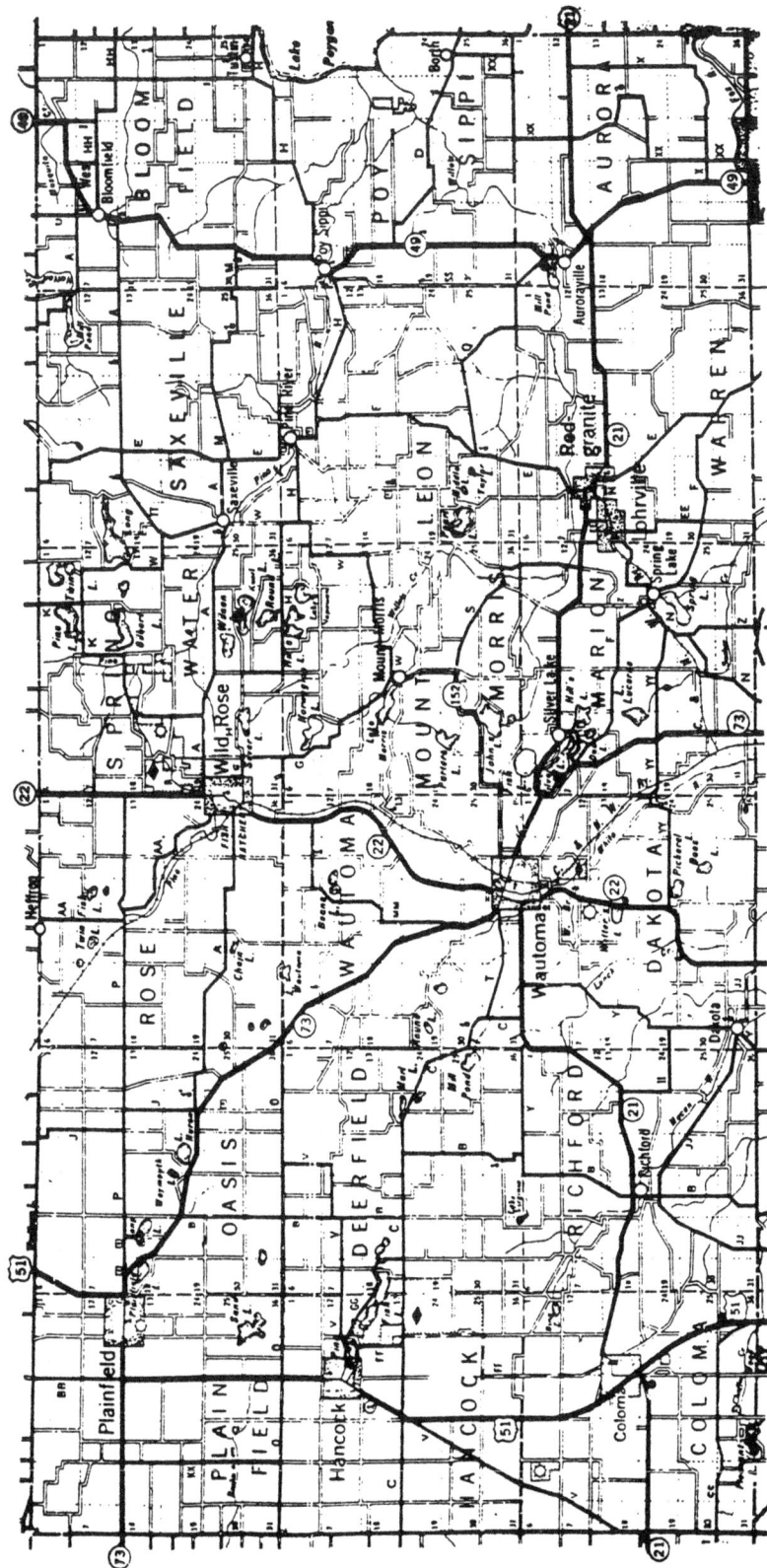

(From COME BACK IN TIME, Vol. I by Elaine Reetz)

Immigrants from the City, County, Administrative District of "Bromberg", Province Posen, Prussia:

1) ERDMANN, Gustav of Manawa (Waupaca Co., Wisc.)- b. "Rezb. (Regierungsbezirk=Administrative District) Bromberg Germany", marr. Emma Janke- b. "Rezb. Bromberg"; at the Town of Bloomfield 1 March (1894) / Vol. D, p. 82, no. 25.

2) FRIEDRICK, Gottfried- b. "Reg(ierungsbezirk=Administrative District) Bromberg", marr. Caroline Fenner at Bloomfield 21 February 1887/ Vol. 3 (1870-1890), p. 71, no. 13.

3) PANKONIN, Herman Albert of Big Flats, Adams Co. (Wisc.)- b. "Bromberg Germany", marr. Bertha Matthilde Marquard- b. "Chicago, Ill."; at Hancock 21 April 1906/ Vol. E, p. 42, no. 56.

4) POMMENKE, Robart- b. "Bromberg Prussia", marr. Wilhelmine Malchow at Bloomfield 7 March 1863/ Vol. 1 (1852-1863), p. 151.

5) RADTKE, Gustavus Robert- b. "Lochowo district of Bromberg Prov. Posen Prussia", marr. Ottilie Amalie S(c)hoeneck at Bloomfield 25 February 1885/ Vol. 3 (1870-1890), p. 61, no. 14.

6) REDMANN, Reinhold Fred- b. "near Bromberg Prov. Tosen Germ."(Posen), marr. Edna Moldenhauer of Berlin, Green Lake Co.; at Berlin 30 November 1905/ Vol. E, p. 30, no. 96.

7) SCHWENGER, Fredrich of Crystal Lake (Marquette Co,, Wisc.)- b. "Bromberg Posen Germany", marr. Matilda Drewes at Dakota 11 May 1878/ Vol. 3 (1870-1890), p. 28, no. 611.

8) TEWS, Andreas Carl- b. "Bromberg Prussia", marr. Frederike Johanne Helm at Bloomfield 12 July 1868/ Vol. 2 (1863-1870), p. 136.

9) TIMM, Frederick T.- b. "Bromberg Prussia", marr. Amelia Beyer at Bloomfield 7 September 1867/ Vol. 2 (1863-1870), p. 118.

10) ZABEL, Frederich A.- b. "Bromberg", marr. Frederike W. Dietrick at Bloomfield 26 December 1868/ Vol. 2 (1863-1870), p. 145.

Immigrants from County Wirsitz, Province Posen, Prussia:

1) BRUCK, Hermann Michael- b. "Guntergost West Prussia(?)", marr. Bertha Emilie Schmidt- b. "Newton, Marquette Co."; at the Town of Richford 3 April 1894/ Vol. D, p. 82, no. 28.

2) DAMROHSE, Martha Ann- b. "Blugowo Germany", marr. August Wruck- b. "Neukronan Germany"; at Coloma 9 May 1899/ Vol. D, p. 185, no. 48.

3) FUNDE?, Gustave F. of Weyauwega (Waupaca Co., Wisc.)- b. "Netzthal Pruesen", marr. Amanda A.B. Timm at Bloomfield 23 August 1890/ Vol. D, p. 11, no. 65.

4) KELLER, Friedrich August of Rushford "Waushara Co." (Winnebago Co.)- b. "Elersport Posen" (may be Elsenort=Aniela Kolonie), marr. Emilie Alvina Wegner at Bloomfield? 16 March 1888/ Vol. 3 (1870-1890), p. 78, no. 33.

5) KIRSCHBAUM, Reinhold- b. "Fredrickshurst (Friedrichshorst) Posen", marr. Maria S. Müller at Richford 26 February 1889/ Vol. 3 (1870-1890), p. 82, no. 17.

6) LAVE, Michael- b. "Sablentz (Lobsens?) Posen Germany", marr. Anna Amelia Berta Ponto in a civil ceremony at Dakota 14 January 1878/ Vol. 3 (1870-1890), p. 27, no. 532.

7) REETZ, Emil R.- b. "Dreidorf Ger", marr. Erna or Ema M. Haase at Poy Sippy 15 March 1889/ Vol. 3 (1870-1890), p. 83, no. 33.

Farmers' Directory of Bloomfield Township

Abbreviations: Sec., section; ac., acres; wf., wife; ch., children; ( ) years in county

Sam Abraham, Weyauwega, R4.
Chas. Bachnman, West Bloomfield, R1.
G. W. Bachnman, West Bloomfield, R1.
Henry Bachnman, West Bloomfield, R1.
Louie Bartel, Poy Sippi, R1.
Henry Bauer, West Bloomfield, R1.
August Boelter, West Bloomfield, R1.
Herman Bowers, West Bloomfield.
John Bowers, West Bloomfield, R1.
John Boyson Jr., Poy Sippi, R1.
Chas. Bradberry, West Bloomfield, R1.
August Ebert, West Bloomfield, R1.
Ferdinand Ebert, West Bloomfield, R1.
Wm. Fisher, West Bloomfield, R1.
Albert Glock, West Bloomfield, R1.
Wm. Godson, Poy Sippi, R1.
Wm. Gollnick, West Bloomfield, R1.
Herman Grambsch, Poy Sippi, R1.
Fred Grimm, Poy Sippi, R1.
August Hanneman, West Bloomfield, R1.
John Hartfield, West Bloomfield, R1.
Albert Hendrich, Poy Sippi, R1.
Wm. Hendrich, West Bloomfield, R1.
Fred Henschel, Poy Sippi, R1.
Clarence Hinchley, Weyauwega, R4.
Ed. Hinchley, West Bloomfield, R1.
Herman Hirte, West Bloomfield, R1.
Albert Howard, West Bloomfield, R1.
Lars Johnson, Poy Sippi, R1.
N. Jorgensen, Pine River, R2.
Wm. Kage, West Bloomfield, R1.
Wm. Kempf, West Bloomfield, R1.
Herman Kissinger, Poy Sippi, R1.
Henry Kleish, West Bloomfield, R1.
Fred Kobiske, West Bloomfield, R1.
John Kobiske, West Bloomfield, R1.
Herman Koehler, West Bloomfield.
Martin Koehler, West Bloomfield.
Herman Koop, West Bloomfield, R1.
Henry Kopiske, West Bloomfield, R1.
August Kuehl, West Bloomfield, R1.
Otto Kuehl, Weyauwega, R4.
Chas. J. Laubenheimer, Poy Sippi, R1.

John Lind, Poy Sippi, R1.
Steve Mueller, Weyauwega, R4.
John Nehring, Poy Sippi, R1.
Wm. T. Neuman, West Bloomfield, R1.
Julius Noak, West Bloomfield, R1.
Wm. Pagal, Weyauwega, R4.
Albert Pagel, West Bloomfield, R1.
Otto Pagel, West Bloomfield, R1.
Alex Pommeranke, West Bloomfield, R1.
Ferdinand Pufahl, West Bloomfield, R1.
Albert Radichel, West Bloomfield, R1.
Herman Radichel, West Bloomfield, R1.
John Radichel, West Bloomfield, R1.
Fred Reinke, Fremont, R2.
John Reinke, West Bloomfield, R1.
Carl Rick, West Bloomfield, R1.
Seth Rogers, Poy Sippi, R1.
John Rucks, West Bloomfield, R1.
Henry Schoenick, Pine River, R1.
Herman Schmidt, West Bloomfield, R1.
Chas. Selle, Poy Sippi, R1.
Otto Standke Jr., Weyauwega, R4.
Otto Standke Sr., Weyauwega, R4.
Henry Strehlow, Poy Sippi, R1.
Albert Strey, West Bloomfield, R1.
Louie Strey, West Bloomfield, R1.
Martin Strey, West Bloomfield, R1.
John Struck, West Bloomfield, R1.
Fred Stuebs, West Bloomfield, R1.
Wm. Tank, Weyauwega, R2.
Henry Teske, West Bloomfield, R1.
Carl Thews, West Bloomfield, R1.
Edwin Thews, West Bloomfield, R1.
Hubert Timm, West Bloomfield, R1.
Herman Wangerien, West Bloomfield, R1.
Frank Wendt, West Bloomfield, R1.
Richard Wendt, Poy Sippi, R1.
Carl Wilke, Weyauwega, R2.
Willis Wolcott, Fremont, R2.
John Yomke, West Bloomfield, R1.
August Young, West Bloomfield, R1.
Edward Zempel, West Bloomfield, R1.

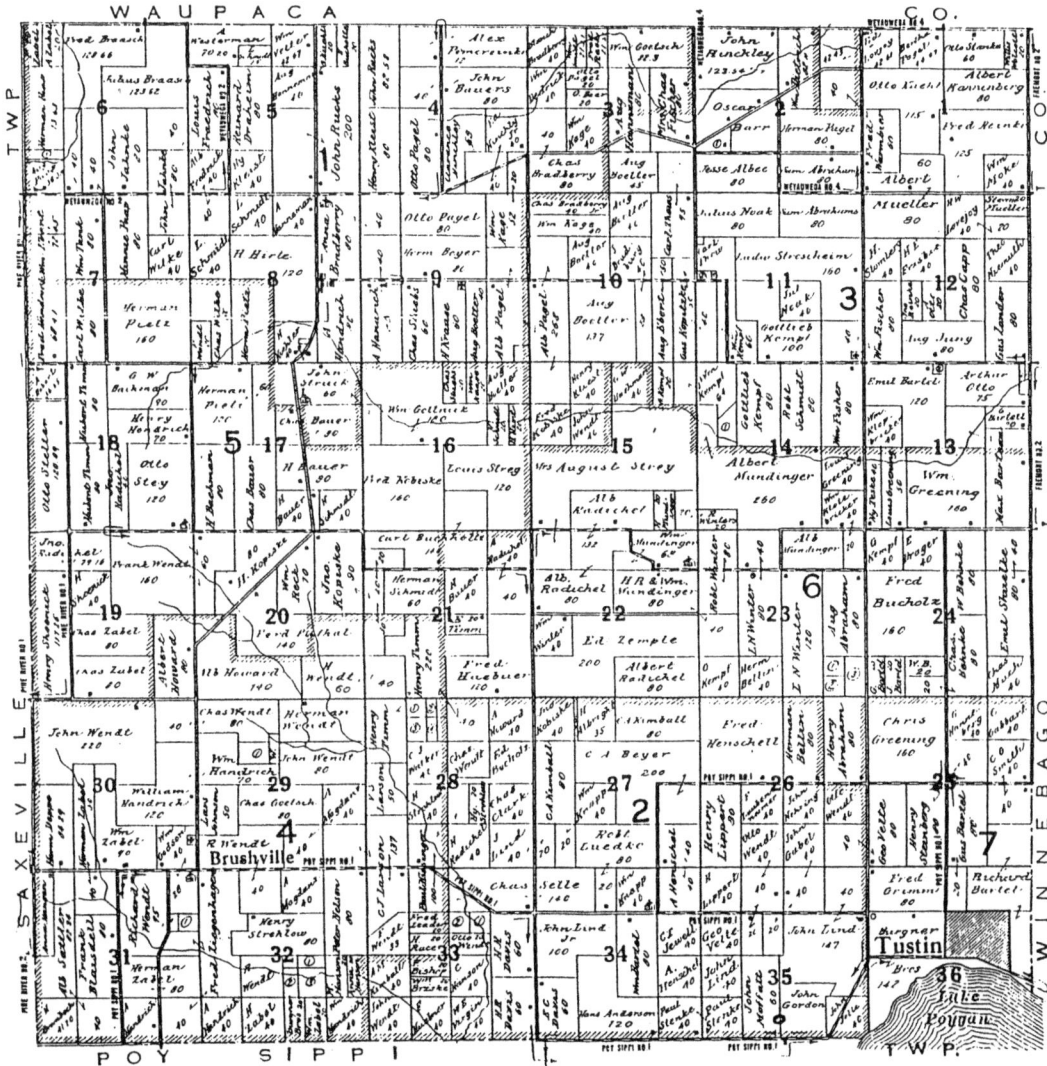

MAP OF
BLOOMFIELD
TOWNSHIP
Scale 1½ Inches to 1 Mile

Township 20 North, Range 13 East of 4th P. M.
WAUSHARA COUNTY, WIS.

Rural Routes shown thus · · · · · · · · · Churches shown thus ·
School Districts · · · · · 2 · · · · · Cemeteries · · · · · · · †
Schools · · · · · · · · · · Corporation Limits of Cities shown thus

List of Small Property Owners in This Township Shown on Map by Numbers

(Michael Bednarek Collection, Wautoma, Wisc.)

Immigrants from County Czarnikau, Province Posen, Prussia:

1) DOEDE, Emil Reinhard- b. "Caroline in Preussen Germany", marr. Elisabeth Louise Timm at the Town of Bloomfield 26 January 1898/ Vol. D, p. 160, no. 14.

2) FREITAG, Heinrich August of Montello, Marquette Co.- b. "Radoline Germany", marr. Emma Amalie Schafer at Richford 9 April 1893/ Vol. D, p. 123, no. 46.

3) KOSLOWSKE, Gustav Karl- b. "Radozin (Radolin?) Provinz Posen", marr. Emilie Ottilie Schwirsinzki at Newton, Marquette Co. 13 "Jany"(1888)/ Vol. 3 (1870-1890), p. 77, no. 5.

4) POCKRANDT, Wilhelmine- b. "Romanshof Germany", marr. Julius Wegner- b. "Neu Danzig (may be Neu-Latzig, Co. Dramburg, Prov. Pomerania) Germany"; at the Town of Coloma 9 August 1898/ Vol. D, p. 172, no. 85.

5) PROESCHER, Karl August- b. "Romanshof Germany", marr. Ottelie Brietzke- b. "Brumgarten (may be Baumgarten, Co. Wirsitz?) Germany"; at Coloma 23 Novemver (1894)/ Vol. D, p. 97, no. 112.

6) SCHULZ, Julius Hermann- b. "15 February 1865 Wornitz (Gornitz?) Kr. Scharnikau (County Czarnikau) Posen", marr. Ella Emelie Brasinsky at Dakota 27 November 1891/ Vol. D, p. 34, no. 139.

Immigrants from County Schubin, Province Posen, Prussia:

1) FREDRICH, Julius of Royalton, Waupaca Co. (Wisc.)- b. "Greenow
(Grünau) district of Posen Prussia", marr. Henriette Werner at
East Bloomfield 22 November 1883/ Vol. 3 (1870-1890), p. 54,
no. 94.

2) HARK, Emilie (widow, maiden name Nilzo?)- b. "in Voronikar (Veronika) Kr. Schubben (Co. Schubin) Posen", marr. Julius Heinrich
(?P)Flugrad- b. "Arnswalde Brandenburg (a county seat)"; at Richford 15 March 1894/ Vol. D, p. 81, no. 22.

3) KRUGER, Gustav Adolph of Wolf River, Winnebago Co. (Wisc.)- b.
"Ruden Reg(ierungsbezirk=Administrative District) Bromberg Ger-
many", marr. Emilie Pauline Jung at Bloomfield 2 April 1883/
Vol. 3 (1870-1890), p. 73, no. 28.

4) STIELMANN, August of Weyauwega (Waupaca Co., Wisc.)- b. "Rans-
dorf*Ab(b)au Posen Preussen Germany", marr. Alvine Adelgunde A-
mande Ebert at West Bloomfield 18 July 1889/ Vol. 3 (1870-1890),
p. 84, no. 57.   (*note actually spelled Rensdorf)

Immigrants from indeterminable locales in Province Posen, Prussia:

1) BLISS, Emma Elizabeth (maiden name Opperman)- b. "Ruhnow (perhaps
Runau, County Czarnikau; or Runowo, Counties Wongrowitz or Schro-
da; or Ruhnow, County Stolp, but Province Pomerania) Posen Ger-
many", marr. Gottfried Emil Valentien of Pine Grove, Portage Co.
(Wisc.)- b. "Gritzendorf (Grützendorf, County Obernick) Posen
Germ"; at Coloma 18 October 1897/ Vol. D, p. 150, no. 82.

2) BUSS, Frederick of the Town of Dubon(?)- b. "Mernsee Posen Ger",
marr. Rosaline Adeline Huf at Bloomfield 2 December 1889/ Vol.
D, p. 1, no. 2.

3) MACHOL, Josephus marr. Catholine BRATKOSKI- b. "Snieradiko Po-
set Germ Europe" at Berlin 25 November 1902/ Vol. D, p. 261, no.
no. 139 (performed by Rev. John C. Bierniatz at St. Mike's Church,
likely Catholic ceremony for Polish couple).

4) MARQUARDT, Friedr. Wilh.- b. "Lehmbin Pos-en, Germany", marr.
Therese Marie Mathilde Fischer- b. "Greifenberg (Co. Naugard,
Prov.-) Pommern Germany"; at West Bloomfield 16 July 1900/ Vol.
D, p. 207, no. 67.

5) RUSCH, Wilhelmine Loisaa- b. "Kisch Rogow Posen Germany", marr.
Alexander Joseph Pommerenke- b. "Nekla (Co. Schroda, Prov. Posen)
Preussen Germany"; at Bloomfield 19 January 1899/ Vol. D, p. 178,
no. 9.

Farmers' Directory of Coloma Township

Abbreviations: Sec., section; ac., acres; wf., wife; ch., children; ( ) years in county

H. Bacon, Coloma.
W. A. Baker, Hancock, R3.
Frank Bandt, Coloma.
Fred G. Bandt, Coloma.
Gust Bandt, Coloma.
Herman Bandt, Coloma.
J. F. Bandt, Coloma.
J. Barrett, Coloma, R1.
George Bartlett, Coloma.
H. F. Bartz, Coloma.
J. Bartz Jr., Coloma.
J. Bartz Sr., Coloma.
G. W. Bassett, Coloma.
Dr. A. A. Beck, Coloma.
H. Belter, Coloma.
J. A. Bishop, Coloma.
L. F. Bishop, Coloma.
Thos. Bishop, Coloma.
B. Blackmore, Coloma.
L. S. Blatchley, Coloma, R1.
Adolph Boesler, Coloma.
H. Boesler, Coloma.
L. Boesler, Coloma.
A. J. Borsack, Coloma.
Chas. Brendlandt, Coloma.
August Britske, Coloma, R3.
Oscar Britske, Coloma, R3.
L. S. Brooks, Coloma.
A. Brown, Coloma, R1.
L. Buchanan, Coloma, R2.
Ray Buchanan, Coloma, R2.
Z. R. Burk, Coloma.
George Burnett, Coloma.
F. Bushke, Coloma, R2.
F. M. Buschke, Coloma.
F. D. Button, Coloma, R2.
Willis Carlton, Coloma, R1.
C. Chesebro, Coloma.
J. Chesbro, Coloma.
John Christian, Coloma.
R. J. Clark, Coloma.
H. Collins, Coloma.
J. W. Collins, Coloma.
L. H. Cotton, Coloma, R1.
F. H. Cramer, Coloma.
W. F. Curran, Coloma.
Carl Damerahse, Coloma.
Emil Denner, Coloma, R2.
Fred Denner, Coloma, R2.
J. W. Dennings, Coloma, R1.
John Devine Sr., Coloma, R3.
Menzo Dimick, Coloma, R1.
B. L. Dulin, Coloma.
H. Eichstendt, Coloma, R1.
R. H. Ely, Coloma.
Walter Ely, Coloma.
Chas. Fearne, Coloma, R1.
John Foat, Coloma, R1.
Darwin Follett, Coloma.
V. Follett, Coloma.
H. Gethers, Coloma.
August Glaska, Coloma.
Emil Glaska, Coloma, R1.
Herman Glaska, Coloma, R2.
Wm. Gloede, Coloma, R1.
E. Gould, Coloma, R2.
F. L. Graichen, Coloma.
Gus. Graichen, Coloma.

Fred Graper, Coloma.
Chester Gray, Coloma, R1.
George Gray, Coloma, R1.
Walter Gray, Coloma, R1.
W. F. Gray, Coloma, R1.
R. Gutsche, Coloma.
H. J. Hawkins, Coloma.
Archie Hayes, Coloma, R2.
V. H. Helms, Coloma.
Wm. Hine, Coloma.
Emil Hoffman, Coloma.
Paul Hoffman, Coloma.
Theo. Hoffman, Coloma, R1.
Wm. Hoffman, Coloma.
J. D. Hollister, Coloma.
John Holtz, Coloma.
Wm. Holtz, Coloma, R1.
C. M. Hopper, Coloma, R1.
A. Hughes, Coloma.
Hiram Humphrey, Coloma.
Marion Humphrey, Coloma.
Warren Humphrey, Coloma.
Wm. Humphrey, Coloma.
Paul Imm, Coloma.
Chas. Jacobs, Coloma, R2.
Fred Jacobs, Coloma, R1.
Herbert Jacobs, Coloma, R2.
John Jacobs, Coloma, R1.
John Jefferson, Coloma.
J. E. Jones, Coloma.
Emil King, Coloma.
F. E. King, Coloma.
Fred King, Coloma, R2.
H. A. King, Coloma, R2.
Herman King, Coloma, R2.
John A. King, Coloma, R2.
J. T. King, Coloma.
Robert King, Coloma, R2.
Theo King, Coloma.
George Kirsenlohr, Coloma.
J. Krause, Coloma, R3.
Amil Krinke, Coloma.
Albert Kromrie, Coloma, R3.
Albert Kromrie Jr., Coloma.
Emil Kromrie, Coloma, R1.
Henry Kromrie, Coloma, R3.
Chas. Kruger Jr., Coloma.
Chas. Kruger Sr., Coloma, R3.
Ed. Kruger, Coloma, R3.
H. Kruger, Coloma.
James Laing, Coloma.
D. W. La Rue, Coloma.
R. La Rue, Coloma.
Chas. Lausch, Coloma.
August Lawrence, Coloma.
Richard Lawrence, Coloma.
Art Lawton, Coloma.
W. C. Lawton, Coloma.
A. Lyon, Coloma.
Joe Machan, Coloma.
A. Manley, Coloma, R2.
August Mantie, Coloma.
Paul Mantie, Coloma.
J. R. McLaughlin, Coloma.
August Miller, Coloma, R1.
W. J. Miller, Coloma, R1.
August Moltke, Coloma, R2.
Asel Monroe, Coloma.

J. C. Moore, Coloma.
Gus. Muschke, Coloma.
J. B. Oliver, Coloma, R1.
John Opperman, Coloma, R3.
C. A. Oppermann, Coloma.
John Otto, Coloma.
Wm. Otto, Coloma.
H. E. Parker, Coloma.
Roy Parkin, Coloma.
Sam Parkin, Coloma.
N. Peck, Coloma, R1.
A. Pekofsky, Coloma.
Arthur Pells, Coloma.
Jerry Pells, Coloma.
F. M. Ploetz, Coloma.
J. Ploetz, Coloma, R1.
Richard Ploetz, Coloma.
Emil Podoll, Coloma.
Theo. Podoll, Coloma.
Wm. Podoll, Coloma.
F. Powell, Coloma.
F. N. Powell, Coloma.
Harry Powell, Coloma.
E. Premo, Coloma.
L. Premo, Coloma.
W. A. Roblier, Coloma.
Frank Runnels, Coloma.
S. C. Runnels, Coloma.
S. H. Runnels, Coloma.
J. Rutkowsky, Coloma, R2.
Albert Rux, Coloma, R1.
Wm. Schmalz, Coloma.
R. Schmudlach, Coloma, R2.
Mike Schrank, Coloma.
Chas. Schultz, Hancock, R3.
Albert Shorey, Coloma.
J. A. Shorey, Coloma.
William Shorey, Coloma.
A. H. Slater, Coloma.
Edgar Slater, Coloma.
E. R. Slater, Coloma.
H. K. Smith, Coloma, R1.
J. W. Smith, Coloma, R1.
L. F. Smith, Coloma.
Wm. Smith, Coloma.
J. F. Spalding, Coloma, R1.
J. N. Spalding, Coloma.
E. E. Stratton, Coloma.
W. H. Tennant, Hancock, R3.
Frank Thompson, Coloma, R1.
R. Thompson, Coloma, R1.
E. Thurber, Coloma, R1.
Leonard Twist, Coloma.
A. J. Uher, Coloma.
E. J. Uher, Coloma.
Albert Vilbaum, Coloma.
T. M. Warner, Coloma.
A. Wedde, Coloma, R1.
Arthur Weiland, Coloma, R1.
A. Welke, Coloma.
A. J. Williams, Coloma, R1.
August Wruck, Coloma.
Wm. Yacht, Coloma, R2.
C. A. Yorkson, Coloma.
Fred Zahn, Coloma.
J. Zuhlke, Coloma.

195

MAP OF
COLOMA
TOWNSHIP   Scale 1½ Miles to 1 Inch

Township 18 North, Range 8 East of the 4th P. M.
WAUSHARA COUNTY, WIS.

Rural Routes shown thus:
School Districts "   2
Schools "
Churches shown thus:
Cemeteries "
Corporation Limits of Cities shown thus:

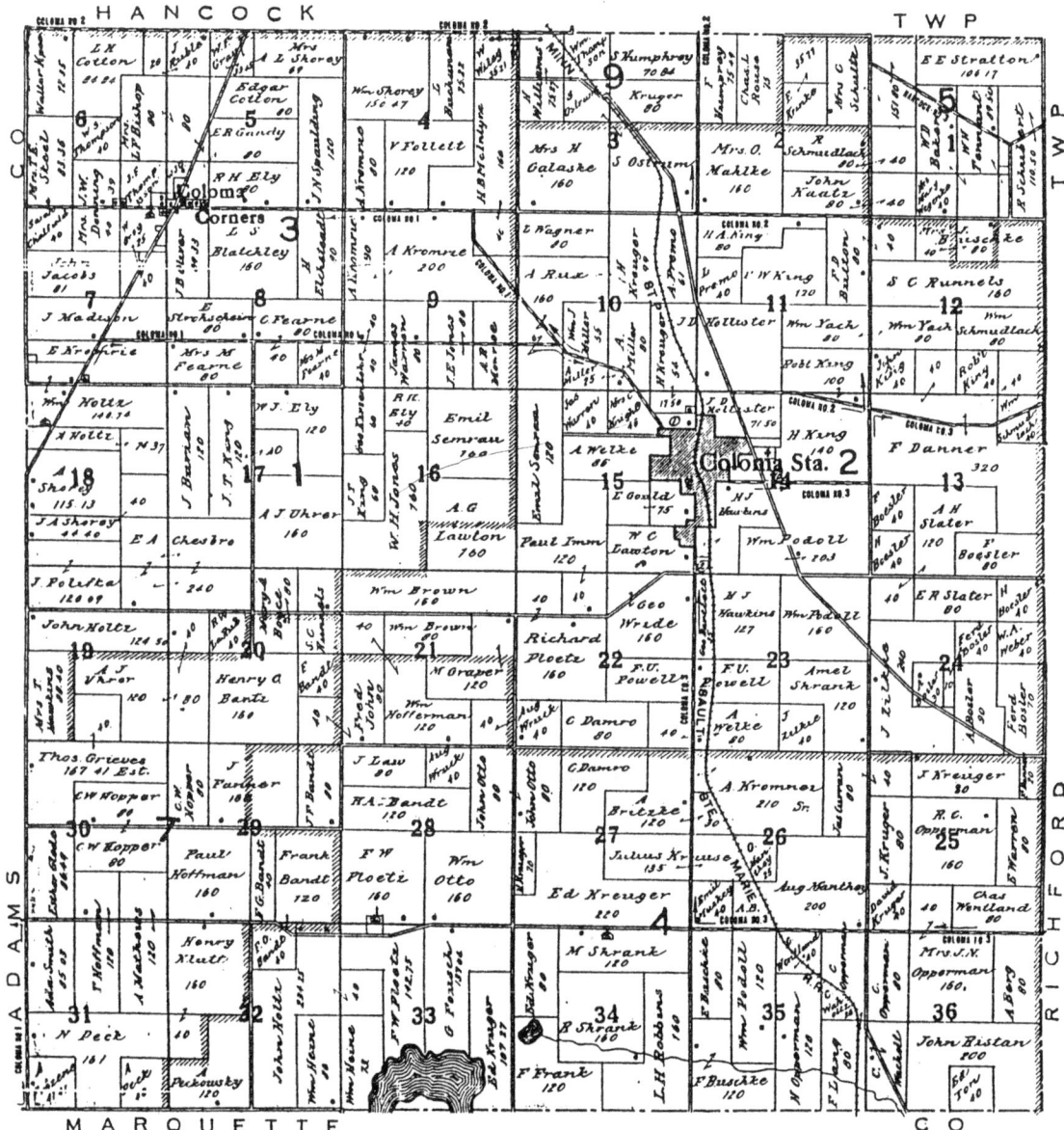

HANCOCK TWP

COLOMA Sta.

COLOMA Corners

ADAMS CO.

RICHFORD TWP

MARQUETTE CO.

List of Small Property Owners in this Township Shown on Map by Numbers

No.	Name	Acres	Sec.	No.	Name	Acres	Sec.
1.	H. Durgin	7	14	1.	E. Menke	7	16
2.	F. Danner	7	14				

6) SACKSCHEWSKI (perhaps Germanized form of Zakrzewski?), Johann Gottlieb- b. "Equart (perhaps Eichquast, Co. Obernick?) in Posen Germany", marr. Juliane Ann Mundinger (widow, maiden name Abraham) at the Town of Bloomfield 24 November 1887/ Vol. 3 (1870-1890), p. 75, no. 92.

*** 7) SCHOENECK, Gustav- b. "Kornelino (County Schubin, should be listed there) Posen Germany", marr. Marie Aspenleiter (maiden name Burger)- b. "Lerach Baden (sotuhwestern) Germany"; at the Town of Bloomfield 15 July 1897/ Vol. D, p. 147, no. 61.

8) WEDDE, Marie (maiden name Berg)- b. "EichKatzberg (perhaps Eichquast, County Obernick?) Germany", marr. August Radüchel- b. "Trutzlatz (Co. Naugard, Prov. Pomerania) Germany"; at ??? 13 June 1905/ Vol. E, p. 23, no. 51.

Immigrants from other identifiable locales in Province Posen, Prussia:

1) GRAMSE, Reinhold- b. "Heide Dombrowke (Heidedombrowka, County Obernick) Germany", marr. Martha Baitel- b. "Germany"; at Richford 12 August 1898/ Vol. D, p. 171, no. 79.

2) HAENSEL, Minnie- b. "Putzig (County Filehne) Germany", marr. August Wehsner- b. "Zachersberg (Zachasberg, County Kolmar) Germany"; at the Town of Richford 13 January 1894/ Vol. D, p. 78, no. 6.

3) KROLL, August- b. "Ludwighorst (County Witkowo?), Germany", marr. Maria Steinberg at Richford 9 November 1883/ Vol. 3 (1870-1890), p. 55, no. 101.

4) NEHRING, John Fred- b. "Polojelewo district of Mogilno Prussia Germany", marr. Anna Juliana Hens(c)hel at Bloomfield 20 "Feby" (1885)/ Vol. 3 (1870-1890), p. 61, no. 15.

5) PIGORSCH, Alf. Aug. Evald- b. "New Strand*Germany", marr. Ber-Maria Caroline Wilke- b. "Pommern Germany"; at Borth Poy Sippi 7 December 1897/ Vol. D, p. 156, no. 117.(*see No. 6 below)

6) PIGORSCH, Gustav Friedrich- b. "Nerr Strand (perhaps Herrnstadt, County Guhrau?) Germany", marr. Henriette Wilhelmine Pofahl at Poy Sippi 16 October 1895/ Vol. D, p. 110, no. 69.

7) POMMERENKE, Alexander Joseph- b. "Nekla (County Schroda) Preussen Germany", marr. Wilhelmine Loisaa Rusch- b. "Kisch Rogow Posen Germany"; at Bloomfield 19 January 1899/ Vol. D, p. 178, no. 9.

8) SCHMIDT, Mary Bertha- b. "Grassloopr (Gross-Lubs, County Filehne) Germany", marr. Georg Albert Wegenke- b. "Kamitz (County Neisse, Prov. Schlesien=Silesia) Germany"; at the Town of Neshkoro (Marquette Co.) 6 April 1907/ Vol. E, p. 67, no. 50.

9) VALENTIEN, Gottfried Emil of Pine Grove, Portage Co. (Wisc.)- b. "Gritzendorf (Grützendorf, County Obernick) Posen Germ", marr. Emma Elizabeth Bliss (maiden name Opperman)- b. "Ruhnow (County Stolp, Prov. Pomerania?) Posen Germany" (or Runau, County Czarnikau, or Runowo, Counties Wongrowitz or Schroda?); at Coloma 18 October 1897/ Vol. D, p. 150, no. 82.

10) WARSINSKI, August- b. "Kramske (Kramsk, County Konin?), Prov. Posen Germany", marr. Jennie Ann Owens at Oasis 5 November 1901/ Vol. D, p. 231, no. 95.(note: Kramske also Co. Dt. Krone, W. Prussia)

11) WINTER, Bernhard of"Lynn"(Lind), Waupaca Co.(Wisc.)-b. "Kolocziewo (Kolodziejewko, County Mogilno?) Prov. Posen Germany", marr. Emma Henriette Reich at Tustin 18 May (1885)/ Vol. 3 (1870-1890), p. 67, no. 35.

Farmers' Directory of Dakota Township

Abbreviations: Sec., section; ac., acres; wf., wife; ch., children; ( ) years in county

Neshkoro Post Office.

Hensel, Mrs. Henrietta, R3, sec 36, ac 160, sec 25, ac 152½, sec 26, ac 26, ch William, Emil, Loris, Ida, Elizabeth, (10).

Hensel, Julius, R3, sec 36, ac 60, Marion twp, sec 31, ac 127, mother Justina, (11).

Nickoley, Henry, R3, box 55, sec 36, ac 110, wf Bertha, ch Evelyn, (46).

Nickoley, W. A., R3, sec 35, ac 360, sec 26, ac 40, sec 36, ac 120, wf Hulda, ch Albert, Ella, Arthur, Herbert, Laura, Herta, (4).

Wautoma Post Office.

Bartel, Fred, R4, sec 7, ac 216, wf Martha, ch John, William, Loretta, Rose, Bernard, (25).

Bartel, Herman, R4, sec 7, ac 216, wf Amelia, ch Minnie, (12).

Bartel, William, R4, sec 7.

Bazing, J., sec 3, ac 120, sec 10, ac 285, sec 9, ac 160, sec 16, ac 160, (12).

Baxter, A. A., sec 1, ac 60, Wautoma twp, sec 36, ac 40, wf Austice, ch Myrtle, Royden, Nellie, Herbert, (17).

Belter, J. H., R5, sec 30, ac 144.73, wf Bertha, ch William, Henry, Louis, (13).

Benjamin, E. L., R6, sec 13, ac 348, wf Clarissa, ch Addie, Mabel, (63).

Bielmeier, John, R4, sec 5, ac 190, sec 12, ac 10, wf Francis, ch John, Albert, Louis, Frenica, Carl, Frank, Henry, Mary, George, (22).

Blader, Alfred, R4, sec 21, ac 210, sec 28, ac 70, wf Annie, ch Max, Charles, Margaret, (38).

Blader, A. J., R5, sec 34, ac 120, sec 17, ac 20, wf Augusta, ch Anna, Edna, (14).

Blader, Fred, R4, sec 27, ac 120, sec 28, ac 120, sec 21, ac 80, wf Elsie, (32).

Brese, Edward, R5, sec 30, ac 100, sec 31, ac 100, wf Elizabeth, ch Milo, (18).

Bushweiler, J. B., R4, sec 13, ac 154, sec 24, ac 40, wf Annie, ch Arlen, Chester, Elmer, Willard, Leroy, (46).

Currier, Frank, R4, sec 11, ac 360, sec 23, ac 40, (54).

Currier, Frank S., R4, sec 11, ac 80, sec 13, ac 80, wf Josephine, ch Ruby, Ellen, (33).

Currier, Roy, R6, sec 12, ac 80, sec 1, ac 14, mother Melissa, (21).

Dee, Albert, R5, sec 32.

Dee, Fred, R5, sec 32, ac 100, sec 16, ac 20, sister Helen, (24).

Dewel, Allen, R4, sec 23, ac 160, sec 24, ac 120, wf Rose, ch Guy, Dora, (50).

Dewel, John, sec 12, ac 80, wf Della, (62).

Dewel, R. H., R4, sec 11, ac 384, wf Emma, ch Ardyn, (45).

Doege, Albert, R4, sec 19, ac 130½, Richford twp, sec 25, ac 80, (32).

Drager, Fred, R4, sec 26, ac 120, sec 23, ac 40, wf Emma, ch Ella, Lydia, Fred, Cora, Lilly, Linda, Della, (24).

Drager, Henry, R5, sec 29, ac 80, sec 30, ac 40, sec 31, ac 40, sec 32, ac 160, wf Lena, ch Martin, Arthur, Clarence, Elmer, (48).

Dravitz, Fred, R5, box 7, sec 27, ac 80, sec 26, ac 120, wf Carrie, ch Lilly, Ollie, Milliard, (57).

Duntley, R., R4, sec 12, ac 119, wf Sarah, ch Delbert, Alfred, (25).

Eichstendt, August, R5, sec 30, ac 167, wf Bertha, (40).

Eichstendt, H., R4, sec 29, ac 200, wf Matilda, ch Leonard, Edna, (35).

Eichstedt, Richard, R5, sec 30, ac 266, wf Amanda, ch Alfred, Lena, (44).

Eichstedt, William, R5, sec 30, ac 266, wf Henrietta, (44).

Flegner, August, sec 16, ac 120, wf Annie, ch Walter, Elmer, Mabel, (4).

Graff, Jacob, R6, sec 12, ac 183.23, wf Minnie, ch George, Lyla, Herbert, Arthur, Helen, (8).

Gramse, William, R5, sec 34, ac 120, Marquette Co., Crystal Lake twp, sec 6, ac 104, wf Ida, ch Stanley, Clinton, Clifford, (31).

Gutche, William, R5, sec 34, ac 160, wf Ida, ch John Tinnie, (3).

Hardel, William Jr., R5, sec 27, ac 200, sec 22, ac 39½, wf Pauline, ch Walter, Elbert, Fred, George, Elsie, Ella, (36).

Hensel, Herrman, R4, sec 25, ac 120, owns sec 13, ac 7, (17).

Hong, Mrs. S., R4, sec 23, ac 60, sec 26, ac 75, ch George Trexell, (60).

Jameson, John, R4, sec 4, ac 160, wf Mabel, ch Mary, Wallace, (45).

Kosloske, August, R5, sec 34, ac 120, wf Bertha, ch Elbert, Lina, Edwin, Clara, William, (30).

Luhm, August, R5, sec 21, ac 20, wf Lena, ch Freda, (24).

Luhm, Charles, R5, sec 22, ac 200, wf Ida, (31).

Luhm, Robert, R5, sec 4, ac 180, sec 9, ac 75, wf Lydia, ch Rennie, Arthur, Bessie, Robert, Ruby, Joseph, Mamie, Roy, Alvin, (24).

Matthies, Herrman, R4, sec 28, ac 120, sec 33, ac 80, sec 21, ac 15, wf Ernestina, ch Ida, Albert, Edwin, (44).

Meyer, Gust, R5, sec 33, ac 200, wf Martha, ch Fred, Arthur, (3).

Meyer, William, R4, sec 28, ac 160, wf Ida, ch Elsie, (17).

Mielke, Fred, R5, box 5, sec 15, ac 179, sec 14, ac 80, sec 16, ac 40, wf Katherine, ch Herbert, Elizabeth, (35).

Miller, Ludwig, R5, sec 17, ac 160, sec 20, ac 160, sec 18, ac 100½, wf Amelia, ch Elsie, Edna, Laura, (44).

Pflugradt, Frank, R5, sec 15, ac 167, sec 17, ac 40, wf Annie, (28).

Pflugradt, Herrman, R5, box 10, sec 15, ac 40, sec 17, ac 20, sec 14, ac 120, sec 11, ac 40, sec 10, ac 40, wf Edith, ch Reinholdt, Mabel, Mamie, Frederick, (20).

Pflugradt, H. E., R6, sec 2, ac 84, sec 11, ac 40, sec 16, ac 20, wf Ida, (20).

Pflugradt, William, R4, sec 2, ac 74, sec 11, ac 40, wf Clara, ch Emma, (20).

Prochnow, J. H., R4, sec 7, ac 117, Richford twp, sec 12, ac 160, wf Johanna, ch Lena, Bertha, Henry, Arthur, (16).

Robinson, Otis, R6, sec 1, ac 104, wf Lula, ch Ray, Laura, Agnes, (44).

Rohde, Frank, R5, sec 8, ac 79, sec 17, ac 60, wf Alvina, (18).

Rohde, F. C., R5, sec 8, ac 280, sec 9, ac 40, sec 16, ac 25, wf Amelia, ch Lucy, Leona, Agnes, Harry, Regina, (44).

Rohde, F. W. G., R5, sec 9, ac 160, sec 17, ac 20, wf Emma M., ch Martha, Anna, Della, Elsie, Emma, William, Ethel, Ernest, Susan, Ruth, Albert, (45).

Rohde, H. C., R5, sec 8, ac 210, sec 7, ac 40, sec 5, ac 80, wf Julia, ch Elizabeth, Edna, Leonard, Laura, Agnes, Reuben, Mary, (50).

Rohde, Richard, R4, sec 28, ac 80, sec 16, ac 20, wf Ella, ch Florence, (23).

Sauer, H. J., R4, sec 6, ac 138, Richford twp, sec 1, ac 40, wf Amelia, ch Edward, Lora, (39).

Schley, Fred, box 221, sec 16, ac 160, sec 9, ac 80, wf Bertha, ch William, Alvina, George, (30).

Schluter, Ferdinand, R4, sec 20, ac 426, wf Gusta, ch Elsie, Elmer, Ruth, Ferdinand, Harvey, Arnold, (10).

Schram, August, R5, sec 31, ac 160, wf Pauline, ch Herrman, Laura, Annie, (32).

Stratton, F., R6, sec 1, ac 90, wf Annie, ch Mabel, Stella, Hazel, Effie, Glen, Elven, Vern, (50).

Thalacker, Paul, R5, sec 31, ac 2, wf Ida, ch Chester, Arno, Archie, Hannah, Loretta, Paul, (12).

Turner, Elwood, R5, sec 3, wf Gertie.

Turner, Mrs. Emma, R5, sec 3, ac 120, ch Elwood, (30).

Wagner, Albert, R4, sec 19, ac 150, sec 17, ac 120, Richford twp, sec 23, ac 80, wf Amelia, ch Albert H., (50).

Wandrey, G. A., R4, sec 5, ac 240, sec 8, ac 40, ch Gustaf R., (46).

Wandrey, Gustaf R., R4, sec 5, ac 240, sec 8, ac 40, wf Mattie, ch Arden, Myron, Elmer, (30).

Weiland, H., R5, sec 17, ac 120, sec 18, ac 80, wf Emma, ch Augusta, Alvina, William, John, (21).

Weiland, Max, R4, sec 21, ac 100, sec 20, ac 80, wf Emma, ch Bertha, Edna, Emil, Martha, Richard, (32).

Werner, Albert, R4, sec 11, ac 124, sec 16, ac 40, wf Tina, ch Laura, Leonard, Hulda, Elsie, (42).

Wilcox, Mrs. Amanda, R4, sec 25, ac 339¼, ch Bert, Agnes, Walter, Chester, Roy, (30).

Wilcox, Bert, R4, sec 24, ac 160, wf Cora, ch Earl, Glen, Austin, Dorothy, (35).

Wilcox, George R., R4, sec 24, ac 194, sec 26, ac 160, wf Daisy, ch Marjorie, Lenmine, Silas, Everett, (37).

Zelmer, R. E., R5, sec 27, ac 200, sec 21, ac 30, wf Lydia M., (22).

Zierke, Herrman, R5, sec 10, ac 74, sec 15, ac 40, sec 21, ac 40, wf Gustaf, ch Marie, (18).

Zuelke, Gust, R5, sec 34, ac 200, wf Bertha, ch Esther, Frieda, Clarence, Chester, (20).

(Michael Bednarek Collection, Wautoma, Wisc.)

MAP OF

DAKOTA

TOWNSHIP

Scale 1¼ Inches to One Mile

Township 18 North, Range 10 East of the 4th P. M.
WAUSHARA COUNTY, WIS.

Rural Routes shown thus: · ——— Churches shown thus: · · · · ·

School Districts " " " 2 Cemeteries " " " ✝

Schools " " " · · · Corporation Limits of Cities shown thus: ⊢⊣⊢⊣⊢⊣

WAUTOMA ———— TWP

MARQUETTE   CO

List of Small Property Owners in this Township Shown on Map by Numbers

No.	Name	Acres	Sec.	No.	Name	Acres	Sec.	No.	Name		Sec.	No.	Name		Sec.
1.	L. H. Ralph		3	5.	S. Thompson		3	1.	H. Hensel	10	13	1.	Max Welland	15	21
2.	D W. Robinson		3	6.	A. Blado	16	3	2.	H. Demer	10	18	2.	H. Mattles	10	21
3.	V. D. Parker	15	3	7.	P. Peterson		3	3.	R. Wertz	10	18	3.	E. Mattles	10	21
4.	T. T.		3	8.	Starch Factory	10	3	4.	J. Beinoeier	10	18	4.	A. Hensel	10	21
								5.	O. J. A. Podall	12	18	5.	A. Henke	7.50	25

(Michael Bednarek Collection, Wautoma, Wisc.)

Immigrants from the City, County, Administrative District, or Province of "Posen", Prussia":

1) ABRAHAM, Samuel- b. "Posen Preus(s)en", marr. Wilhelmine Hermine Meyer at Bloomfield 24 October 1878/ Vol. 3 (1870-1890), p. 30, no. 648.

2) ANKLAM, Adolph of the Town of Lind, Waupaca Co. (Wisc.)- b. "Posen Preussen", marr. Ottilie Timm at Bloomfield 17 April 1883/ Vol. 3 (1870-1890), p. 51, no. 37.

3) ANKLAM, Michael- b. "Posen Prussia", marr. Louise Henriette Bolter at Saxeville 18 June"1842"(?)/ Vol. 2 (1863-1870), p. 40.

4) BARTEL, Ewald- b. "Posen Germany", marr. Minna Krüger at Bloomfield 15 November 1881/ Vol. 3 (1870-1890), p. 44, no. 918.

5) BEUTHLER, Julius of the City of Oshkosh (Winnebago Co.,'Wisc.)- b. "Posen Preussen", marr. Friedericke Schmidt at Bloomfield 29 July 1877/ Vol. 3 (1870-1890), p. 24, no. 524.

6) BLOCH, Fredrick- b. "Posen Prussia", marr. Wilhelmine Pecher at Bloomfield 26 April 1874/ Vol. 3 (1870-1890), p. 11, no. 279.

7) BOELTER, Johannes of Buena Vista- b. "Posser Prussen", marr. Ida Timm at the Town of Bloomfield 9 September 1881/ Vol. 3 (1870-1890), p. 43, no. 898.

8) BOELTER, Wilhelm of the Town of Larabee, Waupaca Co. (Wisc.)- b. "Prov. Posen Germany", marr. Emilie Young of the Town of Wolf River (Winnebago Co)at Bloomfield 21 April 1902/ Vol. D, p. 247, no. 55.

9) BRILL, August of Lind (township, Waupaca Co., Wisc.)- b. "Posen, Prussen", marr. Emilie Handrich at Bloomfield 2 March 1879/ Vol. 3 (1870-1890), p. 31, no. 673.

10) BUCHHOLZ, Edward- b. "Posen Pruessen", marr. Alwine Handrich at Bloomfield 8 December 1882/ Vol. 3 (1870-1890), p. 49, no. 87.

11) BURGER, Johann- b. "Posen Prussia", marr. Emily A. Warmfier (Warmbier?) at Bloomfield 21 November 1873/ Vol. 3 (1879-1890), p. 9, no. 237.

12) DAHLKE, Julius Herman of Utica, Winnebago Co. (Wisc.)- b. "Posen Preussen", marr. Emilie Adolphine Sletter or Stetter (perhaps Stelter?) at Bloomfield 24 January 1879/ Vol. 3 (1870-1890), p. 31, no. 669.

13) DRAEGER, Emma- b. "Prov. Posen, Germany", marr. August Kage at the Town of Wolf River (Waupaca Co., Wisc.) 15 April 1902/ Vol. D, p. 246, no. 54.

14) ERNST, Carl Ludwig- b. "Posen Prussia", marr. Ernstine H. Buss at Bloomfield 18 December 1873/ Vol. 3 (1870-1890), p. 10, no. 246.

15) FANDRAY, Christian of Weyauwega (Waupaca Co., Wisc.)- b. "Posen Prussian", marr. Pauline Warmbier at Bloomfield 17 June 1881/ Vol. 3 (1870-1890), p. 42, no. 878.

16) FREBART, Ernst- b. "Posen Germany", marr. Emilie Hulda Anna Opperman at the Town of Coloma 17 August 1900/ Vol. D, p. 208, no. 73.

17) FREITAG, Johann of Caledonia (Racine Co., Wisc.?)- b. "Posen Pr(e)ussen", marr. Ottilie Scherbath at Bloomfield 25 November 1881/ Vol. 3 (1870-1890), p. 44, no. 921.

18) FRITZ, Ernst Heinrich- b. "Herzogthum (Grand Duchy of) Posen Europe", marr. Ottilie Mathilde Augusta Eilert at Aurora (Ev. As.) 16 November 1885/ Vol. D , p. 65, no. 82.

19) GANGE, Samuel- b. "Posen Preussen", marr. Ernstine Goehrke at Bloomfield 16 February 1875/ Vol. 3 (1870-1890), p. 15, no. 341.

20) GLOFF, Emilie- b. "Posen Germany", marr. Carl Schuelke of the Town of Wolf River (Winnebago Co., Wisc.); at the Town of Bloomfield 26 June (1898)/ Vol. D, p. 158, no. 5.

21) GOEHRKE, August- b. "Posen Prussian", marr. Wilhelmine Behn at Bloomfield 2 May 1878/ Vol. 3 (1870-1890), p. 28, no. 607.

22) GRÜNING, Christoph Johann- b. "Posen Preussen", marr. Amalie Auguste Hens(c)hel at Bloomfield 14 January 1875/ Vol. 3 (1870-1890), p. 14, no. 333.

23) HAFF, Bernhard of the Town of Union, Waupaca Co. (Wisc.)- b. "Posen Prussia Germany", marr. Theresa Augsta Wohlrabe at East Bloomfield 18 August 1885/ Vol. D, p. 64, no. 65.

24) HEDKE, Gustav of Lind (Waupaca Co., Wisc.)- b. "Posen Prussien", marr. Wilhelmine Lipke at Bloomfield 3 June 1878/ Vol. 3 (1870-1890), p. 29, no. 614.

25) HINZ, Wilhelm- b. "Posen Preussen", marr. Mathilde Goehrke at Bloomfield 12 January 1876/ Vol. 3 (1870-1890), p. 19, no. 421.

Abbreviations: Sec., section; ac., acres; wf., wife; ch., children; ( ) years in county

Hancock Post Office.

Bacon, George, R2, sec 5, ac 80, wf Lela, ch Ileta, Merle, (30).

Baker, Ismael, R2, sec 7, ac 89, wf Lena, (3).

Bandt, August, R3, sec 33, ac 120, wf (51). Ida, ch Margaret, Evelyn, (16).

Berry, J., R2, sec 20, ac 80, sec 17, ac 4, wf Maud, ch Francis A., (48).

Bohn, Albert, R2, sec 9, ac 80, sec 10, ac 40, wf Clara, ch Irvin, Alvin, (24).

Bohn, August, R2, sec 3, ac 160, sec 10, ac 80, wf Amelia, (35).

Bohn, Emil Sr., R2, box 26, sec 16, ac 200, wf Bertha, ch Herman, Edward, Otto, (38).

Bohn, Emil, R2, sec 17, ac 80, sec 16, ac 40, (26).

Bohn, Richard, R2, sec 3, ac 160, wf Ida, (32).

Bohn, William, R2, sec 21, ac 160, wf Martha, ch Herbert, William, (32).

Booth, Roy, sec 11, wf Muriel.

Crandell, John, R2, sec 17, ac 80, wf Margaret, ch Mildred, Leonard, (25).

Dehling, H. F., R3, sec 30, ac 110, ch Hilda, Lona, Arlie, Harvey, Lester, (31).

Deuel, Albert, R2, sec 11, ac 120, wf Mary, ch Rennie, Mercedes, (46).

Deuel, Frank, R2, sec 11, ac 80, wf Kate, ch Ellen, Margaret, Anita, (38).

Diggles, N. C., R2, sec 17, ac 220, wf Ella, ch Clyde, Archie, Glen, Ward, Eunice, (47).

Domka, F. J., R2, sec 28, ac 210, wf Minnie, ch Clarence, Arlie, Darwin, (23).

Dudley, Arsey, R2, sec 3, ac 79, sec 10, ac 120, wf Mary, (60).

Eager, W. T., R2, sec 4, ac 120, wf Kate, ch Rolland, Marshall, (22). "Oak Grove Farm."

Engle, N. G., R2, sec 9, ac 180, sec 8, ac 10, sec 16, ac 40, wf Rose, ch Lemrox, Harold, Rita, Sadie, Ensign, (51).

Gibbs, W. A., R2, sec 5, ac 80, sec 8, ac 80, sec 9, ac 20, wf Carrie, ch Marion, Gladys, Lester, Lyle, Shirley, (10).

Goodwin, Mrs. Hattie, R3, sec 30, ac 120, ch Leon, Glen, Hazel, Grace, (52).

Hartford, Frank, R2, sec 22, ac 160, sec 15, ac 40, wf Emogene, ch Harrison E., Hazel M., (33).

Hartford, Lyman, R2, sec 15, ac 210, wf Della M., ch Leila, Lucile, Lillian, Wendell, (45).

Hartford, Robert, R2, sec 23, ac 240, sec 14, ac 40, mother Roxie, (39).

Henne, A., R2, sec 29, ac 200, wf Minnie, ch Sophia, Fred, Melvin, Mabel, Laura, Zelda, Walter, Earl, (45).

Henne, R. J., R3, sec 33, ac 160, sec 28, ac 80, sec 27, ac 70, wf Gustie, ch Frank, Chester, (43).

Hensel, Fred, R2, sec 8, ac 80, wf Minnie, ch Henrietta, Lydia, Leslie, Elmer, (48).

Hine, A., R2, sec 9, ac 90, wf Nata, ch Otis, (41).

Kaatz, Mrs. Emma, sec 19, ac 160, sec 20, ac 120, ch Rudolph, Evald, Theresa, Hulda, (25).

Kitchen, Alvin, R2, sec 5, ac 80, wf Mildred, ch Alice, Doras, Olive, Frieda, (29).

Klabunda, William, R2, sec 19, ac 80, sec 18, ac 40, wf Pauline, ch Herrman, Emil, Annie, (23).

Krueger, Herrman, R3, sec 32, ac 200, wf Tina, ch Fred, Robert, Anna, (5).

Lachelt, Albert, R3, sec 32, ac 20, sec 29, ac 40, wf Emma, ch Richard, Robert, Arthur, Elmer, (33).

Lachelt, William, R2, sec 20, ac 120, wf Elizabeth, ch Herbert, Freda, (8).

Lipke, F., R2, sec 15, ac 120, sec 22, ac 80, sec 21, ac 120, sec 16, ac 80, wf Ida, ch George, Laura, Henry, Lula, Lona, Lillian, (19).

Lipke, Gust, R3, sec 31, ac 80, wf Carrie, ch Francis, (33).

McLoughlin, Mrs. Rose, R2, box 43, sec 11, ac 80, sec 10, ac 40, (50).

Maloney, Mrs. Johanna, R2, sec 16, ac 80, sec 21, ac 80, ch John, Mary, Morris, (41).

Marshall, Bert, R2, sec 8, ac 160, sec 7, ac 90, wf Maud, ch Grace, May, Bonnie, mother Elizabeth, (28).

Marshall, Earl, R2, sec 7, ac 60, wf Jennie, ch Hazel, Ida, Floy, Clifford, Mitchell, (32).

Marshall, F. W., R2, sec 7, ac 401½, sec 8, ac 80, sec 17, ac 52, wf Gertrude, ch Helen, Wilmer, Beulah, Nellie, (35).

Marshall, L. D., R2, sec 8, ac 80, sec 17, ac 76, (59).

Miller, O., R3, sec 32, ac 80, sec 29, ac 80, wf Lydia, ch Alvina, John, Reuben, Dorothy, (11).

Monroe, A. L., R3, sec 31, ac 120, wf Augusta, ch Dane, Harley, Lentus, Orville, Russel, (42).

Monroe, James, R2, sec 30, ac 40, wf Clara, ch Zelda, Arthur, Hugh, Irvin, Clarence, Virginia Esther, (41).

Monroe, R. R., R3, sec 31, ac 80, wf Mary, (58).

Morton, W. W., R2, sec 10, ac 80, wf Mary, ch Doris, Lila, (15).

O'Connor, John, R2, box 31, sec 15, ac 40, mother Elizabeth Parker, (30).

Olson, Martin, R3, sec 34, ac 200, wf Rose, ch Leon, Inez, Gard, (16).

Parker, H. H., R2, sec 18, ac 48, sec 7, ac 20, (52).

Parker, Vern E., sec 18, wf Nina.

Parker, William, R2, sec 7, ac 89, sec 29, ac 80, wf Mary, ch Warren, Carl, Carrie, Ora, Darwin, Neal, (54).

Pionke, M., R2, sec 9, ac 150, sec 16, ac 80, sec 10, ac 40, wf Elizabeth, ch Lawrence, (7).

Pomplum, W., R3, sec 34, ac 120, sec 33, ac 40, Richford twp, sec 3, ac 120, wf Emma, ch Fred, Chester, (46).

Putskey, August, R2, sec 16, ac 80, sec 22, ac 40, sec 26, ac 120, wf Alvina, ch Minnie, Clarence, Albert, Edward, Harley, (21).

Riebe, William, R2, sec 17, ac 100, sec 20, ac 80, wf Emma, ch Fred, Henry, Gustie, Tina, Minnie, Lena, Elsie, Bertha, (22).

Roeski, R., R3, box 29, sec 33, ac 120, sec 32, ac 80, wf Augusta, ch Bertha, Elsie, Julius, Ida, (23).

Rohde, Ernest, R3, sec 34, ac 240, wf Geraldine, (43).

Runnels, Chan. S., sec 29, ac 30, wf Emma, (33).

Runnels, Louis, R3, sec 31, ac 60, mother Agnes, (33).

Scharf, H., R2, sec 17, ac 80, wf Mary, ch Pauline, Julius, Gustie, Tina, (22).

Searl, James, R2, sec 27, ac 120, sec 34, ac 120, wf Daisy, ch Robert, Laton, (20).

Sherlock, George, R2, sec 18.

Sherlock, Jess, R2, sec 18, ac 47, sec 7, ac 100, wf Gertrude, (58).

Silverthorn, B. R., R2, sec 6, ac 80, wf Gertrude, (15).

Spaulding, M., R2, sec 18, ac 193, wf Stella, ch Willard, Marjorie, (38).

Starks, O. M., R2, box 54, sec 9, ac 80, sec 16, ac 40, wf Inna, ch Velma, Metta, Curtis, (32).

Szulczewski, Edward, R2, sec 14, ac 120, sec 13, ac 80, wf Jessie, ch Vina, Gertie, Jennie, Albon, (27).

Szulczewski, Frank, R2, sec 11, ac 80, wf Mary, ch Regina, Alvina, Lucus, Rose, Katherine, Jacob, Ambrose, (27).

Szulczewski, Paul, R2, box 40, sec 11, ac 160, sec 12, ac 80, wf Emma, ch Adeline, (28).

Ueeck, Fred, R2, sec 14, ac 238, wf Anna, ch Ella, Bertha, Edward, Lea, Hugo, (30). "Lake Wood Farm."

Ueeck, Otto, R2, sec 38, ac 120, wf Louise, ch Alice, Arden, Marshall, (30).

Wandrey, John, R6, sec 34, ac 158, sec 33, ac 40, (40).

Whalley, R. H., R2, sec 20, ac 240, wf Amelia, ch Harvey, Clarence, (42).

Plainfield Post Office.

Carey, George, R2, sec 3, ac 120, sec 2, ac 2½, wf Edith, ch Esther, Inez, Nina, Bernice, Alice, Lyle, (11).

Detlor, W. R., R2, sec 3, ac 80, Oasis twp, owns sec 26, ac 40, wf Lula, ch Lena, Ray, Glen, Harvey, (18).

Dudley, F. W., sec 4, ac 80, sec 9, ac 40, wf Nina, ch Lemuel A., Floyd E., Carl C., Archie K., Mary A., Robert F., Hazel D., (40).

Engle, John, R2, sec 2, ac 160, wf Mattie, ch Ora, Arden, (50).

Green, D. F., R2, sec 4, ac 240, Oasis twp, sec 33, ac 120, wf Loula, ch Gladys L., Frank L., (58).

Gustin, Emmet, R2, sec 2, ac 140, wf Flora, ch Roiden, Reed, Norma, Noreen, (37).

Gustin, Ward, R2, sec 2, ac 97½, sec 11, ac 40, wf Lucy, ch Bernard, Marjorie, Harvey, Ivan, Dean, Robert, Hubert, Dorothy, (41).

Masters, A. V., R2, sec 3, ac 47, owns sec 4, ac 47, wf Ida, ch Evelyn, Merle, Alice, (32).

Spawn, Miss E. A., R2, sec 5, ac 140, sec 4, ac 40, (30).

Straw, S. J., R2, sec 4, ac 40, sec 5, at 40, wf Alida, (50).

Wautoma Post Office.

Bartel, H. A., sec 13, ac 160.

Berry, R., R4, sec 36, ac 80, wf Ella, ch Warren, Ota, Archie, Royal, Lillie, Viola, (40).

Boehlke, William, R3, sec 25, ac 140, Dakota twp, sec 18, ac 91½, Richford twp, sec 13, ac 10, wf Hattie, ch Edward, Ella, (14).

Deuel, Alvin, R3, sec 13, ac 160, wf Susan, ch Pearl, Clyde, (44).

Deuel, Clyde, R3, sec 13, ac 160, wf Luella, (21).

Engle, George, R3, sec 1, ac 210, wf Aura, (25). "Oak Lawn Farm."

Groskreutz, Julius, sec 35, ac 200, wf Emma, ch Albert, Martha, Mabel, Mary, (37).

Gustin, R. H., R3, sec 2, ac 160, wf Lena, ch Marion, (42).

Haneman, Hugo, R3, sec 2, ac 82, wf Laura, ch Marcus, (28).

Johannes, John, R3, sec 1, ac 120, wf Ida, ch Mary, Lloyd, Kenneth, (34).

Johannes, Mrs. Mary, R3, sec 1, ac 40, Wautoma twp, sec 6, ac 51, ch Thomas, Elizabeth, (33).

Johannes, M. D., R3, sec 12, ac 80, sec 1, ac 40, wf Grace M., ch Aubrey D., Lyle R., (20).

Johannes, N., R1, sec 1, ac 80, (25).

Kapp, Richard, R3, sec 25, ac 80, sec 26, ac 80, sec 23, ac 40, wf Amanda, (24).

Morton, E. F., R3, sec 12, ac 120, (10).

Morton, Joseph, R3, sec 12, wf Emeline.

Parker, E. A., R3, sec 13, ac 160, wf Edith, ch Earl, Beulah, (40).

Raatz, William, R3, sec 24, ac 100, wf Annie, ch Elma, Elsie, Arno, Hugo, Richard, Lillian, (35).

Reeder, Edward, R3, sec 12, ac 120, wf Amelia, (4).

Ross, William, R3, sec 12, ac 80, wf Deane, ch Rilla, Thorwald, Mary, Clifford, (39).

Smith, Theo, R3, sec 12, ac 80, wf Helen, ch Lilly, (30).

Smith, William, R3, sec 12, ac 80, wf Myrtle, ch Ernest, Elfie, (30).

Souzek, Bernard, R3, sec 23, ac 40, sec 26, ac 80, wf Martha, ch Emil, (1).

Spees, Dana, R3, sec 13, ac 80, sec 24, ac 80, wf Grace, (25).

Wagner, F. E., R3, sec 23, ac 160, sec 10, ac 80, sec 24, ac 80, wf Amelia, ch Elizabeth, Albert, Emil, Annie, Minnie, Herrman, (50).

MAP OF
DEERFIELD
TOWNSHIP

Scale 1¼ Inches to One Mile

Township 19 North, Range 9 East of the 4th P. M.
WAUSHARA COUNTY, WIS.

Rural Routes shown thus: —————
School Districts " " " : 2
School " " " :

Churches shown thus:
Cemeteries " " : ±
Corporation Limits of Cities shown thus:

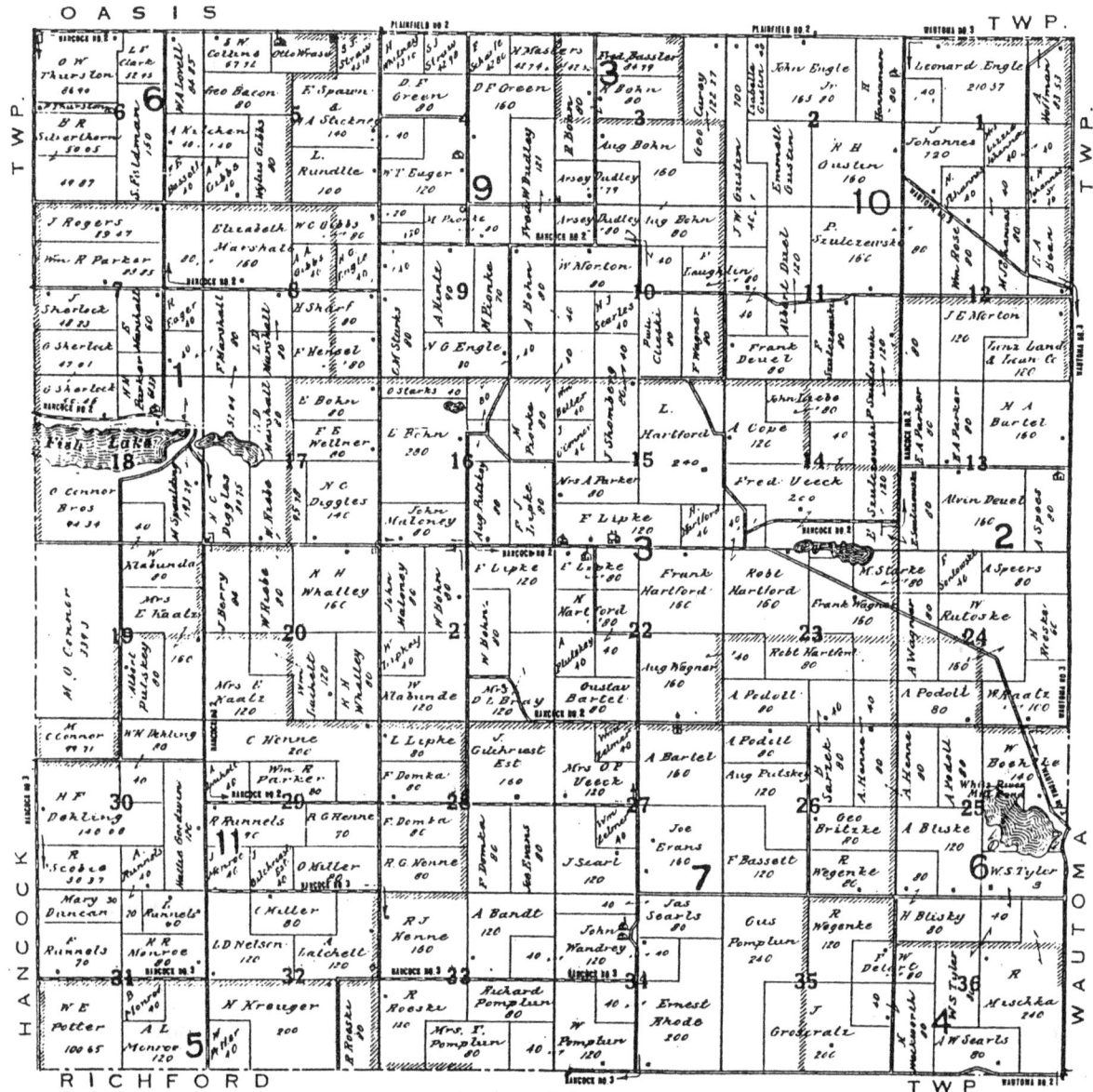

OASIS .... TWP.

TWP. (left side)
HANCOCK (left side)

RICHFORD .... TWP.

WAUTOMA (right side)
TWP. (right side)

Fish Lake

List of Small Property Owners In This Township Shown on Map by Numbers

No.	Name	Acres	Sec.	No.	Name	Acres	Sec.	No.	Name	Acres	Sec.
1.	Clark & Briggs		21	1.	G. P. Walker		25	2.	G. P. Walker		25

(Michael Bednarek Collection, Wautoma, Wisc.)

26) HUEBNER, Reinhard- b. "Posen Preussen", marr. Emilie Puhang (?)
at Bloomfield 29 December 1874/ Vol. 3 (1870-1890), p. 14, no.
335.

27) KIETZMANN, Gustav of Newton, Marquette Co.- b. "Province of Posen, Germany", marr. Wilhelmine Damrohse- b. "Germany"; at Coloma Township 30 August 1898/ Vol. D, p. 171, no. 80.

28) KLEPS, August- b. "Posen Preussen", marr. Emilie Brill at Bloomfield 14 April 1880/ Vol. 3 (1870-1890), p. 37, no. 788.

29) KOPISKE, Julius Rudolf- b. "Prov Posen Germany", marr. Alwine
Jung of the Town of Wolf River (Winnebago Co., Wisc.); at Bloomfield 9 May (1895)/ Vol. D, p. 105, no. 42.

30) KORALESKA, Martin- b. "Posen Germany", marr. Antonia Stahowiak-
b. "Posen Germany"; at Wautoma 1 November 1893/ Vol. D, p. 73,
no. 103.(Roman Catholic, probably Polish)

31) LASCHNER, Gustav Emil- b. "Posen", marr. Pauline Wilhelmine
Krause at Richford 11 March 1892/ Vol. D, p. 41, no. 30.

32) LOHR, Julius of Lind "Waushara Co." (Waupaca Co.)- b. "Posen
Preus(s)en", marr. Wilhelmine Herzyfeld at Bloomfield 24 December 1882/ Vol. 3 (1870-1890), p. 50, no. 7.

33) MALOW, Frederick- b. "Posen. Prussia", marr. Auguste Magdalene
Timm at Bloomfield 9 October 1864/ Vol. 2 (1863-1870), p. 25.

34) MARTEN, Carl of Wolf River (Winnebago Co., Wisc.)- b. "Posen
Preussen", marr. Henriette Boerndt at Bloomfield 7 October 1877/
Vol. 3 (1870-1890), p. 25, no. 541.

35) MILKE, George a farmer of the Town of Lind, Waupaca Co. (Wisc.)-
b. "Posen Preussen", marr. Caroline Loll at Bloomfield 15 October 1883/ Vol. 3 (1870-1890), p. 53, no. 80.

36) MILKE, Wilhelm of Lind (Waupaca Co.)- b. "Possen Pr(e)ussen",
marr. Ernstine Trogan at the Town of Bloomfield 25 August 1881/
Vol. 3 (1870-1890), p. 43, no. 894.

37) MUELLER, Edward- b. "Posen Preussen", marr. Bertha Pagel at
Bloomfield 29 February 1884/ Vol. 3 (1870-1890), p. 56, no. 11.

38) MULLER, Friedrich of Royalton, Waupaca Co. (Wisc.)- b. "Posen
Preussen", marr. Wilhelmine Noack at Bloomfield 7 September 1883/
Vol. 3 (1870-1890), p. 53, no. 69.

39) NOACK, Eduard- b. "Posen Preussen", marr. Emelie Boelter at Bloomfield27 April 1886/ Vol. D, p. 67, no. 32.

40) NOWAK, Ignatius- b. "Posen Germany", marr. Anna Koraleska- b. "Posen Germany"; at Wautoma 1 November 1893/ Vol. D, p. 73, no. 102. (Roman Catholic, probably Polish couple)

41) NOWATNY, Albert- b. "Posen Germany", marr. Mary Mushynski- b. "Posen Germany"; at Wautoma 21 November 1893/ Vol. D, p. 74, no. 106. (Roman Catholic, probably Polish couple)

42) PISCHKE, John Joseph- b. "Posen", marr. Wilhelmine Ernestine Prochnow- b. "Prussia"; at Richford 2 January 1890/ Vol. D, p. 55, no. 2.

43) POMMENKER, Julius- b. "Posen Prussia", marr. W.F.A. Struck at Bloomfield 6 December 1866/ Vol. 2 (1863-1870), p. 84.

44) POMMERNKEE, Julius (perhaps same as above, probably Pommerenke?) -b. "Posen Pr(e)ussen", marr. August(e?) Handrick at Bloomfield 3 September 1875/ Vol. 3 (1870-1890), p. 17, no. 382.

45) QUADE, Gustav of Weyauwega (Waupaca Co., Wisc.)- b. "Posen Preussen", marr. Emilie Loehrke at Bloomfield 21 October 1884/ Vol. 3 (1870-1890), p. 59, no. 70.

46) RADKE, Edward of Nepeuskun (Winnebago Co., Wisc.)- b. "Posen Pr(e)ussen", marr. Emilie Hirte at Bloomfield 1 July 1875/ Vol. 3 (1870-1890), p. 16, no. 374.

47) REECK, Julius H.- b. "Posen Preussen", marr. Emilie L. Muelke at Bloomfield 11 January 1877/ Vol. 3 (1870-1890), p. 22, no. 439.

48) ROENZ, Reinhard J. of Lind, Waupaca Co. (Wisc.)- b. "Posen Preussen", marr. Ottilie M. Jachsmann at Bloomfield 2 August 1876/ Vol. 3 (1870-1890), p. 20, no. 452.

49) RUCKS, Friedrick- b. "Posen Preussen", marr. Wilhelmine Karrow at Bloomfield 4 October 1877/ Vol. 3 (1870-1890), p. 25, no. 539.

50) SCHMIDT, August of Seto, Fond du Lac Co. (Wisc.)- b. "Posen Preussen", marr. Friedericke Glocke at Bloomfield 2 December 1875/ Vol. 3 (1870-1890), p. 18, no. 405.

51) SCHNELL, Johann- b. "Posen Preussen", marr. Juliane Anklam at Bloomfield 9 April 1884/ Vol. 3 (1870-1890), p. 57, no. 26.

52) SCHULZ, Henrietta- b. "Province Posen Germany", marr. Charles Wm. Schrader of Dayton, Waupaca Co. (Wisc.); at the Town of Mt. Morris 2 June 1903/ Vol. D, p. 276, no. 66.

Farmers' Directory of Marion Township

Abbreviations: Sec., section; ac., acres; wf., wife; ch., children; ( ) years in county

Neshkoro Post Office.

Belling, P., R1, sec 14, ac 40, sec 13, ac 40, sec 13, ac 20, wf Minnie, (22).

Bushweiler, Lewis, R1, sec 28, ac 160, wf Henrietta, ch Nancy, (36).

Currier, Elmer, R1, sec 20, ac 160, wf Cora, (40).

Cutts, George, R1, sec 26, ac 80, wf Margaret, ch William, George, Arthur, Florence, (45).

Davis, Edward, R1, sec 19, ac 124, wf Mamie, ch Howard, Carrel, (28).

Dretske, A., R1, sec 33, ac 82, sec 32, ac 20, wf Dora, ch Alma, (26).

Dretske, F., R1, sec 33, ac 90, sec 29, ac 56, sec 32, ac 20, wf Mary, ch Edward, Fred, Walter, Martin, Elizabeth, Annie, Minnie, Alice, (35).

Durke, Thomas, R1, sec 25, ac 105, sec 24, ac 40, sec 22, ac 80, sec 15, ac 17, wf Ella, (45).

Edwards, H., R1, sec 29, ac 164, wf Martha, ch Bill, Henry, Laura, Robert, (22).

Gelhar, J., R1, sec 36, ac 113, wf Amanda, (7).

Hardel, Amiel, R1, sec 14, ac 40, sec 13, ac 80, wf Bertha, ch Dora, Erma, (35).

Hayes, John, R1, sec 19, ac 353, ch George, (52).

Krehn, G. W., R1, sec 23, wf Alma, ch Eunice, Irvin, Ruby, (15).

Krall, H., R1, sec 34, ac 120, wf Susie, ch Edna, Lyle, (13).

Krentz, Joseph, R1, sec 34, ac 120, wf Martha, ch Sadie, (2).

Lehman, M., R1, box 19, sec 34, ac 40, sec 35, ac 79, wf Annie, ch Nathalie, Cecelia, Alex, Stanley, (2).

Leigh, Peter, R1, sec 26, ac 160, wf Anna, ch Paul, Albert, (64).

Ludkey, Fred, R3, sec 34, ac 162.50, wf Alvina, ch Arthur, Lillie, (30).

Ludkey, William, sec 31, ac 197.50, wf Mary, ch Bernice, Bernard, (26).

Marks, John, R1, sec 20, ac 160, wf Gustave, ch Alvin, Edwin, (14).

Marvin, Fred, R1, sec 26, ac 160, sec 35, ac 40, wf Alvina, ch Walter, Edward, (26).

Mills, C., R1, sec 32, ac 56, sec 29, ac 7, sec 31, ac 30, wf Rachel, ch Bessie, Ruth, Edna, Myrtle, (53).

Morrisey, J. C., R1, sec 27, ch Margaret, Mary, Irene, (50).

Mushall, J. F., R1, sec 34, ac 155, (3).

Pritz, William, R1, sec 29, ac 80, wf Philipine, ch August, Frank, Hattie, William, Minnie, Alfred, (12).

Raymond, Hugh, R1, sec 30, ac 146.5, wf Esther, ch Pearl, Mary, Hubert, Bessie, (30).

Rhode, Gust, R1, sec 27, ac 40, sec 26, ac 40, sec 34, ac 5, wf Amelia, ch Alfred, Clarence, Mable, Dora, Grace, (13).

Rieve, Gust, R1, sec 24, ac 120, sec 25, ac 158.60, sec 25, ac 43.40, wf Emma, ch Linda, Emma, Amanda, Gilbert, Alvin, Mildred, (12).

Robinson, Charles, R1, sec 29, ac 160, wf Tacie, ch Clifford, Marion, Hubert, Lawrence, (47).

Rose, Gust, R1, sec 34, ac 80, sec 33, ac 40, wf Minnie, ch Margaret, Lillie, (10).

Ryan, T., R1, sec 35, ac 160, wf Rose, ch Genevieve, Timothy, Margarett, (28).

Sauder, John, R1, sec 22, wf Kate, ch Leigh, (30).

Stanke, Edward, R1, sec 32, ac 200, sec 33, ac 80, wf Ida, ch Irene, Nora, (29).

Stanke, Gust, R1, sec 33, ac 160, sec 32, ac 171, wf Emma, ch Elsie, Carl, Alvin, Arthur, (33).

Swersinske, A., R1, sec 28, ac 200, sec 33, ac 58, wf Amelia, ch Alice, Lillie, Laura, Esther, Elmer, Viola, (35).

Tetzlaff, Herman, R1, sec 25, ac 149, sec 24, ac 120, wf Emma, ch Alice, Alma, Irma, Viola, Clarence, Irene, (21).

Trexell, E. C., R1, sec 30, ac 154, wf Alta, ch Leon, Bessie, Richard, Edgar, (42).

Wallschlager, A., R1, sec 35, ac 160, sec 36, ac 47, wf Alma, ch Irvin, Hattie, (22).

Wallschlager, E., R1, sec 25, ac 160, sec 26, ac 80, wf Emma, (23).

Wentlan, Fred, R1, sec 35, ac 160, wf Lena, ch Edward, Minnie, Ella, Eideth, August, Albert, Henry, Walter, (9).

Wier, J., R1, box 37, sec 21, ac 80, sec 23, ac 108.5, sec 26, ac 30, wf Martha, ch Jessie, Walter, Julia, Harry, Laura, Frank, Eliza, (3).

Zlomke, Hugo, R1, sec 28, ac 40, sec 29, ac 80, wf Lula, ch Mable, (1).

Redgranite Post Office.

Hawks, D., sec 12, ac 160, (40).

Moriarty, M., R2, sec 36, ac 160, wf Rose, ch James, Catherine, John, (40).

Spring Lake Post Office.

Belling, E., sec 23, ac 34.5, sec 24, ac 40.90, wf Bertha, ch Arthur, Emma, Alley, (22).

Fuller, Mrs. E., sec 23, ac 102.41, ch Donald, Mary, (30).

Fuller, L., sec 14, ac 40, sec 23, ac 10, sec 22, ac 5, wf Minnie, ch Irene, Harold, (37).

Fuller, R. R., sec 14, ac 54.50, sec 23, ac 1.50, wf Lyda, ch Howard, Charles, (35).

Krapp, Fred, sec 23, wf Martha, ch Henry, Albert, Stella, (30).

Marks, F. E., sec 14, ac 58.5, sec 22, ac 14, wf Ellen, ch Olga, Alvin, Sadie, Ruben, Harley, Clarence, (37).

Turner, E., sec 23, ac 78, wf Lillie, ch Howard, Pearl, (7).

Wautoma Post Office.

Atkins, O. L., R6, box 19, sec 9, ac 80, wf Myrtle, ch Allie, (30).

Bahn, Mrs. John, R1, sec 5, ac 80, ch Clara, Lillie, Albert, Laura, Ida, Edward, (23).

Beebe, Frank, R4, sec 6, ac 1, wf Clara, ch Emma, (37).

Berry, H., sec 2, ac 100, sec 11, ac 40, sec 12, ac 4, wf Elizabeth, ch Frank.

Booth, Frank, R6, sec 7, ac 80, sec 8, ac 30, wf Nettie, ch Ray, Winnie, Arden, Marie, Daisy, (44).

Booth, Fred, R6, sec 7, ac 80, wf Addie, (35).

Booth, Samuel, R6, sec 7, ac 138.51, sec 8, ac 47, sec 7, ac 23, wf Delia, ch Ward, Silas, Vashti, (47).

Booth, Sanford, R6, sec 8, ac 26, sec 17, ac 40, sec 16, ac 80, wf Clara, (48).

Booth, Ward, R6, sec 8, ac 47, wf Stella, ch Neola, Alice, (24).

Bushwiler, John, R6, sec 16, ac 80, wf Carrie, (7).

Carrol, L. L., R6, sec 16, ac 80, wf Carrie, (7).

Cockerill, John, R6, sec 10, ac 80, wf Adeline, ch Hazel, Cecil, (18).

Coleman, R., R6, sec 17, ac 87, wf Merirn, (40).

Daley, William, R6, sec 17, ac 210, wf Martha, ch William, Ella, (45).

Dretzke, Paul, R6, sec 21, ac 155, wf Anna, ch Arthur, Alvin, Harley, (36).

Dutcher, B. J., R6, sec 4, ac 80, wf Emma, ch Harley, Jay, Irene, (8).

Engan, James, R6, sec 19, ac 80, sec 20, ac 105, wf Celia, ch Jay, Robert, Anna, (60).

Ellickson, Christ, R6, sec 4, ac 73, sec 3, ac 35, wf Emma, ch Jay, Mable, Charlotte, (45).

Ellsworth, C. A., R6, sec 16, ac 80, wf Maud, ch Alice, Florence, (35).

Eckstein, Fred, R1, sec 1, ac 160, wf Nancy, ch Clarence, Fred, Alvina, William, Josie, Fred, (16).

Ferguson, S., R6, sec 14, ac 60, sec 13, ac 13, wf Ruby, ch Evelyn, (16).

Fratzke, Fred, R6, sec 21, ac 160, wf Emma, ch Lenora, Erick, Minnie, (34).

Gaylord, Emily, R1, sec 11, ac 240, wf Rebecca, ch Howard, Oris, (33).

Gaylord, H. H., R6, sec 10, ac 200, wf Idella, ch Floy, (60).

Goodwin, O., R6, sec 7, ac 72, sec 16, ac 37, wf Lottie, ch Blanche, William, Florence, (51).

Grant, R. R., R6, sec 9, ac 120, ch George, (60).

Green, William C., R1, sec 12, ac 181, (26).

Hall, E. M., R6, sec 9, ac 40, (25).

Hanley, Edward, R6, sec 18, ac 80, sec 17, ac 40, wf Emma, ch Lloyd, Marche, Stillman, (36).

Hardel, Robert, R6, sec 20, ac 194, wf Emma, ch Jessie, Stella, (12).

Hayes, Mrs. William, R6, sec 9, ac 120, sec 3, ac 40, ch Francis, Raeburn, William, (45).

Jarvis, William, R1, sec 5, ac 267.71, wf Wilhelmina, ch Sever, Pliny, Henry, Edgar, May, Guida, (53).

Jennings, Frank, R6, sec 16, ac 117, wf Annette, ch Muriel, Mary, Agnes, Alta, (49).

Jennings, John, R6, sec 16, ac 84, (58).

Jones, J., R1, sec 11, ac 91, wf Lucy, ch Kenneth, (36).

Joslin, Ira, R6, sec 15, ac 100, sec 10, ac 40, sec 14, ac 35, wf Ella, ch Sylvia, (38).

Joslin, R., R6, sec 15, ac 40, wf Clara, ch Gertie, (12).

Krapp, Fred, R6, sec 21, ac 160, wf Harmie, ch Elsie, Lillie, Ella, Arthur, Loraine, (28).

Larson, L., R6, sec 4, ac 160, wf Mable, ch Clifford, Leona, Laurice, Verna, James, (45).

Leach, C. E., R6, sec 15, ac 160, sec 22, ac 40, wf Mercy, ch Lyle, Florence, Floyd, (48).

Leach, J. F., R6, sec 10, ac 240, wf Hattie, ch Ruby, Leonard, Lucile, Marion, Grace, (50).

Lehr, F., R1, sec 11, ac 80, sec 12, ac 135, wf Augusta, ch William, John, Walter, Lydia, (45).

Luhm, H., R6, sec 22, ac 160, wf Amelia, ch Eddie, Arthur, Walter, (30).

McBrier, A. J., R1, sec 11, ac 51, sec 14, ac 40, wf Lula, ch Letha, Ila, James, (32).

Miller, E., R1, sec 6, ac 10, wf Minnie, ch Lillie, Lena, Clarence, (4).

Olson, O. A., R1, sec 4, ac 73.45, sec 3, ac 105, wf Ida, ch Nathaniel, (59).

Osterday, Joseph, R1, box 73, sec 5, ac 74, (29).

Post, H. L., R1, sec 14, ac 40, sec 13, ac 160, wf Minnie, ch Edson, (37).

Putzke, Emil, R6, sec 18, ac 80, sec 17, ac 40, wf Jennie, ch Ervin, Escenda, Leona, Elmer, (9).

Pyncheon, George, R6, sec 14, ac 120, sec 10, ac 40, sec 13, ac 26, wf Fannie, (60).

Randall, Libbie, R1, sec 2, ac 70, (28).

Schillert, Paul, R6, sec 9, ac 80, wf Clara, ch Harry, Mable, (11).

Schultz, G., R6, sec 18, ac 160, wf Vern, ch Wilbert, (29).

Schultz, Otto, R6, box 45, sec 21, ac 138.56, wf Minnie, ch William, August, Emil, Edward, (45).

Schwersinske, Henry, R6, sec 7, ac 75, wf Alvina, ch Evaline, Lillian, (35).

Simson, E., R1, sec 3, ac 304.25, wf Adeline, (3).

Simson, L., R1, sec 3, ac 304.25, wf Clara, ch Otto, Lena, (3).

Slovinske, Nick, R6, box 36, sec 14, ac 40, sec 14, ac 20, sec 13, ac 20, wf Elizabeth, ch Clifford, Irene, Linda, (5).

Solvorn, Ole, R6, sec 4, ac 80, sec 5, ac 40, wf Rose, (32).

Spurbeck, Ezra, R6, sec 15, ac 98, wf Anna, (36).

Starke, C. E., box 33, sec 8, ac 226, wf Elizabeth, ch Carl, Lelah, (55).

Sutheimer, R. R., R1, sec 1, ac 210, wf Annie, ch Donald, Etta, (2).

Tetzlaff, Ernest, R6, sec 16, ac 120, sec 13, ac 40, ch Alvin, Vernett, Aurelia, Hilda, Victor, Elenore, (21).

Thorstad, Ole, R6, wf Christiana, ch James, Bertha, Jennie, Clarence, Oscar, George, Alfred, Ella, Clara, (14). "Willow Row."

Wagner, G. E., R6, sec 15, ac 160, sec 10, ac 40, wf Flora, ch Leah, Allie, (21).

Wagner, Otto, R6, sec 18, ac 129, wf Myrtle, (25).

Warner, E., R6, sec 15, ac 65, sec 13, ac 20, wf Alzina, (40).

Warren, Ernest, R6, sec 17, ac 113, (15).

Warwick, Charles, R1, sec 2, ac 171.50, sec 1, ac 4.50, wf Nettie, ch Marvin, Floyd, John, Nettie, Ardella, Charles, (48).

Woodworth, E., R1, sec 6, ac 80.08, wf Agnes, ch Violet, Kenneth, (15).

(Michael Bednarek Collection, Wautoma, Wisc

MAP OF
MARION
TOWNSHIP Scale 1¼ Inches to One Mile

Township 18 North, Range 11 East of the 4th P. M.
WAUSHARA COUNTY, WIS.

Rural Routes shown thus: —————— Churches shown thus:
School Districts " " : ///////// 2 Cemeteries " " :
Schools " " : Corporation Limits of Cities shown thus:

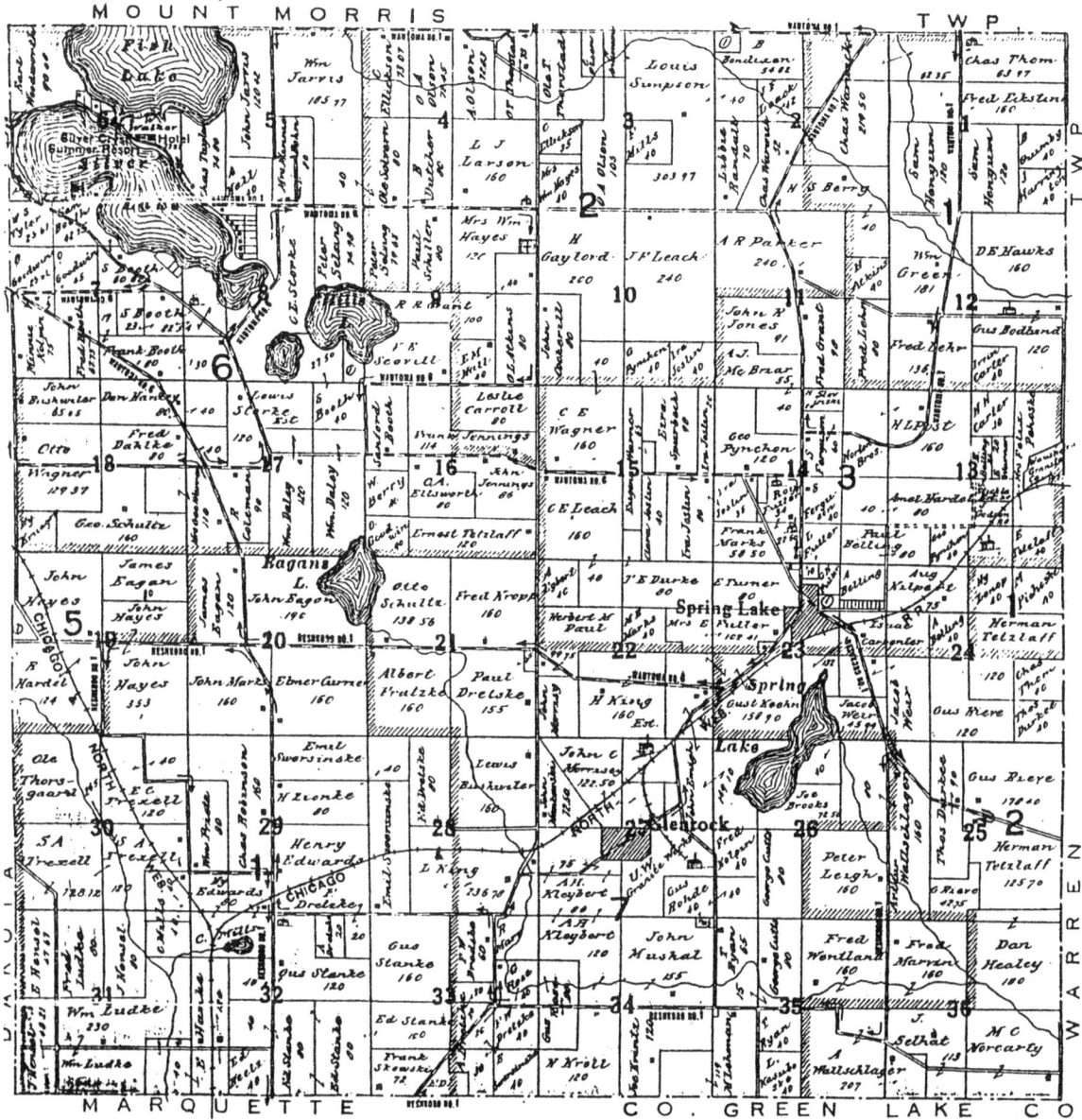

MOUNT MORRIS .... TWP

MARQUETTE CO. GREEN LAKE CO

List of Small Property Owners in This Township Shown on Map by Numbers

No.	Name	Acres	Sec.	No.	Name	Acres	Sec.	No.	Name	Acres	Sec.
1.	John Jarvis	10	2	1.	A. Hall	10	8	1.	J. Williams	5	23
3.	E. Miller		6	1.	B. Currier	4	19				

(Michael Bednarek Collection, Wautoma, Wisc.)

53) SCHWANKE, Edward of the Town of Lind, "Waushara Co."(Waupaca Co.)
- b. "Posen Preussen", marr. Caroline Behnke at Bloomfield 26
December 1883/ Vol. 3 (1870-1890), p. 55, no. 105.

54) SOHER, Wilhelm- b. "Posen Preussen", marr. Ernstine Schenbath
at Bloomfield 27 December 1878/ Vol. 3 (1870-1890), p. 31, no.
662.

55) STAHLBERG, Hermann of the Town of Royalton, Waupaca Co. (Wisc.)
-.b. "Posen Germany", marr. Amalia Henschel (father's surname
Streich)- b. "Posen Germany"; at the Town of Bloomfield 30
March (1896)/ Vol. D, p. 123, no. 47.

56) STEINKE, Fred of the Town of Wolf River, Winnebago Co. (Wisc.)-
b. "Posen Germany", marr. Minna Draeger at the Town of Bloomfield 26 May 1903/ Vol. D, p. 276, no. 62.

57) TESKE, Friedrich Ferdinand- b. "Posen Germany", marr. Caroline
Wilhelmine Gulle at Bloomfield 11 April 1887/ Vol. 3 (1870-1890),
p. 72, no. 31.

58) THOEWS, Carl- b. "Posen. Preussen", marr. Auguste Noack at Bloomfield 9 January 1878/ Vol. 3 (1870-1890), p. 26, no. 572.

59) TURNOW, John F. of New London (Waupaca/Outagamie Cos.)- b. "Posen Prussia", marr. Ernstine W. Schnanke at Bloomfield 29 November 1874/ Vol. 3 (1870-1890), p. 13, no. 319.(Christian ceremony)

60) UHL, August of Lind, Waupaca Co. (Wisc.)- b. "Posen Preussen",
marr. Auguste Paap at Bloomfield 17 February 1885/ Vol. 3 (1870-
1890), p. 61. no. 12.

61) WARGULA, Anthony- b. "Posen (Poland)", marr. Helene Hudziak- b.
"Poland (Prussia)"; at Belmont, Wisc. 24 November 1903/ Vol. D,
p. 292, no. 158. (Roman Catholic, probably Polish couple)

62) WEIDEMAN(N?), Wilhelmin   of the Town of Lind (Waupaca Co.,
Wisc.)- b. "Posen Pr(e)ussen", marr. Emilie Klawitter at Bloomfield 23 May 1879/ Vol. 3 (1870-1890), p. 33, no. 701.

63) WINTER, Gottfried- b. "Posen Preussen", marr. Wilhelmine Rosen-
ow at Bloomfield 7 January 1875/ Vol. 3 (1870-1890), p. 14, no.
336.

64) WINTER, Gustave of Lind (Waupaca Co., Wisc.)- b. "Posen Preussen", marr. Amelia Mueller at Bloomfield 9 December 1879/ Vol.
3 (1870-1890), p. 35, no. 744.

65) ZABEL, Ferdinand- b."Posen Prussia", marr. Emilie Brocks at the
Town of Bloomfield 22 January 1874/ Vol. 3 (1870-1890), p. 11,
no. 261.

66) ZIEMKE, Wilhelm of Blue Earth Co., Minnesota- b."Posen Preussen",
marr. Emilie Engel at Bloomfield 15 March 1885/ Vol. 3 (1870-
1890), p. 62, no. 21.

Immigrants from County Deutsch Krone, Province West Prussia:

1) BERG, Gustav- b. "Appolwerder (Appelwerder) Germany", marr. Auguste Brietzke- b. "Kessburg Germany"; at Richford 9 May 1905/ Vol. E, p. 39, no. 21.

2) GENNRICH, Gustave F.E. of Minnesota- b. "Latzig- " (there was also a Latzig in Co. Rummelsburg, Prov. Pomerania and Latzig-See (Lake) in the Rothen-Klempenower Forst (Forest) in Pomerania), marr. Emilie A. Wedel(1?)- b. "Luchwigshurst Westp(r)eussen" (perhaps Ludwigshorst, Co. Witkowo, Prov. Posen?); at Richford 28 February 1890/ Vol. D, p. 3, no. 16.

3) HAMPEL, Gust. Freidr. Wilh.- b. "Worder (Werder) in Preussen Germany", marr. Alma Wilhelmine Anna L. Bast at the Town of Bloomfield 27 April 1898/ Vol. D, p. 166, no. 50.

4) KOLM, Ludwig- b. "Deutsch Krone Germany", marr. Wilhelmine Koepp (maiden name "Chemicitz"=Kemnitz?) at the Town of Coloma 2 April 1903/ Vol. D, p. 272, no. 37.

5) MIELKE, Friedrich- b. "Salmo (Salm) Germany", marr. Catharina Entriss- b. "Possen Lauer Germany (?)"; at Dakota 11 November 1904/ Vol. E, p. 14, no. 142.

6) NIX, Anna Amanda Alvine- b. "Deutsch-Krone West Prussia Germany", marr. Ernst Wilhelm Roeske- b. "New Lipen (Neu-Lipenfier, Co. Belgard?) in (Prov.) Pom(m)ern Germany"; at Dakota 10 December 1896/ Vol. D, p. 135, no. 119.

7) PFLUGRAD(T?), Auguste- b. "Salm West Prussia Germany", marr. Hermann Zierke- b. "Seeger (Co. Bublitz, Prov.-) Pom(m)ern Germany"; at Dakota 31 March 1898/ Vol. D, p. 164, no. 38.

8) REGEL, Franz Louis- b. "Schloppe in Preussen Germany", marr. Hulda Elisabeth Birkholz at the Town of Bloomfield 18 October 1893/ Vol. D, p. 72, no. 98.

9) ROSANSKY, August Karl of Springfield, Marquette Co.- b. "Dron?? K??ty (Deutsch Krone?) Posen", marr. Hermine Louise Kruger at Coloma Station 27 December 1889/ Vol. 3, (1870-1890), p. 86, no. 94.

Farmers' Directory of Oasis Township

Abbreviations: Sec., section; ac., acres; wf., wife; ch., children; ( ) years in county

Almond Post Office.

Bassler, Jacob, R4, sec 13, ac 80, sec 14, ac 80, sec 1, ac 80, ch Lena, Alma, (33).

Cizinski, Joseph, R4, sec 1, ac 80, Rose twp, sec 6, ac 112, wf Norma, ch Clarence, (36).

Cizinski, W., R4, sec 1, ac 190, wf Julia, (30).

Grimm, Frank, R4, sec 13, ac 135, wf Leila, ch Helen, (37). "Level View Farm."

Hoyt, George, R4, sec 24, ac 210.

Janneck, Mrs. A., R4, sec 11, ac 80, ch Albert, Melia, Sophia, Henry, Fred, (30).

Meyer, Mrs. P. J., R4, sec 25, ac 43, sec 36, ac 187, ch Matthew, Frank, Margaret, (31).

Prochnow, Albert, R4, sec 2, ac 140, sec 1, ac 87, sec 12, ac 80, wf Mary, ch Louis, Alvin, (25).

Prochnow, William F., sec 1, ac 80, wf Etta.

Shaffer, A. C., R4, sec 2, ac 160, sec 11, ac 80, wf Minnie, ch Dana, Margaret, Winifred, Wilma, (24).

Spear, C. E., R4, sec 12, ac 80, sec 11, ac 40, wf Carrie, ch Ruth, (52). "The Lilac Farm."

Styber, Lad, R4, box 33, sec 25, ac 77, wf Marie, ch Miles, Lester, (5).

Urban, John H., R4, sec 13, ac 80, Rose twp, sec 7, ac 40, wf Carrie, ch Orestes, Warnie, (15).

Vroman, P., R4, sec 25, ac 139, sec 26, ac 80, wf Jessie, (45).

Wagner, Henry, R4, sec 14, ac 120, sec 13, ac 25, wf Liddie, ch Floyd, Charles, Clarence, (10).

Waratha, Frank, R4, sec 1, ac 80, sec 12, ac 80, wf Anna, ch Charles, John, Jennie, Martha, Emil, Alvin, (22).

Wittman, William, R4, box 19, sec 12, ac 80, sec 11, ac 40, wf Charlotte, (10).

Wood, B. A., R4, sec 12, ac 80, sec 17, ac 17, Rose twp, sec 17, ac 80, sec 18, ac 40, wf Matilda, ch Albert, Blanche, (52).

Yohn, John, R4, sec 12, ac 80, Rose twp, sec 7, ac 54, wf Anna, ch Walter, Arnold, Leonard, Cora, Lydia, (45).

Young, M. F., R4, sec 11, ac 120, wf Sarah, ch Clarence, Harry, Larina, Albert, Arnold, Leland, Wallace, Clinton, Areland, (21).

Hancock Post Office.

Parkinson, Mrs. P., R2, sec 31, ac 120, ch Elmer, Edgar, Vera, (22). "High Grade Holstein Fresian Cattle."

Plainfield Post Office.

Anselm, Fred Jr., R2, sec 15, ac 78, wf Veronia, ch Mildred, (30).

Bassler, Fred, R2, sec 8, ac 265, sec 9, ac 25, wf Louisa, ch Fred, Charles, Louis, Frank, Mary, Edith, Sophia, (33).

Biegel, Paul, R2, sec 21, ac 85, sec 20, ac 80, wf Kate, ch Frank, Peter, Kate.

Cluth, E. E. R2, sec 23, ac 77, wf Lena, (1).

Collins, F. B., R2, sec 22, ac 197, sec 23, ac 20, sec 15, ac 2, wf Anna, ch Arvilla, Vernon, Hazel, Raymond, Roydon, Harold, (48). "Hickory Grove Farm."

Cornell, J. A., R2, sec 18, ac 14, wf Olivia, ch Roy, Ray, (20).

Eager, L. T., R2, sec 32, ac 80, wf Libbie, ch Ray, (35). "The Old Homestead."

Eager, W. Y., R2, sec 32, ac 100, wf May, (62).

Ebert, H., R2, sec 23, ac 75, wf Hathaway, ch Luella, Edwin, Clarence, William, Ralph, (6).

Foss, W. R., R2, sec 23, ac 80½, wf Dora, ch Thelma, (35).

Gimn, W. H., R2, sec 11, ac 140, wf Katharine, ch Pearl, (31).

Grosse, Gus, R2, sec 11, ac 80, sec 10, ac 40, wf Lena, ch Siegfried, Angela, Leila, (25).

Handschke, Paul, R2, sec 15, ac 80, sec 10, ac 40, wf Nellie, ch Clara, (6). "Lone Oak Farm."

Hellman, H. H., R4, sec 30, ac 80, sec 31, ac 80, wf Philipine, ch Elizabeth, Augusta, Herbert, (2).

Helmrick, H. A., R2, sec 23, ac 83, sec 26, ac 60, sec 25, ac 58, sec 24, ac 3, wf Emma, ch Martha, Edith, (14).

Irish, William, R2, sec 18, ac 58, wf Margaret, ch Mary, (25).

Johnson, George, R2, sec 35, ac 80, (5).

Jorajoske, Mrs. Mary, R2, sec 22, ac 80, sec 27, ac 80, ch Michael, (12).

Kentopp, F. A., R2, sec 14, ac 120, wf Ida, ch Edwin, Carl, Margaret, (7).

King, H. F., R2, sec 35, ac 80, sec 34, ac 80, wf Francis, ch Agnes, Harvey, Harold, Helen, Alice, Arthur, (15).

Klawitter, Charles, R2, sec 27, ac 120, wf Mildia, ch Oscar, Elmer, Jessie, Mabel, (8).

Kortas, John, R2, sec 33, ac 160, wf Francis, ch Joseph, Alex, Celia, (11).

Kruger, F. C., R1, sec 14, ac 80, sec 23, ac 22, wf Amelia, ch Georgian, Esther, Louis, (8).

Kuczmarski, Frank, R2, sec 27, ac 82, wf Mary, ch Edward, Dora, Hubert, (15).

Kuczmarski, John, R2, sec 17, ac 120, wf Anna, ch John, Anton, Luke, Emil, William, Henrietta, Johanna, (16).

Lane, A. D.

Lane, A. D., R2, sec 29, ac 120, wf Abbie, ch William, Elmer, Margaret, Maud, (57).

McLaughlin, De Forest, R3, sec 6, ac 120, wf Anna, ch Arthur, Maud, (50).

Morey, C. T., R2, sec 20, ac 159½, sec 17, ac 141, wf Ella, ch Howard, Chesley, Clarence, Leda, (40).

Ray, B. J., R2, sec 8, ac 80, ch Norma, Lenona.

Ray, C. C., R2, sec 8, ac 80, sec 17, ac 80, wf Adelle, (42).

Reilly, Charles, R2, sec 24, ac 80, wf May, (30).

Sawyer, M. R., R2, sec 27, ac 120, wf Olga, ch Ruth, Marvin, (1).

Schelewski, Peter, R2, sec 26, ac 40, sec 27, ac 40, ch Martha, Joseph, (27).

Sherman, A., R2, sec 17, ac 80, wf Marietta, (24).

Shipley, J. O., sec 16, ac 274, wf Tannie, ch Otto, Nina, (13).

Smith, Millard, R2, sec 21, ac 80, sec 16, ac 80, sec 15, ac 40, wf Motie, ch Jay M., (49).

Spaulding, R. M., R2, sec 23, ac 101½, wf Jennie, ch Edith M., Sidney W., Marjorie E., (45).

Starke, S. F., R2, sec 35, ac 160, wf Helen, ch Leonard, Evelyn, (20).

Storzbach, Fred, R2, sec 28, ac 280, wf Gertrude, ch Emil, Rose, Lenin, Evia, Sadie, (45).

Storzbach, F. A., R2, sec 21, ac 40, sec 16, ac 80, wf Ella, ch Ethelin, (45).

Storzbach, John, R2, sec 21, ac 40, sec 22, ac 57½, sec 27, ac 120, sec 28, ac 240.

Straw, H. E., R2, sec 32, ac 40, sec 30, ac 40, wf Ivy, ch Genevieve, Russell, (20). Breeder of Full Blooded Duroc Jersey Hogs.

Tiffany, W. P., R2, sec 20, ac 200, sec 17, ac 31, wf Lillian, ch Viola, (50).

Tricky, F. B., R2, sec 24, ac 157, wf Lottie, ch Edgar, Edna, Dewey, Murna, Glen, Leon, Blanche, (46). "Broadview Farm."

Vroman T. J., R2, sec 13, ac 80, wf Anna, ch Milton, (30).

Vroman, T. L., R2, sec 16, ac 80, wf Laura E., ch William T., (21).

Walter, John, R2, sec 9, ac 160, wf Mary, ch Adolph, (4).

Walter, J. F., sec 13, ac 80, sec 14, ac 40, (45).

Warsa, Otto, R2, sec 32, ac 100, wf Bertha, ch Lillian, (25).

Waters, Mrs. Joseph, R2, sec 13, ac 80, ch Royal, Ethel, Daisy, (55).

Weiss, Adolph, R2, sec 22, ac 200, sec 26, ac 60, wf Emma, (6).

Whitney, Mrs. J., R2, sec 33, ac 54, ch Henry, (9).

Stevens Point Post Office.

Prochnow, Mrs. Charles, sec 7, ac 80, sec 2, ac 80.

MAP OF
OASIS
TOWNSHIP

Scale 1½ Inches to 1 Mile

Township 20 North, Range 9 East of the 4th P. M.
WAUSHARA COUNTY, WIS.

Rural Routes shown thus · · · Churches shown thus · · · · · 🏠
School Districts " " ▨▨▨ 2 Cemeteries · · · · ✝
Schools " " 🏫 Corporation Limits of Cities shown thus ⊢—⊣—⊢—⊣

PORTAGE CO.

PLAINFIELD

DEERFIELD TWP

List of Small Property Owners in this Township Shown on Map by Numbers

No. Name   Acres. Sec.   No. Name   Acres. Sec.

(Michael Bednarek Collection, Wautoma, Wisc.)

Immigrants from County Flatow, Province West Prussia:

1) BAENSCH, Berthold of Rerelco, South Dakota?- b. "Alt Luebke
(Alt-Lubcza?),Germany", marr. Mathilde Opperman at Springfield,
Marquette Co. 3 February 1903/ Vol. D, p. 270, no. 25.

2) BUHROW, Ferdinand- b. "Dombrowe (Kolonie in Regierungsbezirk=
Administrative District Marienwerder) Germany", marr. Henriette
Groll at Poy Sippi 4 April 1882/ Vol. 3 (1870-1890), p. 46, no.
25.

3) KRUEGER, Julius- b. "New Batrow (Neu-Battrow) West Prussia Germany", marr. Anna Bertha Wilhelmine Radüchel- b. "Trutzlatz
(Co. Naugard, Prov.-) Pommern Germany"; at Richford 10 April
1896/ Vol. D, p. 123, no. 50.

4) RISTAU, Edward Gustav of Newton (Marquette Co.)- b. "Sypemevor
(probably Sypniewo Kreis (County) Flextow West Prussia 3 December 1864", marr. Auguste Louise Opperman- b. "5 June 1871 Taw-
enwke (Tarnowke) West Pr."; at Coloma Station 28 January 1891/
Vol. D, p. 20, no. 105.

5) RISTAU, Johann of Springfield, Marquette Co.- b. "by Franzburg
(probably Vandsburg, larger town east of Sypniewo) West Preusaen",
marr. Pauline Berg at Richford 1 March 1889/ Vol. 3 (1870-1890),
p. 82, no. 16.

213

Immigrants from other locales in Province West Prussia:

1) BLOCK, Godlief (Gottlieb?) of Mansfield, Wisc.- b. "Sirchow (Dirschau, a county seat?) Prussia", marr. Emelia Wise (probably Weiss)- b. "Russia"; at Berlin (Green Lake Co.) 14 October 1901/ Vol. D, p. 229, no. 81.

2) GLASKE, Hermann- b. "Schwetz (a county seat) Germany", marr. Auguste Damrohse- b. "Germany"; at Coloma Township 3 August 1898/ Vol. D, p. 171, no. 78.

3) HOFFMANN, Mathilde Emilie- b. "Rosenberg (a county seat) West Prussia Germany", marr. Wilhelm Heinrich Otto at Coloma 7 April 1896/ Vol. D, p. 123, no. 51.

4) HOFFMANN, Wilh. Julius- b. "Rosenberg (see above) Germany", marr. Ida Louise Fausch of the Town of Springfield, Marquette Co.; at the Town of Coloma 2 April 1902/ Vol. D, p. 245, no. 43.

5) KELLER, Terefil of Berlin (Green Lake Co.), Wisc.- b. "Gryseyn-Carthaus (Karthaus is a county seat) Ger.", marr. Mary Treder- b. "Kichn- Germany"(?); at Berlin 29 April 1902/ Vol. D, p. 247, no. 57 (Catholic ceremony, likely Polish couple).

6) KWIDZINSKY, Eva- b. "Koelln (County Demmin, near Danzig, by Merssen?) Germany", marr. Fredrick Ringling at Bloomfield 3 November 1897 by Justice of the Peace/ Vol. D, p. 152, no. 95.

7) MATHEWS, Albert Wilhelm- b. "Moslin (Mösland, County Dirschau) West Prussia Germany", marr. Wilhelmine Louise Albertine Schlei- b. "Priepkow (Prov.-)Pommern Germany"; at Coloma 7 December 1896/ Vol. D, p. 134, no. 117.

8) TELLAK, Albert Johann August of the Town of Wolf River (Winnebago Co., Wisc.)- b. "Berern or Berem (Berent, a county seat?) Westpreus(s)en Germany", marr. Emilie Auguste Kempf at Bloomfield 30 April 1889/ Vol. 3 (1870-1890), p. 84, no. 44.

9) WEGNER, Julius- b. "Neu Danzig Germany", marr. Wilhelmine Pockrandt- b. "Romanshof (Co. Czarniaku, Prov. Posen, Prussia) Germany"; at the Town of Coloma 9 August 1898/ Vol. D, p. 172, no. 85. (note: see County Dramburg, Province Pomerania listing)

Farmers' Directory of Poy Sippi Township

Abbreviations: Sec., section; ac., acres; wf., wife; ch., children; ( ) years in county

Auroraville Post Office.

Albright, Herman, R1, sec 26, ac 200, sec 25, ac 40, sec 21, ac 40, ch Otto, Harry, Verne, Herbert, Lloyd, Elmer, (26).

Block, William, R1, sec 22, ac 80, sec 27, ac 20, wf Ida, ch Clara, Olga, Richard, Elsa, Linda, William, Adeline, (15).

Braun, Julius, R1, sec 20, ac 80, sec 18, ac 21½, wf Anna, ch Lewis, (15). "Fountain Valley Holstein Dairy Farm."

Cassidy, Frank, sec 28, ac 240, sec 27, ac 80, sec 22, ac 50, wf Julia, ch Joseph, Francis, George, Myrtle, Edward, Laura, Darfine, (55).

Clark, Chas., R1, wf Ann, ch Jay, Lewis, (50).

Costello, Peter, R1, sec 21, ac 160, wf Jennie, ch Martin, Robert, (45).

Cottrell, Carl, R1, wf Myrtle, ch Ruth, Forrest, Sterling, mother Julia Cady, (47).

Gehrke, Mrs. Agnes, R1, sec 29, ac 80, ch Theodore H., Agnes M., Avril A., Judge J., French F., (45).

Handrick, Fred, R1, sec 31, ac 140, wf Martha, ch Ethel, (32).

Handrick, Henry, R1, sec 19, ac 50, sec 30, ac 40, sec 31, ac 30, wf Alvina, ch Leo, Viola, Henry, Lydia, (44).

Hiese, Carl, R1, sec 23, ac 160, wf Bertha, ch Max, Ernest, Emil, Paul, (2).

Hoeft, George H., R1, sec 22, ac 90, sec 9, ac 40, wf Bertha, ch Donald, Lewis, (26).

Hoeft, Henry, R1, sec 26, ac 160, wf Emma, ch Annie, Clara, (35).

Hoeft, Herman, R1, sec 26, ac 160, wf Caroline, ch Edward, grand-daughters Julia, Mabel, (45).

Johnson, Bernard, R1, sec 21, ac 120, sec 28, ac 80, wf Jennie, ch Vesta, Nellie, George, (20).

Kluckman, Herman, R1, sec 32, ac 60, wf Augusta, (10).

Phone 33 Fountain

Apple Trees, Shade Trees
and all kinds of
Small Fruit Plants and Flowering Shrubs

We dig, pack and deliver all stock in the spring. Our plants are never out of the ground more than twenty-four hours.

Fountain Valley Nursery
HOWARD SMITH, Prop.
POY SIPPI, WIS.

Krause, Charles W., R1, sec 29, ac 120, sec 22, ac 10, wf Elizabeth, ch Harold, Edward, (22).

Krause, Herman, R1, sec 32, ac 53, wf Hulda, ch Viola, (22).

Krause, John, R1, sec 20, ac 110, wf Emma, ch Edna, Walter, Mabel, Vernie, Elsie, (20).

Krause, Otto, R1, sec 32, ac 80, sec 15, ac 20, mother Augusta, (27).

Krause, Paul, R1, sec 29, ac 80, wf Bertha, ch William, Frances, Dora, Eleanore, (22).

McCue, Oscar, E., R1, sec 19, ac 100, wf Cora, ch Leland, Leonard, Kenneth, Lillian, Mildred, (48).

Nelson, Charles, R1, sec 30, ac 80, wf Annie, ch Earl, Arnold, Sylvia, (28).

Pagel, Frank, R1, sec 20, ac 80, wf Rose, ch John, Herman, Elizabeth, Heinz, Laura, Arthur, Alfred, (30).

Rodencel, Charles, R1, sec 31, ac 80, sec 32, ac 80, wf Tillie, ch Frank, Paul, Laura, Martin, Herman, (25).

Rucks, Arthur, R1, sec 30, ac 160, wf Mary, ch Arnold, (25).

Sanders, Joseph, R1, sec 19, ac 80, sec 22, ac 20, wf Hattie, ch Daisy, Lillian, Antone, (2).

Sthrey, Julius, R1, sec 19, ac 88, sec 28, ac 10, wf Amelia, ch Lydia, Ella, Walter, (47).

Timm, Charles, R1, sec 31, ac 60, sec 32, ac 51, sec 33, ac 20, wf Flora, ch Herman, John, Theodore, William, Carl, Fred Alma, Martha, (48).

Wendt, Fred, R1, sec 19, ac 52, wf Lena, ch Elmer, Harvey, Wallace, (28).

Werner, Charles, R1, sec 5, ac 9, sec 20, ac 120, sec 17, ac 40, wf Della, ch Arthur, Arleigh, Lyle, Myrtle, Fern, (43).

Werner, Wm., R1, sec 30, ac 40, sec 29, ac 40, sec 20, ac 40, sec 28, ac 10, wf Clara, ch Lawrence, Dorothy, father Fred, mother Bertha, (38).

Pine River Post Office.

Blanchard, Frank R., R2, sec 30, ac 80, wf Ella, ch Cecil, Gard, Irene, Hazel, Miles, Ardin, Bessie, Aaron, (48).

Cate, Nathaniel, R2, wf Gertrude, ch Leon, Ethel, George, mother Mrs. S. L. Cate, (37).

Krueger, William, R2, sec 19, ac 80, wf Clara, ch Dorothy, (18).

Martin, G., R2, sec 19.

Muller, August, R2, sec 19, ac 40, wf Hedwick, ch Alfred, Hattie, (13).

Pigorsch, Alfred, R2, sec 31, ac 40, wf Bertha, ch Alvold, Esther, Lillian, Arthur, Harry, Alfreda, (17).

Rodencil, William, R2, sec 19, ac 80, wf Vina, ch Lona, Edwin, Stella, (25).

Poy Sippi Post Office.

Anderson, Jacob, R1, sec 9, ac 60, sec 16, ac 40, wf Christine, ch James, Gilbert, Arnold, Marie, Alice, (40).

Brey, Herman, R1, sec 6, ac 320, sec 5, ac 100, wf Martha, ch Clara, Elsie, Ida, William, Lewis, Edwin, Arthur, Lillie, Clarence, (35).

Brown, William G., Star Route, sec 7, ac 78, sec 10, ac 20, wf Elizabeth, ch Lillie, Irvin, Edna, (32).

Buchholtz, Edward, R1, sec 7, ac 55, sec 8, ac 239, wf Alvina, (50).

Buchholtz, Lewis, sec 7, ac 109, wf Myrtle, ch Glennie, (28).

Buchholtz, Walter, R1, sec 47, wf Laurna.

Clark, Clarence, Star Route, sec 16, ac 70, sec 18, ac 25, wf Annie, (60).

Clark, Fernado, Star Route, wf Sarah, ch Bert, (50).

Durawa, August, sec 8, ac 102, sec 17, ac 30, sec 16, ac 20, wf Martha, ch Floria, Edward, Harry, Paul, August, Balser, Ralph, Edmond, John, Albertine, Clifford, Sylvester, Josephine, (3).

Gaetch, Edward, Star Route, sec 17, ac 80, sec 18, ac 33, sec 15, ac 25, sec 5, ac 22, wf Annie, ch Alvin, Ella, Clarence, (42).

Gordon, John, R1, sec 2, ac 33, sec 4, ac 20, sec 14, ac 20, wf Bertha, ch Byron, Clara, Lura, (49).

Holsworth, Porter, Star Route, sec 17, ac 40, wf Clara, ch Vivian, Virginia, (28).

Madison, Charles C., R1, sec 9, ac 167, wf Mary, ch Avis E., Guy A., Harold, Leland, Marvin, Francis, Clarence, Arnold, (30).

Madison, Hans, R1, sec 9, ac 100, sec 10, ac 35, sec 5, ac 17, wf Mary, ch Edna, Alice, Blanch, Raymond, Berne, Cora, (40).

Martin, Daniel M., sec 17, ac 50, sec 16, ac 20, wf Mamie, ch Catherine, Ileen, Milton, Henry, Marian, Clinton, (45).

Roggow, August, sec 7, ac 63, wf Mary, ch Charles, John, Lydia, (45).

Sattler, John, Star Route, sec 8, ac 90½, wf Laura, (23).

Schoonover, James F., R1, sec 6, ac 120, sec 5, ac 40, wf Emma, ch Beatrice, Kermit, (20).

Smith, Howard, Star Route, sec 19, ac 40, sec 16, ac 20, wf Minnie, sisters Lottie and Lillian Austin, (27). "Fountain Valley Nursery."

Stafford, William B., sec 18, ac 79, wf Musetta, ch Lettie, (42).

Map of POY SIPPI TOWNSHIP

Township 19 North, Range 13 East of the 4th P. M.

Scale 1½ Inches to 1 Mile   WAUSHARA COUNTY, WIS.

Rural Routes shown thus ·   Churches shown thus: · · · · · ·
School Districts " · · 2   Cemeteries " · · · · · · ±
Schools " · ·   Corporation Limits of Cities shown thus ⊢⊢⊢⊢⊢

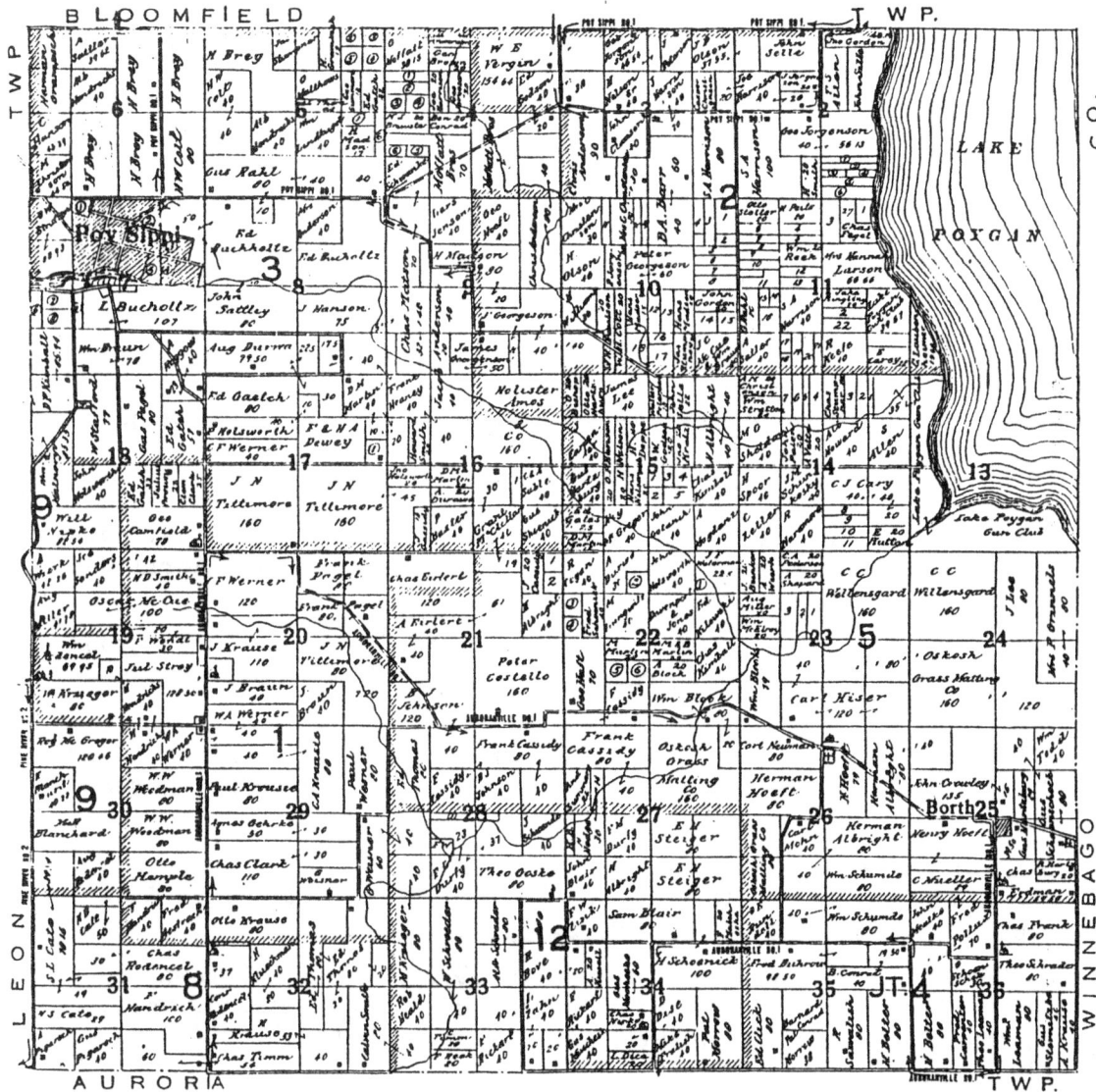

List of Small Property Owners in this Township Shown on Map by Numbers

Immigrants from Province "West Prussia":

1) BERG, Maria Louisa- b. "Westprussian", marr. Karl August Wedde Richford 26 February 1892/ Vol. D, p. 39, no. 15.

2) BLUEMKE, Gottlied- b. "West Preussen", marr. Bertha Timm at Bloomfield 10 September 1877/ Vol. 3 (1870-1890), p. 24, no. 534.

3) BRITZKE, Ida Alvina- b. "West Breussen Germany", marr. Emil Kromrei- resident Coloma, birthplace Springfield, Marquette Co.; at Richford 13 May 1903/ Vol. D, p. 277, no. 69.

4) GE(H?)RKE, Heinrick of Wolf River (Winnebago Co.) - b."West Pr(e)useen", marr. Auguste Abraham at Bloomfield 24 June 1875/ Vol. 3 (1870-1890), p. 16, no. 373.

5) KOBISKI, Johann Julius- b. "West Prussian", marr. Augusta W. Gucht (Gutsch?) at Bloomfield 20 December 1877/ Vol. 3, (1870-1890), p. 26, no. 568.

6) KRAUSE, Auguste Mathilde- b. "West Prussia", marr. Albert Reinhard Roske of Rushford (Winnebago Co.)- b. "Pommern" (Prov. Pomerania); at Rushford "Waushara Co." (Winnebago Co.) 8 April 1892/ Vol. D, p. 43, no. 38.

7) LOHM, August Karl- b. "West Prussia Germany", marr. Minna Antona Bertha Ueckers- b. "West Prussia Germany"; at the Town of Dakota 3 August 1893/ Vol. D, p. 69, no. 75.

8) ROZENSKE, Theodore- b. "V. (West?) Prussia", marr. Johanna Marie Selsing- b. "Norwegian"; at groom's residence- Wautoma 1 November 1906/ Vol. E, p. 53, no. 121.

9) SCHMIDT, Friedrich Wilhelm- b. "West Prussia", marr. Maria Elisabeth Wendland of Portage (Columbia Co.), Wisc. at Coloma Station 27 December 1892/ Vol. D, p. 55, no. 1.

10) SCHORNACK, George Fredrich of Groten (Groton) Braun (Brown) Co. Dacota (Territory, now South Dakota)- b. "Westpreassen", marr. Bertha Ann Martens at Bloomfield 18 March 1888/ Vol. 3 (1870-1890), p. 77, no. 15.

11) SCHROEDER, Albert Carl of Lind (Waupaca Co.), Wisc.- b. "West Pr(e)ussen", marr. Wilhelmine Follendorf at Bloomfield 2 July 1875/ Vol. 3 (1870-1890), p. 16, no. 372.

12) SEMROW, Emil E.- b. "West Prussia", marr. Auguste O. Hinz- b. "Posen"; at Coloma Station 7 April 1890/ Vol. D, p. 6, no. 34.

13) TOKARSKY, Malwine- b. "West Prusken Germany", marr. Johann Shurland of the Town of Wolf River, Winnebago Co. (Wisc.) at Bloomfield 9 June (1897)/ Vol. D, p. 144, no. 48.

Immigrants from County Belgard, Province Pomerania, Prussia:

1) BIRR, Bertha Auguste Alwine- b. "Damen Germany", marr. George Klockzin at Dakota 24 November 1892/ Vol. D, p. 52, no. 92.

2) FRANK, Carl August- b. "Belgard Germany", marr. Anna Rval(?) Buttke at Poy Sippi by a minister of the German Methodist Episcopal Church 13 March(1895)/ Vol. D, p. 102, no. 22.

3) KRUEGER, Bertha Albertine- b. "Belgard Germany", marr. Emil Adolf Werner of Westfield, Marquette Co.; at the Town of Coloma 27 June 1899/ Vol. D, p. 138, no. 54.

4) LAABS, August Bernhardt of the Town of Wolf River, Winnebago Co. (Wisc.)- b. "Lensin (Lensen) in Pommern Germany", marr. Bertha Marie Louise Krehnke (widow, maiden name Diedrich) at West Bloomfield 14 March 1889/ Vol. 3 (1870-1890), p. 83, no. 29.

5) ROESKE, Ernst Wilhelm- b. "New Lipen (Neu-Lipenfier?) in Pom-(m)ern Germany", marr. Anna Amanda Alvine Nix- b. "Deutsch Krone (a county seat in Prov.-) West Prussia Germany"; at Dakota 10 December 1896/ Vol. D, p. 135, no. 119.

Immigrants from County Dramburg, Province Pomerania, Prussia:

1) BARTEL,Emil P.- b. "New Woren (Neu-Wuhrow?) Prov. Pomen Germany", marr. Minna Pflugradt at Wautoma 10 November 1903/ Vol. D, p. 290, no. 150.

2) BLOEDEN, Julius Rudolph Edward- b. "AltWhurow Pommern Prussia Europe", marr. Bertha Henriette Lisette Mu^{e}ller at the German Church- Dakota, in the discipline of the Church of the Evangelical Association of North America; 1 February 1878/ Vol. 3 (1870-1890), p. 27, no. 528.

3) RAATZ, Aug. Hermann- b. "Aulzig Kro. (Kreis=County) Dramburg Pommern", marr. Amrhen Boschen- b. "in Nurkel Prov. Hannover (Prussia, in northwestern Germany)"; at Richford 1 July 1892/ Vol. D, p. 45, no. 52.

4) WEGNER, Julius- b. "Neulatzig (Neu-Latzig) Germany", marr. Ernestine Wilhelmine Krueger at Deerfield township 23 October 1894/ Vol. D, p. 97, no. 113.

Farmers' Directory of Richford Township

Abbreviations: Sec., section; ac., acres; wf., wife; ch., children; ( ) years in county

Carl Bartel, Wautoma, R4.
Otto Bartel, Wautoma, R4.
Fred Belter, Coloma.
Gust Berg, Coloma, R3.
August Bentler, Coloma, R3.
Ed. Blader, Wautoma, R4.
J. E. Blader, Wautoma, R4.
Lewis Blader, Wautoma, R4.
Fred Boesler, Coloma.
A. O. Borst, Coloma, R3.
Fred Borst, Coloma, R3.
Ed. Bruch, Coloma, R3.
Gust Bruch, Coloma.
Herman Bruch, Coloma, R3.
Howard Dulin.
Adolph Ebert, Coloma, R3.
Charley Ebert, Coloma, R3.
Wm. Ebert Jr., Coloma, R3.
Wm. Ebert Sr., Coloma, R3.
Gust Finske, Coloma, R3.
Gust Flegner, Wautoma, R5.
Julius Goetz, Wautoma, R4.
August Groskreutz, Wautoma, R5.
Wm. Gutche, Coloma, R3.
Richard Henne, Coloma, R3.
August Heller, Hancock, R3.
Fred Heller, Hancock, R3.
August Hesler, Coloma, R3.
Henry Hesler, Coloma, R3.
Lewis Hesler, Coloma, R3.
Emil Hintz, Coloma, R3.
Herman Hintz, Coloma, R3.
Ed. Ingalls, Coloma, R3.
Henry Jaschek, Coloma, R3.
John Jaschek, Coloma, R3.
Jacob Jaschek, Coloma, R3.
Julius Jenermann, Hancock, R3.
Lewis Jordon, Coloma, R3.
Rudolph Kapp, Coloma, R3.
Will Krause, Coloma, R3.
Fred Kroll, Coloma, R3.
Herman Lacheldt, Coloma, R3.
Otto Lehman, Coloma, R3.
Ed. Lietz, Coloma, R3.
Fred Lietz Jr., Coloma, R3.
Fred Lietz Sr., Coloma, R3.
Henry Lietz, Coloma, R3.
Emil Matz, Coloma, R3.
Fred Matz, Coloma, R3.
Ed. Meyer, Wautoma, R4.
Otto Mittelstedt, Coloma, R3.
C. G. Nulton Hancock, R3.

Ed. Opperman, Coloma, R3.
A. H. Peevey, Wautoma, R4.
Ranson Peevey, Wautoma, R4.
Otto Podoll, Wautoma, R5.
Reinhold Podoll, Wautoma, R5.
Wm. Potter, Coloma.
Albert Rantz, Wautoma, R4.
August H. Rantz, Wautoma, R4.
Herman Rantz, Wautoma, R4.
John Rantz, Coloma, R3.
Richard Rantz, Wautoma, R4.
Wm. Rick, Coloma, R3.
Herman Roeske, Coloma, R3.
Charley Rogers, Coloma, R3.
Julius Rux, Coloma, R3.
Adolph Schaetzke, Coloma, R3.
Alvin Schaetzke, Coloma, R3.
Chas. Schliepp, Coloma.
C. G. Schmudlach, Hancock, R3.
Wm. Schmudlach, Hancock, R3.
Gotlip Schroeder, Coloma, R3.
Henry Schroeder, Coloma, R3.
Leo Schroeder, Coloma, R3.
Gust Schubert, Coloma, R3.
Herman Schubert, Coloma, R3.
Wm. Schubert, Hancock, R3.
Lewis Schultz, Coloma, R3.
Emil Schwernski, Wautoma, R5.
Ed. Shmudlach, Hancock, R3.
Jul Swanke, Coloma, R3.
Julius Wachholtz, Coloma, R3.
Albert Wagner, Wautoma, R4.
Herman Wagner, Coloma, R3.
Julius Wagner, Coloma, R3.
Will Wagner, Coloma, R3.
Henry Wedde, Coloma, R3.
Richard Wedde, Coloma, R3.
Henry Wedel, Hancock, R3.
Wm. Wedel, Hancock, R3.
Albert Weiland, Coloma, R3.
Earnest Weiland, Coloma.
Julius Weiland, Coloma, R3.
John Wentland, Coloma, R3.
Wm. Whaley, Wautoma, R4.
Herman Wichner, Coloma, R3.
Will Wichner, Coloma, R3.
Wm. Wiesjohn, Coloma, R3.
Emil Wrasse, Coloma, R3.
Fred Zabel, Wautoma, R5.
Wm. Zelmer, Hancock, R3.
Albert Zinke, Wautoma, R4.
Joe Zinke, Wautoma, R4.

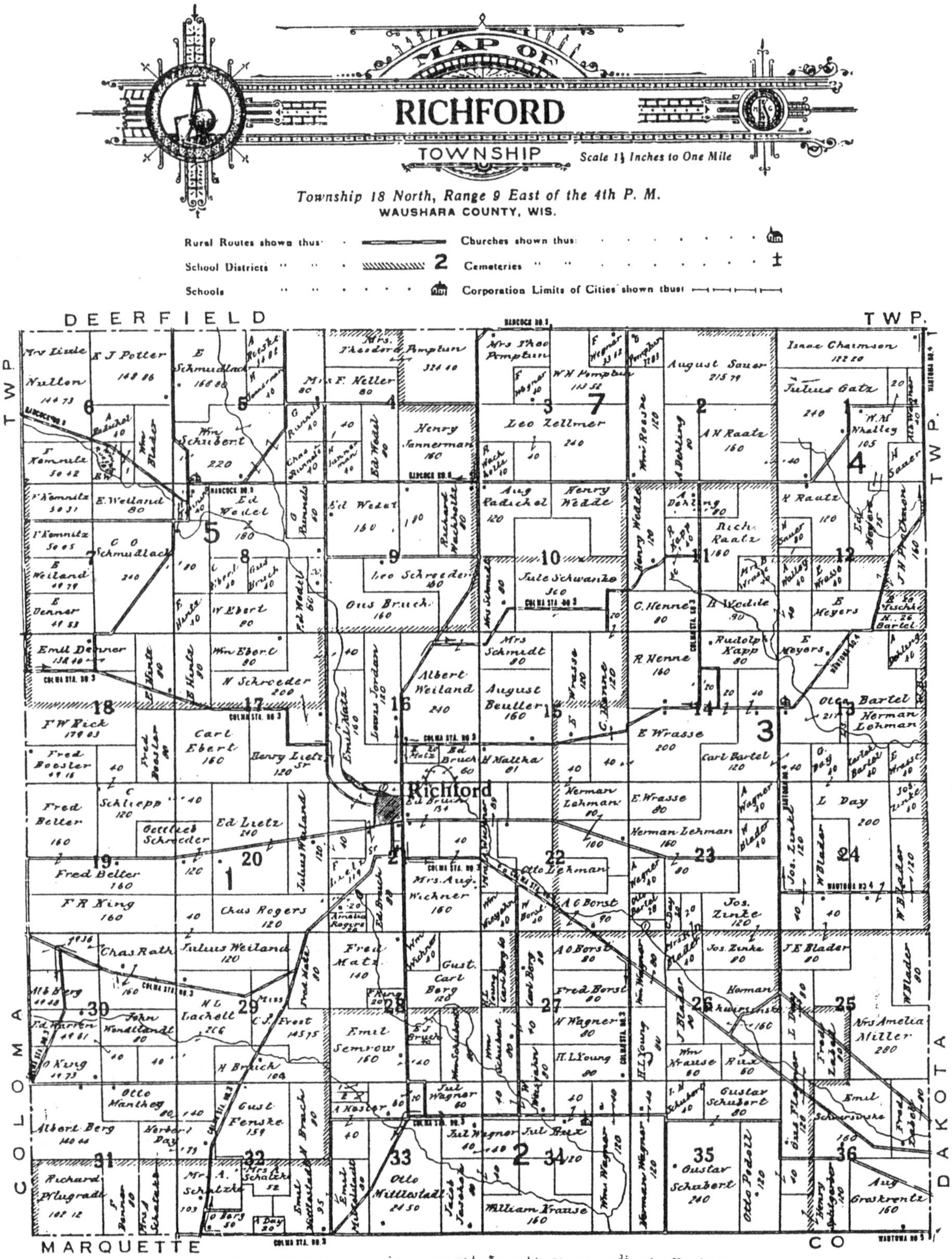
MAP OF
RICHFORD
TOWNSHIP
Scale 1¼ Inches to One Mile
Township 18 North, Range 9 East of the 4th P. M.
WAUSHARA COUNTY, WIS.
Rural Routes shown thus
School Districts
Schools
Churches shown thus
Cemeteries
Corporation Limits of Cities shown thus
DEERFIELD
TWP.
MARQUETTE
CO
COLOMA
DAKOTA
Richford

List of Small Property Owners in This Township Shown on Map by Numbers

No.	Name	Acres	Sec.	No.	Name	Acres	Sec.	No.	Name	Acres	Sec.
1	Wm. Zeimer	12	6	1.	F. Borst	12	33	2.	H. Wagner	10	33
1.	J. Gnatz	10	12	1.	H. Jennerman	10	33				

(Michael Bednarek Collection, Wautoma, Wisc.)

Immigrants from County Naugard, Province Pomerania, Prussia:

1) FISCHER, Therese Marie Mathilde- b. "Greifenberg Pommern Germany", marr. Friedr. Wilh. Marquardt- b. "Lehmbin Pos-en, Germany"; at West Bloomfield 16 July 1900/ Vol. D, p. 207, no. 67.

2) KROEHNKE, Augustus F.G.- b. "Plantika̱w (-ow) Prussia Germany", marr. Bertha L.M. Diedrich at the Town of Bloomfield 13 April 1883/ Vol. 3 (1870-1890), p. 51, no. 38.

3) RADÜCHEL, Anna Bertha Wilhelmine- b. "Trutzlatz Pommern Germany", marr. Julius Krueger- b. "New Batrow (Neu-Battrow, Co. Flatow, Prov.-) West Prussia Germany"; at Richford 10 April 1896/ Vol. D, p. 123, no. 50.

4) RADÜCHEL, August- b. "Trutzlatz Germany", marr. Marie Wedde (maiden name Berg?)- b. EichKatzberg (Eichquast, Co. Obernick, Prov. Posen?) Germany"; at Richford? 13 June 1905/ Vol. E, p. 23, no. 51.

Immigrants from County Stolp, Province Pomerania, Prussia:

1) GUELZOW, Pauline- b. "Stolp Germany", marr. Hermann Kropp- b. "Germany"; at Spring Lake 19 August 1893/ Vol. D, p. 70, no. 84.

2) HAASE, Frederick W.- b. "Ruhnow (a Rittergut, or knight's landed estate) Germany", marr. Bertha Augusta Pel(t)z (widow, maiden name Schons(c)heck) at the residence of the bride's father, Gustav S., Poy Sippi 16 September 1888/ Vol. 3 (1870-1890), p. 80, no. 65.

3) PLOETZ, Aug. Friedr.- b. "Dunow (Dünnow) Germany", marr. Emma Alvine Matz at Coloma 26 April 1895/ Vol. D, p. 104, no. 36.

4) PLOETZ, Franz Wilhelm- b. "Duenow (Dünnow) Germany", marr. Bertha Holz of Niles, Cook Co., Ill.; at Coloma Station 8 May 1891/ Vol. D, p. 27, no. 146.

5) PUFAHL, Fritz Albert Edward- b. "Horst, Pommerania Germany 28 July 1883", marr. Elisabeth Wilhelmine Sophia Braun at the Town of Bloomfield 22 March 1906/ Vol. E, p. 38, no. 34.

Immigrants from other locales in Province Pomerania, Prussia:

1) BEHM, Carl Ernst August- b. "Rothenklempenow (County Randow) in Pommern Germany", marr. Ida Friedericka Caroline Koop- b. "Plietz in Mecklenburg Strelitz Germany"; at the Town of Bloomfield 10 December 1891/ Vol. D, p. 34, no. 191.

2) BEHM, Wilhelm Friedrich- b. "Rathen Klempnow (Rothenklempenow) Preuseen Germany", marr. Ottilie Minna Elsie Oehlke at the Town of Bloomfield 18 December 1889/ Vol. 3 (1870-1890), p. 86, no. 91.

3) BEYER, Lizzie- b. "Paswalk (County Ückermunde) Germany", marr. Wm. Last at the City of Waupaca (a Wisc. County seat) 24 October 1906/ Vol. E, p. 52, no. 115.

4) BORK, Bertha Mathilde- b. "Rotsebuher (Ratzebuhr, County Neustettin) Pom. Germany", marr. Heinrich C. Bartz at Richford 27 February 1900/ Vol. D, p. 200, no. 26.

5) BORK, Johann Friederick of the Town of Royalton, Waupaca Co. (Wisc.)- b. "Landerhow Germany" (possibly Landow, County Rügen?), marr. Emma Adaline Gruening at Bloomfield 26 December (1894)/ Vol. D, p. 99, no. 3.

6) BRAUN, Wilhelm C.- b. "Freienwalde (County Saatzig) Pommern", marr. Karolina Louise Schlief at Crystal Lake Newton, Marquette Co. (Wisc.) 30 July 1889/ Vol. 3 (1870-1890), p. 82, no. 12.

7) DUBRATZ, Gust. Karl Eduard- b. "Schievelb(e)in (a county seat) Germany", marr. Amanda Kneissler at Coloma 5 April 1899/ Vol. D, p. 132, no. 32.

8) FOLENDORF, Wilhelm Friedrick Gottfried- b. "Kollberg (seat of County Kolberg-Körlin) Preussen Germany", marr. Mathilde Charlotte Meir at the Town of Bloomfield 5 December 1889/ Vol. 3 (1870-1890), p. 86, no. 88.

9) HERZFELD, Gustav Wilhelm- b. "Rolenklempnow (Rothenklempenow, Co. Randow) Preussen Germany", marr. Pauline Ernestine Draheim at the Town of Bloomfield 29 January 1896/ Vol. D, p. 117, no. 13.

10) KRESIN, Carl Wilhelm of Oshkosh (Seat of Winnebago Co., Wisc.)- b. "Zackensin (Zackenzin, County Lauenburg i. P.) Preussen Germany", marr. Bertha Albertine Gollnick at the Town of Bloomfield 11 August 1892/ Vol. D, p. 46, no. 56.

11) MUCH, Hermann Johann Adam- b. "Rosalsien (Roslasin, County Lauenburg) in Pommern Germany", marr. Bertha Marie Folendorf at the Town of Bloomfield 2 June 1887/ Vol. 3 (1870-1890), p. 73, no. 40.

Farmers' Directory of Wautoma Township

Abbreviations: Sec., section; ac., acres; wf., wife; ch., children; ( ) years in county

Wautoma Post Office.

Ames, C. W., R3, sec 5, ac 167.18, wf Ida, ch Oliver, Charles. (50).

Anderson, Knute, R3, sec 15, ac 80, sec 16, ac 80, wf Louise, ch Alfred, Hilda, Knuth, Cora, (27).

Attoe, W. E., R2, sec 3, ac 40, sec 2, ac 124.69, wf Florence, ch Irving, Arnold, Audrey, Osborne, Joyce, Edith, Dorothy, Marjorie, (8).

Barnhart, O, R3, box 50, sec 10, ac 80, wf Olga, ch Basil, Vilas, Harris. (32).

Bartel, J., R1, sec 31, ac 100, wf Olga, ch Henry, Harold, Lorena, (34).

Bartz, J. F., R3, sec 28, ac 40, sec 29, ac 80, wf Elizabeth, ch Ella, Amelia, Otto, Alfred, Edith, Martha, (25).

Bauer, L., R3, sec 33, ac 90, wf Mary, ch Joseph, John, Bonnie, (29).

Bendixen, C. O., R1, sec 35 ac 88, wf Thea, ch Lawrence, Dorothy, (48).

Bigsby, Harry, R3, sec 6, ac 40, sec 5, ac 45, wf Essie, ch Lyle, Lloyd, Vira, (30).

Bridgman, C. G., sec 22, ac 200, sec 23, ac 80, (20).

Buschke, W. R., R3, sec 7, ac 150, sec 18, ac 10, sec 17, ac 20, sec 28, ac 10, wf Anna, (21).

Byse, C. M., sec 27, ac 160, sec 26, ac 65.75, wf Dora, ch Gage, Lyman, Georgia, (56).

Charleson, Mrs. Charles, R3, box 27, sec 9, ac 80, sec 4, ac 80, ch Hilda, Elmer, Clarence, Truman, Edna, (56).

Charleson, H., R3, sec 7, ac 80, wf Martha, ch Norman, Neoma, Ruth, (35).

Coleman, M., R3, sec 19, ac 120, wf Anna, ch Gladys, Flossie, Norviel, (45).

Cook, Giles R., sec 27, ac 160, wf Belle, (25).

Daniels, E. A., R1, box 5, sec 36, ac 80, sec 25, ac 40, (16).

Daniels, L., R1, sec 36, ac 80, sec 26, ac 40, sec 25, ac 40, wf Nora, (47).

Darling, Joseph, R1, sec 31, ac 50, wf Minnie, ch Onasita, Bevelin, Callie, Joe, Sever, Jim, Russel, (41).

Darling, Luman, R2, sec 11, ac 240, wf Sarah, ch Gary A.

Drager, August, R1, sec 31, ac 80, sec 32, ac 25, wf Ida, ch Edna, Erma, Irvin.

Drager, J., R3, sec 28, ac 120, (9).

Edwards, C. W., R2, sec 1, ac 120, sec 2, ac 10, wf Ethel, ch Evelyn, (39).

Englebreston, M., R3, sec 20, ac 100, wf Thea, ch Bertha, Selma, Emma, (21).

Engle, Paul, R3, sec 6, ac 160, wf Nettie, ch Ethel, (52).

Feltis, M., R3, sec 7, ac 80, (30).

Frater, Julius, R4, sec 32, ac 120, wf Elizabeth, ch Lena, (27).

Fritz, Oscar, R2, sec 22, ac 40, sec 23, ac 80, (21).

Fritz, O. F., R2, box 60, sec 22, ac 160, wf Louise, ch Mable, Annie, Theodore, Theresa, Martin, (20).

Gaylord, William, R2, sec 26, ac 113, wf Lucy, ch Rarden, Walter, Pearl, (32).

Gilson, Mrs. G., R2, sec 14, ac 40, sec 23, ac 80, ch Victor, Shirley, (30). "Walnut Row."

Gramse, R., R3, sec 28, ac 120, wf Martha, ch Walter, Clara, Mable, (44).

Grendson, G., R3, sec 20, ac 40, sec 21, ac 20, sec 29, ac 40, sec 28, ac 20, wf Gunda, ch Annie, Christ, (9).

Gunderson, George, R2, box 51, sec 10, ac 140, sec 10, ac 10, sec 25, ac 10, wf Anna, ch Lionel, Martha, Edna, Bertha, Justin, Edith, Laura, (30).

Gunderson, James, R3, box 19, sec 21, ac 160, sec 22, ac 80, wf Clara, ch Coleman, Alice, Ina, Clifford, Pearl, Cora, Elmer, (29).

Gunderson, S. C., R1, sec 35, ac 64, wf Emeline, ch Lena, Grace, Gerald Hanson, (4).

Hamlin, W. F., R1, sec 36, ac 120, sec 25, ac 90, wf Malle, ch Hal, William, (58).

Hawks, W. J., R2, sec 1, ac 157, wf Josie, (53).

Hempel, E., R3, sec 18, ac 200, sec 17, ac 95, wf Gusta, ch William, Emma, Elsin, George, Mary, Bertha, (9).

Hensel, A., R2, sec 15, ac 80, sec 9, ac 80, wf Josephine, ch Arthur, Lena, Berna, (47).

Hensel, William, R2, sec 10, ac 88, sec 10, 11, ac 73.55, sec 9, ac 40, wf Josie, ch Fred, Esther, Clarence, Emily, Chester.

Hesnes, E., R2, sec 14, ac 80, wf Annie, ch Agnes, (8).

Hilscher, E., R2, sec 2, ac 120, sec 11, ac 40, wf Theresa, ch Will, Lewis, Alice, Ida, (2).

Jennings, W. W., sec 27, ac 80, sec 26, ac 80, sec 22, ac 40, wf Carrie, ch Mary, (50).

Johannas, Mrs. B., R3, sec 16, ac 120, ch Susan, (35).

Johannas, B., R3, sec 21, ac 120, wf Sarah, ch Bernice, Laurine, Floyd, (35).

Johannas, H., R3, sec 21, ac 80, sec 16, ac 76, (26).

Johnson, Mrs. Margaret, R2, sec 14, ac 193, ch Burnett, Jessie, Ardin, Ira, Carmen, (48).

Keller, Mrs. William, R4, sec 33, ac 135, wf Julia, ch Emma, Lila.

Kingsley, C. A., R3, sec 19, ac 40, sec 20, ac 68, sec 29, ac 80, ch Harry, (50).

Knuteson, S., R3, sec 4, ac 99, wf Tomenn, ch Ernest, Arthur, Luella, (56).

Koeller, William, R3, sec 28, ac 135, wf Minnie, ch William, Harry, Ida, Martha, (15).

Lander, Frank.

Lane, John, R3, sec 8, ac 80, wf Lillian, ch Arnold, Roland, Zadth, Thelma, (44).

Lee, D. N., R2, sec 12, ac 134, wf Bessie, ch Annie, Nellie, Gladys, Ella, (49).

Lee, T. K., R2, sec 1, ac 113.25, wf Betsey, ch Thomas, Johannas, Rodney, Betsey, Irene, Jeanette, Serena, Martha, (15).

Lovedahl, Andrew, R3, sec 21, ac 80, wf Mary, ch Clarence, Genn, Evelyn, (32).

Lovedahl, August, R3, sec 16, ac 160, wf Mabel, ch Leonard, (31).

Lovedahl, Torge, R2, sec 15, ac 120, (30).

Lukas, Frank & John, R3, sec 4, ac 80, sec 3, ac 40, sec 9, ac 160, (3).

McKengue, James, R3, sec 33, ac 120, wf Emily, ch Anna, John, (49).

Miller, William, R3, box 5, sec 20, ac 40, sec 21, ac 60, wf Tillie, ch Julius, Amelia, George, Molly, Violet, (20).

Moon, Mrs. T. R., R1, sec 36, ac 80, ch William, Estel, (46).

Nelson, R., R2, sec 1, ac 90, wf Anna, ch Arden, Florence, Harold, Sadie, Raymond, Edna, (53).

Nelson, S., R3, sec 5, ac 120, wf Lena, ch Noris, Nathan, (36).

Nowotny, A., R2, sec 1, ac 80, sec 12, ac 80, wf Mary, ch Silvesta, Frank, Leo, John, Joseph, (18).

Oliphant, Fred, R3, sec 8, ac 215, sec 26, ac 40, wf Hattie, ch Morton, Harley, Frank, Hazel, Bessie, Charles, Eva, Adeline, Ivan, (36).

Olson, E., R3, sec 22, ac 120, wf Dena, ch William, Chester, Clayton, Lawrence, Bertha, (17).

Olson, Henry, R2, box 49, sec 10, ac 158, wf Anna, ch Lawrence, Kermit, (41).

Olson, N. H., R1, sec 35, ac 28½, wf Hannah, ch Marie, (60).

Peterson, C. S., R2, sec 12, ac 100, wf Laura, ch Naomi, Ruth, (44).

Pierce, E. L., R3, sec 8, ac 4.50, sec 9, ac 160, sec 20, ac 80, sec 17, ac 320, sec 16, ac 120, wf Emily, (55).

Ploenske, C., R3, sec 31, ac 120, wf Amelia, ch Ella, Edith, Martha, Albert, Reinard, Herman, Emil, (18).

Podell, H., R4, sec 33, ac 40, wf Lena, (14).

Porter, L. N., R6, sec 35, ac 4, wf Dell, (57).

Potter, A. J., R2, sec 12, ac 42, sec 13, ac 83, wf Mary, ch Andrew, Minor, Sarah, Alpha, Irene, Arlin, (16).

Raatz, R., R3, sec 30, ac 99½, wf Emma, ch Dorothy, (39).

Riemer, William, R3, sec 18, ac 80, sec 19, ac 80, sec 20, ac 80, sec 17, ac 40, wf Pauline, ch Edward, Henry, Andy, Frank, Ernest, Ruth, Clara, (2).

Robbins Bros., R4, sec 33, ac 106.50, (11).

Roeske, O. L., R3, sec 10, ac 119, wf Marie, ch Harry, Athur, Oscar, (24).

Rolfe, O. N., R2, sec 14, ac 100, sec 23, ac 80, wf Effie, ch Mable, (35).

Rozinske, Theodore, R2, sec 23, ac 80, wf Hannah, ch Jennie, Elmer, (16).

Reud, Charles, R2, sec 12, ac 157, wf Jennie, ch John, Kenneth, (25).

Sander, Andrew, R3, sec 20, ac 80, sec 21, ac 20, wf Margaret, ch Frank, Agnes, Nora, Kate, (30).

Sander, F., R3, sec 21, ac 60, sec 28, ac 30, wf Emma, (24).

Sanesbrie, Paul, R3, sec 32, ac 400, wf Ella, (6).

Severson, C., R2, sec 14, ac 80, (36).

Severson, O., R3, sec 16, ac 80, wf Sophin, ch Agnes, (50).

Shafer, W., R3, sec 6, ac 169.90, sec 4, ac 44, wf Lillian, ch Fred, Vernie, (50).

Simon, J. N., R2, sec 3, ac 40, sec 2, ac 100, sec 10, ac 14.10, sec 11, ac 31.75, wf Mary, ch Luella, Josie, Milton, Gordon, Sidney, Howard, Margaret, Clinton, Stanton.

Smith, I. E., R2, sec 1, ac 86, wf Effie, ch Durward, Adelle, Ethel, Eunice, Dorothy, (50).

Songe, T., R2, sec 11, ac 120, wf Anna, ch Ingwal, Trygve, Emma, Martha, Ragna, Lunsdahl, Anna, Harold, (11).

Spees, Add, R3, sec 18, ac 168, Deerfield twp, sec 24, ac 80, sec 13, ac 80, wf Ruth, ch Fred, Dana, (58).

Spees, Fred, R3, sec 18, ac 168, wf Pansy, (27).

Spees, William, sec 19, ac 80, sec 32, ac 20, wf Cora, (55).

Stewart, Fred, R3, sec 6, ac 80, wf Birdie, ch Russell, Basil, (20).

Taplin, F. A., R1, sec 36, ac 120, wf Carrie, ch Ella, Ray, Agnes, Reid, Dorothy, Frank, (53).

Thompson Bros., R2, sec 12, ac 75, (42).

Thompson, H. F., R2, box 9, sec 24, ac 40, sec 23, ac 20, sec 13, ac 58, sec 14, ac 26, wf Anna, ch Anton, Elmer, (35).

Thompson, H. J., R2, sec 13, ac 86, wf Lila, ch Rosalia, (32).

Thompson, O. T., R3, sec 8, ac 115.50, wf Carrie, (33).

Topping, Mrs. Frank, R2, sec 13, ac 115, ch Eileen, Floyd, Lloyd, (25).

Topping, Fred, R2, sec 12, ac 40, sec 13, ac 85, sec 14, ac 40, wf Clara, ch Eugene, Archie, Vernon, Alice, (39).

Tracey, Charles, R2, sec 14, ac 40, sec 23, ac 20, sec 13, ac 40, wf Amber, (37).

Ueeck, William, R3, sec 7, ac 40, sec 8, ac 85, wf Agnes, ch Elmo, Margarett, (27).

Waala, Edward, R2, sec 24, ac 135, (39).

Waala, Peter, R2, box 52, sec 10, ac 80, sec 15, ac 80, wf Celia, ch Julius, Sarah, (53).

Waala, Samuel, R2, sec 15, ac 160, sec 9, ac 40, sec 15, ac 40, wf Margaret, ch Joseph, Sherman, Clara, Carrie, Ruth, Minor, Ervin, Jeanette, Laura, Lawrence, (31).

Wagner, G., R3, sec 5, ac 80, (8).

Wandrey, William, R3, sec 30, ac 80, sec 31, ac 120, wf Annie, ch Rueben, Erma, Chester, Rubert, Nina, Iven, Margarett, (38).

Wayak, Charles, R3, sec 20, ac 100, sec 30, ac 20, wf Helen, ch Henry, Robert, Helen, Irene, Edmond, Ernest.

Weckwerth, August, R3, sec 32, ac 90, wf Ella, (1).

Wedde, T. A., R3, sec 18, ac 57.14, sec 19, ac 57.15, wf Elma, (23).

Wedell, John, R3, sec 30, ac 122, wf Lena, ch Arthur, Ervin, Martin, (31).

Weeks, John, R3, sec 30, ac 153.33, wf Agnes, ch Marvin, Margaret, (40).

Weigand, Set, R3, box 58, sec 19, ac 59.72, ch Dora, (16).

Wilder, C., R3, sec 17, ac 80, wf Nellie, ch Ray, (46).

Wiler, M., R3, sec 5, ac 47.5, (40).

Williams, B. S., box 162, sec 34, ac 80, sec 27, ac 80, (20).

Wild Rose Post Office.

Erickson, J. F., R3, sec 3, ac 40, sec 2, ac 88.16, wf Mable, ch Howard, Della, (13).

Knuteson, E. E., R3, box 20, sec 4, ac 103.91, wf Emma, ch Ervin, Raymond, (41).

Knutson, Mrs. A., R3, sec 4, ac 80, ch Dolores, Evelyn, Kermit.

Sorenson, Mrs. S., R3, sec 3, ac 120, ch Anna, Ole, George, Thomas, Ingvald, Inga, Clara, (22).

Stee, T., R3, sec 4, ac 140, wf Marie, ch Torney, Julius, Annie, Arnold, Nordis, (14).

Thompson, Andrew, R3, sec 3, ac 80, wf Annie, ch Bernice, Norma, (35).

Thompson, Anton, R3, sec 3, ac 60, wf Hazel, ch Carneth, Laurel, (32).

Yagler, F. N., R3, sec 3, ac 86.47, (33).

MAP OF
WAUTOMA
TOWNSHIP

Scale 1¼ Inches to 1 Mile

Township 19 North, Range 10 East of 4th P. M.
WAUSHARA COUNTY, WIS.

Rural Routes shown thus:
School Districts " " : 2
Schools " " :

Churches shown thus:
Cemeteries " " :
Corporation Limits of Cities shown thus:

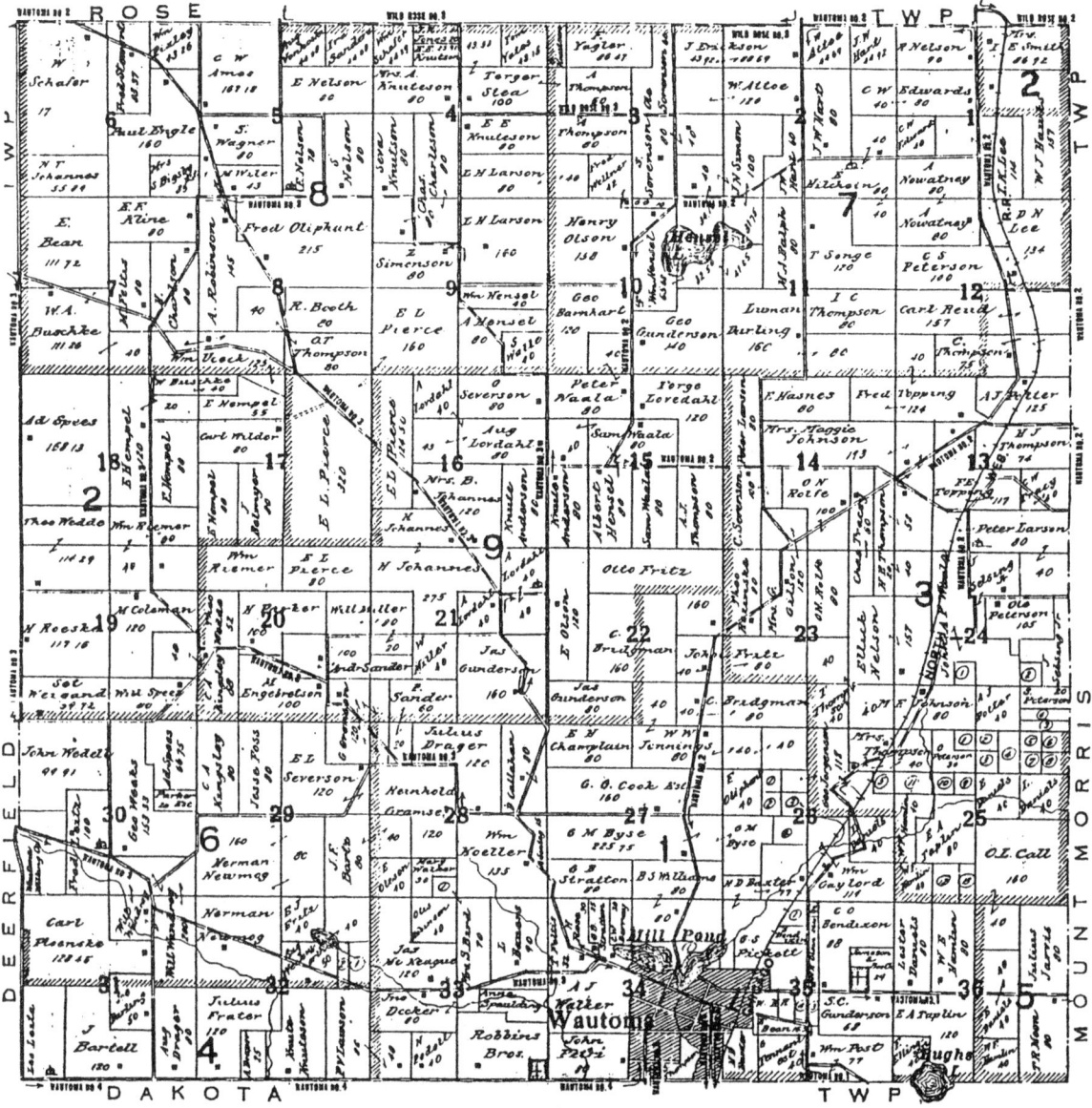

ROSE TWP

DEERFIELD

MOUNT MORRIS

DAKOTA TWP

Wautoma

Mill Pond

List of Small Property Owners in this Township Shown on Map by Numbers

No.	Name	Acres	Sec.	No.	Name	Acres	Sec.	No.	Name	Acres	Sec.	No.	Name	Acres	Sec.
1.	J. Selsing	10	14	4.	E. Nelson	20	15	11.	K. Knutson	20	25	1.	Mrs. S. Bird	10	28
2.	P. Larson	10	14	5.	J. A. Hamre	10	15	12.	Will Putzkey	30	25	2.	Carl Ploenske	10	32
3.	O. Thorstad	10	14	6.	Wm. Topping	10	15	13.	T. R. Moen	10	26	3.	W. Spree	20	32
4.	P. Larson	10	15	7.	W. F. Hamlin	10	15	1.	A. Pomplun	10	26	4.	Cogswell	15	34
5.	P. Larson	10	15	8.	Wm. Putzkey	10	15	2.	F. Chalmson	10	26	1.	F. Teska	35	
6.	G. Gunderson	10	26	9.	B. Johnson	10	26	3.	E. S. Walker	10	26	2.	S. Bendesen	35	
7.	Ole Thompson	10	26	10.	M. Olson	10	26	4.	F. Taylor	17.25	26	3.	H. W. Jameson & Lee	35	
								5.	F. W. Buyce	9	26	4.	O. Nelson	35	

(Michael Bednarek Collection, Wautoma, Wisc.)

12) SCHMIDT, Herman Johann Carl of the Town of Lind, Waupaca Co. (Wisc.)- b. "Barkow (either County Regenwalde or County Grimmen) in Pom(m)ern Germany", marr. Henriette Louise Bertha Gollnick at the Town of Bloomfield 12 May 1887/ Vol. 3 (1870-1890), p. 72, no. 38.

13) TETZLAFF, Hermann- b. "Lebben (County Usedom-Wollin) Germany", marr. Emma Lehr at Seneca, Green Lake Co.; 27 October 1901/ Vol. D , p. 232, no. 100.

14) TIMM, "Gotleib" (Gottlieb) Erdmann of the Town of Lind (Waupaca Co., Wisc.)- b. "Neubork (County Kolberg-Körlin) in Pomerania Germany", marr. Katharina Langenpelser (widow, maiden name Herman?) at West Bloomfield 6 November 1888/ Vol. 3 (1870-1890), p. 80, no. 74.

15) WACHOLTZ, Tielea Louise- b. "Lotten (County-) Neu Steten (Neustettin) Pom.", marr. Wilhelm F. Miller at Crystal Lake, Marquette Co. 18 March 1897/ Vol. D, p. 141, no. 26.

16) ZIEMER, Albert Johann of the Town of Lind, Waupaca Co. (Wisc.)- b. "(Klein-or Gross-)Justin (County Kammin) in Pommern Germany", marr. Ida Albertine Lucht at Bloomfield 16 April 1888/ Vol. 3 (1870-1890), p. 78, no. 30.

17) ZIERKE, Hermann- b. "Seeger (County Bublitz) Pom(m)ern Germany", marr. Auguste Pflugrad(t?)- b. "Salm (County Deutsch Krone, Province) West Prussia Germany"; at Dakota 31 March 1898/ Vol. D, p. 164, no. 38.

Immigrants from indeterminable locales in Province Pomerania, Prussia:

1) HERZFELD, Friedr. J.W.- b. "Freienstein Preussen Pommern Germany", marr. Emma M. Weidemann of the Town of Lind (Waupaca Co., Wisc.); at the Town of Bloomfield 1 December 1898/ Vol. D, p. 174, no. 101.

2) KRUGER, Carl- b. "Belgard Lanenberg Kreis (=County, Belgard or Lauenburg are Pomeranian county seats) Germany", marr. Amelia Neidth at Coloma 7 February 1899/ Vol. D, p. 179, no. 13.

3) MALCHOW, Christian F.W.- b. "Hemmalstate Pommeous", marr. Augusta L. Keitzer at Bloomfield 20 December 1871/ Vol. 3 (1870-1890), p. 4, no. 99.

4) McELREE (maiden name Korth), Auguste- b. "Immenthal by Goldnow Pomern Germin", marr. George H. Evans at the Town of Germania (Marquette Co.?) in the German Methodist Episcopal Church 13 July 1905/ Vol. E, p. 24, no. 55.

5) SCHLEI, Wilhelmine Louise Albertine- b. "Priepkow Pommern Germany", marr. Albert Wilhelm Mathews- b. "Moslin (Mösland, County Dirschau) West Prussia Germany"; at Coloma 7 December 1896/ Vol. D, p. 134, no. 117.

Immigrants from the Province of Pomerania, or "Pommern", Prussia:

1) BACHNMAN, Gottfried- b. "Pomern Preussen", marr. Augusta Malde-
    win at Bloomfield 22 Novemver 1877/ Vol. 3 (1870-1890), p. 26,
    no. 556.

2) BARTEL, Gustav- b. "Pomern Preussen", marr. Albertine Hagemann
    at Dakota 11 December 1876/ Vol. 3 (1370-1890), p. 22, no. 477.
    (Ev.As.)

3) BLADOW, Richard- b. "Pommern Prussia Germani", marr. Mathilda
    Kopps at the Town of Rushford, "Waushara Co."(Winnebago Co.) 19
    April 1880/Vol. 3 (1870-1890), p. 37, no. 787.

4) BOCK, Wilhelm Carl Johan Friedrich of Caledonia (Waupaca Co.)-
    b. "Pommern Preussen", marr. Wilhelmine Maria Kohler at Bloom-
    field 14 January 1875/ Vol. 3 (1870-1890), p. 14, no. 337.

5) BONES, Friedrich of Almond (Portage Co., Wisc.)- b. "Pommern
    Preussen", marr. Ida Maria Zautke at Bloomfield 10 February
    1882/ Vol. 3 (1870-1890), p. 45, no. 12.

6) BOTTOW, Friderich of Nepeuskun, Winnebago Co. (Wisc.)- b. "Pom-
    mern Preussen", marr. Emilie Wilke at Bloomfield 20 September
    1883/ Vol. 3 (1870-1890), p. 53, no. 77.

7) BUCHHOLZ, Carl of Weyauwega (Waupaca Co., Wisc.)- b. "Pomern
    Prussian", marr. Bertha Gruenwald (father's surname Beutler,
    mother's Gruenwald) at Bloomfield 26 December 1881/ Vol. 3 (1870-
    1890), p. 44, no. 932.

8) DALLMAN, Heinrich C.F. of Winchester (Winnebago Co., Wisc.)- b.
    "Pomern Preussen", marr. A.B.E. Bauers at Bloomfield 6 March
    1877/ Vol. 3 (1870-1890), p. 23, no. 499.

9) EBERT, Henry- b. "Pommern Prussia", marr. Wilhelmina Fabel at
    Bloomfield 3 March 1863/ Vol. 1 (1852-1863), p. 151.

10) FIS(C)HER, Wilhelm- b. "Pommern Pr(e)ussen", marr. Auguste Lange
    at the Town of Bloomfield 4 December 1879/ Vol. 3 (1870-1890),
    p. 36, no. 753.

11) FOLLENDORF, Hermann of Lind (Waupaca Co., Wisc.)- b. "Pom(m)ern
    Preussen", marr. Albertine Kobiski at Bloomfield 3 May 1877/
    Vol. 3 (1870-1890), p. 23, no. 509.

12) FREDRICH, Albert- b. "Pommern Pr(e)ussen", marr. Auguste Brasch
    at Bloomfield 15 June 1884/ Vol. 3 (1870-1890), p. 58, no. 44.

13) HANDRICH, Wilhelm- b. "Pommeran Prussia", marr. Christina Ruck at Bloomfield 21 February 1878/ Vol. 3 (1870-1890), p. 27, no. 589.

14) HANNEMANN, August- b. "Pommern Pr(e)ussen", marr. Emilie Ritz at Poy Sippi 13 November 1882/ Vol. 3 (1870-1890), p. 49, no. 84. (Judicial ceremony)

15) HENDRICK, Carl- b. "Pom(m)ern Prussia", marr. Maria Kleps at Bloomfield 29 March 1880/ Vol. 3 (1870-1890), p. 37, no. 731.

16) HERZFELD, Carl- b. "Pommern Preussen", marr. Mathilde Handrich at Bloomfield 7 April 1884/ Vol. 3 (1870-1890), p. 57, no. 34.

17) HERZFELDT, Ernest Friedrich Christian- b. "Pommern Germany", marr. Auguste Louise Draheim at the Town of Bloomfield 13 December 1893/ Vol. D, p. 76, no. 120.

18) HUEBNER, Frank Wm.- b. "Pommern Germany", marr. Ida Louisa Dehling- b. "Berlin (Green Lake Co.), Wisc."; at Deerfield 10 September 1901/ Vol. D, p. 228, no. 77.

19) KENHENBACKER, Hermann- b. "Pommern Germany", marr. Lena Ernst at the Town of Bloomfield 15 March (1898)/ Vol. D, p. 162, no. 30.

20) KLEIST, Albert- b. "Pommern Preussen", marr. Ther(e)se Fischer at Bloomfield 21 December 1875/ Vol. 3 (1870-1890), p. 18, no. 412.

21) KLEIST, August- b. "Pommern Pr(e)ussen", marr. Emilie Wangerin at Bloomfield 1 February 1882/ Vol. 3 (1870-1890), p. 45, no. 10.

22) KLEIST, Friedrich- b. "Pommern Preussen", marr. Auguste Hinz at Bloomfield 14 January 1876/ Vol. 3 (1870-1890), p. 19, no. 420.

23) KNUEPPEL (perhaps Knueppel?), Wilh. of Oshkosh (Winnebago Co., Wisc.)- b. "Pommern Germany", marr. Alma Wilhelmine Anna Bast at Bloomfield 25 April (1898)/ Vol. D, p. 167, no. 55.

24) KRAUSE, Hermann of the Town of Fremont (Waupaca Co., Wisc.)- b. "Pom(m)ern Preussen", marr. Wilhelmine Schwantz at Bloomfield 16 January 1880/ Vol. 3 (1870-1890), p. 36, no. 761.

25) KRUEGER, August of Buena Vista, Portage Co. (Wisc.)- b. "Pommern Preussen", marr. Emilie Gol(l)nick at the Town of Bloomfield 17 July 1881/ Vol. 3 (1870-1890), p. 42, no. 835.

26) LIESNER, Franz (parents' name"Craemer")- b. "Pomeran Prussian", marr. Wilhelmina Peters at Bloomfield 7 January 1879/ Vol. 3 (1870-1890), p. 31, no. 663.

27) LUEBKE, Eduart Hermann Ernst of the Town of Lind, Waupaca Co.-
b. "Pommern Germany", marr. Wilhelmine Er(ne)stine Byer (Beyer
or Baier?) at Bloomfield 4 April 1888/ Vol. 3 (1870-1890), p.
78, no. 22.

28) MAGETANZ, Albert H. of Weyauwega (Waupaca Co., Wisc.)- b. "Pommern Preussen", marr. Auguste H. Noack at Bloomfield 2 April
1877/ Vol. 3 (1870-1890), p. 23, no. 502.

29) PAAP, August- b. "Pom(m)ern Pr(e)ussen", marr. Bertha Hammerman
at Bloomfield 10 May 1879/ Vol. 3 (1870-1890), p. 33, no. 698.

30) PAAP, Ferdinand (parents Jacob & Maria)- b. "Pom(m)ern Prussian",
marr. Bertha Paap (parents Johann & Charlotte) at Bloomfield
10 November 1881/ Vol. 3 (1870-1890), p. 44, no. 919.

31) PAAP, Wilhelm- b. "Pommern Preussen", marr. Wilhelmine Fredrick
at Bloomfield 13 July 1883/ Vol. 3 (1870-1890), p. 52, no. 58.

32) PAGAL, F.J.A.- b. "Pomerian", marr. Johanna Mundinger at Bloomfield 1 November 1870/ Vol. 2 (1863-1870), p. 193.

33) PAGEL, Reinhard- b. "Pom(m)ern Pr(e)ussen", marr. Emilie Draheim at Bloomfield 19 December 1879/ Vol. 3 (1870-1890), p. 36,
no. 752.

34) PASS, Ferdinand Gustav- b. "Pommern Preussen", marr. Caroline
W. Ziel at Bloomfield 28 May 1875/ Vol. 3 (1870-1890), p. 16,
no. 366.

35) PASS, Wilhelm (parents Martin & Henrietta)- b. "Pommern Preussen", marr. Marie Emilie Pass (parents Martin & Katrina) at
Bloomfield 9 April 1875/ Vol. 3 (1870-1890), p. 15, no. 357.

36) RAATZ, Anna Maria Louise- b. "Pommern", marr. Herman Scharf of
"Ellmound" (Almond), Portage Co. (Wisc.); at Richford 6 April
1891/ Vol. D, p. 24, no. 132.

37) RADICHEL, August- b. "Pommern Preussen", marr. Alwine Wendt
at Bloomfield 8 June 1880/ Vol. 3 (1870-1890), p. 38, no. 802.

38) RADICHEL, H.J.A.- b. "Pommern Preussen", marr. B.A.W. Wendt at
Bloomfield 18 April 1876/ Vol. 3 (1870-1890), p. 20, no. 439.

39) RADICHEL, Heinrich- n. "Pommern Prussian", marr. Louise Mus at
Bloomfield 12 September 1878/ Vol. 3 (1870-1890), p. 30, no.
634.

40) RADICHEL, Herman- b. "Pom(m)ern Pr(e)ussen", marr. Martha Bachmann at Bloomfield 13 April 1879/ Vol. 3 (1870-1890), p. 32,
no. 683.

41) ROEHL, Gustav- b. "Pommern Prussen", marr. Auguste Winter at
Bloomfield 3 January 1882/ Vol. 3 (1870-1890), p. 45, no. 9.

42) ROGGOW, August- b. "Pommern Prussen", marr. Maria Bauer at
Bloomfield 6 May 1879/ Vol. 3 (1870-1890), p. 33, no. 697.

43) ROSKE, Albert Reinhard of Rushford (Winnebago Co., Wisc.)- b.
"Pommern", marr. Auguste Mathilde Krause- b. "West Prussia";
at Rushford, "Waushara Co." 8 April 1892/ Vol. D, p. 43, no. 38.

44) RUSCH, Gerhardt; C.C. of Merrill (Lincoln Co.), Wisc.- b. "Pommern Preussen", marr. Emma Amelia Timme at Bloomfield 1 December
1882/ Vol. 3 (1870-1890), p. 49, no. 85.

45) SCHMITT, Gustave of Wausau, Marathon Co. (Wisc.)- b. "Pommern
Prussian", marr. Bertha Malderwin at Bloomfield 16 February
1879/ Vol. 3 (1870-1890), p. 31, no. 672.

46) SCHULZ, Karl Aug. Hermann- b. "Pommern", marr. Christine Maria
Elisabeth Vielbaum (maiden name Bellin?) at Coloma Station 25
September 1892/ Vol. D, p. 43, no. 69.

47) STREY, Fredrick- b. "Pommern Preussen", marr. Ottilie Stielmann
at Bloomfield 3 February 1885/ Vol. 3 (1870-1890), p. 61, no. 9.

48) STRUCK, Friedrich- b. "Pommern Preussen", marr. Caroline Warmbier at Bloomfield 14 March 1875/ Vol. 3 (1870-1890), p. 15,
no. 350.

49) STUEBS, Herman of Waupaca (County seat in Wisc.)- b. "Pommern
Preussen", marr. Elisa Lipke at Bloomfield 10 December 1875/
Vol. 3 (1870-1890), p. 18, no. 406.

50) TREPTOW, F.H.M.- b. "Pom(m)ern Prussia", marr. C.C.E. Brandt at
Poy Sippi "2½ halv o' clock P.M." (no date, but in December
1879)/ Vol. 3 (1870-1890), p. 35, no. 746. (Methodist Episcopal
Church service)

51) WAGNER, Albert of Fremont, Waupaca Co. (Wisc.)- b. "Pommein
Preussen", marr. Alvine Pischer at Bloomfield 12 June 1883/ Vol.
3 (1870-1890), p. 63, no. 49.

52) WILKE, Bertha Maria Caroline- b. "Pommern Germany", marr. Alfred
August Evald Pigorsch- b. "New Strand (perhaps Herrnstadt, County Guhrau, Prov. Posen, Prussia?) Germany"; at Borth Poy Sippi
7 December 1897/ Vol. D, p. 156, no. 117.

53) ZIEMER, Albert of the Town of Lind, Waupaca Co. (Wisc.)- b. "Pommern Preussen", marr. Minna Augusta Tinn at Bloomfield 30 November 1885/ Vol. 3 (1870-1890), p. 65, no. 91.

54) ZIEMER, Ferdinand of Lind (Waupaca Co., Wisc.)- b. "Pom(m)ern
Prussian", marr. Mathilde Hirte at Bloomfield 17 November 1881/
Vol. 3 (1870-1890), p. 44, no. 920.

55) ZIERKE, Julius Friedrich August- b. "Pommeran Prussia", marr.
Charlotte Klara Ludtke at Richford 7 April 1993/ Vol. D, p. 62,
no. 40.

Immigrants from specific locales in Province Brandenburg, Prussia:

1) ARENDSEE, Paul F.W. of Westfield (Marquette Co.)- b. "Durings-
hof (Dühringshof, County Landsberg an der Warthe) Preussen Europe", marr. Elizabeth Mueller at Dakota 10 November 1876/ Vol.
3 (1870-1890), p. 21, no. 468.

2) CZICH, Hermann of the Town of Royalton, Waupaca Co. (Wisc.)- b.
"Kleinraden (Klein-Rade, County West-Sternberg) Preussen German-
ny", marr. Auguste Louise Fandrey at the Town of Bloomfield 3
October 1895/ Vol. D, p. 109, no. 65.

3) NEHRING, Ida- b. "Berlin Germany", marr. Edward J. Falk- b.
"Germany"; at Delavan, Walworth Co. (Wisc.) Methodist Episcopal
Church 20 March 1901/ Vol. D, p. 218, no. 18.

4) PELTZ, Albert August- b. "Zechlin (County Ost-Prignitz) Prussia",
marr. Bertha A. Schonscheck at Poy Sippi 10 September 1882/ Vol.
3 (1870-1890), p. 48, no. 74.

5) POMERANKE, Emma Louisa- b. "Aberwalda (Eberswalde, County Barnim)
Germany", marr. Henry August Carl Schuester of the Town of Harrison, Calumet Co. (Wisc.); at the Town of Harrison 6 February
1902/ Vol. D, p. 242, no. 28.

6) POSORSKI, Fred- b. "Berlin Germany", marr. Rosa Rysup- b."Berlin Germany"; at Aurora 18 August 1900/ Vol. D, p. 207, no. 70.

7) RATZBURG, John Fredrick of Fremont, Waupaca Co. (Wisc.)- b. "Jer-
renthin (Zerrenthin, Co. Prenzlau) Brandenburg Prussia", marr.
Ana Maria Louisa Pagel at Bloomfield 29 May (1885)/ Vol. 3
(1870-1890), p. 63, no. 46.

8) VOIGT, Frank C. of Marion (twp.)- b. "Berlin Germany", marr.
Anna Roehrdanz at Wautoma 8 April 1882/ Vol. 3 (1870-1890), p.
46, no. 36.

Immigrants from indeterminable locales in Province Brandenburg, Prussia:

1) KELLER, William of "Krannville"(Minnesota)?- b. "HasLentz Nm
(Nm.=Neumark, region is eastern Brandenburg)", marr. Alma Winter
at the Town of Bloomfield 25 July 1894/ Vol. D, p. 89, no. 67.

2) LINDEKUGEL, Gottlieb Johann- b. "Langsam e Preussen Germany"
(Langsow, County Lebus?), marr. Christine Debler at West Bloomfield 30 September 1889/ Vol. 3 (1870-1890), p. 85, no. 64.

3) LINDEKUGEL, John Gottlieb of Brushville (?), Wisc.- b. "Rathe-
now (County West-Havelland) Prussia", marr. Maris Schalinski- b.
"Prussia"; at the Town of Saxeville 27 December 1891/ Vol. D,
p. 38, no. 8.

4) WUSTREIK, Henrich Frederich of Brandon (Fond du Lac Co.), Wisc.-
"Neumock (Neumark, a region in eastern Brandenburg) Prussia",
marr. Wilhelmine Auguste Hempel- b."Arnswalde (a Brandenburg
county seat) Prussia"; at the Town of Richford 6 December 1893/
Vol. D, p. 76, no. 117.

Immigrants listed only from Province "Brandenburg", Prussia:

1) KOELLER, Wm.- b. "Brandenburg Germany", marr. Mrs. Minna Luhm
(maiden name Uger)- b. "Germany"; at Dakota 26 December 1899/
Vol. D, p. 197, no. 8.

2) LINDEKUGEL, Johann- b. "Brandenburg Pr(e)ussen", marr. Fredericke Schmidt at Plainfield 20 September 1881/ Vol. 3 (1870-1890),
p. 43, no. 903.

3) MEES, August- b. "Brandenburg Prussia Germany", marr. Hulda Kohler at Bloomfield 6 January 1873/ Vol. 3 (1870-1890), p. 7, no.
193.

4) RATZBURG, Wilhelm of Oshkosh, Winnebago Co. (Wisc.)- b. "Brandenburg Preussen", marr. Emilie Meitzen at Bloomfield 18 May
1885/ Vol. 3 (1870-1890), p. 63, no. 44.

5) STILLER, Otto- b. "Brandenburg Preussen", marr. Pauline Wangerin
at Bloomfield 15 August 1882/ Vol. 3 (1870-1890), p. 43, no. 61.

Immigrants from County Arnswalde, Province Brandenburg, Prussia:

1) DIETRICH, Wilhelm Robert- b. "Radun in Preussen Germany", marr.
Alvine Wilhelmine Auguste Kleist at the Town of Bloomfield 25
May 1893/ Vol. D, p. 65, no. 53.

2) (P?)FLUGRAD(T?), Julius Heinrich- b. "Arnswalde Brandenburg",
marr. Emilie noe Hark (widow, maiden name Nilzo?)- b. "Voronikar. Schubben (Veronika, Co. Schub_in, Prov.-) Posen"; at Richford 15 March 1894/ Vol. D, p. 81, no. 22.

3) HEMPEL, Wilhelmine Auguste- b. "Arnswalde Prussia", marr. Henrich Frederich Wustreik of Brandon (Fond du Lac Co.) Wisc.- b.
"Neumock (Neumark, a region in eastern Brandenburg) Prussia"; at
the Town of Richford 6 December 1893/ Vol. D, p. 76, no. 117.

4) OEHLKE, Albert Gustav- b. "Nemsehoff (Nemischhof) Neumark Germany 6 February 1867", marr.Martha Caroline Loehrke at the Town
of Bloomfield 26 April 1904/ Vol. D, p. 301, no. 42.

5) ROSE, Gustav Emil Hugo of Glen Rock, Wisc.- b. "Glambeck, Germany 2 June 1874", marr. Wilhelmine Dretzke of Neshkoro (Marquette
Co.) at Neshkoro 6 December 1906/ Vol. E, p. 55, no. 135.

Immigrants from indeterminable locales across "Prussia":

1) BUTT, Hermann Ferdinand Erdmann from the Town of Waupaca, Waupaca Co. (Wisc.)- b. "Libenow (may be Liebenow in Counties Arnswalde or Landsberg an Warte, Prov. Brandenburg; or County Greifenhagen, Prov. Pomerania) in Preussen Germany", marr. Mathilde Timm at the Town of Bloomfield 1 September 1892/ Vol. D, p. 46, no. 58.

2) FRITZ, Otto Paul- b. "Zumeschnow Preussen Germany", marr. Louise Wilhelmine Auguste Kleist at the Town of Bloomfield 12 March 1896/ Vol. D, p. 121, no. 34.

3) GORTSCH, Eduard Carl Friedrich- b. "Hetbraeck Preussen Germany", marr. Anna Johanne Marie Struck at the Town of Bloomfield 14 March 1896/ Vol. D, p. 121, no. 36.

4) GRUNING, Friedresh Wilhelm- b. "Wunsorfh (either Wunstorf, Neustadt dist. of Prov. Hannover or Wunsdorf, Co. Teltow, Prov. Brandenburg), Pr(e)ussen Europe", marr. Ida Muller at Bloomfield 22 January 1864/ Vol. 2 (1863-1870), p. 11.

5) KAATZ, Reinhold A.- b. "Schulit (perhaps near Schulitz stream, running by Bromberg, Prov. Posen into Prov. W. Prussia?) Preussen Germany", marr. Tena A. Boerke at West Bloomfield 19 May 1902/ Vol. D, p. 250, no. 76.

6) KIENERT, Joh. Aug.- b."Rotenburg (either county seat in Prov. Hannover or on the Fulda River in Prov. Hessen-Nassau) Preussen Germany", marr. Louisa Friedricki Magdanz-b. "Bransberg*(perhaps Bromberg?) Preussen Germany"; at the Town of Saxeville 6 July 1897/ Vol. D, p. 146, no. 58. (also, there is Braunsberg in CountiesNeu-Ruppin/Potsdam Administrative District or Naugard, Prov. Pomerania/Administrative District Stettin; or also a county seat in Prov. East Prussia)

7) PIOTTER, Hermann Carl- b. "Gieseintz (perhaps Gieseritz, Salzwedel dist., Prov. Saxony-Anhalt or Giesebitz, County Stolp, Prov. Pomerania?) Preussen Germany", marr. Anna Amanda Handrich at West Bloomfield 24 May 1901/ Vol. D, p. 222, no. 38.

8) POFAHL, Anna Emilie Henriette- b. "Horst (one of 18 places) in Preussen Germany", marr. Wilh. Joh. Friedrick Berg at the Town of Bloomfield 19 June 1897/ Vol. D, p. 146, no. 57.

9) STREIGE, Johann of Lind (Waupaca Co., Wisc.)- b. "Kisch Kags (?) Preussen Germany", marr. Augusta E.J. Pagel of Wolf River (Winnebago Co., Wisc.); at Bloomfield 8 February 1899/ Vol. D, p. 179, no. 12.

10) ZIBELL, Leopold of Oshkosh (Winnebago Co. seat)- b. "Schattkower in Prussia Germany", marr. Wilhelmine Gollnick at West Bloomfield 21 October 1888/ Vol. 3 (1870-1890), p. 80, no. 69.

Immigrants from "Prussian Poland" and its variant names:

1) BARRON, Jacob of Marshfield (Wood Co., Wisc.)- b. "Prussian Poland", marr. Sefronay Srulcrevki (?-Barbara Thomas given as fa-
ther-?)- b. "Prussian Poland"; at Plainfield 24 February 1902/
Vol. D, p. 241, no. 24. (Catholic ceremony, likely Polish couple)

2) GOLNIK, Francis- b. "Tuchola (in Poland) Europe", marr. Frederick
William Gura of Oasis- b. "Boston Massachusetts"; at Polover (Plo-
ver) Portage Co. (Wisc.) 24 October 1899/ Vol. D, p. 192, no. 88.
(Roman Catholic ceremony, likely Polish couple)

3) KROUSE, Alvina- b. "Polnis(c)h Russia", marr. Albert Arthur Smith
at Poy Sippi 12 March 1907/ Vol. E, p. 64, no. 31.

4) RYBICKI, George- b. "Poland (Germany)", marr. Katie Szambelan- b.
"Poland (Germany)"; at Belmont (Portage Co.) Wisc. 28 July 1903/
Vol. D, p. 233, no. 105.

Immigrants of German descent from "Russia":

1) OEHLKE, Theodor of Princeton (Green Lake Co.)- b. "Russia Europe",
marr. Clara B. Luedtke at the Town of Marion 5 November 1901/ Vol.
D, p. 235, no. 118.

2) WEISS, Daniel- b. "Russia", marr. Minna Roggow at Poy Sippi 7 December 1905/ Vol. E, p. 31, no. 99.

3) WISE (probably WEISS), Emilie- b. "Russia", marr. Godlief (Gott-
lieb?) Block of Mansfield, Wisc.- b. "Sirchow (Dirschau, a W.
Prussian county seat?) Prussia"; at Berlin (Green Lake Co.) 14
October 1901/ Vol. D, p. 229, no. 81.

4) WEISS, Olgo (Olga?)- b. "Russia", marr. Wm. Carl Roggow at Poy
Sippi 7 November 1905/ Vol. E, p. 29, no. 87.

5) WEOSNER, Delia- b. "Russia", marr. Carl Frederick Erdmann- b.
"Germany"; at Poy Sippi 22 March 1900/ Vol. D, p. 201, no. 35.

(all ceremonies listed here were Lutheran or Protestant)

233

Immigrants from locales in central Germany:

1) BERG, Alb. Robt. Edward- b. "Priesnits (Priessnitz, Borna dist-
    rict, Saxe-Meiningen state by Kamburg) Germany", marr. Hulda Lau-
    ra Mats at the Town of Coloma 23 February 1899/ Vol. D, p. 183,
    no. 36.

2) DEUTER, Jakob- b. "Loukos (Luko, Zerbst district, Prov. Saxony-
    Anhalt, Prussia) Germany", marr. Emma Hulda Ida Ploetz of Cale-
    donia (Waupaca Co.?) Wisc.; at Coloma Station 12 April 1901/ Vol.
    D, p. 220, no. 25.

3) GERLACK, Joh. Aug. Fre^{e}derick- b. "Saxony (either independent
    Kingdom or Prussian Province?)", marr. Augustie E. Schoenack at
    Bloomfield 6 September 1868/ Vol. 2 (1863-1870), p. 138.

4) KOOP, Hermann Johann Friedrich- b. "Ploetz in Mecklenburg Streh-
    litz-Germany", marr. Alvine Albertine Mueske at West Bloomfield
    2 January 1889/ Vol. 3 (1870-1890), p. 32, no. 5.

5) KOOP, Ida Friedericka Caroline- b. "Plietz in Mecklenburg Stre-
    litz Germany", marr. Carl Ernst August Behm- b. "Rothenklempenow
    (Co. Randow) in (Prov.) Pommern Germany"; at the Town of Bloomfi-
    eld 10 December 1891/ Vol. D, p. 34, no. 191.

6) STEPHAN, Alvena- b. "Mohrenbach (Gehren district, Thuringia) Ger-
    many", marr. John Heaney at Saxeville in a Congregational cere-
    mony 21 October 1900/ Vol. D, p. 211, no. 92.

Immigrants from Province Hannover, Prussia in northwestern Germany:

1) BOSCHEN, Amrhen- b. "in Hurkel Prov. Hannover", marr. Aug. Her-
    mann Raatz- b. "Aulzig Kro. (Kreis=County) Dramburg (Prov.-) Pom-
    mern"; at Richford 1 July 1892/ Vol. D, p. 45, no. 52.

2) BRAMMER, Heinrich of Manawa (Waupaca Co., Wisc.)- b. "Han(n)over
    Preussen", marr. Caroline Mathias at Bloomfield 3 January 1881/
    Vol. 3 (1870-1890), p. 40, no. 836.

3) GOOK, Wilhelm of Sheboygan (a Wisc. county seat)- b. "Han(n)over
    Prussian", marr. Anna Straub at Bloomfield 13 September 1878/
    Vol. 3 (1870-1890), p. 30, no. 635.

4) GRUNDMAN, Fred. of Milwaukee- b. "Hanover Germany", marr. Emma
    Belter at Poy Sippi 25 October 1905/ Vol. E, p. 28, no. 82.

Immigrants from the Kingdom of Bavaria, in southern Germany:

1) BAUER, Anton- b. "Bavaria Germany", marr. Francis Bielmeyer at
    Wautoma 19 November (1888)/ Vol. 3 (1870-1890), p. 81, no. 80.
    (Catholic ceremony)

2) BIELMAIER, Mr. John- b. "Unterviechtach (flowage running from
    Niederbayern to Oberpfalz districts?) Bavaria Germany", marr.
    Miss Francis Stoeger (illegitimate: father- Michael Mueller,
    mother b.-"Germany") at Wautoma 12 February 1896/ Vol. D, p.
    118, no. 21. (Catholic ceremony)

3) FRITZ, Anna- b. "Gunzburg (Schwaben district) Germany", marr.
    Richard Jones of Berlin (Green Lake Co.), Wisc.- b. "GlanMor-
    ganshire S. Wales"; at Aurora 15 September 1898/ Vol. D, p. 173,
    no. 90.

4) STUMPNER, Johan Georg of Loyal, Clark Co., Wisc.- b. "Mitteldoff
    (Mitteldorf?) Baiern (Bayern=Bavaria) Germany", marr. Alvine
    Christine Braun at the Town of Bloomfield 4 March 1899/ Vol. D,
    p. 180, no. 17.

5) UHER, Mathias (names reversed on record?)- b. "Bavaria (Bohemia)",
    marr. Mary Nepodal (names also reversed) at Friendship,(Adams
    Co.)"Dane Co." 22 May (1883)/ Vol. 3 (1870-1890), p. 52. no.
    52. (Catholic ceremony, probably Bohemian-Czech couple)

Immigrants from other locales across western Germany:

1) ASPENLEITER, Marie (maiden name Burger)- b. "Lerach (Grand Du-
    chy of) Baden Germany", marr. Gustav Schoeneck- b. "Kornelino
    (County Schubin, Prov.)Posen (Prussia) Germany"; at the Town
    of Bloomfield 15 July 1897/ Vol. D, p. 147, no. 61.

2) BECK, Henry, a minister from"Naperville, Wisc." (Ill.?)- b.
    "Hoheback Kuenzelaw (Hohebach, Künselsau district, Kingdom of
    Württemberg) Germanie", marr. Lda Lau at the Town of Coloma 15
    August 1906/ Vol. E, p. 47, no. 87.

3) GOLLNICK, Johan- b. "Salz in Germany" (either Unterfranken dis-
    trict of the Kingdom of Bavaria, or Unterwesterwald county in
    Wiesbaden district of Prov. Hessen-Nassau, Prussia?), marr.
    Auguste C. Hartfiel at Bloomfield 29 April 1882/ Vol. 3 (1870-
    1890), p. 46, no. 37.

4) KUETZING, Frances F.A. of New Ulm (Brown Co.), Minnesota- b.
    "Bern Switzerland", marr. Ella Lucy Porter at Mt. Morris in
    the Methodist Episcopal Church 16 September 1882/ Vol. 3 (1870-
    1890), p. 48, no. 65.

5) MUNDINGER, Jacob F.- b. "Kingdom of Würt(t)emberg", marr. Emi-
    ly Prellwitz at Bloomfield 21 March 1867(Evangelical Lutheran
    ceremony)/ Vol. 2 (1863-1870), p. 100.

6) NEUMANN, Philipp- b. "Dangendorf (Grand Duchy of) Hessendarm-
stadt (Hessen-Darmstadt)", marr. Amande Clementine Flor.(entine)
Timm at Bloomfield 7 February 1865/ Vol. 2 (1863-1870), p. 37.

7) RATH, Carl of the Town of Almond, Portage Co. (Wisc.)- b. "Baden" (a Grand Duchy), marr. Emilia Theresia Jung at the Town of
Oasis in the Methodist Episcopal Church 14 April 1887/ Vol. 3
(1870-1890), p. 73, no. 39.

8) WESTERMAN, August- b. "Detmold Lippe" (Principality and State),
marr. Auguste Kossman at Bloomfield 11 May 1884/ Vol. 3 (1870-
1890), p. 57, no. 38.

Immigrants from indeterminable locales across "Germany":

1) BAST, Mina Avline Helema (maiden name Schmidt?)- b. "Grabow (one of 15 places) Germany", marr. Friedrick Mundinger- b. "Margstadt Germany"; at Bloomfield 7 December 1890/ Vol. D, p. 19, no. 99.

2) BRIETZKE, Ottelie- b. "Brumgarten Germany", marr. Karl August Proescher- b. "Romanshof (County Czarnikau, Prov. Posen, Prussia) Germany"; at Coloma 23 November (1894)/ Vol. D, p. 97, no. 112.

3) CRAFT (KRAFT?), Herman Friedrich- b. "Buchholz (one of many places) Germany", marr. Theresa Pickert at Berlin, Green Lake Co.; 18 November 1903/ Vol. D, p. 290, no. 147.

4) ENTRISS, Catharina- b. "Possen Lauer (perhaps someplace in Prov. Posen?) Germany", marr. Friedrich Mielke- b. "Salmo (Salm, Co. Deutsch Krone, Prov. W. Prussia) Germany"; at Dakota 11 November 1904/ Vol. E, p. 14, no. 142.

5) FEHSER, Julius Frederick of Little Wolf, Waupaca Co. (Wisc.)- b. "Carshedelle Germany", marr. Emilie Ottilie Gerentine Gruening at Bloomfield 11 December 1890/ Vol. D, p. 19, no. 98.

6) GLASKE, Emil- b. "Garingen Germany", marr. Bertha Heiman of Chicago, Ill.; at Coloma 26 December 1906/ Vol. E, p. 60, no. 10.

7) GRIMM, Frederick- b. "Wuss (either Wussow, Counties Lauenburg or Rummelsburg, Prov. Pomerania, Prussia; or Wust, County Jerich, Prov. Brandeburg, Prussia?) Germany", marr. Wilhelmine Laubenheimer at the Town of Bloomfield 10 October 1894/ Vol. D, p. 93, no. 91.

8) KAPP, Carl- b. "Wetsernhausen (either in Kingdom of Württemberg, or County Quedlinberg, Prov. Saxony-Anhalt, Prussia; or County Melle, Duchy of Oldenburg) Germany", marr. Claudia Emigh at the Congregational Parsonage in Pine River 21 January 1897/ Vol. D, p. 139, no. 16.

9) KWIECEYRISKE, Lucie- b. "Kerno Gurcrus Germany-Europe", marr. Stanishaus Markofski at Berlin 11 November 1902/ Vol. D, p. 261, no.140. (likely Polish couple)

10) MANTHEY, Otto Georg- b. "Friedland (one of 9 places) Germany", marr. Agathe Ottilia Mina Bartz of Crystal Lake (Marquette Co.); at Richford 5 May 1904/ Vol. D, p. 303, no. 54.

11) MITTELSTAEDT, Ernst Eduard- b. "Zeden A.O. (probably an Oder River, Prov. Brandenburg, Prussia) Germany", marr. Bertha Emilie Auguste Behm at the Town of Bloomfield 30 May 1895/ Vol. D, p. 106, no. 45.

12) PFAFF, Louisa- b. "Vogelsang Germany" (one of 9 places), marr.
Herman Raatz of the Town of Wolf River, Winnebago Co. (Wisc.);
at Bloomfield 2 March (1895)/ Vol. D, p. 101, no. 18.

13) SOHN, Gustav Wilh.- b. "Oshomveo(?) Germany", marr. Louise Shef-
fert of Montello (Marquette Co.); at the Town of Coloma 2 December 1903/ Vol. D, p. 293, no. 168.

14) TOEWS, Franz Richard- b. "Hohenstein (one of 11 places) Germany",
marr. Emelie Amelia Jerick- b. "Laskowo (Co. Kolmar, Prov. Posen) Prussia Germ."; at Berlin, Green Lake Co.; 11 September
1901/ Vol. D, p. 227, no. 70.

15) WINDT, Albert- b. "Sovelwete Germany", marr. Elezabeth Wirth at
Leon in a congregational ceremony 14 January 1885/ Vol. 3 (1870-
1890), p. 61, no. 13.

16) WOHES, Louise, b. "Karpenhoff Germany", marr. Georg Kopitzke at
the Town of Bloomfield 6 November 1894/ Vol. D, p. 95, no. 103.

17) WRUCK, August- b. "Neukronan Germany", marr. Martha Ann Damrohse-
b. "Blugowo (Co. Wirsitz, Prov. Posen, Prussia) Germany"; at
Coloma 9 May 1899/ Vol. D, p. 185, no. 48.

238

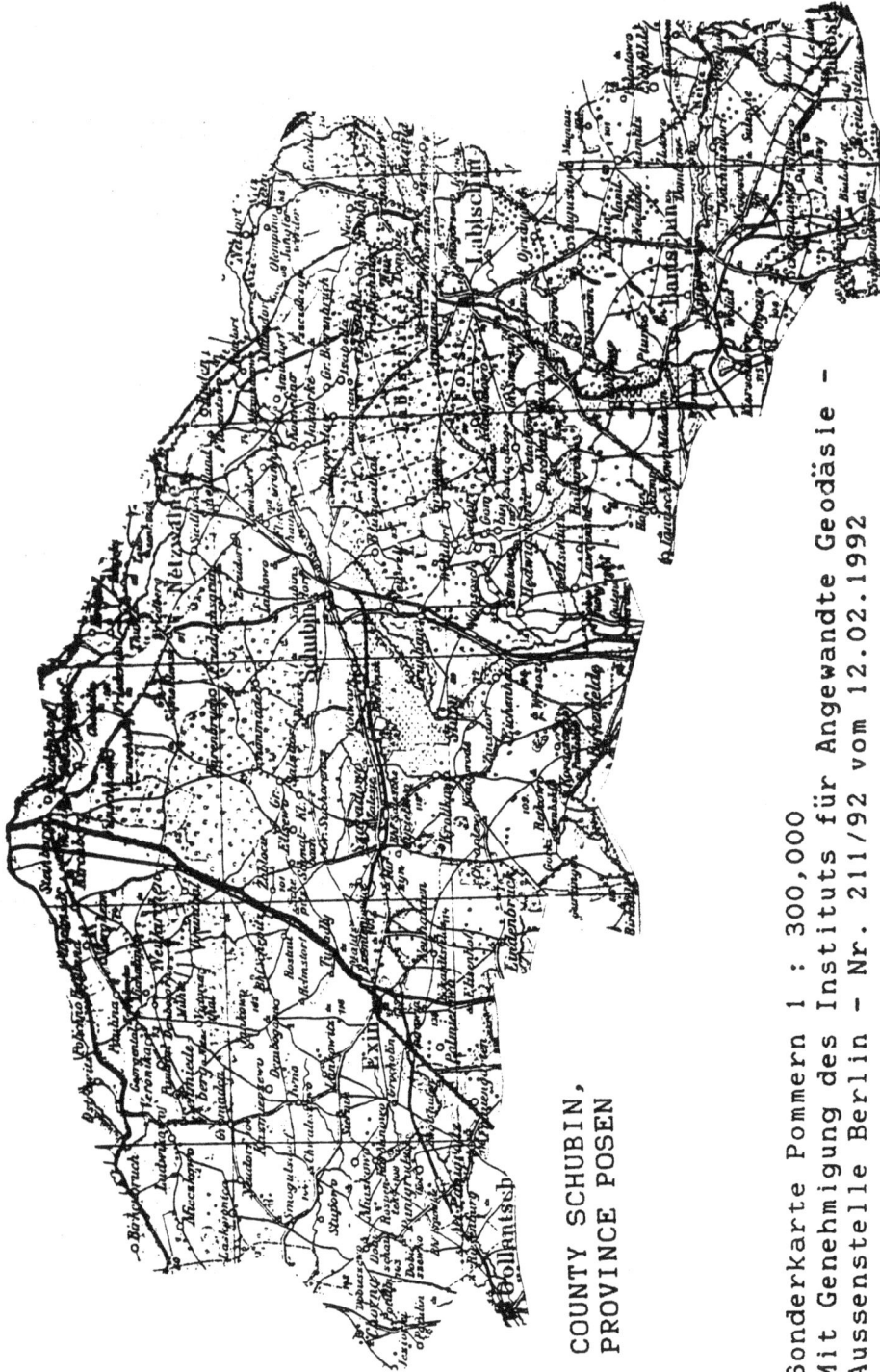

COUNTY SCHUBIN,
PROVINCE POSEN

Sonderkarte Pommern 1 : 300,000
Mit Genehmigung des Instituts für Angewandte Geodäsie –
Aussenstelle Berlin – Nr. 211/92 vom 12.02.1992

THE NORTHERN 7/8 OF
COUNTY WONGROWITZ,
PROVINCE POSEN

(Note the estate
community of Podolin
in the upper right)

Sonderkarte Pommern 1 : 300,000
Mit Genehmigung des Instituts für Angewandte Geodäsie -
Aussenstelle Berlin - Nr. 211/92 vom 12.02.1992

240

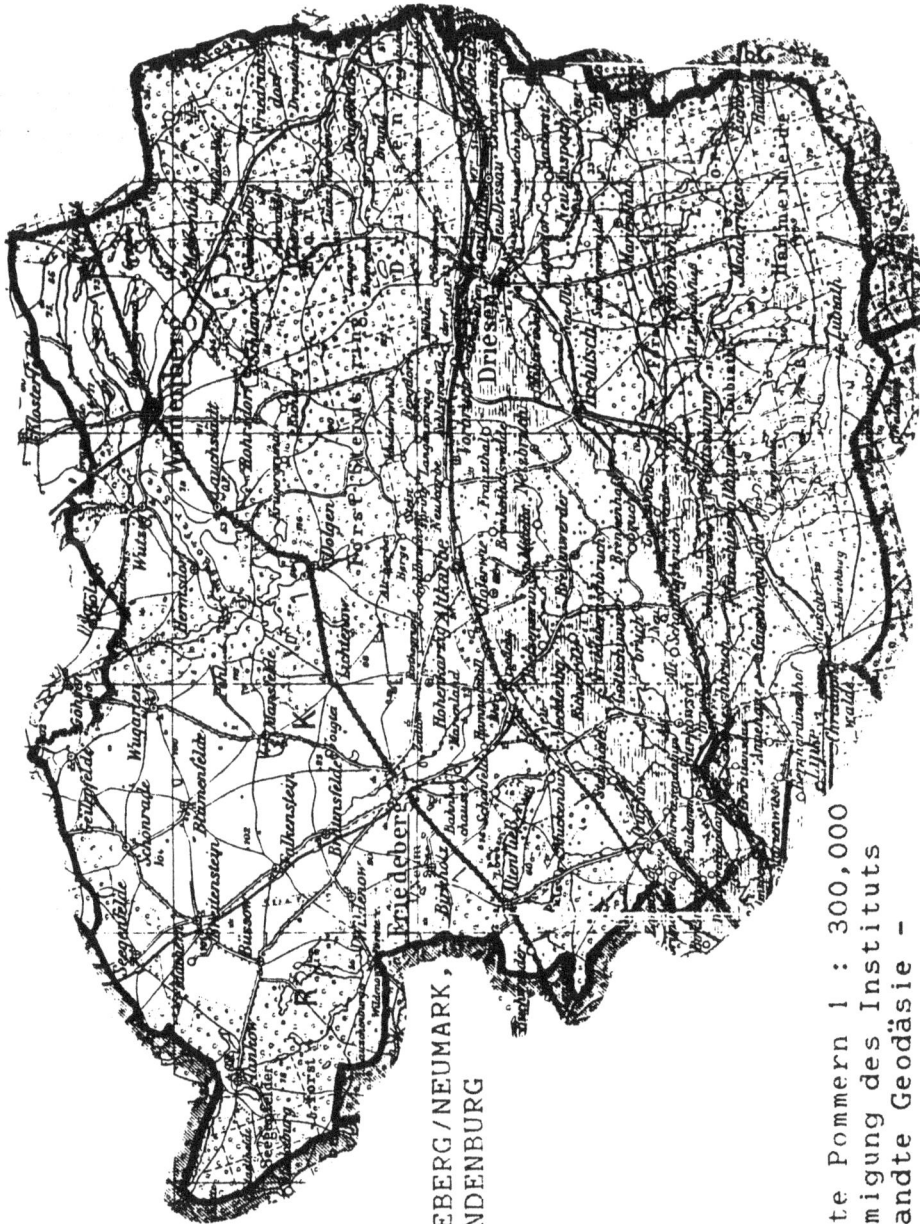

COUNTY FRIEDEBERG/NEUMARK,
PROVINCE BRANDENBURG

Sonderkarte Pommern 1 : 300,000
Mit Genehmigung des Instituts
für Angewandte Geodäsie –
Aussenstelle Berlin – Nr. 211/92 vom 12.02.1992

Der Netzedistrikt 1772/74

•••• Grenze zwischen den Großkreisen Dt. Krone und Kamin 1773

Grenzlinien im Netzegebiet

•••• Nordgrenze des Herzogtums Warschau von 1807
––– Demarkationslinie von 1919 (16. 2.)
––– Grenze von 1920

Changing borders, from the original two greater counties of the Netze District to the Post-World War I demarcations (Couresty *DIE ANTLITZ UND GESCHICHTE DES KREISES KOLMAR (POSEN)* HKG KOLMAR, W. Germany)

www.ingramcontent.com/pod-product-compliance
Lightning Source LLC
Chambersburg PA
CBHW080235270326
41926CB00020B/4242